The True Interpreter

L. G. Kelly

The True Interpreter

A History of Translation
Theory and Practice in the West

St. Martin's Press · New York

All rights reserved. For information, write:
St. Martin's Press, Inc.
175 Fifth Avenue
New York, NY 10010
First published in the United States of America in 1979

ISBN 0-312-83057-7

Library of Congress Cataloging in
Publication Data

Kelly, Louis G
  The true interpreter.

  Bibliography: p. 253
  Includes indexes.
  1. Translating and interpreting—History.
  I. Title.
P306.K45 1979   418'.02   79-4179
ISBN 0-312-82057-7

Printed in Great Britain

VIRIS ERUDITISSIMIS
MAGISTRISQUE CARISSIMIS
EDWARDO MUSGRAVE BLAIKLOCK
ET
GULIELMO FRANCISCO MACKEY
QUIBUS DUCENTIBUS
TUM ANTIQUAS TUM HODIERNAS
TIRO DIDICI
ARTES MINERVAE

Contents

viii *Contents*

Preface

It would be churlish to forget my apprenticeship in *linguistique différentielle* under M. Jean Darbelnet at l'université Laval, Québec, and to pass over in silence my debt to the *Stylistique comparée du français et de l'anglais* by himself and Jean-Paul Vinay. Dr. George Steiner, by his incisive comments from a less pragmatic viewpoint than mine, and Sir Basil Blackwell, by his interest and shrewd advice, caused major changes in the thrust of the book. Among my colleagues at Ottawa, I received much help from Mr. Thomas Henderson of Linguistics, Dr. Bernhard Maurach of Modern Languages, Mrs. Susan Treggiari of Classics and Dr. Michael MacConaill of Medicine. At Cambridge, Christopher Ryan of St. Edmund's House helped me with the Italian material, and the Department of Linguistics provided several occasions for airing parts of the book. Dr. Gregor Maurach of Pretoria gave valued assistance with the work of German translators from classical languages. Several generations of students at both Ottawa and Cambridge have seen the work grow, and their reactions have suggested interpretations that would otherwise have escaped me.

Most of the research was done in the university libraries of Ottawa, Cambridge and Harvard, with visits to St. Paul's University (Ottawa), Queen's (Kingston) and the Eastman School of Medicine (Rochester, New York). Important material came from the British Museum and the National Libraries of Canada and France. Mme. Conchita Belmonte-Proulx and Mme. Clémence Tondreau of the Ottawa Department of Linguistics typed the final manuscript with their usual cheerful efficiency and inspired interpretation of corrections and scribblings. And my wife Joy, by her understanding and encouragement in the face of what was, at times, an almost hopeless task, took a major hand in reducing the mountain of files to something readable.

With its usual generosity, the Canada Council provided two Summer Research Grants to enable me to visit Harvard, and a Leave Fellowship for 1973–4, which was spent at Cambridge.

To all of these, and to the many others who have knowingly and unknowingly contributed to this work, I offer my warmest thanks.

Acknowledgements

Collect for the Sunday of the Passion: Palm Sunday
1. Extrait du *Missel romain*, © Association Episcopale Liturgique pour les Pays Francophones, Paris 1969–74.
2. Taken from the English translation of the Roman Missal © 1973, International Committee on English in the Liturgy, Inc. All rights reserved.
3. Taken from the *Book of Common Prayer* (Proposed) Copyright © 1977 by Charles Mortimer Guilbert as Custodian of the Standard Book of Common Prayer. All rights reserved. Reprinted by permission.

Pound, translation of Dubellay, *Les antiquités de Rome II*,
   Taken from Ezra Pound, *Translations*. With an Introduction by Hugh Kenner. Copyright © by Ezra Pound. Reprinted by permission of Faber and Faber Ltd, London; and New Directions Publishing Corporation, New York.

Schadewalt, translation of Anacreon
   Taken from *Hellas und Hesperien* I. Reprinted by permission of Artemis Verlag, Zürich & Munich.

Steinberger, translation of Moore, 'The Last Rose of Summer'
   Taken from *Vita latina* 37 (May 1969) 31. Reprinted by permission of Editions Aubanel, Avignon.

von der Vring, translation of Herrick, 'To Dianeme'
   Taken from *Die Kunst der Übersetzung*, Oldenbourgh, Munich, 1963.

Zukofsky, translation of Catullus, Ode 27
   Taken from *Gai Valeri Catulli Veronensis Liber* © 1969 by Louis & Celia Zukofsky. Reprinted by permission of Jonathan Cape, Ltd., London.

Introduction

Western Europe owes its civilization to translators. From the Roman Empire to the Common Market, international commerce and administration has been made possible by translation; the first Christian translators were the four Evangelists who recorded in Greek what Christ and his disciples had said in Aramaic; and it is only since the early nineteenth century that scientists have ceded to professional translators the responsibility of turning essential books into the language of their fellow-countrymen. Yet in spite of this, writers from Republican Rome to the present have consistently treated translation as merely a branch of literature. It is little wonder then that a comprehensive theory of translation has proved elusive. For through neglect of non-literary work, significant thought and practice have been suppressed and forgotten.

But first, what is translation?

In its simplest terms, it is 'the interpretation of verbal signs by means of some other language' (Jakobson 1966, 233). The key word here is 'interpretation', as Jakobson comments:

> If we were to translate into English the traditional formula, *traduttore traditore*, as 'the translator is a betrayer', we would deprive the Italian rhyming epigram of all its paronomastic value. Hence a cognitive attitude would compel us to change this aphorism into a more explicit statement, and to answer the questions: translator of what messages? betrayer of what values?

Obviously, translators have answered the first question by pointing to the genre and subject of their source text. As all texts are message-bearing, any discussion of theory rests on the second question; for the user of language seeks from an utterance not only what it contains, but also why it was said. Rarely are these issues explicitly formulated in translation; they depend on relationships instinctively placed between content, reader and expression.

A complete theory of translation, then, has three components: specification of function and goal; description and analysis of operations; and critical comment on relationships between goal and operations. Few writers have presented a universally applicable theory of translation.

Indeed, the only example that comes readily to mind is George Campbell (1719–96), principal of Marischal College, Aberdeen, whose 500-page introduction to his 1789 translation of the Gospels discusses a practical theory of semantic and grammatical equivalence within the frame of both literary and spiritual goals of scriptural translation.

Most of those mentioned in this book treat one facet of theory to the exclusion of others. For the majority, translation is a literary craft; from the prologues of the dramatist, Terence (190?–159 B.C.), to Jiri Levý, the most common focus of attention has been the creative aspect of translation. A curious legacy of this is the almost universal custom in libraries of classifying books on translations with manuals of literary criticism. Reciprocal influences between form and content, ramifications of source and target texts in their respective literary traditions, the rights and duties of the translator, all are constant themes since Cicero's discussions in *De finibus* and *De optimo genere oratorum*. Except for a continual fascination with the rights and wrongs of literal and free translation, this stream of theory has analysed aims and results without paying much attention to the linguistic operations involved.

In contrast, linguists and grammarians have identified theory with analysis of semantic and grammatical operations. The major tradition of this type, lasting from St. Augustine (354–430) to the twentieth-century European structuralists, sees meaning in terms of the dualistic Aristotelian model of the sign. During the twentieth century, this was challenged from two quarters. American structural linguists, denying that a linguistic sign 'contained' meaning in the Aristotelian sense, saw the translator's task as creating a language structure which would evoke the same reaction in a target-language reader as the original had in its readers. On the same assumption, the London School of J. R. Firth sought linguistic equivalence through creating an utterance that would fit into the same social context ('context of situation') as the original. In each case, translation is regarded as an application of linguistics: the aim of creating a text of equivalent meaning is assumed, and the object of theory is to describe and validate lexical and grammatical manipulations meant to attain that meaning.

The third approach, hermeneutics, treats language and its signs as creative energy. Though the concept of the Word (λόγος) is Platonic in origin, and came into Jewish and Christian theology through Philo Iudaeus (*fl.* 20 B.C.), it enters translation theory through Johann Gottlieb Herder (1744–1803) and the German Romantics. The Romantics began reversing the priorities of traditional sign theory; where traditionally the word had existed solely as an index to a concept, in the thought of Wilhelm von Humboldt (1767–1835) it shaped concepts and cultures. Romanticism was an ideology which, by identifying language and nation, was later to fuel the nationalist movements of Europe for the next century and a half.

For in their eyes, history of language went hand in hand with history of nation, because the vigour of its language forged the identity of a nation and every aspect of its culture. What the Romantics sought through translation was to transfer the creative power of great writers of other languages into their own. Thus translation was not primarily production of a text, but interpretation and contemplation of Language at work. Friedrich Hölderlin (1780–1843), seeing individual languages as realizations of 'Pure Language', made of translation a search for the kernels of meaning which composed this basic tongue. Under the impetus of this tradition, German linguistic philosophers of the early twentieth century dismissed the Saussurean concept of language as inadequate and untrue to its generative power. Thus when Martin Heidegger (1889–   ) speaks of language as 'the House of Being', he is redefining the Romantic tradition in terms reminiscent of Roman Catholic sacramental theology, in which signs are not merely indicators, but also *signa efficientia*.

Each one of these theories of translation falls short: for the literary and epistemological directions of the first and third groups leave aside technique; and the linguistic theories assume a very generalized purpose for translation. Furthermore, in their present forms, they all have an unrealistically restricted view of their own section of theory. In the case of the literary theorist, not all uses of language are literature; and so there is a large body of translation resting on uncreative language functions and purely objective transfers of information. Likewise, in the form which has most influenced translation, hermeneutic theory biasses its object by assuming that all uses of language are essentially creative, that all language signs are primarily *signa efficientia*. This is patently absurd: as daily life demands from language everything from automatic routines to the sublimest of utterances, inspiration of the type taken for granted by Heidegger and Meschonnic is rarely called on. Thus the literary theorist is not concerned with the ordinary uses of language; and the hermeneutic theorist has misinterpreted the nature and function of the linguistic sign.

Nor can the linguist escape unscathed. He too has misinterpreted the nature of the linguistic sign by seeing its auditory component purely in relation to the concept, rather than having significant value in its own right. His vision of sign-function is likewise narrow: in concentrating on lexicon and grammar, he has, until recently, neglected the wider question of discourse. In addition, it is only since the appearance of sociolinguistics as a separate discipline, that the social implications of Saussure's dichotomy between *signification* and *valeur* have brought home to linguists that the subjective and objective information carried out by the linguistic sign is not as consistent as is usually made out.

In the polemic between these three groups of theorists, only a

few individuals have perceived that their approaches are complementary. Fortunately, good translation has never depended on adequate
theory.

A translator moulds his image of translation by the function he assigns
to language; from function, one extrapolates to nature. Thus those who
translate merely for objective information, have defined translation differently from those for whom the source text has a life of its own. Hence, our
account of how theory and practice have evolved begins with a summary
of European thought on the nature and function of language as it has
affected translation. The models and definitions of chapter 2, then, depend
on purposes and functions of language as they are revealed in actual
translations. It is significant that practice has usually come before theory,
so that the first attempt at definition occurs in Quintilian (A.D. 90) (see page
44, below), though intuitive models of translation had already been
reflected in practice for some 300 years. In chapter 3, the different genres of
translation are related to Karl Buhler's three functions of language: objective information, self-expression and persuasion.

Chapters 4, 5 and 6 are concerned with the second component of theory,
specification of operations. Translation involves a double interpretation.
Its first element, usually instinctive, assesses the balance of communicative
function; then interpretation focusses on 'content', and the way it is
coloured by function. The lexical and grammatical operations following
this act of interpretation are described according to the Geneva School's
stylistique comparée, one of the most comprehensive modern linguistic
approaches to translation practice.

In order to relate principles and technique, chapters 7 and 8 focus on
texts themselves, rather than on the ideologies and techniques so far
exemplified; and chapter 9 discusses the evolution of translation theory
from Roman times until the present. Thereby, achievements of translators
are measured against theory and purpose as they have differed between
genres and periods. The snippets of translation were largely chosen at
random with little regard to quality. Unintelligent application of principle
is often as revealing as subtle mastery: the pretentious insensitivity of
Desfontaines is as illustrative of the eighteenth century as Tarteron's
delightful Horace. In an effort to cast the net as far as possible and to
maintain a difficult balance between the various fields of translation,
interesting texts, even if obscure, have been included when they best
illustrate points at issue. Where possible, translations have been checked
against recensions of the original extant during the translator's lifetime; for
modern critical texts often differ significantly. Where the original does not
appear in the text with its translation, it will be found in the Appendix,
referenced to other translations quoted. Passages in classical languages
have been translated into English; in the case of illustrative passages, this

translation is merely a crib, whose function is glossing the words rather than elucidating the content.

If in its own time and for its own purposes, every competent translation is judged adequate, it is clear that, given differences between periods and genres, adequacy in translation is a concept at the mercy of intellectual fashion and pragmatic need. It is therefore the intention of this book to criticize, rather than to evaluate. For evaluation would necessarily entail measuring the past against the standards of the present: in so measuring one's predecessors, one is tempted to read difference as deficiencies. And it is this act of evaluation, which, mistaken for dispassionate evaluation, is the instrument of the evolution we are about to trace.

One

Translation and Language Theory

In the Western world, theories about language depend on two complementary ways of knowing, characteristic of different ways cultures have of approaching reality.[1] The first, represented by linguistics, systematizes observable speech phenomena to arrive at analysis of the means of expression. It is strongly empirical, and at least three times in the last 2,000 years has attempted to take on the trappings of an exact science: the thirteenth century saw linguistics fall under the influence of Aristotelian philosophy; during the eighteenth century it was dominated by logic; and during the twentieth, it took its orientation first from the social and behavioural sciences, and then from symbolic logic and mathematics. Linguistics assumes that language is an instrument, and that its essence can be described by relating observed behaviour to scientific models.

Where linguistics concentrates on the means of expression, the complementary hermeneutic approach analyses the goal of linguistic interactions. The focus here is anti-empiricist: the central reality is not the observable expression, but the understanding of the cognitive and affective levels of language through which communication takes place.

For translation theory these complementary approaches to language set up two tensions against which Jakobson's 'values' can be assessed at each period. The first is that between language as instrument and language as λόγος, a division that is far from contradictory. The second is that between different conceptions of the scope of translation theory. The adequacy measures of the linguist are drawn from analysis of the two linguistic codes involved, while the philosopher and man of letters takes the means represented by these adequacy measures for granted, asking whether the translation communicates in a way befitting the original.

I.I LANGUAGE AS INSTRUMENT

Early formulations of translation theory rest on characteristics of the word and its representative function, leaving structure in a theoretical limbo. The first coherent theory of this type comes from St. Augustine (354–430), who tried to create a theoretical framework for the two main teaching activities of the early Church, preaching and translation. His most important works here are *De magistro*, an early dialogue with his son Adeodatus; *De doctrina christiana*, an early work on scripture published near the end of his career in 427; and the *Enarrationes ad psalmos*, a series of sermons on the psalms.

Augustine begins *De magistro* by characterizing the goal of language as teaching and learning. On one hand, this is a direct reminiscence of Cicero's habitual *docere* (to teach) in the sense of forensic argument; on the other, it is an amplification of Aristotle's sign theory, which originally had relevance only to rhetoric. Augustine takes the word to be 'a conventional sign pertaining to the ear'. Aristotle's σημαινόμενον becomes the *significatio*, and his σημαῖνον the *sonus* (i.e. signified and signifier). The *significatio* is a mental construct derived from perception of reality, while the *sonus* is the group of vocal sounds associated with it. Within the word itself, the *sonus* is the sign of the *significatio*, a link as arbitrary as that of the whole sign with the thing signified.

From the arbitrary or conventional nature of the sign there flow a number of important consequences. The first is that one cannot 'know' words without having direct or indirect experience of what they signify. The second is that more than one *sonus* can be the sign of a single *significatio*, thus producing synonymy; and more than one *significatio* can be expressed through a single *sonus*, thus producing transferred senses. And third, the mechanism which controls these arbitrary links and keeps them meaningful is the linguistic habits or customs of the community, a crucial application of the Roman concept of *mos maiorum* to the Christian community.

As an example of the first problem, Augustine quotes Daniel iii. 94: 'Et saraballae eorum non sunt immutatae' (*De magistro* x. 33), noting that, though he assumes *saraballa* to be a head covering, never having seen the object concerned, he cannot be sure. His scribes unwittingly drive home his point, for, though the accepted reading is *capitum tegmina*, there is a well-supported variant, *pedum tegmina*. Obviously the scribes were no better informed on the matter than he was. To deal with synonymy, he invokes the arbitrary nature of the sign. In his comment on Psalm vi. 2, where he discusses the Greek words, θύμος, and ὄργη, and their Latin translations, *furor* and *ira*, he establishes first that the four words denote the same reality; and then, arguing from the essential arbitrariness of the sign linkage, states that the word of God was not harmed by the personal preference of translators while the sense remains intact. The third issue, that of transferred senses, he takes back to the principle of divine illumination which will aid the translator in analysing the substantive sense behind the *sonus*.

Yet Augustine seems uneasy about his theoretical postulates. Though he assumes that different languages share *significationes*, he admits that certain Hebrew words, e.g. *Amen* and *Racha*, have no Latin equivalents, and sanctions borrowing them. He is also forced to admit that *significationes* can vary according to modalities of perception. In the title of the Gradual Psalms, for instance, the Greek term, ἀναβαθμῶν, implies that the steps concerned lead upwards. And indeed they do; for these are the main steps leading to the Holy of Holies in the temple of Jerusalem. But the Latin *graduum* does not have this directional sense. Augustine writes this off as a gap in the resources of Latin, but in the light of many similar examples, his explanation rings hollow.

Another major problem rises from his habitual overt identification of the linguistic sign with the word. Certain passages in the *Enarrationes in psalmos* treat Greek bound morphemes as independent signs: for example in Psalm cxviii. 43, Augustine commends *supersperavi* for the Septuagint's ἐπήλπισα, because, although the form is rare, it conforms to 'the necessity of translating truth'. A glance at the Vulgate shows that the translator thus singled out was probably St. Jerome (347–419). But there are times when Augustine's scruples over bound morphemes show up even Jerome in a bad light. In Psalm lxxvii. 31, Jerome has *impedivit* for συνεπόδισεν. Augustine objects on two grounds: first the Greek συν is translated by *cum*, not *in*; second, God's anger did not merely impede, it actually led the Israelites into slavery, which is one of the senses of *compedivit*. In his Hebrew Psalter, taken direct from the Hebrew text, Jerome writes *incurvavit* (to bend under the yoke), a much more accurate rendering. Augustine was certainly no more favourable to literal translation than Jerome, but his choice for the more transparent *compedivit* over the imagery of *incurvavit* shows more regard for the form and make-up of the sign than Jerome considered necessary, or even helpful.

Augustine's theories had little immediate effect on translation, the practice of St. Jerome receiving more publicity and a certain amount of imitation. It is not until the second half of the Middle Ages that Augustine's sign theories are quoted as a possible basis for discussions of translation. Among philosophers and grammarians the Augustinian theory of the sign was common property. In Part III of his *Opus maius* Roger Bacon (1220–92), no friend to translators, argues against the very possibility of translation from an Augustinian base, claiming that differences in the semantic coverage of Greek, Hebrew and Latin made translation a patchwork of errors and misunderstandings. Bacon's arguments reappear a century and a half later at the Council of Oxford (1401) as a flail with which to beat the Lollards. Butler, an official theologian, sees three major causes of error in interpreting signs in the Biblical text: acquaintance with words without knowing the things referred to; knowledge of things without knowing the word, and ignorance of both word and thing (Deanesley 1920, 405). The Lollards' errors are categorized under each of these three headings.

Until the twentieth century, there is little practical advance from the medieval reading of Augustine. The Humanists and their successors repeated incessantly that full knowledge of word-meaning entailed direct or indirect experience of the thing signified. There seems to be a slight change during the late seventeenth century owing to the development of *la grammaire générale*. Charles Rollin, rector of the Sorbonne, writes in his *Traité des études* (III. iii):

> Les pensées sont les images des choses, comme les paroles sont les images des pensées.

Pensée here has more than its modern sense of *thought*, including any mental act, even emotions. Despite their working hypothesis that all languages were cast in the same logical mould, scholars of the Age of Reason were painfully aware of specific language differences. By various applications of casuistry, they found their way around the problem, gradually coming to the point of conceding that the meaning of a word was a many-faceted affair. With more acceptance of language differences, the emphasis moved away from attempts to 'correct' the situation towards methods of symbolization and explanation, of which the Venn diagram seems to be one of the earliest, being cited by Schopenhauer (1861, 101–2).

During the twentieth century, theories of meaning applied to translation take two forms. Beside the traditional sign theory, which we shall lay aside for a moment, rise positivistic theories based on observations of behaviour. Such theories of meaning reject the traditional dualism, relating their object to three readily analysable characteristics of language: relevance in the social situation in which the utterance is produced; role of the utterance within a unit of psychological behaviour; and relationships of linguistic units to context. The philosophical background to the movements adopting these positivistic theories is a fragmented one: in England, the primary source was Wittgenstein's '. . . the meaning of a word is its use in the language' (*Philosophical Investigations* I. 43); and in America, the behaviourist movement in psychology, which attempted to reduce all human actions to bodily processes. It is no secret that meaning is the area of linguistics that this group of theories treated least effectively.

The first element of meaning that came under the notice of our two groups of theorists was its relevance to social situation. Bloomfield, indeed, explicitly defines meaning of a linguistic form as '. . . the situation in which the speaker utters it, and the response it calls forth from the hearer'. The Firthians term this element of meaning 'the context of situation'.[2] This, the first aspect of Wittgenstein's ambiguous word, 'use', came to Firth from the anthropologist, Malinowski. The point here is that as language is used only in some sort of situation, Malinowski assumed that the situation generated the meaning of linguistic utterances attached to it. Thus, the word 'cow' means something different in a milking shed from its use as an unflattering description of an old lady in a post office queue. Firth nuanced Malinowski's rather simplistic model by classifying the observable elements of the situation, i.e. participants, effects, non-verbal acts.

The Bloomfieldian approach did not make as much of the context of situation, but nuanced it against the responses of participants, which can be an internal reaction (Nida 1964, 41–2). For translation, Bloomfield's definition led immediately into communication theory, which has considerable relevance to the anthropological cast of the American tradition in both linguistics and translation. Punya Sloka Ray (1962, 182) reflects these concerns in his fourfold division of the aspects of meaning. His first division, 'meaning as information', is the commonplace of the first-year linguistics class: later investigators of translation divided it into explicit information, which is what the words of the passage say, and implicit information, which is background information assumed to be shared by the speech community (Taber 1970, 1). 'Meaning as impact' derives from the affective focus of words in text: for instance, the famous 'four-letter words' of English (and the equally notorious *cinq lettres* in French) have an impact quite different from their technical and medically correct synonyms. 'Meaning as legitimacy' has the double face of concordance with the context and acceptance by the receiver. And 'meaning as locality' takes into account language features peculiar to certain geographical areas and social strata.

It is within this tradition that Quine produced his concept of 'stimulus meaning'. It is clear from his *Word and Object* that he conceives translation as a search for the meaning structures of a language through examination of behaviour, or as he himself described the task of the anthropological linguist: 'the recovery of a man's current language from his currently observed responses' (Quine 1960, 28). While both Firth and Bloomfield take meaning as a *datum*, Quine (ibid. 32) has meaning arise from the assent of the receiver of a stimulus to its truth or verisimilitude. Translation is then based on what he calls 'analytical hypotheses' concerning the degree to which one has correctly interpreted the stimulus and then matched it. Hence, as Kirk (1969, 321) points out, Quine impugns the philosopher's assumption that meaning is an objective entity. Quine's reasoning in defence of his position is based very largely on the Sapir–Whorf hypothesis and on twentieth-century models of communication: meaning turns on behaviour and socially relevant factors, not on the traditionally objective sign-function. Quine also points out that there are many accidents that can happen on the way between the words uttered by his native and the notebook of his linguist. Superfluous information can completely skew the data, so that assent can be given to the wrong-meaning result. Unfortunately, this is the experience of every translator at some time or other.

In this connection, there is an interesting passage in Ebeling (op. cit. 95ff). In pointing out that even a common language is no guarantee of understanding, Ebeling notes that language is used to lie as easily as to tell the truth. This does not come into Quine's model, as a linguistic researcher must be able to assume that his subjects are telling the truth if his research is to have any grounds at all. But, more relevantly to Quine's thesis, Ebeling discusses the misunderstandings that can arise when one discusses the same thing in the same language but with different postulates on which word-meaning is based. In this, he enunciates the common sociolinguist's dictum that the divisive and separative function of language is as important an object of study as the communicative. Hence, the indeterminacy argument, or its consequences, is one of the constant factors of a translator's professional life. And despite his rather mechanistic consideration of it, Quine affords an opening towards the rival hermeneutic theories to be examined later in this chapter.

The second element in the definition of meaning for the American structuralist and Firthian schools is what Catford (1965, 35) calls 'formal relations'. The first of these is distribution, 'collocation' in Firth's terms: a word is known by the company it keeps. For some linguists, this was the unarguable method of defining word-meaning. Firth added to this 'set', a paradigmatically related group of words that pertained to the same context of situation, and could be used in the same type of collocation and make sense. For Firth and his school, these formal relations were a second major tool in defining word-meaning, but their relevance was not exploited in translation theory to the same extent as the context of situation.

Modern versions of the ancient theory of signs widened their scope to take in the functionalist concerns just discussed. There are two main concerns: the first, normally associated with Saussure, to the complete exclusion of philosophers such as Charles Pierce, is a reiteration of the traditional dualist sign model and the way it functions; the second is an investigation of the question of subsidiary meaning, or *valeur*. The first theory in the field was the *stylistique* of Charles Bally. Though Bally himself specifically excluded the written language from consideration, Jules Marouzeau applied his principles to Latin, showing the way to others who developed a Saussurean stylistics to the written language, and eventually translation.

The most important legacy of Bally was a carefully considered debt to the nineteenth-century *Völkerpsychologie*. In discussing vocabulary, he characterized vocabulary differences as modes of seeing peculiar to each language: words in Germanic languages tend towards a picture, reflecting a physical type of vision; while those in Romance define, resting on a mental vision (Bally 1912, 89). On the plane of the *signifiant*, Bally noted that German prefers *motivation explicite*, i.e. a transparency of derivation that French does not exploit to the same extent. Malblanc (1968, 118) goes further: he marks a definite dichotomy between French, which is by preference *arbitraire*, and German, by preference *motivé*. Vinay and Darbelnet extend this principle to English; for example, to the German and English, *blind*, correspond respectively *Blindheit* and *blindness*, while to the French *aveugle* corresponds *cécité*.

Differences on the systematic level of *signifiant* reflect similar differences on the level of *signifié*. Malblanc (1944) reworks the over-used and somewhat jejune designation of French as a 'logical language', to arrive at the principle that French prefers an intellectual vocabulary, while German prefers an affective. Again Vinay and Darbelnet concur as far as English is concerned. The root cause of this is that words can be *signes* or *images* (Malblanc 1968, 33). The *mot signe* is a simplification or intellectualization of the real, while the *mot image* attempts to evoke sense impressions and unmediated linkage with experience. Again we can oppose French and Germanic languages: French tends towards stasis because of this preference for mediated analysis, which freezes movement; German because of its opposite preference for *image*, which implies immediacy, tends towards dynamism in word reference.

Vinay and Darbelnet (1958) adopted this distinction, finding the same preference for *image* in English as in German: for instance, to the neutral word, *bruit*, English can oppose an equally neutral word, *noise*, but given the right context can oppose *thump*, *swish*, *thud*, *crack*, *rattle*, etc., all of which have a certain pictorial value modifying the onomatopoeia. In the Vinay–Darbelnet version, however, their distinction between the *plan de l'entendement*, based on the *mot signe*, and the *plan du réel* based on the *mot image*, applies both concepts to grammar as well as lexicon.

Where traditional sign theory had assumed the presence of the person mentally making the sign, Bally and his successors had based the making of the sign on perceptions which varied according to a system characteristic of each language. This laid the ground for one of the most notable achievements of *stylistique comparée*, its absorption of certain social elements from contemporary positivist linguistics. To do this Vinay and Darbelnet altered Saussure's sign diagram slightly, to show how the sign was integrated into the situation of utterance (see fig. 1). In so doing, they take up both Firth and Bloomfield. Their discussion of metalinguistic relevance (Vinay and Darbelnet 1958, 259) is an almost standard repro-duction of the Whorf hypothesis, but it pays careful attention to both social and interior reactions of speaker and hearer and, in the context of

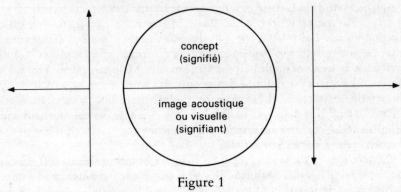

concept
(signifié)

image acoustique
ou visuelle
(signifiant)

Figure 1

translation, author, translator and reader. It is against this background that the question of *valeur* is discussed. There is little change from the basic dichotomy of intellectual and affective put forward by Bally, except for deriving from it finer oppositions such as *normal/technical*; *popular/learned*, etc.

Stylistique comparée was early marked down as a linguistics of *parole*, and derided in certain quarters as 'un livre de recettes'. In one sense this is unjust, as it does not take into account the way the authors carefully related expression to habits of perception and conception. In another sense, the accusation has some basis in that their continual specification of techniques hides theoretical postulates.

Attempts to transcend this pragmatic concern begin with Mounin (1963), who takes his analysis of word meaning from Hjelmslev and Prieto. The basis of a possible translation theory is the 'unité de signifi-cation', which exists in the Hjelmslev concept of *figura*, i.e. an abstract relationship which is part of the content associated with expression. These *figurae* are usually isolated by commutation tests: thus the Latin word *vir* is opposed to both *homo* and *mulier*: *homo* has a generic *figura* of 'humanness' opposed to the specific maleness of *vir*; and the maleness of *vir* is opposed to the specific femaleness of *mulier*.

The reaction against *stylistique comparée* continued with Vernay (1974), who attempted to put into practice Saussure's conception of linguistics as a section of the more general science of semiology. His discussion proceeds from two re-readings of the Ogden–Richards schema in the light of

Saussure's slightly simpler model. The starting point is comparison between the Ullmann and Baldinger versions of Ogden and Richards:

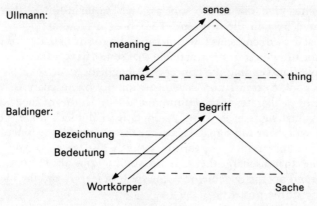

Figure 2

As in the traditional model of the sign, the meaning of a word is not
identical with the thing to which it refers. Hjelmslev's *figurae* in the work
of later linguists became *semes*, which are of two types, those of specifically
semantic reference (which make up the *sememe*), and those of grammatical
reference (which make up the *classeme*). Sememes of universal reference
were termed the *noeme*. This model of meaning, the *signifié*, in Saussure's
terms, is linked to a lexeme, which is Saussure's *signifiant*, Ullmann's name'
and Baldinger's *Wortkörper*. Vernay (1974, 30), gives the last word to Klaus
Heger by quoting his diagram (Fig. 3).

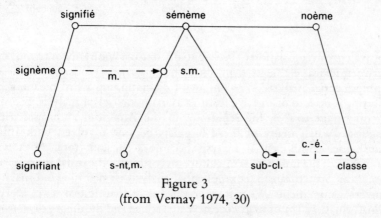

Figure 3
(from Vernay 1974, 30)

By assembling all the elements of the *signifié* into one unit (represented by the abbreviation *m.*), the linkage between *signifiant* and *signifié* (*signème*) becomes a unit in which all the various semes and sememes are united. It is then represented by a unitary *signifiant* (s-nt,m). The grammatical semes in the sememe give rise to the subclass, whose inclusion in the class is represented by *i* in the diagram. The concept of seme (*figura*) is thus functional in two senses: its function can be linguistic in that it has a role to play in the utterance; or pragmatic, in that semes have a social communicative role transcending the concerns of linguistic structure.

Application to translation depends primarily on an analysis, whether intuitive or deliberate, of the communicative functions of the text and of the individual signs in it. Vernay adopts Karl Buhler's three functions, symbol, symptom and signal. It is in the discharge of these functions that the roots of universality rest: the functions themselves are universal as are the noemes that discharge them. In Saussurean terms, the balance between function and noeme or sememe is an aspect of *langue*, and the method of expressing it the property of *parole*.

The translator's problem then becomes one dealing with the different ways in which *figurae* are combined. Words can have elements of meaning in common or share some *figurae* without sharing others, a point brought out in Baldinger's diagram of synonymy through interlinked Ogden–Richards triangles (see fig. 4). Vernay takes the problem of

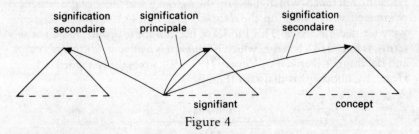

signification   signification   signification
secondaire   principale   secondaire

signifiant   concept

Figure 4

equivalence in translation to be essentially one of synonymy or paronymy between lexical elements from different languages. Under the name of 'componential analysis', a technique of diagramming word-meaning by splitting it up into distinctive features as in phonological analysis, became an important tool in the repertoire of the American anthropological linguists. When many of these linguists became involved with Bible translation, componential analysis became a constant tool. As it was conscious of the uniqueness of cultures according to the usual approach of American Structuralism, componential analysis tended to avoid making universal judgements. When it was refined as a semantic analysis model by transformational grammar, little new was added and the theory of translation certainly drew no further benefit from it.

Unlike philosophical theories of the word, theories of grammar were slow to rise in Europe. 'Grammar' for the ancients was concerned largely with morphology, while questions of sentence and discourse structure seemed to be more the concern of rhetoric. For translation theory, the point at issue is a simple one: are morphology and syntax merely a device for arranging words, or have they some representational function?

For the ancient grammarian, morphology was merely a device to fit the word to enter syntax; and the first appearance of contrastive grammar in the shape of the Macrobius *De differentiis et societatibus graeci latinique verbi* (*c.* A.D. 400) did not alter the situation. The only references to morphological problems during the Middle Ages were oblique: Cassiodorus (560?, 43) advises his monks to avoid putting Latin flexions on Hebrew proper nouns; and Hilduinus (835, 15) quite clearly tells his patron, Louis the Pious, that comments on the grammar of his Latin translation are beside the point. The *grammatica speculativa*, which was one medieval attempt to make of Latin flexional patterns something more than a sort of linguistic glue, was not applied to translation, even if traces of it appear in Roger Bacon's Greek grammar (1272?). An extremely utilitarian approach to morphology remained current until the twentieth century, suiting the anti-mentalist orientations of Structural linguistics and Firthian linguistics adequately, and creating a tradition in which morphology was one language resource that transformational-generative grammar handled with considerable difficulty.

The other way of approaching morphology is to see it as the embodiment of a certain category of meaning which reflects a particular world view or a particular way of viewing the relationships between elements of experience symbolized by the words in the utterance. There are hints of such an approach to morphology in the *Völkerpsychologie*, but they remain undeveloped until the beginning of the twentieth century.

Let us illustrate from the categories of tense and aspect in the verb. Bally labels tense as 'la localisation du concept du procès'. Events are usually localized in relation to one's own place in time, which becomes the present; what has already happened is the past; and what is still to happen is the future. While tense can thus be conceived as horizontal, aspect is the vertical, running from inception up to completion: in Bally's view, 'le concept du procès est quantifié par l'aspect du verbe'. From a purely descriptive point of view, verbal systems of different languages can be sorted into those expressing aspect, those expressing tense, and those expressing both. But classification is not theory: mentalist theories of verb flexion begin from statements such as that of Mario Wandruszka (1968, 113), 'l'aspect est le record de l'expérience humaine', a principle that applied equally well to tense and to the balance each language achieves between tense and aspect in the mental representation of time. A second balance is that between flexional representation and syntactic within the verb system.

Stylistique comparée relates the nature and use of morphological features in different languages to preferences for the *plan de l'entendement* or the *plan du réel*. In this, morphological tendencies follow lexical. Thus French, which prefers the *plan de l'entendement*, organizes its vision and expression of time according to logical priorities: the continuum represented by time is cut into distinct *tranchées* (slices) (Vinay and Darbelnet 1958, 130). In contrast, English and German have a much less intellectual concept of time: and the expression of time follows the priorities of sense impressions. Indeed Malblanc (1968, 83) speaks of the 'tactile concept of time' in Germanic languages. In the light of this it might be better to see the *plan du réel* as the *plan du visuel*, while the *plan de l'entendement* is the *plan du logique*:

> cf. Je vous attends depuis une heure / I have been waiting for you for an hour.

Not only is the perfective continuative of English a paradox, but in English the view taken looks back to the past, when the wait began; while French concentrates solely on the observable fact that the speaker is still waiting, and infers continuity from the past. This sort of judgement leads to the specification of technique, and is the reason why *stylistique comparée* was widely accused of concentrating on *parole*. It never makes judgements on morphological forms outside structure, taking for granted the system of time, aspect and tense as it is put forward by Bally (1932).

Other schools of European structuralists treated morphology as a sign system that had value apart from structure. Hjelmslev and the Glossematists developed the concept of grammatical *figurae* parallel with semantic *figurae*, and so tense and aspect equivalences depended on a matching of relevant *figurae*. Guillaumean linguists went in a slightly different direction to contrast the actual nature of time with time systems in languages. According to Guillaume himself the present separates the past from the future. And in so doing, it has elements of both past and future in it:[3] hence the possibility of *je vous attends depuis une heure* and *je vous attends pour une heure*, which are past and future in reference respectively. English, on the other hand, divides time into past and non-past, and the future becomes a special case of the non-past:[4] e.g. *I have been waiting for you for an hour* and *I'll be waiting for you at one o'clock*. This sort of approach was not fully applied to translation theory, morphology being intensely difficult to separate from syntax; but attempts begin with the Prague Circle in the 1930s, and, after thirty years of near neglect, reappear in the late 1960s.

The perceptive Classical practice of translation had produced no contrastive syntax; a lack which was felt 1,500 years later by the Humanists: John Palsgrave, for example, writes in the preface to his *Acolastus* (1540, 6) that the 'chiefe thynge the scholemaster should travayle in' is the different sentence and period patterns in Latin and English. While this was a classroom commonplace, neither teaching nor translation developed a structural theory out of it before the seventeenth century. One of the reasons was that syntax was not considered to be message-bearing, and stylistic studies were more the property of the rhetorician. We find this view again among the positivist schools of linguistics already referred to; so that syntactic contrast in their hands becomes a series of *ad hoc* precepts.

The opposite view, that syntactic arrangement was not fortuitous, affected translation very deeply from the beginning of the seventeenth century, mainly through the *petites écoles de Port-Royal*. Contrastive grammar and rhetoric were in the air as part of a scholarly climate which was attempting to show that the modern languages were as supple literary vehicles as Latin and Greek. Flexional morphology was not an issue: by several brands of casuistry, the Latin and Greek flexional system was assumed to be universal. The issue was syntax, which, being logically based, was universal at least in essence. The features of syntax common to all languages were termed *syntaxe de convenance*, those belonging to individual languages only, the *syntaxe de régime*. As put forward by Daniel Huet (1661, 45), language differences are to be found in differing grammatical patterns, which come roughly under Port-Royal's *syntaxe de régime*, and also in different degrees of freedom in figures of speech, an element that caused considerable debate in the eighteenth century.

For Port-Royal, the central point of theory was *'l'ordre naturel'*, i.e. an order of words which reflected the progression between subject and predicate in a logical proposition. By a fortunate but unexplained series of events, the only language which consistently reflected the natural order was French. Other languages which did not observe this order, like Latin, or consistently disturbed it, like English, showed evidence of lack of logical rigour.

Several assumptions underlie the Port-Royal version of *l'ordre naturel*. Language is, for them, essentially rationalistic: style is something added on to provide 'beauty'. Expressive affective priorities are definitely in second place. For Charles Batteux (1713–80), it was clear that a natural universal word order existed but, in the light of the strong rationalism of the period, his view was little short of scandalous. His basic principle (Batteux 1747–8, v. 219) was that there were many *ordres naturels* deriving from 'la nature de l'homme', and that in man's nature affectivity was at least as important as logic. Therefore the universal element was not grammar, but word order. The corollary was that grammatical structure was controlled by sentence order, and that, in a case of conflict, grammatical structure was sacrificed.

Towards the end of the eighteenth century, there comes an awareness of the freedom of word order possible through flexional morphology, one of the important treatments of the question outside French being George Campbell's *Rhetoric* (1776). But the old habit of thinking in fixed word orders made the type of dislocation and inversion common in classical languages hotly debated subjects. In the Tenth Fragment, Herder (1767, 182) makes the word order characteristic of a language depend on the *Volksgeist*, so that, as the spirit of a people is characteristic, so is the type of syntax preferred in the sentence.

Batteux's ideas on a variable *ordre naturel* were developed a century later by Henri Weil (1844, 5), who started from the principle that, as the words were signs of ideas, following the original word order entailed preserving the priority of ideas in the original. Be it a simple or complex sentence, a proposition will always contain *une notion initiale* and *un but*, even if they do not consistently occur in a logical order (ibid. 38), but on occasion appear in an order determined by subjective priorities of the speaker. Weil's *notion initiale* is not the first term of a logical proposition, but 'l'être dont l'action émane', and other parts of the proposition act as qualifiers. All languages, in his view, possess two orders of syntax: an ascending order from *notion initiale* to *but* and an opposite descending order; the first is designed to show the essential unity of the complex thought behind the sentence, the second the parts and their relationships.

The analytical consequences of this are the following: first, there are two orders in the sentence: an objective order expressed by grammatical relationships, and an affective order expressed by word order; secondly, in modern languages, in contradistinction to ancient, the order of words also expresses certain syntactic relationships; and third, despite this semi-identity, the two orders of syntax and word-sequence are entirely independent, a consequence with which Batteux and his contemporaries had played, but did not adopt. As a practical consequence, the prior element in a sentence is the affective order of ideas, and the grammar is adapted to suit, especially when translating (Weil 1844, 21).

Though Weil's ideas had some currency among classicists, he himself remained relatively unknown, and the credit for propagating this separation of word order and syntax went to the *Völkerpsychologie*. In a long series of articles Georg von der Gabelentz developed the ideas of psychological subject and psychological predicate, which correspond in all respects to Weil's *notion initiale* and *but*. In developing this theory, von der Gabelentz relies heavily on Herder's notion of the way in which the *Volksgeist* determines preferences in sentence shape, and beyond that, the basic shape of the grammar. Sentence shape reflects priorities in ideas and feelings, and is basically a psychological and not a linguistic reality. Word order is meaningful in these terms, and has to be respected.

We are faced then with a situation where two disparate groups were teaching almost the same theory of language without being aware of the other, or so it seems. Weil is cited in several late-nineteenth-century Latin grammars and in translation manuals such as Cauer (1893) and Tolman (1901). The *Völkerpsychologie* stream, while ignoring the classicists and being ignored by them, was the one on which several significant twentieth-century theories were built.

Twentieth-century discussions of syntax in translation fell into four groups: the first follows naturally from *Völkerpsychologie* and is strongly influenced by Saussure; the second comes from American structuralism; the third from the followers of Firth in England; and the most recent, and so far the least fruitful, is transformational-generative grammar.

European structuralism begins its interest in translation theory in a climate that is ambiguous. Literary stylistics was interested in the repercussions of sentence shape, but Charles Bally deliberately avoided the written language as an artificial construct. Bally takes over Weil's distinction 'entre l'ordre grammatical, relevant de la langue, et l'ordre psychologique relevant de la parole, et parfois aussi de la langue' (Vinay and Darbelnet 1958, 201). The actual theory of the sentence is developed by Sechehaye in *La structure logique de la phrase* (1926) and Bally's *Linguistique générale et linguistique française* (1932) as far as strict Saussurean theory is concerned. They adopt for the two parts of the sentence the terms *thème* and *propos*, which Vinay and Darbelnet (loc. cit.) define as follows: 'Le thème est un terme connu, le sujet psychologique à propos duquel on énonce un fait'; and 'le propos est le prédicat psychologique, point culminant du syntagme'.

Prague took over the same idea but tried to remove the psychological overtones by dividing the sentence or syntactic unit into the determined and the determiner, which correspond to Bally's *thème* and *propos*. They were later to be called 'theme' and 'rheme' (cf. the Greek ῥῆμα), or 'topic' and 'comment'. It is not easy to assign the credit for this: Mathesius, Karcevskij and Artymovic all seem to have had a hand in it. This last model was modified by Paul Garvin (1961, 288) to a dynamic model of a whole sentence supported on a fulcrum, which presupposes 'a grammatical code organized in terms of the potential syntactic functioning of the words, rather than in terms of their morphological origin'.

While this worked well for fixed-word-order languages, Marouzeau found it unsuitable for free-word-order languages like Latin. While fully agreeing with the premiss that word order is an issue apart from grammar, he did not see the Latin sentence as the linear progression necessary for the Bally theory of *démarche*. In classical Latin, the last word of the sentence, very often the verb of the main clause, acts as the cap-stone of an arch to close all dependencies. The order of the sentence is based on the 'valeur plastique ou dramatique' of the ideas concerned, so that there is considerable scope for disjunction and other spectacular sentence orders (Marouzeau 1935, 291–302). Both Saussureans and Prague developed their theory by analysis of the simple sentence: but, as Bally (1932, 56) remarks, 'Deux phrases sont coordonnées quand la seconde a pour thème la première'. One can also descend to the phrase level, and note that an adjective is the *propos* of its noun. It is in the Bally shape that the theory was developed into a comparative stylistics for French and German by Albert Malblanc, for French and English by Vinay and Darbelnet, and for German and English by Rudolf Jumpelt. There is a distinction to be drawn between internal *démarche* (i.e. that of sentence and phrase) and external *démarche* (that of the discourse unit). This does help in the analysis of sentence linkage, especially where the resources and techniques of a language are different. The mentalist approaches typical of this approach to comparative grammar were reduced to their barest essentials by Georges Mounin (1963), who based his syntactic theory of translation on the three universal fundamental relations of coordination, subordination and selection.

In English-speaking linguistics, syntactic elements in translation tended to be reduced to mere arrangements of meaningful units. Bloomfield's *immediate constituent analysis* was developed by Nida and Voegelin into a discovery procedure for isolating the meaningful units of the source text, assessing their grammatical function and forging equivalents in the target text. Nida developed Bloomfield's model of syntax by re-reading it in the light of communication theory, seeing syntax as the bearer of the message, rather than as an element which can become part of the message itself, as Vinay and Darbelnet make it. The important function of syntax in this view, is to create sufficient redundancy in the transmission channel to bear the message efficiently, keeping in mind that the message in most utterances is not only referential but also affective. As we find it in Catford, syntactic theory is based on M. A. K. Halliday's article, 'Categories in the Theory of Grammar' (*Word* 17, 1961, 241–92). This model of analysis adopts a single set of levels or 'ranks', which serve to compare languages. The levels appropriate to grammar begin with the sound, and increase in complexity up to the sentence, each rank being an immediate constituent of the one above it. Both Catford (1965) and Shillan (1970) use this analysis to suggest ways in which languages can be compared, and as a theoretical frame in which to build translation techniques. Again, the problem these two approaches shared with *stylistique comparée* was that they did not seem capable of progressing into universal principles. Catford especially has some brilliant descriptions of translation techniques; but there does not seem to be any deepening of this beyond statements about social function. Nida does not even have this, his catalogue of 'adjustments' being nothing beyond a list of things to do in awkward situations.

Yet in Nida (1964, 57–69) there is what could have been a promising development, the long section based on functional analyses of parts of a sentence, which contains certain elements of case-grammar. Nida adopts a functional classification of parts of speech based on categories of symbolic logic. His four classes are words indicating objects, events, attributes and relations. These are subdivided according to functions in the sentence like agent, circumstance, recipient, etc. He postulates, then, that the passage from one language to another is carried on by transforms from 'kernel structures' which find ways of expressing similar sentence functions in the target language. Something similar was put forward by Bolinger (1966), who regards translation in the more Chomskyan light as an operation built on structural transformations and assumes a common deep structure.

Transformational-generative grammar, however, has had next to no influence on translation theory. One of the stated aims of this theory was the isolation of linguistic universals, which should have served as a basis for translation theory,[5] but in *Aspects of Theory of Syntax*, Chomsky had already attempted to short-circuit discussion on possible applications to translation.[6] However, whether Chomsky's reserves on the matter had an effect or not, very little work relevant to translation theory has come from transformationalist sources. The axiomatic assumption is that all languages share a common deep structure, defined as

> . . . a level of linguistic analysis where (i) basic grammatical relations
> between fundamental grammatical categories are defined; (ii) selectional
> restrictions and co-occurrence relations are stated; (iii) appropriate
> grammatical categories receive lexical representations; inputs to
> transformational rules are provided (Krzesowski 1971, 38).

Krzesowski follows Lakoff here, rather than Chomsky, noting that in this connection deep structures are a good deal more abstract than was previously supposed, and placing certain semantic elements in deep structure beside the grammatical elements first postulated. Where this has so far failed is in the very point which the founders of transformational grammar stated as the goal of linguistic theory: the specification of invariant linguistic universals. Vinay's brief examination of transformational grammar, a reaction to the criticism that *stylistique comparée* dealt only with *parole*, never got beyond a proposal to reexamine his principles in order to arrive at 'les motivations profondes qui poussent les auteurs, écrivant en anglais et en français, à rédiger des textes différentes en nature' (Vinay 1966, 5).

As a discipline, stylistics has contributed little to translation. Despite its name, and the slightly different *grammaire comparée* developed by Darbelnet in the early 1960s, *stylistique comparée* is really a branch of contrastive linguistics, the only important element of stylistics in it being the difference between *servitude* (i.e. an obligatory equivalence) and *option*. Most linguists who have attempted to build an instrumental theory of style, agree that style is choice or deviation from a norm. But the question is choice of what, and deviation from what norm. One important theory is that flowing directly from Firth, that style is a language use suitable to a specific situation: style is identified with the sociolinguist's register, and is characterized by the linguistic features, ranging from phonological factors like rhythm to semantic features, which are customarily associated with given subjects, purposes and interlocutors. The problem is not one of lack of effort, but the sheer impossibility of reducing to objective terms the intuitive judgement of the ordinary speaker or writer on what is fitting use of language. Quite rightly, in this area, translators, like writers of all types from the civil servant to the poet, have been guided by their own sense of what was fitting in the circumstances of their texts.

What does the linguist have to offer the translator? The most obvious is analysis of equivalence, and some objective justification of the translator's intuitions. Augustine, for instance, set up a certain theoretical basis in taking it for granted that if a *sonus* or *vox* in Latin could be traced to the same *significatio* or to one which shared a significant number of characteristics, there was translation equivalence between them. This rough measure of equivalence remained unchallenged and largely unsupplemented until the late eighteenth century.

Among twentieth-century linguists two types of equivalence, dynamic and formal, were developed. Dynamic equivalence is characterized by Nida (1964, 166) as 'the closest natural equivalent to the source-language message', while formal equivalence is correspondence between linguistic units independent of any idea of content. The contrast between them is clear from the following table given by Beekman (1965, 88):

Types of Correspondence	Illustration of Types		Meaning
	Source Language	Receptor Language	
(1) correspondence of form and function	form ⟷ function ⟷	form function	correct
(2) correspondence of form but not of function	form ⟷ function	form function	wrong or at best obsure
(3) correspondence of function but not of form	form function ⟷	form (if present) function	correct if form irrelevant
(4) no correspondence of either form or function	form function	form function	zero

Both types of equivalence can coexist in the same item; and this is not as rare as some proponents of free translation would contend. There are three ways of assessing equivalence: the basic one is the Augustinian principle of a shared *significatio*; the second is equivalent social functions of the object referred to; and the third is equivalence on the affective level.

The first equivalence measure is so obvious that it is not worth tracing, and indeed shows little development from Augustine to Vernay. The second measure is an important one, attracting the attention of George Campbell (1789, I. 41). At this point in his introduction to the Gospels, and in considerable detail further on, he discusses vocabulary in relation to the purpose for which it is introduced into text. Thus, while giving the Roman *denarius* the formal equivalence of sevenpence-halfpenny, he notes that in Matthew xxii. 19, such a translation misses the mark, as it is the role of the denarius as 'the tribute coin' that is Christ's point, not its purchasing power (Campbell 1789, I. 346). Similarly in Matthew v. 15, the capacity of the bushel measure under which the candle is placed is of no consequence; what is important is that the light is obscured (ibid. 345). Hence his translation is 'corn-measure'. This is obviously a forerunner of Firth's *context of situation* and Ray's 'meaning as locality' and 'meaning as legitimacy'.[7] Two hundred years later this became the first element in dynamic equivalence as discussed by Nida; and was made one of the central pivots of translation equivalence by *stylistique comparée*.

The third measure of equivalence is the question of affectivity. Following Bloomfield's behaviourist theories, Nida sees that as an aspect of dynamic equivalence. A well-translated text will produce in its reader the appropriate cognitive and emotional reactions, i.e. its meaning will have what Ray calls the right 'impact'. This angle is partially covered by Firth's context of situation, partially by links between collocations and contexts of situations. This received recognition by Vinay (1952, 54) in his comment that the search for *mot juste* is conditioned by seeking *le context linguistique juste*. European structuralists from Bally to Vernay see this as a question of manipulating *valeur* in a way appropriate to both source and target language. The lack of complete fit between languages remains a minor issue in the more theoretical semantic discussions; but Vinay and Darbelnet, followed by Jumpelt, nuance their discussion by emphasis on functional parity in the task of expression, rather than a more 'exact' parity that can be linguistically measured.

Obviously, the values that instrumental theories of language seek in translated texts depend on the expressive means used. The assumed end is reduced to transfer of information, though this in the context of affectivity is extremely wide, wider indeed than the 'information' of communication theory. The basis for equivalence is parity of expressive function in the linguistic units used: parity of means will ensure parity of result.

1.2   LANGUAGE AS Λόγος

To the comfortable assumption that language is an instrument, there is opposed the concept of language as a creative entity, as λόγος in the Platonic sense. As a term in Jewish and Christian philosophy, λόγος is first of all, Philo Iudaeus' 'rich and manifold union of myriad ideas'. To this platonic concept, Philo adds the specifically Jewish doctrine of λόγος as the mind of God, and finally as the instrument of Creation.

Here we have two themes based on two differing but not entirely separate views of language as a creative entity. The first, which has had an obvious effect on translation, is the theory of language as a creative entity, what Heidegger calls the 'House of Being'. The second view treats language as the entity which forges human relationships, which forms the human being by giving him the tools to express his experience of the real. This second view has been overshadowed by the first and absorbed in it; and its effect, though hidden, is not without importance.

There are hints in Plato that language has the creative power of λόγος; and much of the difficulty of Augustine's discussion of the *verbum mentis* and its expression, the *vox verbi*, in the *De trinitate*, is due to an unadmitted conflict between the instrumental view Augustine taught, and half-understood implications of his statements on the power of language over human beings and their relationships. Little relevant is added to this until the late eighteenth century.

The end of the eighteenth century marks an intellectual and social upheaval in which ideological realities crumbled. Concepts of absolute truth, analysed by philosophers and theologians and, in our case, grammarians, had proved to be the stuff of literature. It had been Man who had governed language, and hence the rationalist analysis of language that had begun again with the early seventeenth century had quickly moved into prescription. Various attempts had been made to rebel against this: the Rollin–Batteux reworking of the concept of *ordre naturel* was a beginning (see page 19, above), but the most effective revolt came from Germany: first with Herder, then with Humboldt and his Romantic colleagues. For Herder, working in a frame set by the struggles of German to find its identity as a language, language ruled Man; and the poet's contemplation of language was little different from the ordinary man's, if much more subtle and powerful. Thus perception of truth, if such was completely possible, was no longer the prerogative of the philosopher, theologian and scientist, but of the poet. Not that this was universally obvious: our previous section shows that many of the supplanted did not realize how gravely they had been challenged, and continued as before, and not without fruit.

But the poet, in Romantic eyes, became a seer of hidden reality; one whose approach was through feelings as well as reason. In one sense the enormous ego of a large number of Romantics bulldozed them into speech and print. But the essential aim, as is clear in the best of them, is to destroy the old concept of Man as the complete measure of things, and to emphasize him as the channel through which perceptions of deeper intellectual, social and artistic forces bring a truer vision of the world.

As far as translation theory is concerned, the view of language as λόγος is the property of the German Romantics, and the credit given largely to Humboldt. But this is a case where it is of little importance what Humboldt thought: it is what people thought he thought that had various influences on translation. Where different emphases lie in interpreting his thought can be seen from comparing the account of Humboldt in R. H. Robins' *History of Linguistics* (1967), and the account in Steiner (1975). Robins (174) writes:

> A language is to be identified with the living capability by which speakers produce and understand utterances, not with the observed products of the acts of speaking and writing; in his words it is a creative ability (*energeia, Tätigkeit, Erzeugung*), not a mere product (*ergon, Werk, Erzeugtes*).

With this we should compare Steiner (1975, 81): '. . . language is the true and only verifiable *a priori* framework of cognition'. The other differences are of a piece; while Robins and Steiner both link Humboldt's *innere Sprachform* and *Weltansicht*, Robins produces a simple model of the *innere Sprachform* being essentially the 'grammatical and semantic structure' of the language which results from experience, whereas Steiner chooses the interpretation of a reciprocal influence in which language 'generates a complex structure of human understanding and response . . .' (Steiner 1975, 83). Other less critical elements of exposition are common to both authors, except for Steiner's mention (ibid. 81) of language as a 'third universe' between the 'empirical world' and the structures of consciousness. The facts reported in both these accounts of Humboldt are the same; it is the different interpretations that have each, in their own way, contributed. The 'linguist's view' appears in various guises ranging from the Saussurean mentalism of Vinay–Darbelnet to the positivism of Firth, and having, as we have seen, an important role in certain translation norms. What we have attributed to Steiner is also traditional, and had its first influence during Humboldt's lifetime.

The various faces of the Romantic view of language are illustrated in Goethe's depiction of Faust struggling with the opening of St. John's Gospel: Ἐν ἀρχῇ ἦν ὁ λόγος (In the beginning was the Word). Faust begins by translating λόγος as *Wort* (word) and immediately rejects the rendering as impossible. His next attempt, *Sinn* (meaning), seems to make of λόγος something in potency which precedes action; and thus the translation implicitly excludes the creative action of God's Word; it is not therefore the agency that 'alles wirkt und schafft'. *Kraft* (skill), his third attempt, does not unmistakeably transmit the idea of action. Faust, then, finally settles on *Tat* (deed), reflecting probably unconsciously Philo's 'whatever God says is not words, but deeds' (*De cal.* II. 47).

Each of these attempts by Faust reflects one facet of the view of language current in the Romantic circle. Language as *Sinn* is developed in the work of Hölderlin. The essence of language for him was meaning, a numinous *Grund des Wortes*, and all uses of language are an attempt to find this meaning by interpretation. This meaning is not the derivative image the mind makes by its reaction with things, but the reality one finds through experience of life, society and other people. Thus whereas in the instrumental theory of language, meaning is a term relative to the speaker, in Hölderlin and his contemporaries it is an absolute. From this flow the other attempts Goethe depicts: *Kraft* is the skill by which one seeks this hidden meaning; *Tat* is the act of seeking. But in seeking one makes: on another level, this is the experience of every social scientist whose presence as a fieldworker inevitably biasses his experiment.

Language as *Schöpferung* runs through Schleiermacher's thought on translation. He develops Herder's postulate that the history of a people and its language are so interpenetrated that one is the record of the other, that one even formed the other. The idea, for all the natural-science basis of the *Völkerpsychologie*, is an uneasy presence in von der Gabelentz's analyses of syntax, for syntax is the expression of language as an *Einfluss der Seele*, and the strong Darwinian cast of mainstream nineteenth-century linguistics did not allow for such things. In any case, historical linguistics was intensely data-oriented, while those theories of language with an influence on translation were theory-oriented, and tended to deal with the intangible.

Language as λόγος and the hermeneutics involved are an essentially German preoccupation. Language was the one unifying factor in the chaotic political situation of nineteenth-century Germany. Another element of interest is the influence of Jewish thinkers in this tradition: the line begins with Philo Iudaeus and culminates in the modern poet, Paul Celan. In a history marked by centuries of social and political upheaval, Hebrew is the sacred language which formed their society and culture, and which was revived as the most important social link in the modern State of Israel.

Let us pursue the question of language as the root of existence. Karl Vossler attacks Saussure and his pupils for conceiving language as a series of signs in the Aristotelian sense. It is the 'outer form' of language which is thus; the 'inner form' is the universal element of meaning (Vossler 1925, 182). This is parallel with Hölderlin. As far as the idea of language as

Schöpferung is concerned, if we look at Augustine's *De trinitate*, and the sacramental theology of the twelfth century, we find a concept of signs that exactly concord with Vossler's objections to Saussure. Augustine and later theologians had developed the theory of a sacrament as a *signum efficiens*, i.e. a sign which creates what it signifies. The Aquinas discussion of sacraments in *Summa theologica* 3, question 60, makes the point that under the observable words and actions of a sacrament there lies hidden sacred effect. Thus in a sacrament such as the marriage ceremony, the exchange of promises is both a sign of the contract and the instrument by which it comes about. So in the thought of Heidegger, language is not a sign for what exists in the mind, but a thing which creates new existences. It therefore becomes a vital energy in which man participates.[8]

Both literary practice and anthropological theory were leading to this point. In art and music, form and its internal relationships were the predominant concern, and under the impulse of symbolism, were becoming so in literature. In anthropology, Lévi-Strauss's concern with semiotics or symbolic values of things in social behaviour, was revaluing objective reality in terms of what it meant in the frame of daily life. Therefore, like words, things became symbols for other realities. The importance of an activity or an artifact was not, therefore, what it was, but what it stood for in a scale of social values. Therefore, both language and social behaviour rest on movement from interpretation to expression, essentially a translation reflex.[9] Tangible reality, then, was merely the route through which one discovered meaning and, indeed, was as much a symbol as the language describing it.

The essence of symbolism is contemplation of symbols to create realities transcending everyday existence. Symbolism uses much of the language of religious mysticism to convey similar attitudes.[10] It is a development of the Romantic view of literature, and like that type of hermeneutics, was applied to language. The best-known stream of hermeneutic theory is that of Martin Heidegger, which had a deep effect on some translators in the Continental tradition. For Heidegger and Buber, the contemplation inherent in language is not a passive reception of impressions, but an active symbolization and interpretation of the object of contemplation. Language is an underlying reality to be sought through the use of speech, or in Heidegger's terms, must be experienced by submission to it. This element came from Hölderlin's numinous view of language, and there is every indication that Heidegger tended to think of language as a divine presence, an idea reappearing in Steiner (1975). For both Heidegger and Buber, 'use' of a language, creating literature, and growing up in one's society, all become part of the same process in which language plays a central part.

Heidegger exploits the strongly motivated type of sign in German, whose words tend to be an agglutinated string of transparent bound morphemes. He takes a very etymological view of words, a fact not too peculiar in German, but thrown into rather startling relief in translations of Heidegger by his disciples, who treat words in English or French as if they were still fully motivated and thus transparent: e.g. spellings like pro-duction, trans-lation. Their point is that the creative power of the word is made doubly clear when the ancient bound morphemes become obvious, as they still are in the German equivalents of the words *Erzeugung* and *Übersetzung*. This, of course, imitates Heidegger's own handling of Ger-man, in which philosophical points turn on unexpected decompositions of compound words.

The other symbolist element in Heidegger is his view that the silence so necessary to art and contemplation is the essence of language itself. In the *Unterwegs zur Sprache* (59) he claims that language is at its most essential when we cannot find words for what we want to say. This 'essential being of language' is Humboldt's 'pure language' that is so important in this stream of hermeneutic thought. There is in Heidegger an obvious concern with universals, but contemporary translators, especially the French, have parallels to Heidegger which point up rather the peculiarity of the inner form of specific languages. In a manner uncannily similar to the *stylistique comparée*, French translators who wrestled with Shakespeare describe the problems of penetrating him from a metaphysics which is entirely differ-ent, and at times repugnant to the strong classical ideology which has endured even through French romanticism and symbolism. For Pons (1960, 117), a French translation of *Hamlet* is an excellent illustration of the metaphysical gulf between French and English. This theme is taken up by Yves Bonnefoy in his *Postface* to *Hamlet*. He remarks that while the English word is *ouverture*, the French is *fermeture* (1962, 239), a distinction almost coterminous with the Vinay–Darbelnet distinction between the *plan du réel* and the *plan de l'entendement*. For he begins his discussion of the French word by remarking that it deliberately excludes the diversity of real existences by reducing the object to a logical construct (ibid. 243). Then, in language recalling that of the practitioners of *stylistique comparée*, he remarks how English seeks to put before both speaker and hearer 'l'aspect tangible des choses', a reminiscence of Malblanc's word, *tactile*, in the description of German.

One of the most difficult problems in the history of translation is this mixture of mysticism, aesthetics and philosophy we find in Heidegger, Walter Benjamin and their colleagues. Part of the difficulty is that some attributes of God, including the fact that he is unknowable, have become those of language: the old distinction between sign and thing developed by instrumental theories of language is rejected, as language transcends man, and to some extent creates him. The effect on the usefulness of this theory is clear: hermeneutics as taught by Heidegger, Benjamin (1923) and Steiner (1975) is not adequate as a full theory of translation,[11] and indeed merely serves to deepen the gulf between the two 'professions' so mourned by Citroen (1966).

The second stream of hermeneutic theory of importance to translation is that of Martin Buber. To a large extent Buber does accept the Romantic concept of language as a vital assembly of units with real existence and the power to create. But his most characteristic difference from the thorough-going symbolists is his emphasis on experience. This is not passive receiving of impressions or the symbolist stillness, but an active participation in the reality experienced. His point is that to experience something is to change it; so that our experience with language changes it. Buber rejects Heidegger's divine dimension of language, nuancing symbolist mysticism by the simple expedient of placing language between two people, as both tool and environment of a human reaction.

It is this element of social hermeneutics that is built on by Ebeling (*Introduction to a Theological Theory of Language*, op. cit. 163):

> . . . speaking and listening are complementary aspects of the same situation.
> Speaking is basically oriented towards listening, and listening to speaking.
> To speak is to cause someone to apprehend and to listen is to apprehend.
> Because the two aspects of the one event in language are complementary, in the concrete use of language they are inseparable.

Ebeling begins his treatment of the hermeneutics of language with the person speaking, the 'I', a being conditioned by its own history and the history of its culture. The hermeneutic movement begins with an assessment of self, basically the question: 'What is my right to speak?' The most radical answer is to conclude that one has no right, and thus keep silence. But in monitoring oneself in the act of speaking, one assesses the apprehension that has caused one to speak, its relation to one's own experience or lack of it, and an assessment of one's own powers in the situation of the utterance. One might add to this an assessment of one's right to hear, but Ebeling does not go this far.

The second element passes from rights to responsibilities (ibid. 169). The question here is whether the speaker is producing an utterance that fulfils his responsibilities to himself, the addressee and the subject spoken about. To perform this act of analysis, one must know what one's responsibilities are, whether to give information (or conceal it), and the affective language movements of expressing extreme closeness or distance. Ebeling quickly discards the idea that what is suitable to a situation is always courteous and innocuous. The speaker's responsibility to language is a dynamic one:

What helps us to understand the situation and see it so clearly that the very word it requires come at the right moment with the power to set it to rights? (ibid. 173)

Ebeling's third element is the challenge to understanding, which is not merely coming to know the relationship between the form and content of language (ibid. 158). The encounter of two persons through language always takes place through a particular matter. Where the *I* situates the speaker in place and time, the object of his statement sets up a relationship with the *you*, the hearer. It can be a relationship that is oriented purely to the matter of the statement; it can be a relationship between the participants, in which the matter is merely an excuse to begin exploring the other person. Basically this understanding is one of perception of levels. The objective level is the easiest to perceive; the perception of subjective levels, if they are there, is the essence of a hermeneutic approach to language in normal situations.

The term of an information process is the person addressed. Whether there is true information within the communication model depends on whether the hearer takes from the utterance what the speaker wants to transmit. In saying this, we are assuming that the speaker's intentions are honourable, and that what he wants to transmit coincides with truth. Hence, the mutual understanding here is a complex in which the speaker understands both himself and his listener, and the listener both himself and the speaker, to the level demanded by the message and its intent. Problems arise when the levels of understanding are not quite complementary, and one party in the reaction understands more than the other would wish, or admit. In this case, the concomitant information tends to bias communication into somewhat unexpected channels.

For Ebeling, the main dimensions of a comprehensive theory of language are these four: the authority to speak, the responsibility for language, the challenge to understanding and the achievement of mutual understanding. Where Quine speaks of *indeterminacy*, Ebeling speaks of *ambivalence* (ibid. 95ff), which arises from the importance of language in human relations. Quine, with the solemnity of a philosopher, assumes that the natives his anthropological linguist comes in contact with, do their best to tell the truth. Ebeling, with a more sober view of the human being, points out that truth is not an unvarying quality of language. Even setting aside deliberate attempts to lie, there are enough areas of privacy in a person to ensure that full understanding of what he says cannot be guaranteed, and enough preconceptions to bias any message received. Yet language is powerful enough to penetrate the whole of human existence; and in this Ebeling makes a link between the hermeneutic school and the analytical linguist. His respect for linguistics is manifest, his parallelism with sociolinguists like Basil Bernstein and Halliday obvious. The essential difference between Ebeling and Heidegger is that one places the person at the centre of living, the other places language.

For the development of a holistic theory of translation, one must go beyond both the linguist's analysis of technique, and the kabbalistic mysticism of Heidegger. The question asked by Ebeling is a simple one: what do I experience in the reaction between this person's language and mine? In Jakobson's terms, what is the message, what are the values? And it is on this basis that we can bring both theories of language, the instrumental and the hermeneutic, down into the marketplace of translation to see how one contributes to the other, and how translators have behaved before their originals.

Two

Models and Definitions

To each stream of language theory, there corresponds a theory of translation. Linguists' models assume that translation is essentially transmission of data, while hermeneutic theorists take it to be an interpretative recreation of text. It is hardly surprising then, that each group, sure that it has the whole truth, lives in isolation from the other.[1] This is a problem peculiar to the nineteenth and twentieth centuries, and few hold the pre-Romantic view that there is an essential complementarity between these views. For if, as Govaert (1971, 436) writes, a translator is a person who knows how to read and who teaches others, no matter his theory, his practice must have the essential elements of both views of language.

2.1 TRANSLATION AS TRANSMISSION

Modern linguists, among them Roman Jakobson and J. C. Catford, distinguish three types of translation: intralingual (rewording in the same language), interlingual (rewording in another language) and transmutation (reworking in another code altogether). Here, though the other types of translation have had some bearing on theory, we are concerned with the second type. A typical instrumental theory of interlingual translation is that of Vinay (1975, 40):

> The problem of translation theory could thus be depicted schematically by a series of levels like the following:
> 1. Grammatical structures
> 2. possessing lexical structures
> 3. creating a certain effect
> 4. leading to a certain sense
> 5. within the framework of a given style and genre
> 6. reflecting the personality of the author.

What makes this typical is the progression from means to end. It would thus be an error to see instrumental theories of translation as entirely neglecting the ends of translation: they merely do not specifically formulate them.

And this is what we find in Augustine, 1,600 years before Vinay. As set out in the *De doctrina christiana* III.i.1, his requirements for translation are knowledge of the two languages involved and of the subject-matter of the text, some skill in textual criticism, and care for accuracy. The model of the translation process put forward is essentially a two-stage one of reading the message in Greek, and writing it out in Latin. For some purposes this remained current until the twentieth century, being the model on which Warren Weaver based his famous rationale for machine translation: In his memorandum of 1949 (18) he writes:

> . . . one naturally wonders whether translation could conceivably be treated as a problem in cryptography. When I look at an article in Russian, I say: 'This is really written in English, but it has been coded in some strange symbols. I will now proceed to decode.'

This decoding model, a constant at least in aspiration, assumes that there is consistent one-to-one correspondence of small units. Take, for instance, the following passage from the preamble to Justinian's *Institutiones* in a late thirteenth-century Old French version:

> Justice est volentés ferme et pardurable qui rant a chascun sa droiture, et senz de droit et connoissance des choses devines et des humainez et esciences de droit et de tort.

> Iustitia est constans et perpetua voluntas ius suum cuique tribuens. Iuris prudentia et divinarum atque humanarum rerum notitia, iusti atque iniusti scientia.[2]

Such translations exemplify a tradition of absolute neutrality towards information and its linguistic expression deriving ultimately from the Jewish translators of the Old Testament.

From this model rose two related attitudes: that translation was essentially copying; and that translators had no right to 'comment' or 'interpret'. Both rest on an intellectualized view of language and its purpose: Tytler (1790, 9), for instance, describes the translator's task as giving 'a complete transcript of the ideas of the original'. The word, *copy*, appears in the literature fairly constantly from the beginning of the seventeenth century, last being used, it seems, by Ferri de St-Constant (1808, 1) and being later replaced by the word, *portrait*. Simple as theory seems to be, practice assumes a fair degree of creativity. In Saurin's 1699 translation of the Latin hymns of Jean-Baptiste de Santeuil, there is a printed letter in which de Santeuil recognizes the French as a 'perfect copy' of the original. For the eighteenth century, copying certainly did not entail literality, but a recreation in terms of the other language. De Santeuil's simple Ambrosian verse becomes an almost Cornelian declamation, a redrafting with the same creative spirit as Dryden's Vergil and Tarteron's Horace.

The other issue, the prohibition of 'interpretation', is very old, going back at least to the Septuagint translators. Its earliest expression seems to be Scotus Erigena's denial in a letter to Charles the Bald (in 860?) that translators had the right to avoid obscurities by using their own judgement. The case against this defeatism is argued at greatest length and with least asperity by George Campbell (1789, I. 383), who attacks Théodore de Bèze for flagrant 'interpretation' in Acts i. 14. There the Apostles are waiting in the upper room after the Ascension σὺν γυναιξί. De Bèze translates as *cum uxoribus suis* (with their wives), a reading the Greek can bear. Campbell castigates the translation as twisting the Greek in order to attack the Roman Catholic law of clerical celibacy. Even if, as is possible, de Bèze was right, there is no warrant for his reading from text. Campbell's attitude was shared by the Romantics: by 'commentary' they obviously mean reading into the text what was not there in either tone or meaning.

As it had been by Jerome and Rufinus before him, the issue was tied by Campbell to the controversy over 'literal' and 'free' translation. But from the beginning of our period, most translators espoused one cause or the other. For while Cicero was castigating literal translation as the work of the unskilled (*De finibus* III.iv.15), the Jewish translators of the Bible and Talmud saw it as the only way to accuracy. They were followed by the early Christians and by medieval philosophical and theological translators. In the religious and political crisis following the Great Schism of the eleventh century, translators were assigned a critical role in attempts to bring the Western and Eastern Churches together again. Their singular lack of success proved deeply disturbing, and to give translators some guidance philosophers developed a model from Aristotelian psychology. As it appears in Humbertus de Romanis (1274, 696H), a thirteenth-century General of the Dominican Order, it has the dual Augustinian structure of reading and expressing. But while his second stage, that of *significatio*, is the standard 'showing forth of thought', his first, *excogitatio*, is described as the organizing of what is known or learnt for expression. In this, there is a glance forward to the Romantics. In this form it is a constant until the twentieth century, being of particular interest to machine translators (cf. Andreyev 1964).

Even in instrumental terms, one of the major difficulties with the two-stage models was what, if anything, went on between the reading/understanding phase and the writing phase. Nida (1964, 146) postulated a 'transfer stage' without really detailing what this was. The diagram he arrived at is shown in Figure 5. The focus, as in similar models, e.g. that of Luigi Heilmann (1967, 905), is on the translator as a member of two speech communities. In the source language, he acts as a listener, decoding the message and then acting on it; in the target language he acts as a speaker, encoding his message from the product of the transfer phase and speaking or writing it.

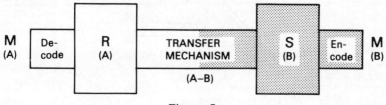

Figure 5

The content of the transfer phase was a problem which exercised many. Some used an Ogden–Richards model, as in Haas (1962, 208):

$$\frac{\text{Sign I}}{\text{Sign II}}$$

Expression I → meaning → Expression II.

This model is, on the surface, heavily influenced by Saussure, but in amplifying his middle term, *meaning*, Haas inserts:

Expression I → Reference I → Referent → Reference II → Expression II.

This would assume that referents are identical for all languages, which is somewhat questionable. To get round this problem, concepts of translation equivalence based on Hjelmslev's *figurae* were proposed, as we have seen in the last chapter. But these, being strongly mentalist, had little effect on the American anthropological tradition.

Reflecting his anthropological approach to translation, Nida proposed a supplementary model (see fig. 6) that depicts the operation, including the transfer phase, as sociolinguistic adaptation of text (1964, 147). Nida assumes here that, in line with the normal practice of the United Bible Societies, the translator will be translating with the help of an informant into a language he does not know well and that cultural adaptation will be filtered through his mother tongue. One inherent difficulty of all these models is that, through assuming an almost exclusive relationship between text and translator, the whole question of relationship between original text and new reader was very lightly skimmed over. And this leads to a second dubious assumption that information is constant and objective. In religion especially, information is highly emotively charged, and it is rather the native who is in the position of Quine's linguist

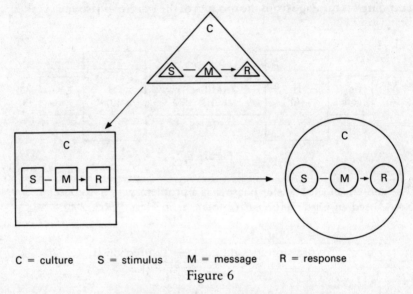

C = culture   S = stimulus   M = message   R = response

Figure 6

observing the missionary's reactions to words like *Christ, sin, Heaven* and *Hell*.

Some of the work in machine translation resulted in almost parallel models and definitions. In a lecture delivered in late 1974, Alexander Ludskanov, of the Bulgarian Academy of Sciences, sought to bring translation into the sphere of semiotics. The central act in translation became that of 'semiotic transfer' defined as:

> . . . replacement of the signs encoding a message by signs of another code, preserving (so far as this is possible in the face of entropy) invariant information with respect to a given system of reference.

Like Nida, he uses ideas from communication theory and includes both the original author (as sender) and final reader (as receiver) in his model, a necessary refinement as each person in the chain generates his own fund of 'meaning' (cf. Jiri Levý, 1969, 33). His assumption is that there is a common fund of information to be transferred, but at the same time he opens up his model towards hermeneutics by distinguishing two types of understanding: the 'substantive', i.e. the identification of information in the sense of content of the language, and the 'linguistic', i.e. the analysis of language units to find the relationship between them and their content.

One revealing line of research, exploited by Jiri Levý, was game theory (1966, 1171):

> From the teleological point of view translation is a process of communication. . . . From the point of view of the translator at any moment in his work, it is a decision process: a series of a certain number of consecutive situations . . . imposing on the translator the necessity of choosing among a certain (and often exactly definable) number of alternatives.

Translation is thus 'a game with complete information . . . a game in which every succeeding move is influenced by the knowledge of previous decisions' (ibid. 1172). In terms of game theory, the translator's 'situation' is the immediate problem posed by the unit in front of him; his 'paradigm' is the range of possible solutions and the constraints imposed by previous decisions and future contingencies. Translation drills which detail action from the first comprehension phase to the last touch of revision (cf. Kuič 1970, 1824) take much of Levý's ideas for granted, while expressing them in a less technical manner.

The second major type of translation model includes the reader. Such models exist in germ in St. Augustine's concern with the reaction of the hearer to linguistic signs. For unless this reaction was congruent with that intended by both translator and author, teaching would not take place, for the translation would not be a translation. Fifteen hundred years later, Louis Bonnerot (1963, 1–2), professor of English at the Sorbonne, diagrams the 'processus d'une traduction':

SC	T.LD	S'C'	T'LA	S"C"

S is the situation passing through the brain (C) of the original author, which produces the *thème* (T) as presented in the source language (LD). S'C' represents the metamorphosis going on in the brain of the translator, producing the *thème* in the dress of the target language (LA). In its turn it is further processed by the reader, producing a third state of the information, S"C". The intimate connection Vinay and Darbelnet see between an utterance and its context underlies the whole equation (cf. Levý, 1969, 33, quoted p. 64).

Other theorists based their models on the Shannon–Weaver model of communication (Richards 1953, 250) (see fig. 7). After quoting this, Richards adapts it to translation by subordinating the middle terms to what he calls 'comparison fields' (ibid. 251) (see fig. 8). He defines the 'comparison fields in Figure 9 (ibid. 253). Working from a simplification

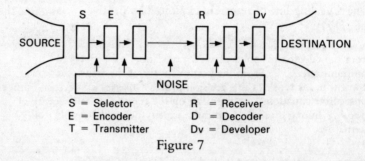

S = Selector   R = Receiver
E = Encoder   D = Decoder
T = Transmitter   Dv = Developer

Figure 7

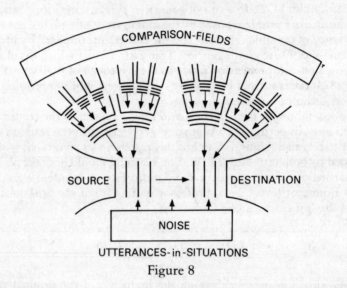

Figure 8

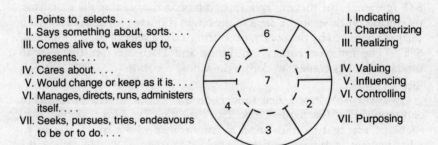

I. Points to, selects. . . .   I. Indicating
II. Says something about, sorts. . . .   II. Characterizing
III. Comes alive to, wakes up to,   III. Realizing
    presents. . . .
IV. Cares about. . . .   IV. Valuing
V. Would change or keep as it is. . . .   V. Influencing
VI. Manages, directs, runs, administers   VI. Controlling
    itself. . . .
VII. Seeks, pursues, tries, endeavours   VII. Purposing
    to be or to do. . . .

Figure 9

of the Shannon–Weaver model by Hayakawa, Rudolf Jumpelt (1961, 176) suggested the following:

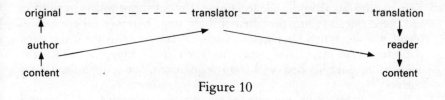

Figure 10

These two approaches were combined in a diagram by M.- O. Houziaux (1965, 119) (see fig. 11).

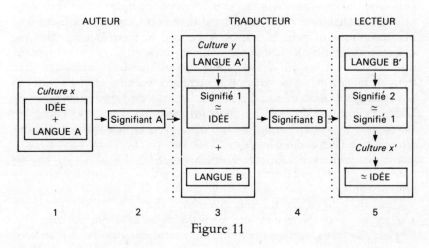

Figure 11

Other more pragmatic models settled on an analysis of operations which separated content from style. This seems to have been a legacy of the medieval language classroom in which techniques of construing, i.e. producing a series of exact lexical and grammatical matchings which is then polished for both sense and elegance, appeared during the fourteenth century. This is widely recommended during the sixteenth and seventeenth centuries in language teaching. As a principle of translation it appears in Rollin (1725, 33), who recommends first seeking a translation that is 'simple, claire et correct' and then working 'à l'orner et à l'embellir'. Pope's conviction that the sense was the author's and the 'Diction and Versification' the translator's responsibility is another statement of the same principle. This stage of *orner et embellir* could be long; it is said that Vaugelas spent about thirty years on his Quintus Curtius before he was satisfied. But long after the death of the seventeenth-century attitude, this construing drill was recommended (cf. Gourdin 1789, 134), and translators like Letourneur (1770) and Shelley (1822) printed their literal versions to illustrate attitudes and technique. Though the original justification had been style, a feeling that the polishing stage removed other types of blemish is illustrated by a series of school classical texts from the Paris publisher, Hachette, during the late nineteenth century, in which the editor confronts his text with two translations, 'l'une littérale, l'autre correcte'.

But the question of transference became tied up with the old quarrel between literal and free, and added another dimension to the image of translation as copying. For most translators of the seventeenth century there was no real problem for the literary translator and the religious or philosophical translator were so convinced of the rightness of their own professional habits that they translated as their principles took them; and like most men of principle, they were sure of their ground. But the seventeenth century had begun to make distinctions: Dryden recognized three types of translation: *metaphrase* (literal transfer), *paraphrase* (free translation) and *imitation*, which was making a working of one's own out of the original. A more usual classification was the opposition made by Diderot's *Encyclopédie* (and by the many who translated into Latin) between *version*, a literal transfer, and *translation*, which was a conscious attempt to go beyond the literality of the version. These are mere classification possibilities, but George Campbell (1789, 1. 20) adds a censorious note, seeing literal and free as opposing ends of a continuum, both equally reprehensible.

Until the end of the nineteenth century the focus of any polishing activity, especially in France, had been the rights of the target language. English classicists, while paying due honour to this attitude, emphasized the duty of full understanding of the original, so that as Souter (1920, 8) puts it, one can find 'the most effective English in which to express the meaning'. Gilbert Murray (1923, 421) goes further, describing the sacrifices translators will have to make in the transfer which, unless their examination of the original has been thorough, will be wrong. From this point of view few critics have stated the problem more clearly than Procházka (1942, 96). A translator has three duties: (1) 'thematic and stylistic' understanding; (2) reconciliation of two different linguistic structures; (3) reconstruction of the stylistic structures of the original.

The particular conditions of translation had kept stylistic considerations as an element in themselves, to the extent that the school drill of a construe followed by writing a sound text was taken as endemic, even late in the twentieth century. In an article speculating on the application of transformational grammar to translation, Walmsley writes (1970, 195):

. . . translation can be considered to be a *two*-dimensional operation. That is, as well as translating from one *language* to another, we are also translating into a particular stylistic level of the second language.

Thus, he sees three steps, valid at least as a training procedure. First, the text is to be rewritten in the source language using sentence patterns of the target language in an effort to isolate the deep structure. Then, the text is to be rewritten in the target language following the first structures exactly. Finally, the complete text is to be stylistically reconstituted by applying appropriate transformations. The close analogy with the classical construe is obvious, and further, it bears a family resemblance to the French seventeenth-century idea of redrafting texts in *l'ordre naturel* before producing a finished text from them. Whether it adds anything to traditional views of translation as transmission is very doubtful.

The pragmatic view adopted here makes it difficult for some theorists to accept translation as an art; and, indeed, such a refusal is made easier by the sheer volume of translation outside literature. This one point seems to have aroused all the obstinacy a theorist blinded by his own postulates is capable of. On the one hand, we have a long tradition of translation criticism in which all translation outside creative literature and religious work is ignored; and on the other the rabid linguist. Simpson (1975, 252), for instance, speaks of this issue as 'another point of past controversy: the idea that translation belongs in the realm of art'. Few of his authorities give grounds for taking this flagrantly biased statement as true. Marouzeau (1931, 5) speaks of translation as 'sinon une science, du moins une technique'. His theme is developed by Vinay and Darbelnet, Mounin and Vernay who take it to be 'un art fondé sur une science' (Mounin 1963, 17). The scientific backing is a complex one, founded not only on a type of contrastive linguistics, but also on sociolinguistics and communication theory.

But are these models adequate as anything but a description of process? Their main weakness lies in taking the human element as a variable that can be controlled: the only models we have quoted that come near to escaping this criticism are those of Bonnerot, Jumpelt and Houziaux. Another weakness is the assumption that what is communicated is objective information. The problem posed by lacks of equivalence between cultures is partially covered by Nida and Vinay and Darbelnet; but again, there is the immense problem of equivalence through compensation that is only touched on here. The last lack in these models is the question of goal: there is no allowance made for the reason why one translates a given text, and what one does to one's text under the influence of the fate one intends for it and the function it is to fulfil. But, for all these serious gaps, these models are useful in delineating the actual process of translation, and the steps through which one goes.

2.2 TRANSLATION AS CREATION

Coexisting with these utilitarian views of translation is a group of models based on concepts of translation as literary creation. There are two broad themes to be traced here. The first is a view of translation as a relationship between translator and original text, or between translator and language. The second is an image of translation which assumes that one is setting up a relationship between oneself and the author of the original, with the two languages, source and target, as mediators.

These themes are far from self-exclusive, and the problem of separating them exists already in Quintilian's *De institutione oratoria* x.v.4:

> Neque ego paraphrasin esse interpretationem tantum volo, sed circa eosdem sensus certamen atque aemulationem.[3]

Rivalry with the Greeks was the central concept in the Roman approach to building a literature in Latin. In the fourth Tusculan, Cicero had defined it as 'imitation of outstanding qualities'. This was further exemplified by Horace who, in *Odes* iv.ii, details the problems of rivalling Pindar, and proceeds to apply his precepts in *Odes* iv.iv, a brilliant Pindaric pastiche on an essentially Roman theme. It was not a given work that was imitated; but the art of *aemulatio* consisted in bending the techniques of another author to one's own subject and language. As far as original composition is concerned, this had been made clear by Cicero. And as translation was an aspect of general literary activity, the consequence of forging a personal relationship with the author followed naturally on perceptive penetration of his text.

Cicero himself followed his own dictates closely. His Homer on page 81, below, is completely Roman and a forerunner of Vergil; and his Plato on page 163 is at one and the same time Cicero and Plato. Three hundred years later, St. Jerome in following Cicero, did much the same sort of thing to Origen. Though Jerome never seems to have used the *aemulatio* figure, in his letter to Pammachius he speaks of 'transferring the meanings into one's own language by right of conquest', an echo of Quintilian's idea of struggle which, though found in writers on language up to the present, seemed hardly congruent with the reverence due to sacred writings. Here is how he put his ideas into practice in dealing with Origen's first homily on the Prophet Jeremiah (385?: 225):

Deus ad beneficiendum promptus est, ad puniendos autem eos qui poena
digni sunt dissimulator. Cum possit quippe tacens sine contestatione venturi
punire eos quos semel dignos supplicio iudicavit, numquam hoc facit; sed
etiamsi condemnaverit, dicit quod sibi semper dicere propositum est, ut
liberentur a condemnatione per poenitentiam qui condemnati fuerant per
delictum.

Ὁ θεὸς εἰς ἀγαθοποιίαν πρόχειρός ἐστιν, εἰς δὲ τὸ κολάσαι τοὺς ἀξίους
κολάσεως μελλητής. δυνάμενος γοῦν ἐπαγαγεῖν τὴν κόλασιν τοῖς ὑπ' αὐτοῦ
καταδικαζομένοις μετὰ σιωπῆς, μετὰ τοῦ μὴ προδιαμαρτύρασθαι, οὐδαμῶς
τοῦτο ποιεῖ· ἀλλὰ κἂν καταδικάζῃ λέγει, τοῦ λέγειν αὐτῷ προκειμένου ἐπὶ τῷ
ἐπιστρέφαι ἀπὸ τῆς καταδίκης τὸν καταδικασθησόμενον.[4]

With its care for both matter and audience, this passage is Ciceronian in
method, even if the style is an educated fourth-century one, as indeed the
Greek is Hellenistic rather than classical. The sense of Quintilian's 'rivalry
and struggle' over the same meaning pervades Jerome's explanatory
rephrasing of some of the more cryptic passages of the Greek. Jerome's
former friend, Rufinus, used the same approach in his St. Basil (see page
100, below), but disagreed on a complex ground of doctrinal difference,
broken friendship and jealousy with what Jerome was doing. But the
sheer energy of fourth-century translators' prose recalls Cicero, and
through its attempt at compensating for the loss suffered in transfer,
marks intense differences with the *Vetus latina* and other early Christian
translators.

Yet, were Jerome and Rufinus translators, or what Quintilian had called
paraphrastes? Each accused the other; and Jerome admitted that hostile
critics would readily apply the label of paraphraser to him. Accuracy was
clearly in the eye and emotions of the beholder.

From this point until the sixteenth century, there is little precept on this
issue. But, when we come to examine practice, we shall see to what extent
the vernacular translators of the Middle Ages believed in their rights to
interpret and create. Humanist translators found themselves torn between
the ideals of creation and transmission. Many of them so far misunderstood their adored classics as to think that translation was imitation. Yet
there is reason to believe that what they called 'imitation', Cicero would
have called '*aemulatio*', and while remaining under the impression that
their task was essentially one of transmission, many of them took liberties
with their texts, and challenged all comers to prove them wrong. Edmund
Becke writes in his preface to Erasmus:

For some heretofore submytting themselfe to servytude, have lytle respect
to the observance of the thyng which in translatyng is of all other most
necessary and requisite, that is to saye, to render the sense and the very

meaning of the author, not so religiouslie addicte to translate worde for
worde, for so the sense of the author is sometimes corrupted and depraved,
and neyther the grace of one tongue nor yet of the other is truly observed
or aptlie expressed.

What actually happened was recreation in terms as subtle as Cicero's
dealings with the Greeks. Becke exemplifies his principles by giving his
public a translation they could react to and identify with. Here is the
opening of one of Erasmus's *Colloquia* in Becke's 1550 version:

Eulalia: God spede, and a thousand mine old acquaintance, Xanthippe.
Xanthippe: As many agayn, my dere heart, Eulalia, me semeis ye ar
waxen much faire now of late.

E.   Salve multum, exoptatissima mihi Xanthippe.
X.   Salve tantundem, mihi charissima Eulalia. Videre mihi solito
formosior.[5]

The language is pure Tudor, but its flavour is suggested by the Plautine
extravagance of the Erasmus original. As with the Chaloner text (see page
143, below), which is contemporary, recreation of text was made through
functional equivalence seen in social terms, rather than through lexical
matching.

Following this lead, the seventeenth century rejected the image of
imitation out of hand. Cowley introduced his *Pindarique Odes* by explicitly
denigrating 'exact imitation, which being a vile and unworthy servitude, is
incapable of producing anything noble'. Likewise, Isaac Lemaistre de Saci
(1613–84), a key figure in Port-Royal, taught that the ultimate crime in
translation was 'un assujetissement qui dégénère en servitude, et qui rend
une traduction semblable au modèle . . . comme un homme mort est
semblable à un homme vivant'. Though granting imitation a place as a
literary technique, Dryden (1680, 240) took it as out of place when labelled
'translation', calling it in his preface to Ovid's Epistles (1680) 'the greatest
wrong that can be done to the memory and reputation of the dead'
(Dryden, ed. Ker 1961, 240).[6]

The issue was the basic one of what translation was. The old pejorative
term, 'paraphrase', had now become respectable, just how respectable
it is easy to judge from the three versions of *Aeneid* iv. 1–5 on page 89,
below. For attention was focussed on content, and it was this that was the
goal of criticism. The point is made with particular clarity by Ezechiel
Spanheim (1629–1710), a German diplomat gallicized by long contact
with France, who distinguishes between the duties of translator and critic,
and then states that good translating demands both skills. He continues his
preface to Julian the Apostate (1660) by a long section reminiscent of Ezra

Pound, in which he sees the translator as the intermediary between author and reader, rather than between author and text. To do this, literal translation must be nuanced by a critical creativity.

Spanheim belonged to a select group of seventeenth-century translators who had some suspicion of the doctrine of *le bon goût*. De Segrais notes in his introduction to Vergil that judging the Ancients by seventeenth-century standards was rash, not a popular sentiment; and Dryden has in the introduction to *Sylvae*:

> For, after all, a translator is to make his author appear as charming as he possibly can, provided he maintains his character, and makes him not unlike himself. Translation is a type of drawing after life; where everyone will acknowledge that there is a double sort of likeness, a good one and a bad.

But the assessment of good or bad likenesses depended on ethnocentric approaches to the task of criticism. This is particularly true of Dryden's own attempt at Vergil (see page 89, below), and indeed, of most of the literary translation of the seventeenth and early eighteenth centuries. In the translations ascribed to Smollett, and especially in the immense preface George Campbell writes to his Gospels, the tone required in a critical translator changes; for, instead of criticizing by measuring the foreign against the translator's own cultural norms, there are genuine attempts to assess the text translated against its own cultural norms and to bend the target language and culture to fit. Campbell (1789) in several passages traces this to the great French Hebraist, Houbigant, but it is a constant in Batteux (1747), Smollett on both Cervantes and Lesage, and Nugent on Montesquieu.

It is in this cultural atmosphere that Herder writes of the translator's duty and mission. Ostensibly, he begins from the idea of transfer: the translator's mission is to make foreign books understandable to the unilingual reader, a task summed up by the word *Erklärung* (explanation). This is not merely teaching, but, in the Augustinian mode of 1,500 years before, leading the reader to knowledge. Comprehending the text is the first step from which a good translator takes the reader to an intuitive understanding of the foreign language, and finally to insight into the foreign nation and its historical development. In the *Volkstimme* of 1774 he put his principles into practice. Here is his version of Ariel's song from *The Tempest*:

> Fünf Fad'n tief liegt der Vater dein!
>   Perlenglanz sein Auge ward
> zu Korallen sein Gebein,
>   liegt in Meergrund schön erstarrt.

Unverwelklich! prächtig! hehr!
  hat ihn gewandelt das Zaubermeer,
Und Stund' auf Stunde läuten ihm
  Nymphen die Totenglock – – Bim! Bim!

Full fathom five thy father lies;
  Of his bones are coral made;
Those are pearls that were his eyes:
  Nothing of him that doth fade,
But doth suffer a sea-change
Into something rich and strange.
Sea-nymphs hourly ring his knell:
                    Burthen: Ding-dong.[7]

What we see here is an extremely allusive approach to *Erklärung*. Herder does not seek to explain through paraphrase or expansion in the sense of Jacques Delille (a pet hate of Goethe's), Pope or Dryden, but throws light on the original through using the resources of German that are closest to those of the English poem.

The sense of *Erklärung* moves towards the semantic field of *klar* (clear, lucid). Herder's aim of revealing what is already there is translated by imitating Shakespeare's poetic form, by the consistent attempts to use German phonemes acoustically like the English, and by semantic equivalences like *Totenglock* for *knell* and the decomposition of *sea-change* into the verb, *wandeln*, and the noun, *Zaubermeer*. The essential distinction between commentary and *Erklärung* was the etymological sense of κρίνειν, which means to judge or appraise without passing moral judgements. The only problem was that the basis of critical *Erklärung* had changed; for Dryden's Vergil had been as clear to his contemporaries as it was opaque to the Romantics. Hence, Schleiermacher, in distinguishing between *Paraphrase* and *Nachbildung*, directs the first towards the language-learner, and the second towards the seasoned reader. For the first assumes concern with the surface mechanism of language, the second with a critical penetration into the translated work. This critical penetration has two goals: the first is Herder's *Erklärung*; the second is the search for Hölderlin's *Grund des Worts*, the numinous *Ursprache*. This approach is found very widely; among its many guises is an echo of Quintilian x. v. 4 (see page 44, above) in Melchiore Cesarotti's Italian translation of Homer (1802?): 'Il copista serve all'erudizione, e l'emulo alla poesia.'

The eighteenth century had assumed that the basic universal in language was a logical arrangement of meaning and meaningful units. For the Romantics, however, the basic universal was a creative energy which expressed itself in meaning; this was what was to be called 'pure language'. Through the historical development of peoples and languages it had taken on surface differences which obscured the essential unity of human language and experience. This gives rise to Goethe's conviction, discussed in *Dichtung und Wahrheit*, that a plain simple translation is always the best, and that a translation that tries to compete with the original merely a learned diversion (cf. his Diderot, page 93, below). It is the word 'compete' that sums up the difference between what the eighteenth century had tried to do, and what Goethe and his colleagues were about.

One loses count of the number of times eighteenth-century translators tried to produce 'a French Vergil', 'an English Homer'. In contrast, the Romantics aimed to reproduce Vergil and Homer in their own languages, to show the foreign poet as he was, or rather, as he related to the basic energy of the 'pure speech'. Only in this way could translation be an experience which changed language. If the translator sought to find what was already there, and to present it as it was, the original became present in a way the eighteenth century had found impossible. A most important indication of Goethe's attitude is his own description of his attitude to Shakespeare: 'my own joyful acknowledgement of something higher floating above my reach . . .'.

For the Romantics regarded completely adequate translation as an impossible ideal. The compliment of 'something higher' was paid to Goethe by Gérard de Nerval whose 'appréciation' of *Faust* was admired by the Master himself. French Romantics tended to be bothered by obstinate classical attitudes, and de Nerval found himself 'forcé alors d'en donner l'interprétation, plutôt que le sens', a truly eighteenth-century sentiment which is, by an artistic paradox, also completely Romantic. Here is what he makes of the Archangels' Chorus:

> Le soleil répand sa lumière
> En chantant le Dieu qu'il chérit;
> Rapide comme le tonnerre,
> Sa vaste course s'arrondit;
> O Dieu! tes regards adorables
> Soutiennent de tout leur amour;
> Et tes oeuvres inexplicables
> Sont belles comme au premier jour.

It is not literal in Goethe's sense of parody, nor is it the re-reading so loved by the previous two centuries. What de Nerval does is re-express Goethe's images of sunlight, song and God's power in a series of quick tableaux which reproduces Goethe's form and the bareness of Goethe's German, but also casts a nod towards what was going on in the French poetry of the time. It is flavour he is seeking, if one takes a surface approach; on a deeper level he is attempting to find in French what Goethe found in German.

De Nerval illustrates very well the ambiguity of the early nineteenth century. The French and English were prisoners of their history in a way the Germans were not; and so de Nerval shies away from some aspects of Goethe's compression and graphicness (cf. *regards adorables* for *Anblick*). The force of tradition in French struck Jean-Louis Burnouf (1775–1844), who commented that he and his colleagues tended to judge Vergil 'avec les mêmes sens et les mêmes habitudes' with which they approached Racine. His own Tacitus (1827) comes over as the work of an urbane neutral scholar, which Tacitus obviously was not; here is the beginning of *Annals* I. 3:

> Auguste, pour donner des appuis à sa domination, éleva aux dignités d'édile curule et de pontife Claudius Marcellus, fils de sa soeur, à peine entré dans l'adolescence, et honora de deux consulats successifs M. Aggripa, d'une naissance obscure, mais grand homme de guerre et compagnon de sa victoire.

> Ceterum Augustus subsidia dominationi Claudium Marcellum sororis filium admodum adulescentem pontificatu et curuli aedilitate, M. Agrippam, ignobilem loco, bonum militiae et victoriae socium, geminatis consulatibus extulit.[8]

What Burnouf brought from the Age of Reason was a deep insensitivity to the power of innuendo. The Tacitus sentence is an angry account of nepotism. But the juxtaposition of Marcellus's age with his offices, and the damning snobbery of *ignobilem loco* (of low birth) are both ignored: what Burnouf transmits is the objective fact: and in this he is at the opposite pole from the Romantics who transmitted objective fact if it did not get in the way of 'truth'. At the same time, however, Maillet–Lacoste (1843, 18), an equally respectable academic, was referring to translation as

> . . . cette sorte d'entretien où, mis en rapport avec les esprits les plus distingués, vous les écoutez dans leur langue pour parler dans la vôtre.

An odd mixture of old and new with its seventeenth-century emphasis on distinguished minds (*esprits distingués*) and the very Romantic image of translation as listening (*écouter*). But at the same time, scientific translation was probably the best illustration of what the Romantics were driving at. For example, the German and English translations of Lavoisier (see pages 164 and 171, below) have all the subtlety of the Romantic manner and its instrumental techniques.

England was facing problems similar to those in France. The need to 'critically master' one's text was a commonplace (cf. Pattison 1860, 134); and the Romantic ban on commentary was being rejected as unworkable. Rossetti, for instance, writes in *Dante and his Circle* (1861) that as translation settles many points in the original without discussion, 'it remains the most direct form of commentary'. But the major problem was what one critically mastered. Even if the ramifications of the text were perceived, and the Victorians could be astonishingly perceptive, the Romantic theories relating to the form of text often produced language teetering between bathos and incomprehensibility: Browning's *Agamemnon* is an excellent example. For the problem was what one listened for, and what one sought to produce. And one of the caricatures of criticism was such denaturing of English in the name of a critically authentic content or style.

It is not clear when translators began to lay claim to the status of artist. The main ground seems to be the concept of parallel creation one finds in critics as far distant as Cicero. His claim that one was to treat translation as a branch of oratory is repeated constantly as a justification for translators' freedom. But the aspect of this that was most prominent at the beginning of the twentieth century was that translators created a new series of forms in their target language. The essential element of artistic creation remains Herder's *Erklärung*.

In the hands of the great classical translators of the early twentieth century there is almost a collective '*mea culpa*': J. S. Phillimore, for instance, expects a translator to have the sensitivity to find the 'pitch' of an author, that is his linguistic and artistic peculiarities; an approach often neglected in translation from classical languages during the nineteenth century, but preached in translation towards classical languages by R. C. Jebb. The strong social-history orientation of classics also acted as a link with movements outside the discipline; and what came later to be known as the Sapir–Whorf hypothesis was current long before the appearance of Whorf's *Language, Thought and Reality*. Indeed, in Charles Péguy's *Les suppliants parallèles* (1908, 425) is expressed a view of the power of language that combines both the Romantic idea of the poet as seer and the Horatian theme of permanence:

C'est le propre du poète, c'est un don du poète que de saisir d'un mot, que de ramasser en un mot toute la réalité d'un événement, la réalité profondément essentielle d'une histoire, d'un mouvement, d'un geste individuel ou collectif.

This 'classical' approach to translation continues among those such as Ronald Knox, for whom the translator was to be 'ruled by his determination to *write* to produce a work of art' (Knox 1957, 9). The ideals proposed for imitation were those of the English Renaissance, that is the power of communication sought by Urquhart, Florio and their contemporaries. And as we have seen Edmund Becke make a completely Tudor scene out of Erasmus, so Knox's New Testament treats Christ as a raconteur with the suave touch of the Oxbridge common room. Here is the beginning of Luke xvi. 19–21 from St. Jerome's Latin:

> There was a rich man once, that was clothed in purple and lawn, and feasted sumptuously every day. And there was a beggar, called Lazarus, who lay at his gate, covered with sores, wishing that he could be fed with the crumbs that fell from the rich man's table, but none was ready to give them to him; the very dogs came and licked his sores.

Such translation rests, as the Bells remark in their volume of Welsh poetry (1942, 71), on an attempt to recreate the mood of the author through reliving the experience. On a more philosophical plane, Wandruszka (1971, 14) remarks that translations is not replacing one instrument by another, but searching underneath the instrumental surface to find common mental structures, a theory very close to Hölderlin's pure language.

Just what content was for these translators is not entirely clear. There was a lingering element from scientific translation that marked content down as the agglomerate of meanings, semantic and grammatical, in the original. Knox and those like him did not reject this view, but saw it as a necessary road to parallelisms in creative experience. Insight into the emotional, social and intellectual consequences of the experience which the text relates, is only the beginning; what is meant here is an actual sharing in the experience of artistic creation, an insight into the purposes of the writer, and a deliberate bending of one's own resources to follow.

It is this that lies behind Procházka (1942, 96) when he speaks of vivid awareness of language differences, and Valéry Larbaud's image of translation as 'la balance où nous pesons ces mots . . .'. For through 'weighing-out' words one takes complete possession of the text, by penetrating to its very centre (Larbaud 1946, 74). The problems raised by this line of thought were discussed within a frame resting on a type of applied linguistics viewed through literary needs and priorities. What emerges is the conviction that the purely linguistic transfer task is of less importance than that of dealing with the work as an artistic entity. Critics of the 1960s and 1970s were intensely aware of the difficulties of 'fit' between the two traditions, with the double problem of dealing respectfully with the content of their texts, and ensuring that any implications in the language itself of the text were rendered in a telling and undistorted fashion. A second group of problems associated with this major one was the question of the reader. If a translation was to enrich a language, it was to transcend linguistic accuracy.

The other point of view is one owing its being to Symbolist tendencies of varying force. In a slightly diluted form we find them in Ezra Pound's translations and prefaces that almost span the first half of the twentieth century. As did St. Augustine, Pound took translation to be essentially teaching, the central element being Herder's *Erklärung*. The various facets of the image run through his writings: he praises Laurence Binyon's Dante for 'shedding more light on Dante' than any other translation he had seen. This, too, is a point he makes of his own Cavalcanti: that any 'atrocities' in his translation are there to 'drive the reader's perception' far under the surface of the original. The translation is meant to come alive, to make the background of the original contemporary. On his Cavalcanti he writes:

> It is conceivable the poetry of a far-off time or place requires a translation not only of word and of spirit, but of 'accompaniment', that is, that the modern audience must in some measure be made aware of the mental content of the older audience, and of what these others drew from certain fashions of thought and speech.

If a translator was to make his audience aware of this 'mental content', the translator then had to tread the narrow line between explanation and wilful changing of the author to the translator's own image. But, Pound's problem, as set out in the same preface is that 'it is not always expeditious to approach the same goal by the same alley'. Here is Pound's version of Sonnet III of *Les antiquités de Rome* by Du Bellay:

> O thou newcomer who seek'st Rome in Rome
> And find'st in Rome no thing thou canst call Roman;
> Arches worn old and palaces made common,
> Rome's name alone within these walls keeps home.
> Behold how pride and ruin can befall
> One who hath set the whole world 'neath her laws,
> All-conquering, now conquered, because
> She is Time's prey and Time consumeth all.
> Rome that art Rome's one sole last monument,
> Rome that alone has conquered Rome the town,
> Tiber alone, transient and seaward bent,
> Remains of Rome. O world, thou unconstant mime!
> That which stands firm in thee Time batters down,
> And that which fleeteth doth outrun swift time.

Nouveau venu, qui cherches Rome en Rome
Et rien de Rome en Rome n'aperçois,
Ces vieux palais, ces vieux arcs que tu vois
Et ces vieux murs, c'est que Rome on nomme.
Vois quel orgueil, quelle ruine, et comme
Celle qui mit le monde sous les lois
Pour dompter tout, se dompta quelquefois
Et devint proie au temps, qui tout consomme.
Rome de Rome est le seul monument,
Et Rome Rome a vaincu seulement.
Le Tibre seul, qui vers la mer s'enfuit,
Reste de Rome. O mondaine inconstance!
Ce qui est ferme est par le temps détruit,
Et ce qui fuit, au temps fait résistance.[9]

What is the 'mental content' which the Pléiade could rely on? The first element is the Renaissance consciousness of the glories of classical times and the decadence which followed in the later years of the principate and during the Middle Ages. This is contrasted with affirmations of Rome's greatness, as in the Roman Odes of Horace, *Odes* III, and the famous passage, *Aeneid* VI. 851–3, where Vergil describes Rome's mission of civilizing the world. Hence the heightened images of decay which Pound assumes a French humanist of the sixteenth century would have sensed: *vieux*, for instance, becomes *worn old*, and *made common*. For Pound, they are all the more cogent through his own disgust at the tourist trap modern Rome has become.

Pound's point is that the translator has to lead the reader round the poem and all its ramifications, even those the poet was unaware of. Hence his own technique is close to that of Herder: he retains Du Bellay's balance between the parts of the sonnet by imitating its form as exactly as he can, while using dynamic translation techniques. 'Light is thrown' on the original by parallelism in function, and deliberate avoidance of literality.

Most translators would agree with the linguist's view of language as an assembly of phonic signs for mental concepts. Indeed, this is the first of André Martinet's *deux articulations*. The second is linkage of vocal forms in utterances. So far, translators had respected both articulations and Martinet's order. But Symbolist theory, aided by the anthropologist's destruction of the boundary between things and symbols, turned this model on its head; and the linguist's ranking of the first articulation over the second, of the communicative over the expressive, and indeed, of the human being over the text he had created, was called radically into question.

As we see the Symbolist approach to translation in Walter Benjamin's *Aufgabe des Übersetzens*, it is one indifferent to anything beyond the units of the text, including an intended reader. Benjamin begins with a blunt denial that translation is meant for a reader, and that there is a 'content' that can be communicated without damage to the integrity of the task. Thus at the outset he restricts his object to literary translation, and to translation in the Symbolist sense of commuting word to word. There is little attempt to define translation in this essay, but there is a description of the task: it is to find that intended effect in the target language which produces in it the echo of the original. For translation is a mode of its own, which is not really concerned with anything objective. In true Symbolist fashion, what is objective is regarded as surface, under which the mind must penetrate to find the truth. And this truth is Humboldt's 'pure language'. Translation, then becomes the manipulation of linguistic units as symbols of another reality which is also a symbol. Underneath a translation one must see the movements of the original. In this way, through the clash between the surface structure of the two languages, one will find what they have in common, which is the pure language, the λόγος. Then, by a play of the two meanings of the Greek word, Benjamin ties translation down to a rendering of words rather than meanings. The other essential element in Benjamin is the conviction that original and translation share a continuity of existence:

> A real translation is transparent: it does not cover the original, does not block its light, but allows the pure language, as though reinforced by its own medium, to shine upon the original more fully.

In the hands of the Symbolist translator this sets up a relationship between the translator and the *numen* of language to which the translator must submit. In the most extreme form of this theory, language is identified with its phonological form, so that its sign function, in at least the traditional sense, is denied. Equally important, the affectivity of language is made to predominate over any objective content.

As an example, let us take the Catullus of Celia and Louis Zukofsky (1961). Their preface is probably one of the shortest on record for a translation of a major poet:

> This translation follows the sound, rhythm and syntax of his Latin . . . tries, as is said, to breathe the 'literal' meaning with him.

Here is Ode 27:

> Minister wet to lee, pour the Falernian
> and gear me chalices, ah my bitterest,
> the law's Postumia, you bet magistral,
> eh breezy kin a grape-loving breeziness.

Adieus qualifying between water and
wine are pernicious, let the odd serious
migrate: high! pure the thigh on us's the wine god's.

Minister vetuli puer Falerni
inger mi calices amariores,
ut lex Postumiae iubet magistrae,
ebrioso acino ebriosioris.
at vos quolubet hinc abite, lymphae,
vini pernicies, et ad severos
migrate: hic merus est Thyonianus.[10]

Whereas translators traditionally have seen the outer form of language as a
vehicle for meaning or content, and have bent the expressive resources of
their target language to fit, the Zukofsky's have reversed priorities and
have treated meaning and sense as vehicles for the sound of Catullus's
Latin as they perceive it. And it is this Latin, pronounced in the Classical
style with an American accent, that reappears in English.

Approach to an original assessment of what is important, is what is
meant by hermeneutics. In Steiner (1975), the 'hermeneutic movement'
has four stages: trust, aggression, incorporation and restitution.

His first stage, that of trust, is obviously a necessary preliminary to any
attempt to penetrate the original. It is usually couched in terms of 'What
does this text say?' And what the text can be trusted to say will vary
according to genre or to the purpose for which it is translated, quite apart
from the attitude of the translator to his function. Confidence in the good
sense, taste and accuracy of an original has varied constantly. Religious and
scientific translators, in the main, tend to take their author as they find him.
Literary translators of the classical age, Renaissance and nineteenth century usually translated closely. But there are grounds to doubt that the
medieval literary translator, the translator of the Age of Reason and certain
moderns are as confident in their originals as a good translator should be.

As we shall see in dealing with medieval translators, their intentions
were good, their methods idiosyncratic. The Age of Reason, however,
presents the sorry spectacle of a large number of translators apologizing
for their authors. The French in particular tended to act like an embar-
rassed mother introducing a plebeian son-in-law, especially when dealing
with English literature.[11] But the times were changing even as they wrote:
Goujet in an article in the *Année littéraire* for 1756 denied that the translator
had the right to 'supprimer les fautes de son auteur' and, the following
year, he was followed by Grosier who wondered whether the taste of
translators was as infallible as had heretofore been believed.

This censorious attitude to authors had not existed among scientists or
religious translators, and the Romantic reverence for the original was, in

effect, a continuation of the scientist's care for exact terminology. Though the most extreme Romantic attitude remained rare, all genres of translation since show a flexibility of attitude within the bounds of respect for the author that might have surprised the eighteenth century and the Romantics alike.

The second movement, that of aggression, is perhaps the most ancient hermeneutic movement to have been isolated: we find it in Jerome's image of taking the meaning of the text captive. As discussed by moderns, the idea is Hegelian (cf. Steiner, 1975), in that it gives rise to a third force, a synthesis, between thesis and antithesis. Inside this view we can place Yves Bonnefoy's 1962 *Postface* to *Hamlet*, which sees this aggression as a clash between two languages, two forms of thought, within the intuition of the translator. His attitude is almost the Bacchic image of the poet and seer one finds in classical literature.

This battleground is also one proper to language outside translation. Ebeling speaks of 'wrestling for verbal expression', and makes this struggle not something independent of the meaning, but something that is an integral part of one's understanding of the meaning. There is a place to distinguish two sorts of aggression: that inspired by genuine trust in the source text; and that inspired by the censoriousness abroad in the Age of Reason. The only real way of judging depth of trust and the movement of aggression is in Steiner's third stage, that of incorporation.

Both the Middle Ages and the Age of Reason, and to some extent the twentieth century, suffer from an egocentrism which reduces everything to the terms of contemporary vision. What went on during the Middle Ages is best described in the chapters on the instrumental techniques of translation; it merely suffices here to remark that acclimatization was hardly uncongenial in either literature or religion; though in science it was frowned on.

The fourteenth-century *Ovide moralisé* is a typical example of medieval adaptation to audience. Here is the beginning of Book VI:

Pallas avoit doné s'oreille
A escouter ceste merveille
Que la Muse li vait contant,
Qui li recorde le contant
Des neuf Muses et des neuf pies,
Et dit que bien se sont vengies,
Si loe lor desputoison
Et qu'il orent droit et raison,
Puis dist em bas, que nulz ne l'oc:
„Que me vault ce que ie vous loc?
Pourquoi me lessé-ie despire?
Moult ai grant despit et grant ire

De ce qu'Araigne me desprise
Par son sens et par sa mestrise,
Dont el se vait orgueillisant.
Bele ouvriere est et bien tissant:
Pour ce ne me deigne obeir.
Je l'irai, certes, envaïr,
Si comperra s'outrecuidance,
S'el ne me porte reverance."[12]

Given that this sort of epic narrative was orally delivered, the narrator had
first of all to work within the conventions of oral recitation which had to
compensate for short memory spans. Hence the careful link with the end
of Book v, and the delineation of Arachne (*Bele ouvriere et bien tissant*) to act
as a well-remembered pivot on which to hang the story. Similarly, the
four lines of Ovid to which this corresponds, present too compressed a
cameo to accord with the leisurely medieval style of narration. The
thirteenth-century French *Pater* from the Bibliothèque nationale MS 2431
tickles the ears of the groundlings in as culturally peculiar a manner:

Pere nostre qui es en ciels,
Li tien nom soit saintifié
Viegne tez permanables regnes.
Que tu touz tens mais sur nos regnes.
Que ton voloir plenierement
Faisomes tuit comunalement.
Done nos pain de sostenance,
De dotrine et de penitence,
Pain del sacrement del autel
Qui nos guart de pechié mortels.
Fai nos de noz pechiéz pardom,
Si con nos a autrui pardonons.
Fai que pechié ne nos enyvre,
Et de trestous mal nos delivre.
Done nos yces requestes,
Qui trestous autres biens nos prestes.

Pater noster, qui es in caelis, sanctificetur nomen tuum. Adveniat regnum
tuum. Fiat voluntas tua, sicut in caelo, et in terra. Panem nostrum
quotidianum da nobis hodie. Et dimitte nobis debita nostra, sicut et nos
dimittimus debitoribus nostris. Et ne nos inducas in tentationem: sed libera
nos a malo.[13]

The translator's purpose here is not to produce a liturgically correct
translation, but to provide a text which would guide the faithful to
meditate on the link between the *Our Father* and the way to salvation

provided by the Church. Hence we have emphasis on the Eucharist, doubtless prompted by the variant reading in Matthew vi. 11 (*panem supersubstantialem*), and heavy emphasis on repentance for sins as a condition of divine forgiveness. But most important to our purpose is the adaptation of a simple prayer to the full rigour of popular sacramental theology.

What the Middle Ages shared with the Age of Reason was the conviction that the universally human could only be understood in the familar terms of their own society. Hence we find Pope making a division between content and expression: he insists in his preface to the Iliad that he is giving 'his author entire and unmaimed'. But because he reserves 'Diction and Versification' as his own responsibility, Homer struts in borrowed plumes. The beginning of the *Iliad* becomes this:

Achilles' Wrath, to Greece the direful Spring
Of Woes unnumber'd, heav'nly Goddess, sing!
That Wrath which hurl'd to *Pluto*'s gloomy Reign
The Souls of mighty Chiefs untimely slain;
Whose Limbs unbury'd on the naked Shore
Devouring Dogs and Hungry Vultures tore.
Since Great *Achilles* and Atrides strove,
Such was the Sov'reign Doom, and such the Will of *Jove*.
Declare, O Muse! in what ill-fated Hour
Sprung the fierce Strife, from what offended Pow'r?

This is Homer in a powdered wig declaiming in a baroque theatre. But, to be received by the eighteenth-century public which believed that it was the acme of taste, Homer had to suffer such incorporation, based on an unconscious lack of trust in his ability to communicate outside his own group. The end of the century showed a notable swing towards a more 'scientific' standard, mainly because the Romantics believed that the creative writer, as the seer of truth, could not help but communicate. Hence, keeping *eine gewisse Farbe der Fremdheit*, as Humboldt put it, was essential. Far from distorting the target language, it entailed, as we can see from Goethe's Diderot and Chateaubriand's Milton, using the resources of the target language that were closest to those of the source. The method ran riot in the 'Wardour Street translators' of nineteenth-century England who went to the other extreme of adulation of their authors's texts and distorted English in a way that can only be described as a parody of the resources of the language (cf. Browning, on page 78, below).

This collective sense of nineteenth-century guilt is nowhere more obvious than in Croce's refusal to recognize the possibility of translation. His view of what inevitably goes wrong is taken from the assumption that the translator obtrudes through the text, a reaction against both the strong-willed Age of Reason and the inept self-effacement of many nineteenth-century translators: both approaches had cast the same opaque curtain between author and reader (Croce 1902, 68):

> Indeed every translation either diminishes or spoils, or it creates a new expression, by putting the former back in the crucible and mingling it with the personal impressions of the so-called translator.

The problem is that an utterance and its content are not entirely coincident: Ezra Pound's distinction between 'what a man sez' and 'wot a man means' is an ancient nightmare. It is here that we have one of the roots of translation indeterminacy. Incorporation, though a mental operation, is signalled by linguistic technique; and it is the reality behind technique that is important. In technical translation the task of incorporation is not too difficult; one operates on only one level, the objective and intellectual. In literary and certain types of religious translation, one has incorporation on many levels, a number of them purely intuitive, and at the mercy of the person translating.

Steiner's fourth movement, that of restitution, consists in putting back what was already there, a compensation for loss in the passage between the two languages. It seems to have been the Russian, Federov, who used the word first. But the idea had been in translators' minds for centuries. This was at the root of Cicero's famous claim in *De optimo genere oratorum* that he translated like an orator, and of Jerome's casuistic twinning of the Evangelists with Cicero in the letter to Pammachius. Jerome's argument is based on Mark v. 41, where Christ raises the daughter of Jairus. He quotes the Hebrew, *talitha kumi* (Girl, get up) and notes that Mark translated it into Greek as 'Girl, I say to you, get up'. As this is a legitimate attempt, in his view, to penetrate to the sense of urgency in Christ's command, it is allowable. In this matter, therefore, Mark, like Cicero, is translating with all the flair of an orator.

Rufinus might have swallowed a precedent from the Evangelists; he was outraged at Cicero. Yet how different was his own work? In his *Apologia* 106 he admits readily that he added matter from other parts of his originals to clarify his translations: '. . . I have merely given back to the author what was his'. This remains a constant theme: it appears in Sorbière's More, in Dryden's *Sylvae*:

> . . . I desire that the false critics would not always think, that those thoughts are wholly mine, but that either they are secretly in the poet, or may be fairly deduced from him.

But there was an awareness that text and translation were different, and translators concerned over what they were doing to their authors alternated their attention between matter and style. Some were certain that they took texts as they found them, others were equally convinced that texts had to be remade.

The comfortable assumption of difference, as far as literature was concerned, was shaken by the Romantics. Translation was a reinterpretation of symbols by other symbols, a search for the λόγος just as the original had been. In Hölderlin's view it was an emendation, externalization, correction, a bodying-forth of implicit meanings. The clearest twentieth-century statement of this is Süskind's comment on von der Vring's *Herrick* (see page 97, below), that the changed imagery of the German lies in the English, in its *Urgrund*. But its aspect has been re-read, emended.

But after one has finished emendation, the original is still there, and from this view of the text as a Proteus under the hand of a translator, came the view that there was a continuous life between original and translation, based on language constants. It is the search to restore the continuity of life that seems to be what Steiner (1975, 395) means by restitution, rather than the more easily understandable instrumental view we saw in Procházka. Steiner's model in its entirety is a Hegelian one based on thesis, antithesis and synthesis; the thesis and antithesis being the two languages involved and the synthesis being the final translation.

Rather like British law, Steiner's is an adversary model of translation, but it is not the only literary or even hermeneutic model with roots running back to the beginning of translation. There had, in fact, developed a 'friendship' model of translation, which first surfaces as a conceit in Roscommon's *Essay on Translation* (1684):

> Then seek a poet who your way do's bend,
> And chuse an author as you chuse a Friend,
> United by this sympathetic Bond,
> You grow familiar, intimate and Fond;
> Your thoughts, your Words, your Stiles, your Souls agree,
> No longer his interpreter, but he.[14]

The German Romantics gave this critical commonplace a new twist by interpreting the symbol of lover and friend very literally. And since then, the recommendation that one translate what one loves, or would like to have written, has been often and tediously repeated. There are, however, some remarks to be made: Hölderlin's view that each new translation was a 'correction' of the original has its counterpart in Francklin's concern with hiding faults and softening blemishes; and Roscommon's last line has its echo in Novalis.[15]

All this was well and good for literature, but it is somewhat difficult to find the 'modest latent beauties' of an author like Lavoisier. But, for all that, both hermeneutic approaches should be examined in the light of the more pedestrian uses of translation. Part of the approach already exists in Maillet-Lacoste's image of translation as an *entretien*, and in a gentler interpretation of the Hegelian term of aggression. Like any use of language, translation is an experience with another person and with language, and such experiences, as Vossler, Buber and Ebeling are well aware, can take place on all levels, from the mere passing of information to a complete interpenetration of insights and experience. The less objective the insight and experience to be shared, the more the being of the translator is engaged and his skill channelled into a creativity guided by both the personality of author and the community of goal between translator and author (cf. Vossler 1925, 201).

Approach to another is not the peaceful process of legend, but often a violent assessment of self in relation to the other person. In application to translation it has a brief mention in Jerome's attack on Rufinus, who, Jerome claims, had not come to terms with himself, and then seems to remain implicit until Bonnefoy (1962, 242), for whom translation is a struggle of the language with itself, a questioning of its whole being. In a paper delivered to the Royal Society of Literature in 1962, Cecil Day Lewis takes the issue to be one of knowing one's own resources and their applicability to the foreign text:

> . . . the original is used to mediate between [the translator's] own imagination and some field of experience hitherto unexplored or unsatisfactorily worked over—to clarify his own ideas.

It is parallel to Ebeling's 'right to speak'. Further, in a manner close to that of Day Lewis, Ebeling conceives 'wrestling for verbal expression' as 'wrestling to understand'. Both Ebeling and Day Lewis speak of the expression problems caused by the differences in the person addressed or author translated.

If a translator finds an author refractory, it is certain that the translator is not the pale imitation of a writer many think he is. Basic to any act of translation is an act also basic to friendship: the sharing of goal and insight. As Day Lewis describes his state of mind when translating Vergil's *Georgics*, he seems to be following C. S. Lewis's exposition of sharing friendship from *The Four Loves*. Under the pressure of war, Day Lewis found in Vergil's attitude to Rome his own attitude to England. And so he came to have the same insight into him as one has into a friend. Even more important to our purpose, Day Lewis's sharing of insight fulfilled another condition of friendship, the wish to widen the circle by sharing it with others. C. S. Lewis sees this as the distinction between friendship and love.

Sharing between friends is not merely informational: friends add to the information they share, a joy in the act of recounting it and a vicarious sharing of each other's experience on terms special to the friendship. It is within this framework that Day Lewis develops the old idea that translator and poet are collaborators, and that the translation is subdued to the same imaginative process as the original. This, of course, can be taken in a large number of ways. As there are varying depths of friendship, there are varying depths of translation, ranging from the necessary exchange of courtesies in technical translation to the deep passion of the Catullus translation of Sappho (see page 192, below). This view means a reworking of Steiner's third movement of incorporation: it is not annexation, but sharing. It is here that we have one essential difference between approaches to translation throughout history. What one can share depends on the cultural cast of the person one has to share with; and different translators have shared different aspects of their author's work. Some translators have dictated the manner of sharing, instead of attempting to approach the author on his own terms. Cecil Day Lewis is an example of the other sort of translator. In his discussion of Proust on Ruskin (Day Lewis 1962, 20), he makes the point that the task of translation brings out the best in the translator, provided he works with the mixture of humility and confidence with which one seeks friendship.

Translation then becomes an interaction between translator and translated; for the ruling question is what does the translator want? Is it the passing touch of an informant, or deep communion with a kindred spirit? Texts, like translators, offer opportunities for all types of contact. Day Lewis (1962, 30) does not claim that collaboration with the original is easy: he too speaks about wrestling, this time with the author. And the final act, that of compensation, cannot be separated out. For once one has wrestled down the author, one has to restore his dignity, as it were. Day Lewis and Ebeling both base the compensation inherent in translation and human interaction on interpretation of need.

It is therefore better to see this compensation as giving. For if one gives on terms intuitively learnt from friend or lover, one is actually enhancing oneself. Day Lewis, then, presents us with a Dido understated and almost meditative in terms not at all different from his own original poetry:

> But now for some while the queen had been growing more grievously
>   love-sick,
> Feeding the wound with her life-blood, the fire biting within her.
> Much did she muse on the hero's nobility, and much
> On his family's fame. His look, his words, had gone to her heart.
> And lodged there: she could get no peace from love's disquiet.

Of all the versions of Dido quoted this is the quietest, the least rhetorical.

There is yet another metaphor to describe the translator's task, and that is the comparing of the translator with a musician or an actor (cf. Zilahy 1963, 285). This goes back at least to Dr. Johnson's remark about Pope playing Homer on a flageolet, while Homer himself used a bassoon. This metaphor rests on a certain understanding of the nature of interpretation. In music, full entry into a work comes through friendly, but just criticism and empathy. It is not for nothing that one speaks of Boult's Elgar or Beecham's Delius. They are every bit as alive as Chapman's Homer or Urquhart's Rabelais. As in translation, the composer is present only in spirit, and his only revenge for inept handling arises from obvious failure on the part of the performer to please, while an abused friend can always snap back.

What is the balance between these three models? The immediate difference between the Benjamin model and the others is its exclusivity. It therefore falls under the Francklin figure of a mistress, rather than the Roscommon of a friend. But the most serious weakness of the Benjamin model in the face of the diversity of translation is its kabbalistic nature. Much translation is aimed purely at factual communication rather than reinterpretation of symbols; and most literary translation is done for an audience. It would seem then that the figures of performance and friendship are truer to the reality, as they honour the reader in a way that the kabbalistic view of hermeneutics rejects. This has been well captured by Jiri Levý's model (see fig. 12), and this is repeated by a very large number of translation theorists (cf. Bonnerot & Houziaux, pp. 39 and 41 above).

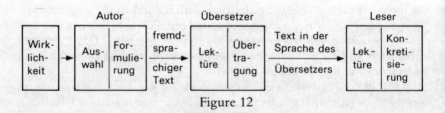

Figure 12

Translation viewed in this light chooses a balance between C. S. Lewis's 'need-love' and 'gift-love'. When Cecil Day Lewis (1962, 19) says that 'the desire to gain a fuller knowledge of that poem is the translator's prime motive for translating it', he is assuming that need-love predominates. But, complementing that is Testard (1975, 54), who writes that beyond professional conscience, there is in a good translator 'une générosité plus profonde, un don de soi'. But a translator relying purely on need-love imposes himself and wrests out of the author his own image. The result is often a shallow journeyman's work that need not lack brilliance, but lacks the original author's voice. This accusation can be levelled at minor figures in all periods, but is especially applicable to the great eighteenth-century figures of Pope and Voltaire. A translation based purely on gift-love produces a caricature of both author and translator himself, as in certain of the less brilliant passages of William Morris's *Aeneid* and the general run of nineteenth-century English classical translations. It is only the brilliant and intensely human translator, possessing both, who has made a comparative success of the task in literature, in that the best in author and translator interact. In other types of translation, the essence of hermeneutic approaches is knowing what the author has to give, asking only for that, and not being disappointed when no more is proffered.

This type of model places a heavy responsibility on the means of expression, a theme constant in writings on translation from the very beginning. Two thousand years of discussion is summed up in Campbell's dictum:

> To express the sense well, and to give it in proper words are in my apprehension, very nearly, if not entirely, co-incident. (1789, ii. 261)

It is here that instrumental theories of translation have always been found wanting: the essence of good translation is not linguistic technique, but the skill with which it is used. And as is clear from the aggressive article by Simpson (1975, 253), translation was considered to 'belong to linguistics', since the juxtaposition of two different statements of the same message can inform the analyst about a whole range of elements, from grammar to culture. Yet twelve years before, Edouard Cary (1962–3, 229) had already characterized views like those quoted as 'une vie partielle qu'on prend pour une vue totale'. Moreover, it was a sterile occupation to reduce problems of translation theory to contrastive linguistics (Cary 1962–3, 11). At the same time, Cary counters those who would see translation as solely a literary problem by requiring that translation theory be based on as wide a sample of translation types as possible (1962–3, 10). The problem of those who rest translation theory solely on linguistics is that it is fatally easy to confuse technique with theory; and when Vinay, Darbelnet, Catford and Nida are accused of concerning themselves solely with *parole*, their real crime is hiding theory behind transfer formulas. Likewise, theories relating to purpose are wanting since, like the instrumental theories, they artificially separate means and end. Translation theory has always been a branch of applied linguistics. But as one must understand that application demands subordination to an end, it is also a branch of literary theory or philosophy. Purpose without technique means groping, technique without clear purpose, sterility. Hence the wiser view is that of Etkind (1967: 'La traduction peut être considérée comme la création littéraire au second degré. Elle ne peut donc pas être exemptée des problèmes linguistiques.'

Our two groups of theoriests are not really contradictory, but contrary; many perceptive critics have seen them as complementary. Thus Capmany Suris y de Montpalau (1776, viii) distinguishes three *caracteres* in a language: the grammatical or logical; 'el usual', and 'el moral', which includes under it the poetic. Capmany's contemporary, Herder, definitely takes the same line; and the split comes with the Romantics, whose main interest was with results, not means. The positivist orientation of the nineteenth century did not help in a rapprochement, though, paradoxically, the separation into two camps did foster the development of useful and evocative ideologies with points of contact that could be exploited. Finding of points of contact begins during the 1930s with I. A. Richards's statement that the results of translation must be judged according to two scholarships, one in each of the source and target languages (Richards 1932, 249). Similarly the instrumental interpretation of Humboldt sensitized linguists to the creative power of language, useful work being done by the Prague Circle, which combined both analytical linguists and literary scholars. The results of the work of Prague are evident in Mounin (1963, 17):

> Toute opération de traduction . . . comporte à la base, une série d'analyses
> et opérations qui relèvent spécifiquement de la linguistique . . . la traduction
> reste un art—mais un art fondé sur une science.

Such statements on the nature of translation rise from the common ground between linguists concerned with means, and critics concerned with ends. That translation begins in an interpretation of source text, this is taken for granted; the major differences between theorists resting on the significance accorded the translator's repertoire of linguistic skills. It is in the movement of 'incorporation' that this repertoire begins to have its effect. A valid fourth hermeneutic movement, not a 'restitution' but a revelation of both power and respect, comes through refusing violent aggression, and taking the time to comprehend author and self. For from this last movement comes the act of criticism which controls techniques. For in failing an author, a translator has failed himself; in revealing the best of an author, the translator has enhanced himself beyond the need to compensate for any damage.

It is only by balancing the means of translation against its end that one can arrive at a comprehensive theory of translation. Such balancing goes on in the mind of every translator who sits down in front of his text and reaches for his dictionary. Few have had the time or patience to construct a theory; but all have tried to avoid betraying 'values'. It is the values they seek to preserve, the values they see in the texts before them, the balance between means and end, the degree to which they have judged themselves true and faithful that are the stuff of a theory of translation. And it is inevitable that theory and practice will change according to needs and ideology.

Three

Translations and their Functions

All functions of language and of translation are exchanges of information,[1] which Karl Buhler divides into three classes: *'symbol'*, 'object-centred, representational, intensional, referential'; *'symptom'*, 'self-expression, source-centred, the subjective element'; and *'signal'*, 'persuasion, recipient-centred, impressive, an appeal, a summons' (Newmark 1973, 3). These functions are rarely separated one from the other: one senses the functions of an utterance and reacts according to the balance perceived between them. Analogous attempts to characterize translation functions have given rise to typologies such as 'scientific' and 'literary', Postgate's 'retrospective and prospective'.

Operationally, there are two critical moments in translation. In acting as a receptor of his author's message, the translator makes judgements about him, and about his purpose in speaking. Then, in casting himself as the author, the translator takes on his authority and the attendant responsibility for assessment of message and reader. That he discharge these responsibilities on the author's terms is desirable, but far from inevitable. Yet it is in assessment of the author's purpose that translators lay the foundation for a translation that will be good or bad, adequate or inadequate, faithful or unfaithful.

3.1 SYMBOL

Symbol entails transfer of information without anything but intellectual commitment. Translators show such commitment in two ways. The first is subjection, complete and often abject, to the expository modalities of the original. The second is extraction of raw information. Full commitment to the author is impossible by this means as there is no affirmation of equality, nor attempt to break down interpersonal barriers. Not that this type of translation is *ipso facto* defective, provided that the immediate aim of symbol fulfils the purposes of both author and translator.

Thus symbol as subjection was characteristic of the Jews who translated the Scriptures into Greek. For, according to their concept of divine inspiration, the texts were the direct creation of God, who had taken over the faculties of the human author. As the word of God, the Old Testament was an objective historical account expressed in the most adequate way. Therefore, as Philo Iudaeus puts it in his life of Moses, Scripture translation was akin to that of science: there is 'a wording which corresponds with the matter', and is therefore the only one adequate. This espousal of literal translation was taken to extremes by the first-century Greek proselyte, Aquila, who rejected as blasphemous the slight attempts by the Septuagint to adapt to Greek linguistic structure. But, as the text he arrived at was unworkable, Christian translators adopted the Septuagint method.

This was all the more possible as they had at their disposal a highly Hellenized register of Latin. A fair example of it is Luke xvi. 19–21 as quoted by Augustine in Sermon xxxiiia, one of the versions under the rubric, *Vetus latina*:

Erat quidam dives, qui induebatur purpura et bysso, et epulabatur cotidie splendide. Erat autem quidam pauper, nomine Lazarus, qui iacebat ante ianuam ipsius, ulceribus plenus, et cupiebat saturari de micis quae deiciebantur de mensa divitis, et nemo illi dabat; sed et canes veniebant, et linguebant ulcera eius.

This dates from about a hundred years after the *Pastor Hermae* (see page 99, below), which shares some of its characteristics. Both passages show close patterning of Latin semantic and grammatical features on Greek. In the *Pastor Hermae*, one has merely to note the Hellenized word order; in the Gospel passage, the same type of word order and the use of Hellenisms like *sed et* where a classicist might expect an adversative like *tamen* and the free use of participles of subordination. For the early Christians such linguistic subjection was the result of not only rejection of classical rhetoric, but also a keen sense of the juridical role of the New Testament Epistles in setting norms of conduct and belief: translators were creating the beginnings of theological and liturgical expression; and hence they preferred to be cautious.

After the first wave of persecutions gave way to official state protection under the Emperor Constantine, the Church could afford to allow its organization to develop publicly and to acquire the trappings of legal entity. Documents like the early Creeds were translated from Greek with an exactness of terminology that is juridical in relevance rather than mystical, as in St. Hilary of Poitier's version of the Nicene Creed (*c*. 365):

Credimus in unum Deum Patrem omnipotentem, omnium visibilium et invisibilium factorem. Et in unum Dominum nostrum Jesum Christum,

Filium Dei, Natum ex Patre unigenitum, hoc est, de substantia Patris, Deum de Deo, Lumen de Lumine, Deum verum de Deo Vero, natum, non factum, unius substantiae cum Patre, quod Graeci dicunt homoousion; per quem omnia facta sunt quae in coelo et in terra; qui propter nos homines et propter nostram salutem descendit, incarnatus est et homo factus est, et passus est; et resurrexit tertia die, et ascendit in coelos; venturus judicare vivos et mortuos. Et in Spiritum sanctum. Eos autem qui dicunt: 'erat, quando non erat', et 'antequam nasceretur, non erat', et 'quod de non exstantibus factus est', vel 'ex alia substantia' aut 'essentia', dicentes 'convertibilem et demutabilem Filium Dei', hos anathematizat catholica ecclesia.

Πιστεύομεν εἰς ἕνα θεὸν Πατέρα παντοκράτορα, πάντων ὁρατῶν, τε καὶ ἀορατῶν ποιητήν. καὶ εἰς ἕνα κύριον Ἰησοῦν Χριστόν, τὸν υἱὸν τοῦ θεοῦ, γεννηθέντα ἐκ τοῦ πατρὸς μονογενῆ, τουτέστιν ἐκ τῆς οὐσίας τοῦ πατρός, θεὸν ἐκ θεοῦ, φῶς ἐκ φωτὸς, θεὸν ἀληθινὸν ἐκ θεοῦ ἀληθινοῦ, γεννηθέντα, οὐ ποιηθέντα, ὁμοούσιον τῷ πατρί· δι'οὗ τὰ πάντα ἐγένετο, τά τε ἐν τῷ οὐρανῷ καί τε ἐπὶ τῆς γῆς· τὸν δι'ἡμᾶς τοὺς ἀνθρώπους καὶ διὰ τὴν ἡμετέραν σωτηρίαν κατελθόντα καὶ σαρκωθέντα καὶ ἐνανθρωπήσαντα, παθόντα, καὶ ἀναστάντα τῇ τρίτῃ ἡμέρᾳ, καὶ ἀνελθόντα εἰς τοὺς οὐρανούς καὶ ἐρχόμενον κρῖναι ζῶντας καὶ νεκρούς. καὶ εἰς τὸ Ἅγιον Πνεῦμα. Τοὺς δὲ λέγοντας, ὅτι ἦν ποτε ὅτε οὐκ ἦν, καὶ πρὶν γεννηθῆναι οὐκ ἦν, καὶ ὅτι ἐξ οὐκ ὄντων ἐγένετο, ἢ ἐξ ἑτέρας ὑποστάσεως ἢ οὐσίας φάσκοντας ἔιναι, ἢ κτιστόν, τρεπτὸν ἢ ἀλλοιωτὸν τὸν υἱὸν τοῦ θεοῦ, τούτους ἀναθεματίζει ἡ καθολικὴ ἐκκλησία.[2]

Because Hilary is conscious that he is defining theological terms at a critical stage in the development of Latin Christianity, he uses formal lexical equivalences, as *incarnatus* and *omnipotens*; and in the most difficult case of all, *homoousion*, he repeats the Greek word as a definition procedure.

Despite his reputation as a new broom, Jerome too conceived his Scriptural work as reporting, and aimed at accurate transference of both matter and vocabulary. Hence his Biblical translations vary little from the *Vetus Latina* (see his Vulgate, page 134, below). No fourth-century Christian would have found any cultural oddities in either text: the ostentatious rich, the beggar with serious skin diseases at the door, the pariah dogs, all were to be seen every day. But this, in view of Jerome's practice elsewhere (see page 45, below), does not explain his literality. In Epistle 106, 12 to Sunnia and Fretella, Jerome notes that, in translating the Psalms, he worked for an unsophisticated readership that was easily put off by the unfamiliar, even if it was correct. So, to avoid upsetting ingrained religious habits, he kept the old readings where it made no difference to the sense. He could have said the same about translating Scripture in general, for his public used what the British sociologist, Basil Bernstein, calls a 'restricted code', whose salient features are flight from semantic and grammatical abstractions and reduction of language to a tool of limited allusiveness. In

Jerome and the *Vetus latina*, then, we have grammatical concretizations like *ulceribus plenus* for ἡλκωμένος, which could have been translated by an adjective, and the characteristic reduplication of grammatical words, as *sed et* for ἀλλὰ καὶ. Not that any of Jerome's friends or enemies saw literality as the only road to salvation: Augustine is especially clear on this, as in the comment on Psalm lxvii. 69, where for the Greek εἰς τὸν αἰῶνα he argues that both *in aeternum* and *in saeculum* are correct, and is even willing to tolerate *in saecula*.

But following the destruction of the Roman Empire and much that was valuable in its legacy, Augustine's theories were largely ignored. The central figure in this retreat from classicism was Manlius Boethius (480?–524). In his preface to Porphyry, he sets out the symbol aim: one seeks in certain works 'knowledge of matter' rather than 'the charm of style'. So, in order to express the 'uncorrupted truth', he demands word-for-word translation. His stand is reminiscent of the dictum on translation from Philo Iudaeus. How he put it into effect, we see in the extract on page 134, below. His interest was that of Cicero, the formation of a philosophical terminology in Latin.

After Boethius, medieval translation was not concerned with anything but intellectual information, and so had little use for any function but symbol. The readership was a highly professional one with an administrative and technical jargon all of its own, and attitudes to match. Yet, beginning with Gregory the Great in the sixth century, there is growing uneasiness over the unthinking attitude that symbol demanded literality. It continues in the work of Anastasius Bibliothecarius, papal librarian, who in a letter written to Pope John VII in *c.* 850 accuses his contemporaries of not only distorting the target language by literal translation, but also putting the reader off. It reaches its peak in the fulminations of Roger Bacon, whose rejection of even the possibility of translation may follow from the thirteenth-century condemnations of the Latin Aristotles translated from Arabic. And indeed, the appearance of texts taken from the Greek caused some reexamination of current techniques, a matter that became urgent with the Great Schism of 1054. Thus in the foreword to his *Contra errores graecorum*, Thomas Aquinas accuses the literal school of sacrificing clarity to formal matching, and thus contributing to the continuation of the schism. Was Aquinas behind the attempt by Humbertus de Romanis to suggest the basis for theory (see page 36, above)?

The suitability of the symbol aim to certain restricted purposes is obvious from the far-reaching effect of the Latin Aristotles of the thirteenth century, and its unsuitability to anything else by the fate of Latin versions of Greek Uniate liturgies in Southern Italy. The twelfth-century translations of the liturgies of St. Basil and St. John Chrysostom were originally meant as information; but some official of the Roman chancellory tried to impose them on the Greek churches in the South. They failed; and the reason is clear from the following extract from the Eucharistic anaphora of St. John Chrysostom as translated by Leo Tuscus:

> Vere dignum et iustum est, te benedicere, tibi gratias agere, te adorare in omni loco dominationis tuae: tu enim es deus ineffabilis, ignotus, invisibilis, incomprehensibilis: semper es, similiter existens tu et unigenitus filius tuus, et spiritus sanctus.[3]
>
> ἄξιον καὶ δίκαιον σὲ ὑμνεῖν, σὲ εὐλογεῖν, σὲ αἰνεῖν, σοὶ εὐχαριστεῖν, σὲ προσκυνεῖν ἐν παντὶ τόπῳ τῆς δεσποτείας σου· σὺ γὰρ εἶ θεὸς ἀνέκφραστος, ἀόρατος, ἀκατάληπτος, ἀεὶ ὤν, ὡσαύτως ὤν, οὐ καὶ ὁ μονογενής σον υἱὸς καὶ τὸ πνεῦμά σου τὸ ἅγιον.

The Greek approach to religion was emotionally rich and cogent, while the Roman liturgy fostered a staid, austere relationship between God and Man. The root error was in not recognizing this; and the above version with its several echoes of the Roman Canon was never in any position to compete. In our terms, Rome had attempted to impose a translation whose purpose was symbol, where a signal translation was called for. Vernacular scientific translators followed the norms set by their Latin colleagues. The medical work of the French court physicians (see the Henri de Mondeville passage on page 136, below), the Justinian passages already quoted and the Aristotle of Nicholas Oresme (1330–82), one of the greatest translators at the French court of Charles v, all show a bending of French syntax to Latin, and some borrowing. In all cases the reason was the same: fear of going outside the 'intention' of the author.

Bitterly as the Humanists criticized their medieval predecessors, in technical terms the results were much the same. In comparison with the Asiatic flourish of Apuleius (page 140, below) some 1,200 years before, the Pseudo-Aristotle of Guillaume Budé (1467–1540) is intensely literal:

> Mundus est compages e coelo terraque coagmentata, atque ex iis naturis, quae inter ea continentur. Dicitur etiam aliter mundus, ordo et digestio universorum quae a Deo et per Deum asservatur. Huius situm medium immotum et stabilem Terra vitae foecunditate praedita sortita est: animantium quidem illa omnifariam distinctarum sedes et parens.[4]

And, indeed, the same remark can be made about Bruno Aretino and Thomas More. Such caution, appropriate to teaching translations, was passed on to Erasmus, whose New Testament is quoted below. In an early letter to the Earl of Warwick, he writes that he preferred to be meticulous, rather than adventurous, a true index of the symbol aim.

Though they started in philosophy, the Humanists were a new breed whose interests went beyond pure intellect, and they very soon went into literary translation, which they at first approached with the same symbol norm. Though this stage lasted only a couple of generations, it left behind it some important work. One of the peculiarities of work into the vernaculars was that all translation was instructional in aim, and therefore almost literal even when a literary work was involved. Thus Delaigne's Caesar (see page 167, below) was translated for both amusement and instruction, and the carefully nuanced literality of the technique shows it. Similarly, culturally important and instructive works were translated to raise the tone of the English bourgeoisie and upper classes. One such was Thomas Hoby's translation of *Il cortegiano*. Our passage is from that on the duties of women (Hoby 1516, 216–17):

> Leaving therfore a part the vertues of the minde that ought to be commune to her with the Courtier, as wisdome, noblenes of courage, staidenesse, and manie mo, and likewise the condicions that are meete for all women, as to be good and discreete, to have the understanding to order her husbandes gooddes and her house and children whan she is maried, and all those partes that beelonge to a good huswief: I say that for her that liveth in Court, me thinke there beelongeth unto her above all other thinges, a certein sweetnesse in language that may delite, wherby she may gentlie entertein all kinde of men with talke woorth the hearynge and honest, and applyed to the time and place, and to the degree of the person she communeth withall; accompaniyng with sober and quiet maners and with the honestye that must alwayes be a stay to all her deedes, a readie livelines of wit, wherby she may declare herselfe far wide from all dulnesse: but with such a kinde of goodnes, that she may be esteamed no lesse chaste, wise and courteise, then pleasant, feat conceited and sobre: and therfore must she kepe a certein meane very hard, and (in a maner) dirived of contrarie matters, and come just to certein limites, but not passe them.

The literal character of Hoby's technique is manifest: and his sobriety in strong contrast with the panache of Clerke (see p. 183). It is in translation of this sort that we find the germs of what was during the next century to become Royal Society prose. Its development can be traced through Salusbury's Galileo, Sir Thomas Nugent's legal translations of the mid-eighteenth century, to productions like Henderson's version of Victor Cousin (see page 185, below). As with the subject matter, so with translation. Both were the concern of gentlemen.

But while the sixteenth century was preparing to improve this world by translation, many translators were casting a close eye on access to the next. Erasmus had innocently started the debate with his edition and translation of the Greek New Testament, which, despite his deep respect for Jerome, was meant to rectify the mistakes of the Vulgate. Here is what he makes of Luke xvi. 19–21:

> Homo quidam erat dives, qui induebatur purpura et bysso, et epulabatur quottidie splendide. Erat autem quidam mendicus, nomine Lazarus, qui iacebat ad ianuam eius ulcerosus, cupiens saturari de micis quae cadebant de mensa divitis. Sed et canes veniebant ac linguebant ulcera eius.[5]

Apart from some critical emendations to Jerome's Greek text, differences are few, but those that there are betray a totally different purpose. While Jerome's was for the Latin-speaking marketplace, for a population speaking largely a restricted code, Erasmus was working for a scholarly population with Bernstein's elaborated code. Hence, instead of Jerome's colourless *et* for δὲ at the beginning of the second sentence, Erasmus has *autem*, which gives a definite adversative and directional sense to the link. Jerome's *ulceribus plenus*, a typical restricted-code concretization, is replaced by the more abstract *ulcerosus*, proper to an elaborated code. A final touch is in the use of *ac*, a literary form, in the last sentence instead of *et*.

With an eye on the vernacular, the battle lines were drawn by Sir Thomas More in his *Dialogue* on heresies (1528):

> . . . it is dangerous to translate the text of Scripture from one tong into another, as Holy Saint Ierome testifieth, for as much as in translation it is hard alway to kepe the same sentence [i.e. sense] whole.

The obvious answer was to protect oneself by translating literally, as the translators of the English Geneva Bible claim in their preface to the 1560 edition:

> Now as we have chiefly observed the sense and laboured always to restore it to all integrity, so we have most reverently kept the propriety of the words, considering that the Apostles who spoke and wrote to the Gentiles in the Greek tongue, rather constrained them to the lively phrase of the Hebrew, than enterprised far by mollifying their language to speak as the Gentiles did. And for this and other causes we have in many places reserved the Hebrew phrases that they may seem somewhat hard in their ears that are not well practiced and also delight in the sweet-sounding phrases of the Holy Scripture.

Literal they were, but like Jerome before them they had an eye to their readership. Here again is Luke xvi. 19–21:

> There was a certeine rich man, which was clothed in purple and fine linen,

and fared wel and delicately everie day. Also there was a certeine beggar named Lazarus, which was laied at his gate ful of sores. And desired to be refreshed with the crommes that fell from the rich man's table: yea, and the dogs came and licked his sores.

Like St. Jerome, the Geneva translators had to deal with a largely restricted-code population. Hence the translation is concrete: εὐφ-ραινόμενος λαμπρῶς (indulged himself splendidly) is concretized to 'fared wel and delicately', for example.

The Reformation was naturally a time of definition of belief, and in some ways the outlook of its translators resembles that of the third- and fourth-century ecclesiastical translator. The problem of impending error, and the cure by abject submission to the source text, is obvious in Thomas Norton (1532–84), who writes in his preface to Calvin's *Institutes of the Christian Religion* (1561):

> If I should follow the words, I saw that of necessitie the hardnesse of the translation must needs be greater than was in the tonge wherin it was originally written. If I should leave the course of the words, and graunt myself libertie after the natural manne of my own toung, to say in English which I conceived to be his meaning in Latine, I plainly perceived how hardly I might escape error, and on the other side in this matter of faith and religion, how perilous it was to erre.

His version is plainly one for the study—here is the opening of Book III. 3:

> Albeit we have already partly taught how fayth possesseth Christ, and how by it we enjoy hys benefytes: neverthelesse it were yet dark, unless we did also make declaration of the effects that we feele thereby.

> Etsi iam aliqua ex parte docuimus quomodo fides Christum possideat, et per ipsam fruamur eius bonis: hoc tamen adhuc obscurum esset nisi effectuum, quos sentimus, accederet explicatio.

Who was Norton translating for? It was probably not the ordinary lay-man, whose interest in theology during the sixteenth century was as rudimentary as in our own time. For the Calvinist clergy? Or was it for the Anglican authorities who were as hostile to Calvin as to the Pope and Luther? Close as this translation is, there are several grammatical differences between it and the original. Its essential aim is reporting; its commitment an intellectual one to doctrine with all its exactness of terminology.

It was Daniel Huet, Bishop of Avranches, who, in his history of translation, gave the clearest expression to such a commitment as the only possible in translation. He attacks St. Jerome for basing a case for free translation on Cicero, Horace and the dramatists (Huet, 1661, 100–1): the sense, in his view, could only be transmitted by language modelled on that of the source text. With an eye to contemporary literary translators, Huet (ibid. 20) forbids any discretion in word-choice or alteration in order, for such 'deviations' from text would be deviations from matter. His norms were followed mainly by scientific translators writing in Latin. The Dutch mathematician, van Schooten (1610?–60?), writes an introduction that could almost have been written by Huet, laying out his intention to keep the 'form' of the words in order not to hide truth in the darkness caused by an elegant style; he was ironically successful in his translation of Descartes' Geometry:

> Et quemadmodum arithmetica tota ex quattuor aut quinque solummodo operationibus constat, ut sunt Additio, Subtractio, Multiplicatio, Divisio et Radicum extractio, (quae pro quadem Divisionis specie haberi potest): Ita similiter in Geometria, quod spectat ad lineas, quae quaeruntur, praeparandas, ut cognitae fiant, aliud faciendum non est, quam ut vel ipsis addantur, vel ab iisdem subtrahantur aliae; . . .

> Et comme toute l'Arithmétique n'est composée, que de quatre ou cinq opérations, qui sont l'Addition, la Soutraction, la Multiplication, la Division, et l'Extraction des Racines, qu'on peut prendre pour une espèce de Division: Ainsi n'a-t-on autre chose à faire en Géométrie touchant les lignes qu'on cherche, pour les préparer à estre connuës, que leur en adiouster d'autres, ou en oster, . . .[6]

The purpose of this was to widen the professional readership through the use of Latin, at that time still a relatively universal language. But this manner of translation carried within it the seeds of its own destruction. Not only is the Latin inelegant, but it is also unclear. And in proportion as modern languages acquired exact terminologies, scientific translation in Latin lost its advantage and disappeared.

Yet for all this, there was still the strong belief that, in technical translation at least, one had to reproduce the features of the source text. And, indeed, in expert hands, that could happen, as is evidenced by the remarkably literal version of Pitot by Edmund Stone (see page 173, below). Neither was it impossible in Latin. Charles Houbigant (1686–1783) repeats most of Daniel Huet's opinions in his preface: the *proprietas* of the words was sacrosanct. But on what constituted *proprietas verborum* there seems to be a theoretical difference. Huet (1661, 109) requires a translator to keep the *compositio* of the words, that is, as his examples demonstrate, to use a strict formal equivalence. Houbigant (1753 I. clxxij) rejects this as an abusive use of etymology: for him the *proprietas verborum* is kept when the reader can recognize not only the Hebrew root in the Latin, but also the meaning in context. Yet his translation of the deutero-canonical *Book of Wisdom* shows no startling innovation in literal transla-tion practice:

> Diligite iustitiam, qui iudicatis terram, de Domino recte sentite, & in simplicitate cordis quaerite illum. Nam invenitur ab iis, qui eum non tentant, & praesens adest eis, qui sibi non diffidunt.

> Ἀγαπήσατε δικαιοσύνην, οἱ κρίνοντες τὴν γῆν,
> φρονήσατε περὶ τοῦ κυρίου ἐν ἀγαθότητι
> καὶ ἐν ἁπλότητι καρδίας ζητήσατε αὐτόν.
> ὅτι εὑρίσκεται τοῖς μὴ πειράζουσιν αὐτόν,
> ἐμφανίζεται δὲ τοῖς μὴ ἀπιστοῦσιν αὐτῷ.[7]

Houbigant's Latin Old Testament is intended to reflect the movement of the Hebrew or Greek, which he printed in parallel columns. That he arrived at an approximation to the style of Jerome's Vulgate is not in itself remarkable; but to do so during the eighteenth century in Biblical work shows a definite symbol aim. His criticism of Arius Montanus and Aquila, who were notorious for their literality, approaches Goethe's somewhat equivocal attitude to complete literality. And his justification for avoiding free translation prefigures Goethe's attack on the 'parodistiche' manner of the eighteenth century (see page 92, below).

The most important vernacular Bibles of the period shared Houbigant's attitudes and techniques. The most successful English version of that time was that of George Campbell. His preface to the Gospels asks of a trans-lator that he unemotionally translate the clarity of the Greek into English; which had not been done, as far as Campbell could see, in the Reformation versions. Yet his version of Luke xvi. 19–21 is not much more objective than the others already quoted:

> There was a certain rich man, that wore purple and fine linen, and feasted splendidly every day. There was also a poor man, named Lazarus, covered with sores, that was laid at his gate; and was fain to feed on the crumbs which fell from the rich man's table; yea, even the dogs came and licked his sores.

Campbell here is drifting over into symptom, i.e. clothing the message in a personally relevant guise. 'Poor man' is less emotionally charged than 'beggar', which in eighteenth-century England could imply that the per-son was violent; 'gate' for πυλῶνα is closer to the reality of the older parts of Aberdeen, with a discreet house set back from a city street behind its own gate and walls. Objectivity? Yes certainly, but not to the extent that Campbell says is possible in his preface.

The Romantic espousal of the Houbigant–Campbell type of literality will be discussed in the next section. Suffice it to say here that the reaction against the excesses of the eighteenth century was severe. One of the illustrious who went too far was Robert Browning. In his preface to *Agamemnon* he writes:

> I have spared no effort to be literal at every cost save that of absolute
> violence to our language. . . . I would be tolerant for once—in the case of so
> intensely famous an original—of even a clumsy attempt to furnish me with
> the very turn of each phrase in as Greek a fashion as English will bear.

He opens the play with almost a schoolboy crib:

> The gods I ask deliverance from these labours,
> Watch of a year's length whereby, slumbering through it
> On the Atreidai's roofs on elbow,—doglike—
> I know of nightly stargroups the assemblage,
> And those that bring to men winter and summer. . . .

> Θεοὺς μὲν αἰτῶ τῶνδ᾿ ἀπαλλαγὴν πόνων,
> φρούρας ἐτείας μῆκος, ἣν κοιμώμενος
> στέγαις Ἀτρειδῶν ἄγκαθεν, κυνὸς δίκην,
> ἄστρων κάτοιδα νυκτέρων ὁμήγυριν,
> καὶ τοὺς φέροντας χεῖμα καὶ θέρος βρότοις.[8]

Indeed, the version is so literal that a crib is not necessary. It is the Goethe 'interlinear version' without commitment to the mother-tongue, or as Brower (1966b, 187) notes, sharing in the experience of the tired watchman.

As twentieth-century education increasingly came to neglect the past, technical translation found itself with a double responsibility. The first was the normal transmission of science and technology between language groups. In the shock following the Second World War, many (e.g. Weaver 1949, 18) saw this type of translation as a way of avoiding future confrontations. In the second third of the twentieth century, worldwide scientific reporting became an urgent priority: as Adkinson (1963, 102) put it, '. . . translators are an integral part of the total research process . . .'. The other responsibility, a perpetual one in the case of the Bible, was linkage with the past. And with the decline in classical studies, the tools to forge such linkage were disappearing. Hence there appeared modern versions of Galileo, Descartes and other great scientific thinkers of the past. In general the technique was a nuanced literality.

By a curious pathology of language this literality reappears in Vladimir Nabokov (1955, 512), whose ideal is

. . . the absolutely literal sense, with no emasculation and no padding—I
want such sense and such notes for all the poetry in other languages that
still languishes in 'poetical' versions, begrimed and beslimed with rhyme.

The attitude here is a complex one: it is partially due to viewing words as
unidimensional objective things which match exactly between languages;
it is probably a hangover from his experience of translating from his own
language into English: there are the same problems in the Greek-speaking
translators of the Sicilian courts who translated into Latin during the
twelfth century. The result is a commitment of the translator to his text as
slave to master.

3.2   SYMPTOM

While the main commitment of the symbol aim is to intellectual content,
symptom transcends this by depending on personal commitment, what
Testard (1975, 54) calls 'un don de soi'. Thus translation with the symptom
aim resembles closely the friendship model discussed in the last chapter.
Hence, the deeper the commitment, the higher the risks and satisfactions.

In the fulsome acknowledgements of the Greek contribution to Roman
culture, we have the constant theme that translation of the symptom type
is an apprenticeship through which all great literatures pass; it is a school in
which writers come to understand the greatness of what they are translating and improve the power of their own language. Most Roman writers
follow the line taken by Pliny's Seventh Epistle (c. A.D. 100) in which he
sees translation as an unrivalled rhetorical exercise. But the more perceptive Cicero and Horace had already seen that translation taught a whole
series of essential literary concepts and behaviours.

But the beginnings had been rough and somewhat ham-handed. The
preclassical dramatists of Rome had made of translation a form of creative
composition. Roman political expansion had left a fascination with things
Greek. But the question was making from the more delicate Greek taste a
vehicle to amuse the more earthy Roman. Here is what Caecilius Statius
(d. 168 B.C.) makes of a speech from Menander (Williams 1968, 363–5):

Is demum miser est, qui aerumnam suam nescit occultare
foris: ita me uxor forma et factis facit, si taceam tamen indicium,
quae, nisi dotem, omnia quae nolis habet: qui sapiet de me discet,
qui quasi ad hostis captus liber servio salva urbe atque arce.
quae, mihi quidquid placet, eo privatum it me, servatam velim?
cum eius mortem inhio, egomet inter vivos vivo mortuus.
ea me clam se cum mea ancilla ait consuetum. id me arguit:

ita plorando orando instando atque obiurgando me optudit.
    illam uti venderem. nunc credo inter suas
    aequalis et cognatas sermonem serit:
    'quis vostrarum fuit integra aetatula,
    quae hoc idem a viro
    impetrarit suo, quod ego anus modo
effeci, paelice ut meum privarem virum?'
haec erunt concilia hocedie: differat sermone misere.

ἐπ' ἀμφότερα νῦν ἡ 'πίκληρος ἡ κ⟨αλὴ⟩
μέλλει καθευδήσειν. κατείργασται μέγα
καὶ περιβόητον ἔργον· ἐκ τῆς οἰκίας
ἐξέβαλε τὴν λυποῦσαν ἣν ἐβούλετο,
ἵν' ἀποβλέπωσι πάντες εἰς τὸ Κρωβύλης
πρόσωπον, ἥ τ' εὔγνωστος οὖσ' ἐμὴ γυνὴ
δέσποινα. καὶ τὴν ὄψιν ἣν ἐκτήσατο·
"ὄνος ἐν πιθήκοις" τοῦτο δὴ τὸ λεγόμενόν
ἐστιν. σιωπᾶν βούλομαι τὴν νύκτα τὴν
πολλῶν κακῶν ἀρχηγόν. οἴμοι Κρωβύλην
λαβεῖν ἔμ', εἰ καὶ δέκα τάλαντ' (ἠνέφκατο,
τὴν) ῥῖν' ἔχουσαν πήχεως. εἶτ' ἐστὶ τὸ
φρύαγμα πῶς ὑποστατόν; (μὰ τὸν) Δία
τὸν Ὀλύμπιον καὶ τὴν Ἀθηνᾶν, οὐδαμῶς.
παιδισκάριον θεραπευτικὸν δὲ καὶ λόγου
†τάχιον† ἀπάγεσθ' ὧδε †τισαρανπισαγαγοι†.[9]

Two characteristics stand out. The first is a withholding of trust: Menander has something to say, but Caecilius assumed he knew better how to say it to the Roman public. Hence, there follows aggression and incorporation in their most violent senses, and the last movement of restitution is not the sort, one suspects, Menander would have welcomed. Menander's exposition is relatively logical and ominously calm: that of Caecilius is rich and extravagant. Underlying this there is a difference in psychological perception. The figure of an unkind wife is amusing, but has in it the seeds of tragedy which a relatively unsophisticated audience might miss. That of the henpecked husband raging against his fate to all and sundry is the stuff of farce; and this is what Caecilius, with all the tricks of parody at his command, aims at.

    This element of violence to the original disappears in Cicero. In a famous passage from *De optimo genere oratorum* v. 14, which as been quoted since to justify everything from inspired insight to wilful remoulding, Cicero claims the right of an orator to express the foreign text in words conformable to Roman customs of speech. It follows, therefore, that word-for-word translation is to be avoided and that the inmost nature (*genus omne vimque*) of the words must be kept. Let us see how he exercises his privileges. In his lost *De fato*, savagely criticized by Augustine (*De civitate dei* v. 8), he translates *Odyssey* xviii. 136–7:

> Tales sunt hominum mentes, quali pater ipse
> Iuppiter auctiferas lustravit lumine terras.[10]

Cicero, an excellent advocate because his understanding of both client and opposing counsel, brings this sort of insight to bear on Homer's couplet. According to Augustine, he assumes that this is a reference to Divine Providence, a theory he rejects. But, hostile as he was, he has a typically Roman vision of Zeus as father of Gods and Men. It is not intensely interesting that Zeus becomes Jupiter: any hack would have done the same. But the image of Zeus leading men in the daylight suddenly becomes one of purification through light (*lustravit lumine*): a completely Roman image, evoking the *lustrum*, the five-yearly purification ceremony that was the responsibility of the censors.

Clearly, *aemulatio* is another way of describing the fourth hermeneutic movement; but it would be a mistake to identify it completely with a technique of dynamic equivalence. It does appear in early Christian translation; for outside Biblical translation, there does occur sharing of insight. Just how different such insights could be is illustrated by two standard Latin versions of St. Basil's *Hexaemeron*, translated about fifty years apart: the first was done in about 390 by St. Ambrose of Milan (*c.* 340–97), the second by Eustathius, a follower, it seems, of St. Jerome, in about 440.

> Conveniens principium est mundi structuram narraturo, narrationi suae principium quo res visibiles exornatae sunt, praeponere. Etenim caeli terraeque tradenda creatio est, quae casu, ut quidam opinati sunt, producta non est, sed a Deo originem traxit.

> Conveniens exordium de mundi compositione narraturus assumpsit decorationem gestorum operum, sui faciens sermonis initium. Caeli enim terraeque factura referenda est non sponte formata, ut quidam opinati sunt, sed ex Deo causas propriae nacta substantiae.

> πρέπουσα ἀρχὴ τῷ τῆς τοῦ κόσμου συστάσεως μέλλοντι διηγεῖσθαι, ἀρχὴν τῆς τῶν ὁρωμένων διακοσμήσεως προθεῖναι τοῦ λόγου. οὐρανοῦ γὰρ καὶ γῆς ποίησις παραδίδοσθαι μέλλει, οὐκ αὐτομάτως συνενεχθεῖσα, ὥς τινες ἐφαντάσθησαν, παρὰ δὲ τοῦ θεοῦ τὴν αἰτίαν λαβοῦσα.[11]

Ambrose, prompted by aspirations towards objectivity, stands back and uses a type of indirect speech: he is so much of a mouthpiece that his translation is symbol. Eustathius, on the other hand, tries to provide us with a picture of Basil preaching (cf. the finite verb, *assumpsit*) and there is a direct intrustion of comment in *sui faciens sermonis initium*. In both there is an attempt to transmit, but Eustathius' movement is towards the circle of readers, towards involvement in a way the more cautious Ambrose does not attempt. The Eustathius type of approach reappears in Cassiodorus's monastery, the *Vivarium*, in the late sixth century, and then disappears.

Three hundred years later, as the Carolingian Renaissance woke Europe up to some of the old classical values, Anastasius Bibliothecarius (fl. 850) complained in a letter to Pope John VII that, 'having left the idiom of both languages, they have so followed word for word that their text can not be understood' (850?, 195). Those translations we definitely know to be his are undistinguished, but the minutes of the Fourth Council of Constantinople, at which Photius was deposed, were translated either by him, or at least under his direction. The final speech in the condemnation of Photius was given by Pope Hadrian II. It would seem that the report of it given in the *Acta conciliorum* v:1083 was transmitted in Greek and that the Latin is the translation. Here is the opening of the Pope's summation of the affair:

> Iam, dilecti fratres et consacerdotes, in proxima huius magnae et sanctae synodae actione declaratum est, quo pacto Photius, qui a foro et curia profectus, ecclesiam Constaninopolitanam per vim invasit, admonitus sit, uti se submitteret, verboque et scripto delicta sua fateretur, scriptaque impia et acta bis contra sanctam Patriarcham Ignatium detestaretur. . . .

> *ἤδη πεφανέρωται, ὦ ἠγαπημένοι ἀδελφοὶ καὶ συνιερεῖς, ἐν τῇ προλαβούσῃ πράξι ταύτης τῆς ἁγίας καὶ μεγάλης συνόδου πῶς παρῃέθη ὁ Φώτιος ὁ ἀγορῖος καὶ βουλέυτικος, καὶ ἐπιβήτωρ τῆς Κωνσταντινουπολιτῶν ἐκκλησίας, τοῦ ὑποκλιθῆναι, καὶ λόγῳ καὶ γραφῇ ἐξαγγεῖλαι τὰ ἁμαρτήματα αὐτοῦ, καὶ ἀναθεματίσαι τὰ παρανόμως γραφέντα καὶ πραχθέντα ὑπ᾽ αὐτοῦ δὶς κατὰ Ἰγνατίου τοῦ πατριάρχου αὐτοῦ. . . .*[12]

Obviously, the translator is trying not only to report the objective facts of this crisis, but also to give some flavour of the occasion by attempting a Ciceronian pastiche in which some sense of periodic construction is evident, and there is a definite evocation of law-court oratory.

Outside Romance Europe, translation into the vernacular begins relatively early, and Romance Europe follows suit at about the eleventh century. The professed aim, as in Latin, is objectivity; the performance is variable. Jehan de Vignay, a Hospitaller of St. John, claims in his preface to Vegetius, that he is 'following the pure truth of the letter'. But in his *Evangéliaire* (1350) he provides a jolting contribution to Luke xvi. 19–21:

> Il fu un homme qui estoit riche, et estoit vestu de pourpre et de bougeran, et mengait chascun jour tres plentureusement. Ore avoit il un mendiant lequel avoit nom Lazarus, qui gisoit a sa port plain de bosses, qui avoit

desire d'estre saoulez des miettes qui cheoient de la table du riche, et nul homme ne lui en donnoit, mais les chiens venoient et lechoient sa roigne.[13] (Original Latin on page 134, below.)

Though Jehan de Vignay might have thought he was objective, he is not. For like a large number of medieval translators he is rebuilding the situation through the world he knew: *byssus*, for example, becomes the thoroughly medieval *bougeran*, a luxurious fabric used only by the rich. Further, there is a deliberate attempt to involve his public emotionally through his experience of the more hideous skin diseases rampant in both medieval and Biblical times: *ulcera*, a normal word for a skin lesion, becomes the graphic *roigne* (mange), a not inapt touch in the presence of the ubiquitous stray dog.

In this way the late medieval period prefigured the early Humanists. Leonardo Bruni Aretino, in an inflammatory preface to Aristotle, makes his position clear: Aristotle was not an abstract set of doctrines: he was a person, and it was the translator's duty to get involved. And from this principle of 'looking at Aristotle face to face' flow all the other requirements of humanist imitation of style: in a word, dealing as creatively with Latin as Aristotle did with Greek.

Though their performance in prose seems relatively innocuous, it was in poetry that they moved closer to classical *aemulatio* with its mixed air of kinship and struggle. An early example is the Latin version of Petrarch's Sonnet CII by the Florentine diplomat, Alessandro Braccese (1445–1503) (1477?, 21):

> Caesar, honoratae cervicis proditor illi
>   Postubi Niliacus tristia dona dedit,
> Gaudia nota tegens lachrymas expressit inertes,
>   Ex oculis, docet ut pagina prisca, foras.
> Hannibal, imperio postquam tot fluctibus acto
>   Sors foret ut vidit facta molesta suo,
> Moesta inter, simulans, lachrymosaque lumina risit,
>   Ut premeret luctum corde gemente magis.
> Sic animas cunctas vario sub tegmine curas
>   Nunc tegit ore hilari, nunc tegit ore nigro.
> Invita quare siquando splene cachinnos
>   Exprimo, quin etiam carmina siqua cano,
> Id facio, quoniam nobis via nulla supersit,
>   Haec nisi, qua lachrymas tristitiamque tegam.[14]

Through exercises such as this for learned colleagues, Latin was revitalizing itself through translation, and thus the history of the classical period was repeating itself. One can see in the Braccese version the hand of the apprentice: the sense of poetry is there, but the elegiac verse is rough, appropriate though it is by classical convention, and there is constant tension between grammar and form, as in line 4 where the *ut* is misplaced to avoid lengthening a syllable.

Vernacular translators did not underestimate the value of translation as a literary apprenticeship. Translation taught everything about what was good in another culture. Peletier du Mans (1555, 106) speaks about the riches translation brings; Pasquier (1576, 125) thought of translation as the instrument through which one participated in 'les belles et nobles conceptions des estrangers'. But the simplest tribute comes from Sir John Harington in his preface to *Orlando Furioso* (1591):

> . . . the Earle of Surrey and Sir Thomas Wiat, that are yet called the first refiners of the English tong, were both translators out of Italian.

The question to be settled was the stamp put on what one learned. The Braccese sonnet, like so many early Humanist productions, is a cautious piece of work; and does not really show much attempt to do any more than linguistic transfer. However, when translators tried to share their fascination with people outside their circle, the literary apprenticeship aspect began to compete with remnants of the old medieval freedom. Let us look at the first stanza of Horace's *Odes* I. v. in the French version of Luc de la Porte, a Paris lawyer of the 1540s, and in the Spanish of the Franciscan, Fray Luis de León:

> Quel graile enfant en maintes roses
> De molles odeurs fres-ecloses
> Oinct, soubz ton antre gratieux,
> O Pyrrhe, ton blanc marbre presse?
> A qui ta belle blonde tresse
> Tors-tu d'un noeud delicieux,
> Simple d'une monde parure?

> ¿Quién es, ò Nise hermosa,
> Con aguas olorosas rociado,
> El que en lecho de rosa
> Te ciñe el tierno lado?
> ¿Con simple aseo pura los cabellos
> Anudas?

Our concern here is how the two translators proceed from differing insights. Luc de la Porte's Pyrrha is not unlike the famous portrait of Diane de Poitiers: her skin is white, not a detail that appears in the Latin, and her blonde hair is done in the sophisticated Renaissance fashion. Her swain is a fashionable teenager, whose behaviour in the rose-covered bower is physically as well as verbally passionate. It is a vivid scene that heightens and coarsens all of Horace's hints. Luis de León, the better classicist, gives us another picture. The brash worldliness of Luc de la Porte is replaced by a hint (in the word *ciñe*) that the boy is emotionally involved; and the scene is a tender private one on a couch scattered, as Roman festive couches were, with rose-petals. The image of the girl is different. Blondes in Rome (and very often in sixteenth-century Paris) were women of fashion with dyed hair. Luis de León omits this point with its reflection on the girl's sophistication. Of the two versions, the Spanish is the gentler, even to the point of blunting some of the quietly amused malice of Horace.

Some technical translation depended on shared experience too. Delaigne, a Gentleman of the Bedchamber at the French court, writes in his preface to Caesar (see page 167, below) that he wished to provide his colleagues with 'une lecture . . . non seulement delectable, ains commode et fructueuse'. That this was a normal aim in technical and scientific translation is clear from Thomas Salusbury's preface to Galileo's *Massimi sistemi* (1661):

> The book being for subject and design chiefly for gentlemen, I have been careless of using a studied pedantry in my style, as careful in contriving a pleasant and beautiful impression.

It was from the attitude of such translators, that we have the guiding principle of organizations like the Royal Society, who saw science as the pursuit of gentlemen, and placed as much emphasis on efficient and graceful reporting as on good research. Salusbury's Galileo is an excellent example of Royal Society prose:

> Indeed, these men do not deduce the conclusions from the premises but accomodate, or, to say better, distort and subvert, the premises and arguments to make them speak in favour of preassumed and pertinacious conclusions.

> Questi dunque non deducono la conclusione dalle premesse, nè la stabiliscono per le ragioni, ma accomodano, o per dir meglio acomodano, e travalgon le premesse, e le ragioni alle loro già stabilite, e inchiodate conclusioni.

There is a curious sense of a law-court argument about the balanced synonyms of this passage. In an anti-Catholic age that was well aware of the persecution of Galileo, such an imagined polemic in which Galileo was finally allowed to plead his own case would have seemed fitting.

But scientific theory was accorded a treatment that was not repeated on the more practical and plebeian level. In experimental science, especially pharmacology and chemistry, the running of laboratories seems to have devolved more and more on laboratory assistants and apprentices whose Latin was suspect enough to require vernacular handbooks. One of the most influential Latin originals was the *Basilica chymica* (1609) of Oswald Croll, a follower of Paracelsus. Here is his preparation of potassium sulphate, in the French of the otherwise obscure Jean Marcel de Boulenc (1624):

> Prens par exemple, quatre onces de sel de tartre bien blanc, dissoult deux ou trois fois (selon qu'enseigne la Chymie) lequel soit filtré et espoissi avec eau d'agrimoine, resouls le par apres en une eaue, dessus le marbre, ou avec huille de tartre bien pur, par le benefice de la chauffe, par laquelle tu le couleras: ayant cest huille pur, prens deux onces d'huille de vitriol bien rectifié, lequel tu distilleras goutte à goutte dessus l'huille de tartre en un verre assez capable, et alors tu verras une congelation tres-blanche, sur laquelle l'humidité nagera, et apres le chauffant peu à peu et à petit feu, tu rendras sec ton sel. Voyla comme se faict le tartre blanc fixe de vitriol.

> Recipe salis tartari albissimi, aliquot vicibus secundum artem Chymicam dissoluti, filtrati & coagulati cum aqua agrimoniae, exempli gratia, uncias quattuor, resolve in cella supra marmor, aut beneficio manicae in oleum. Habito hoc oleo puro accipe olei Vitrioli optime rectificati uncias duas, illudque guttatim supra tartari oleum in vitro capaci instilla: tunc fiet coagulum albissimum. Humiditas supernatans evocetur lento calore ad siccitatem Salis, ita habetur Tartarum album Vitriolatum fixum.[16]

Croll was writing for experts; Marcel de Boulenc for their assistants: his French, though factually and linguistically equivalent, interprets the somewhat convoluted grammar of Croll's original, providing a step-by-step exposition of the process.

Much scientific translation, similarly simplified, was done for the layman, continuing the Renaissance drive toward secularization of education. For example, Nicholas Culpepper translated professional literature, including some Galen, for the ordinary householder. He was out to break the monopoly of the medical profession, who, he claims in the preface to his Galen deliberately used Latin to hide the truths of medicine from their patients, behaviour as reprehensible as that of the Papists whose religion was clothed in Latin. In his introduction to Galen (1648) he writes:

> Time was when all Physitians wrote in their mother tongues, time was when they thought it their glory to instruct others in matters belonging to their own health . . . time was when he would have been considered a

monster and unfit to live in a Commonwealth that should have attempted such a thing as to hide the Rules of Physick from the Vulgar in an unknown tongue. . . .

Ostensibly, his purpose was objective information, but his sense of mission produced symptom shading off into signal.

Chapter 2 of the Galen *Ars medica* begins:

Medecine is the Knowledg of things Healthful, not Healthful and Neutral. This definition is nothing else than if you should say, Medecine is the knowledg of things belonging to the Sick, 'tis not one whit more nor less.

Ἰατριχή ἐστιν ἐπιστήμη ὑγιεινῶν, καὶ νοσωδῶν, καὶ οὐδετέρων. οὐ διαφέρει δὲ οὐδ' εἰ νοσερῶν τις εἴποι.[17]

In contrast to Salusbury, who assumed that his readers had a scientific culture equal to his own, Culpepper takes his readers as being a little dense. Indeed he shows the technique of an elementary teacher; his second sentence is stretched by an expository repetition to drive home his point in as conversational a tone as necessary to an unsophisticated readership.

By the end of the eighteenth century the professional and lay streams of scientific translation were merging. Latin scientific translation was safely dead by 1750, but vernacular translations of modern originals, such as the works of Locke, Lavoisier and Faraday, were contributing to the spread and development of both physical and social science. Translators tended to regard themselves as teachers: Lieutenant John Clarke of the Royal Marines translated Vegetius's *Art of War* as a model for his colleagues, and the French Revolution called forth the patriotism of translators such as Sheperd, whose translation of the *Strategems* of Polyaenus (1793) was meant to provide a textbook for the army in general. In the same spirit important books on economic theory and practice were either commissioned by legislative bodies, or forced on them by eager citizens.[18] The translator's commitment here is a many-sided one. Commitment to matter, inevitable in the circumstances, is matched by commitment to reader. That to the author is shown through the sharing of the translator's own fascination.

In many ways, the best of seventeenth- and eighteenth-century translation is here, rather than in literature or religion. The reason can be found in *The Appeal to Truth* (1622) by the London schoolmaster, Joseph Webbe, quoting Georgius Haloinus Cominus, a contemporary of Erasmus. Webbe is writing primarily about language teaching, but his complaints apply to translation as well. He sees 'fower especiall reasons . . . why fewe, or none, perceiue the custome of the Aucients': literal translation; the use of what was later to be called 'l'ordre naturel'; rash repudiation of these faults without the guide of a sense of language; and slavish adherence to the rules of grammar. His version of Cicero's letters to Tiro attempts to make of this exchange between friends a normal piece of educated English: here is the end of *Ad fam*. xvi. 5:

> Wee long all, but I above the rest, to see you presently, but in no case without your health, good Tiro. And therefore make no haste, I shall think I have everie daie seen you, so you come lustie and strong unto us. I can doe, what is to bee done, withoute your helpe, and therefore suppose not, that mine own benefit drives mee, to desire your health, so much as the love I beare you. Farewell, Cicero.

The aim here is to step into the shoes of Cicero, much as Cicero attempted to become Demosthenes; and to seek an English equivalent in meaning and social function to the original Latin.

That this aim was general is abundantly clear from the inaugural address to the Académie française by one Claude-Gaspard Bachet de Méziriac (1635, 419):

> Celui qui péche par ommission, témoigne de la négligence, plutôt de la malice. Celui qui change, et met une chose pour une autre, fait voir son ignorance, et qu'il n'entend pas bien la matière dont son auteur traite, ou la langue en laquelle il écrit. Mais celui qui ajoute quelquechose mal à propos, se montre plein d'arrogance et de témérité.

But with the exception of German, the culturally important languages of Europe were suffering from an adolescent sense of their own maturity. Hence, in interpreting the unexceptionable statements about fidelity from the beginning of the century, one must take care to read them against documents like l'abbé Perrin's preface to the *Aeneid* (1648):

> Pour te faire trouver Virgile en Virgile, et son Héros travesty de l'habit, non pas d'un barbare tel qu'il a paru dans les anciennes traductions, ny d'un faquin, comme tu l'as veu nouvellement, et comme il est au pouvoir des plus misérables, mais d'un Cavalier François avec la pompe des plumes et des clinquants.

The standard image is one of restitution: in the words of Nicholas Perrot d'Ablancourt, 'nous ne devons point craindre de lui donner celles [i.e. les beautés] de nostre pays, puisque nous lui ravissons les siennes'. The extent to which this was done is obvious from what happened to

Vergil's *infelix Dido* (*Aeneid* IV. 1–5) in the hands of Perrin, de Marolles and Dryden:

> Mais la Reyne Didon cruellement blessée,
> D'un amoureux soucy qui trouble sa pensée,
> Nourrit depuis lontems l'ulcère dans le coeur,
> Et flestrit d'une molle et secrète langueur.
> L'amour à sa mémoire incessamment retrace,
> La vertu de son hoste et l'honneur de sa race;
> Elle y porte gravez ses traicts et ses propos,
> Et ce trouble à ses yeux ne laisse aucun repos.

> La reine agitée depuis longtemps d'une violente inquiétude, nourrissoit sa playe dans ses veines, et sentit son âme éprise d'un feu secret. Toutes les grandes qualités de Prince revenoient en son esprit, les traits de son visage, et la douceur de son entretien: Tellement que ses soucis ne laissoient à ses membres aucun moment de repos.

> But anxious cares already seiz'd the Queen:
> She fed within her veins a Flame unseen:
> The heroe's Valour, Acts and Birth inspire
> Her soul with Love, and fann the secret Fire.
> His words, his looks imprinted in her Heart,
> Improve the Passion, and increase the Smart.

There is, in each of these versions, a sense that Vergil could not be allowed to get away with portraying the human element in a noble woman: a curious standing-off, as if Dido is a lay figure in a Gainsborough portrait. Apart from some lexical watering-down (as in the dilution of *virtus*, a many-sided concept, to which Michel de Marolles in his flat way comes closest), there is a characteristic choice of the more colourless of grammatical alternatives: *venis*, for instance, is taken by all three translators as an ablative of place (cf. Dryden's 'within her veins'). With more justification it can be taken as an ablative of instrument, 'fed with her veins'. Not a grammar mistake, but an obvious attempt to present a Vergil with all the seventeenth-century virtues. As in Caecilius, there is a certain lack of trust in the power of the original to communicate and a corresponding twisting in the movement of commitment.

Composition in classical languages was a common recreation for the man of letters, and translations of poetry into Greek and Latin were part of many poets' stock in trade. For several English scholars, it was also an attempt to overcome the low stature of English as a European language by turning its best poets, e.g. Edmund Spenser and John Milton, into Latin. In so doing, the Roman love for ornamental epithet and grace was fused with similar but grosser qualities current among eighteenth-century poets. Here is the opening of William Cowper's 1779 translation of Prior's *Euphelia and Chloe*:

> Mercator, vigiles oculos ut fallere possit,
>   Nomine sub ficto trans mare mittit opes;
> Lene sonat liquidumque meis Euphelia chordis,
>   Sed solum exoptant te, mea vota, Chloe.[19]

One might expect an initial hermeneutic movement of complete trust: Prior and Cowper were almost contemporary, and their cultural ambience was much the same. But the problem is one of visualization of Roman classical convention. Seventeenth-century classicists regarded Roman ornamentation as all-pervasive, instead of as a series of deft effects in an otherwise sober fabric. Hence, Cowper's fault is imposition of his vision of Roman poetry through misplaced virtuosity: Prior's trifling wit becomes the laboured grace of Eliza Doolittle. But this caricaturing of the original was demanded by the norms of the period; and Lemaistre de Saci, as quoted in Fontaine (1738, 138), had the gall to lament that, if a translation was rigorously exact, 'il y aurait du danger qu nous n'écrivissions alors vraiment que pour nous-mêmes, et non pour les autres . . .'.

The gravest problem for the eighteenth-century literary translator arose from this conflict between his stated aims and cultural objectives. Voltaire, for instance, writes in his preface to *Juies César* (1736, 366):

> Pour bien faire connoistre un poète, pour donner une idée juste de sa
> langue, il faut traduire non seulement ses pensées, mais tous les accessoires.

A sentiment worthy of Cicero, Jerome and many others before and since, but the extract on page 199, below has a most un-Shakespearean sobriety with its diluted imagery and regular Alexandrine.

Unexceptional as theory may have been, practice followed the intense ethnocentrism of the time, which was entertainingly described in his *Lettres françoises et germaniques* (1740) by Eleazar de Mauvillon, a precursor of Daninos' Major Thompson: '. . . les François veulent qu'on leur parle clair et net, qu'on leur donne rien à deviner, en un mot, qu'on leur parle *François*.'

In this light, the teaching function of translation had shifted from improvement of the language to that of the pupil, and no less a radical than Charles Rollin (1725, I. 93) could write:

> Rien ne peut estre plus utile aux jeunes gens pour leur apprendre les règles

et les beautés de la langue françoise, que de leur faire traduire de pareils
endroits d'auteurs, et de comparer ensuite leurs traductions qu'on a en main,
en y joignant les réflexions nécessaires.

In the pages of *L'Année littéraire*, however, French critics were coming to
grips with the problem posed by the undisciplined English, whose literature had only just penetrated across the Channel. In his *Nouvelles lettres
angloises* Fréron (1755, 137) warns his compatriots:

Dans un bloc informe de bois ou de pierre, dit un Auteur Italien, il y a
toujours une belle statue renfermée: la difficulté est de l'en tirer; tout l'art
consiste à lever l'enveloppe qui la couvre. Cette idée peut s'appliquer à la
plupart des livres Anglois. Sous une rude écorce, ils ne laissent pas de
renfermer de vrais beautés.

He follows this by stating that the skill of a translator is measured by the
extent to which he can 'les dépouiller de tout ce qui peut blesser notre
délicatesse' (1762, VII. 61).

The English tended to be a little more respectful, at least where they
were dealing with writers of major reputation. 'D.Z.' writing in the
Gentleman's Magazine for 1771, regretfully concedes that even in Vergil
and Homer some of the baser passages will have to be made less uncouth,
but reserves his fire for poets of minor reputation:

But in poets of less eminence he may use greater liberties. He must exercise
his taste to discover their defects, and his art to conceal them. He must lend
them spirit where they are dull, and correct that which is too ardent. He
must labour to heighten their beauties, and, where they are wanting, he may
venture to supply them.

But even before 'D.Z.' a reaction was setting in. In 1750 a certain P. Francis
writes (Draper 1921, 248):

. . . the misfortune of our translators is that they have only one style, and
that consequently all their Authors, Homer, Virgil, Horace, Ovid, are
compelled to speak in the same numbers and the same unvaried expression.
This unclassical kind of versification would be particularly most unnatural
in Horace. It would make him argue in couplets, and the persons of his
dialogues converse almost in epigrams.

But *L'Année littéraire* was changing too. In 1756 Goujet had embarked on
heresy: 'Un traducteur ne peut plus supprimer les défauts de son auteur
qu'un historien ne doit taire les fautes de son héros' (West 1932, 346); and

twenty years later the reform was in full swing. L'abbé Grosier (1777, 308) criticized Cavailhon's Ariosto for embroidery and cutting, crowning his review:

> En se constituant le juge des beautés et des défauts de son auteur, quel garant, en effet, le traducteur peut-il nous donner de la justesse de son discernment et de l'infaillibilité de son goût?

And, six years later, the final blow came from Geoffroy (1783, 87):

> Il faut traduire les littéraires . . . dans la costume de leur pays; je ne les reconnois plus, habillés à la françoise. . . . Cette manière de mutiler les ouvrages . . . me paroît extravagante. . . . Notre goût et nos moeurs sont-ils donc la règle du beau?

Behind all this was a shift in purpose towards casting light on the author instead of teaching the target language. Already in 1770, Bitaubé (1770?, I. 59) was demanding 'traductions fidèles, sans être barbares' which would facilitate understanding the beauties of the original.

But schoolmasters such as Bitaubé were already being overshadowed by the Romantics. Apart from some close imitation of the worst aspects of French classicism by Gottsched at the beginning of the century, the German attitude had been that the translator had a responsibility towards his mother tongue: he was to be the 'morning-star of a new age in our literature', through his abilities as philosopher, poet and philologist (Herder, *Fragmente* II. 7). While critics outside the Romantic movement were concerned with the more immediate questions of education (witness Bitaubé), Herder passed on to Goethe and his contemporaries the view that translation was penetration to the inmost *Geist* of a work. Hence Goethe's three types of translation: the informative, that brings over the message 'in our own sense'; the parodistic remaking of a work according to the cultural norms of the translator; and the 'interlinear version', in which the translator penetrates to the essence of the original through close imitation of language use. In the light of this numinous quality language had for Goethe and his circle, the translator becomes 'ein Prophet in seinem Volke', with both the divinity of a prophet and his total subjection to a divine presence, in this case, Language.

It has long been assumed that Romantic interlinearity necessarily demanded literality. This is not the case. Michele Leoni (1776–1858) gives us a *Giulio Cesare* (1811) in which dynamic equivalence consistently overrides formal. And yet, his translations had a formative influence on Italian Romanticism. Goethe, likewise, did not translate literally, even if his dynamic equivalences were less pervasive than those of Leoni or Gérard de

Nerval, whom he admired. The linguistic technique entailed is clear from his version of Diderot's *Le neveu de Rameau*:

> Es mag schön oder häßlich Wetter sein, meine Gewohnheit bleibt auf jeden Fall, um fünf Uhr abends im Palais Royal spazieren zu gehen. Mich sieht man immer allein, nachdenklich auf der Bank d'Argenson.

> Qu'il fasse beau, qu'il fasse laid, c'est mon habitude d'aller sur les cinq heures du soir me promener au Palais-Royal. C'est moi qu'on voit toujours seul, rêvant sur le banc d'Argenson.[20]

Clearly, not an interlinear version in the sense of the schoolroom. For giving life to this instrumental concordance there was recognition that parallelism of experience and temperament with the original gave rights—Diderot's picture is clearly one resembling Goethe's own *Werther*. This was certainly not accidental; and Chateaubriand claims in his Milton preface that, as Milton had written in a period of revolution, and as therefore there was a close concordance of ideas and attitudes, literal translation was the only safe way of signalling this resemblance. For all his agreement with his German mentors, Chateaubriand shows a sense of strain, taking care to remove 'ce qu'elle a de sauvage' from his literal version of *Paradise Lost*. He begins:

> La première désobéissance de l'Homme et le fruit de cet arbre défendu, dont le mortel goût apporta la mort dans ce monde, et tous nos malheurs, avec la perte d'Eden, jusqu'à ce qu'un Homme plus Grand nous rétablît, et reconquît le Séjour Bienheureux, chante, Muse céleste.

Chateaubriand has caught the Latinate, Biblical flavour of Milton's English not only in the shape of his words, but also in dignified and heavy balance of his prose. This stylistic similarity reflects similarities between Chateaubriand's own approach to his religion as we see it in *Le Génie du christianisme* and Milton's view of the relationship between Church, God and Man. And it is on such emotional and intellectual kinship that the rationale of the 'interlinear version' rests. Thus, though the technique of Goethe, Chateaubriand and their colleagues is exactly that of Houbigant, the aim is different: Latin, as a 'dead language' or as a language of study, was beyond the regenerative power the Romantics saw in translation; though it seems clear from Campbell's praise of Houbigant, that he did cast considerable light (in the sense of *Erklärung*) on Biblical Hebrew, and E. Haupt's Latin versions of Goethe's lyric poems are models of Romantic interlinearity in both language and form.

The Romantic interlinear version remained an ideal until late in the century—what Astre (1870, 148) calls 'une littéralité littéraire'. Carlyle

attempted it in his version of Goethe's *Helena*, and wrote his attempt
off as a failure because, though formally close, it missed Goethe's tone.
Carlyle's example, however, inspired the American, Bayard Taylor
(1825–78). Here is his version the Archangels' Chorus from *Faust* (1870,
11):

> The sun-orb sings in emulation,
> 'Mid brother-spheres, his ancient round;
> His path predestined through Creation
> He ends with step of thunder-sound.
> The angels from his visage splendid
> Draw power, whose measure none can say;
> The lofty works, uncomprehended,
> Are bright as on the earliest day.

In comparing this with de Nerval and Shelley (pages 49, above; 150,
below), this is much more of an 'interlinear version'. First, Goethe's
compound words, *Brudersphären* and *Donnergang* are translated here by
compounds. Secondly, Goethe's poetic form, pulse, images and words are
more exactly reproduced in Taylor than in the other two. The phonological shape of the French sentence, with its accent at the end of the phrase,
tends to give de Nerval a slightly faster pace, while Shelley and Taylor
move, as Goethe does, more slowly. The essential contribution of the
Romantics to the ideology of translation was to stress personal involvement in the creative process, and the ability of symbols to have views of
their own.

The problem of the personal contribution of symptom appears differently in four late nineteenth-century renderings of Horace's *Ad Pyrrham*
(cf. and contrast de la Porte and Luis de León on page 84, above). These
are by Richault (1879), Menendez y Pelayo (1882), Giuseppe Chiarini
(1890?) and Binder (1855).

> De parfums inondé, quel svelte et jeune amant,
> Sur des roses, Pyrrha, dans un antre charmant
> Te presse, et simple en ta parure,
> Pour qui relèves-tu ta blonde chevelure?
>
> ¿Qué tierno niño entre purpúreas rosas,
> Bañado en oloroso ungüento,
> Te estrecha, Pirra, en reglada gruta,
> Cabe su seño?
> ¿Por quién sencilla y à la par graciosa
> Enlazas las flexibiles trenzas?

Chi è, dimmi, il giovine stillante balsami,
Che te sul talamo di rose abbraccia,
Pirra, nel grato speco?
Per chi t'annodi l'aureo
Crin monda e simplice?

Welcher Knabe so hold küsset, o Pyrrha, dich,
Reich mit Rosen bekränzt, duftend von Wohlgeruch,
Im Helldunkel der Grotte?
Welchem knüpfst du das blonde Haar,
Einfach, neidlich geschmückt? . . .

Horace's ambiguous *antrum*, which can mean 'divan' as well as 'cave', is read by all four as a grotto. But, in an effort to make the scene more graphic, Chiarini translates the word twice: in line 2 as *talamo* (bed) and in line 3 as *speco* (cave). The roses are a problem: Richault and Chiarini obviously have the picture of a Roman feast with rose-petals strewn around. In this way, Chiarini's *talamo* makes good sense. But Pelayo is vague, and Binder has the boy wear them as a garland. It is the picture of the girl that is most interesting. One assumes that Pelayo had had no experience of blondes, not at all surprising in Spain. In both the Spanish and Italian, *religas* is culturally neutral. In French, however, we find *relèves-tu*, a sure sign of a nineteenth-century belle preparing for an evening out; and Binder's *knüpfst* recalls a hairdo still not uncommon in certain parts of Germany. The commitment is to parallel experience, and to one's own conceptions or even memories of such a situation, and not to language as such. Hence there is a specific rejection of the *tertium datum* of the beginning of the century.

One crucial legacy the Romantics left, which crossed with other similar stirrings in England, was a historical sense of language. The Pre-Raphaelites approached ancient classical epic as 'primitive' poetry, and so William Morris's *Aeneid* attempts to use a nineteenth-century English inspired by *Beowulf*. Here again is Dido (*Aeneid* iv. 1–5)—one of his best moments:

Meanwhile the Queen, long smitten with sting of all desire,
With the very heart's blood feeds the wounds and wastes with hidden fire.
And still there runneth in her mind the hero's valiancy,
And glorious stock; his words, his face, fast in her heart they lie:
Nor may she give her body peace amid that restless pain.

Clearly not an interlinear version, if only for the high degree of oblique translation. Yet, the essence of what Goethe had hoped translators would achieve is there. There is a feel of antiquity, an approach to Vergil's power, and a careful reinterpretation of human experience: the alteration of *venis* for *heart's blood* is the type of insight into the meshing of symbol and reality the Romantics had sought. In this passage at least, as in the modern version by Day Lewis, there is language the contemporary reader could react to and an image he could savour.

Such fusion strengthened the attitude that languages were served and transformed through translation, and the opinion that translation enriched a language appears in many later Romantics, including Hugo's introductions to his son's Shakespeare. Another Romantic idea, that of the translation as a continuation of the life of the original, became increasingly important in criticism as the century progressed. The 'interpretative' or 'corrective' role of translation is at its clearest in translation into Latin verse, as one can hardly change Latin in the sense that the Romantics tried to change living languages. Here then is the first verse of *Euphelia and Chloe* as translated by John Kells Ingram (1823–1907), Vice-Provost of Trinity College, Dublin:

> Fictis, ut sibi sospitet,
> Cautus vector opes sub titulis tegit;
> Versus Aemiliam mei
> Laudant, sed penitus depereo Chloën.[21]

For the nineteenth-century classicist, the fascination of matching mood and convention proved to be one of the closest forms of commitment. Ingram has chosen his resources to fit Prior's small scale and lack of seriousness: a Horatian lyric metre with short lines and linguistic resources whose classical perfection reflects well the amused tone Horace often brought to lyric idealizations of romantic trifling. To a classicist, this rendering with its light touch assimilates Prior's grace and deprecation of self to the qualities which make Horace so attractive.

During the early twentieth century, the approach to symptom translation was strongly affected by another element: that 'good translation' was a cultural artifact whose norms did not remain constant. Warren (1895, 333) puts down the constantly changing climate of translation to the fact that 'each age feels the original in its own way'. Seventy years later Douglas Knight (1966, 198) speaks of this feeling as an insight which the reader 'can interpret in the composite matrix of their world and that of the original'. Both views are reflected in T. S. Eliot's 1936 essay on Baudelaire. In remarking that Arthur Symons in his English translation had made Baudelaire a man of the 1890s, Eliot pays tribute to Symon's skill in making something foreign live with the life proper to those times. But, at the same time he notes that what Symons saw in Baudelaire is not what the generation of the late 1930s will see; and that therefore a new translation is needed for the conditions of 1936. It was against this background that the hoary issue of the freedom of the translator was analysed yet again. Attitudes varied from the practice of individualists like Pound and his admirers to echoes of Goethe's advocacy of the interlinear translation. Julien Green (1942, 110) sees in the translators of the Authorized Version of 1611 the Symbolist attitude:

> . . . they understood that in the case of such a book as the Bible, only a literal translation would do.

And beside him, one can place Benjamin, Buber and Nabokov (see page 79, above).

There were, however, many who refused to see symptom translation as excluding the reader. Among many literary theorists was a revival of Maillet-Lacoste's *entretien* in Lefevere (1970, 77), for whom the translator is to 're-establish the dialogue between author and reader'. Parallel with this was the linguist's test of gauging the worth of a translation by its effect on the reader (see Nida and Tabor 1969, 1), and the liturgies of the mid-twentieth century for whom the reaction of a certain type of congregation was the acid test.

In Bayard Taylor and William Morris, there is an unconscious beginning of the Symbolist approach to literary translation; for they insist on the role of intuition in interpretation. Their attitude remains alive and active in moderns like Day Lewis (1962, 20), who remarks that the translator works from the impressions made on him, as these are 'guides to the poem's meaning, and motives towards finding an equivalent for it'. But at the same time, this intuition did not exclude the reader, and symptom translation of this sort does fall within the friendship image, as the translator is seeking to share with like-minded readers what he makes of the poem. In this vein, a large number of modern translators seek to perpetuate the Goethe interlinear version as the sole means of balancing respect for manner with that for matter. Herrick's *To Dianeme*, as translated by Georg von der Vring (1889–1968), is a fair example:

Sei du nicht stolz auf dein schön Aug
Darein sein Blau der Himmel taucht;
Nicht stolz, ob auch, selbst unbesiegt,
Manch Herz vor dir bezwungen liegt;
Nicht stolz auf dein Gelock, nun dich
Ein Windhauch anrührt, liebessich;
Denk: der Rubin, ob unbedankt
Er unterm zarten Ohr dir schwankt,
Verbleibt ein Funkler königlich
Wenn die schönheit längst entwich.

Sweet, be not proud of those two eyes
Which starlike sparkle in their skies;
Nor be you proud, that you can see
All hearts your captives; yours yet free:
Be you not proud of that rich hair
Which wantons with the lovesick air;
Whenas that ruby which you wear,
Sunk from the tip of your soft ear,
Will last to be a precious stone
When all your world of Beauty's gone.

The beautiful flirt is always with us, and the warnings of the ravages of age a poetic commonplace. Von der Vring wants to put before the reader his own reaction to Herrick's language, as well as Herrick's picture of the girl. This is an interlinear version in Goethe's sense, with the submission to the original nuanced by intuitively re-reading linguistic symbols: from the free handling of the star image in line 2, to the emotional dimension of tenderness that *zart* adds to *soft* in line 8. And this is all framed by a verse-form which exactly follows Herrick's.

While translation such as this falls within the gregarious friendship image through its concern with the reader, the extreme symbolism of Benjamin resembles Francklin's image of a mistress in that his denial that the readership is a major factor in translation assumes kabbalistic communion between author and translator, which resembles the privacy of a love relationship. The second important element in Benjamin is, as we have seen, his reversal of priorities:

> . . . a translation, instead of resembling the meaning of the original, must lovingly and in detail incorporate the original's mode of signification, thus making both the original and the translation recognizable as fragments of a greater language. . . .

One can then distinguish two types of symptom in translation. The first, which we have seen in such translations as Cicero and Goethe, is an expression of self through a participation in the original on its own terms, whether they be the intellectual values of science or the emotional cogency of poetry. The other, the imposition of self on the original, is obvious in the work of Caecilius, the Old French *Pater noster* (see page 58, above), and the Vergils on page 89, above. While the second can produce great literature, it is only the first that produces great translation.

3.3 SIGNAL

One can impart information, one can seek to share the being of another person, and finally one can seek to influence his thoughts and way of action through signal. Translators have often been persuaders, through either strong self-interest, or commitment to a political or religious cause. Technically, signal demands departure from literality; and sometimes changes in matter and emphasis.

At its crudest, this function depends on twisting the message, as in the Greek text of the *Momentum Ancyranum* (19 B.C.). When Augustus began consolidating his *coup d'état*, one of his greatest problems was the East, which in Julius Caesar's civil war had supported Pompey, and in his own, Antony. His *Res gestae*, carved on the walls of what is now a mosque in Ankara, was a successful piece of propaganda for Romans, but it took translators to adapt it to the East. Two things had to be done: first, specifically Roman elements had to be softened; second, Caesar's assassins had to be represented as murderers.

Hence, the typically Roman concept of *respublica* is consistently rendered πατρίς (homeland), thus appealing to the Greek identification of a citizen with his homeland, and all references to Augustus's conquests in the East are transformed to the idea of liberation. On the second point Augustus's word *factio*, refering to Brutus and company, is translated as τῶν συνομοσαμένων (conspirators), and its context has oblique references to oppression of the East (which had supported the wrong side) before it was lucky enough to fall under Augustus's rule.

On a more ethical level, while the early Latin translations of the Bible were meant as coldly accurate reporting, those of contemporary doctrinal and mystical works were aimed at forming religious opinion and behaviour. One of the earliest is the *Shepherd of Hermas*, a second-century mystical work:

> Audi nunc, insipiens, quemadmodum tristitia cruciat Spiritum sanctum, et quo modo salvum facit. Cum dubius inciderit in negotium aliquod, et non proveniat illi propter dubitationem, tristitia haec intrat in hominem, et tristem facit Spiritum sanctum, et vexat eum.

> ἄκουε οὖν πῶς ἡ λύπη ἐκτρίβει τὸ Πνεῦμα, καὶ πάλιν σώζει. ὅταν ὁ διψύχος ἐπιβαλήται πρᾶξαί τι, καὶ ἀποτύχῃ διὰ τὴν διψυχίαν αὐτοῦ, ἡ λύπη ἐκπορεύεται εἰς τὸν ἀνθρώπον, καὶ λύπει τὸ πνεῦμα τὸ ἅγιον, καὶ οτενοχωρεῖ αὐτό.[22]

Like the *Vetus latina*, the Latin shows insight into the restricted code readership (most Christians in Rome at the time were lower-class or slaves). There is a rejection of the abstract for the pictorial, or semantic synthesis for analysis. Hence the Greek, σώζει becomes *salvum facit*, despite the existence of *servare* and *salvare*; λύπει for which the elaborated code form is *contristat*, comes out as *tristem facit*. One could hardly expect to spread spirituality in a type of language that ignored the characteristics of the population.

While taking St. Jerome's biblical translation as symbol, we see his work on the Greek Fathers (see page 45, above) as signal. Firstly, the nature of the originals was such that a persuasive approach was indicated. Secondly, the public had to be moved by the peculiar disciplinary and mystical riches to be found in these writings. Hence, Jerome passed on their doctrine through his own perceptions, falling foul of the traditional party: signal does demand explicit or implicit interpretation and the reformulation of the target text in modes assimilable by the public.

Though, so far, Christian translators had tried to hide what they were doing, St. Jerome brought things to a head by claiming in his letter to Pammachius that 'from my youth I have consistently translated not words, but matter' (Letter 57). To some extent he can be convicted of lack of honesty: for, though in Letter 22, he claims to have abandoned Cicero after a nightmare, he argues for his translation model from classical precedent. But this went further than a mere justification for free translation. By Jerome's time the clergy had become professionalized and his translation of Origen (page 45, above) is in a fourth-century elaborated code: a characteristic quite clear from the care for all the tricks of prose composition one finds in the work.

Jerome's debt to the great classical translators was obvious enough even without parading Cicero and Horace through the pages of the letter to Pammachius. Cicero had shown some delicacy in his approach and gives the reader room to move within the transformations he makes: the translation from Homer on page 81, above, gives room for a large number of interpretations within the semantic field of *lustrare*: Jerome leads his reader in his passage from Origen by his explanatory parentheses, *per poenitentiam* and *per delictum*, to his own austere view of salvation.

In reaction to this Rufinus (340?–410), his critical senses sharpened by hostility, accused Jerome several times of 'falsification': 'propaganda' might be a better translation. Yet Rufinus himself was no different, and certainly no less expert. Here is the beginning of his version of St. Basil's first homily on Psalm I (400?, 1723):

Omnis scriptura divinitus inspirata utilis est ad docendum: hac ipsa de causa a Spiritu sancto conscripta, quod velut ex communi quodam sanctitatis fonte, omnes nobis ex hac remedia propriis passionibus assumamus. Sanitas enim, inquit, compescit peccata multa.

πᾶσα γραφὴ θεόπνευστης καὶ ὠφέλιμος, διὰ τοῦτο συγγραφεῖσα παρὰ τοῦ Πνεύματος, ἵν᾽, ὥσπερ ἐν κοινῷ τῶν ψυχῶν ἰατρείῳ, πάντες ἄνθρωποι τὸ ἴαμα τοῦ οἰκείου πάθους ἕκαστος ἐκλεγώμεθα. Ἴαμα γὰρ, φησί, καταπαύσει ἁμαρτίας μεγάλας.[23]

To indicate the Biblical provenance of St. Basil's thought, Rufinus adds *ad docendum* to complete the headquote from II *Timothy* iii. 16, and the medical imagery of the original becomes more consistent in Latin, although *passionibus* for πάθους has mystical overtones more explicit than those of the Greek.

Translation as signal disappears until the late Middle Ages. Translators into the vernaculars saw their role as transmitting the teachings to be found in Latin texts to their readers or hearers: Jacques d'Amiens (fl. 1250?) prefaces his translation of Ovid's *Ars amatoria*, a favourite book, with protestations of complete fidelity:

> He teaches you thirty-five rules, whose content I shall relate closely, and as conscientiously as I can, I shall follow his intent according to the skill of his book. For I wish to put in nothing of my own.

As a profession of literary faith, this section of the preface recalls Cicero and St. Jerome: Ovid's matter is to be translated, his literary intentions are to be respected. But let us see what Jacques does with *Ars amatoria* I. 659–60:

> et fai, que te voie plourer
> tenrement et fort soupirer:
> Teux coses moult bien le feront
> amolir et l'esmouveront
> a cou, k'elle ait merci de toi.

> Et lacrimae prosunt: lacrimis adamanta movebis.
> Fac madidas videat, si potes, illa genas.

Much as it might have amused him, Ovid was regarded as an ethical teacher, and the *Ars amatoria* as a serious treatise on the art of love. In our French passage, Ovid's progression is made more consistent by combining the first hemistich with the second line. The impersonality of *Et lacrimae prosunt* is abandoned in favour of a direct command. The two words, *adamanta movebis*, are expanded into three lines to shift attention to the tenderness required of a lover, and needed by him.

Religion offers a logical field for signal translation, while often giving the impression that the translation intention is the scientific one of symbol. We see this in the translation of the *Pater noster* quoted on page 58, above, and in the hymn texts on page 106. Among the orthodox churchmen of the fifteenth century, translation for the laity was indeed recognized for the inspirational material it was: the late medieval translations of devotional works abound in calls to sanctity through reading the books in question. Likewise, in the Lollard movement, there is strong insistence on presenting the Bible in the vernacular. An anonymous Lollard tract circulated about 1410 seems to extend this principle to worship in general:

> And on this seith the doctor Lire: if the people understood the preyour of the prest, it schal the better be lade into God and the more devotedly answere amen.

Basically, Lollard theology of salvation flowed from the same postulates as that of the official Church in that the influence of God through Grace was a commonplace. For the Lollards, this came from reading the Scriptures in English:

> For Holy Scripture in latyn, greek or frenche to an englische man is as a dark cloude til he have lerned and understanden these spechis. But whenne by the voys of his owne langage hit entreth into hys soule, hit moysten alle hys wittis bothe bodily and gostly, and make him to bere fruit.[25]

This from Cambridge MS Ii.vi.f108. And in their advocacy of free translation in the same work they echo Aquinas' condemnation of literality.

One would expect from the immense amount of para-liturgical translation recorded in the hymn collections of Kehrein that worship in the vernacular was not discouraged, nor expressing there a popular theology of a sort less scholarly than that in vogue in the clergy. Certainly, the *Pater noster* quoted is a complete dose of sacramental theology, and the Poitiers version of *Jesu dulcis memoria* on page 193, below, reads much into the hymn: the image of Christ as comfort of the sorrowing has little warrant in the Latin, almost as little as the reading of *praesentia* in the last line as the vision of Christ in Heaven. But this theology had official backing.

The fifteenth century also saw continuation of efforts to heal the Great Schism of 1054. To this end, John Bessarion (1389–1472), a high-ranking Byzantine churchman, arrived in Rome in the mid-fifteenth century, changed sides and became a Cardinal. He formed the centre of a Greco-Latin circle concerned with patristics, theology and Church unity. We can assume that the original of his *Oratio dogmatica de unione* was in Greek. In the following passage, the Greek reads like an admonition to come to one's senses and abandon one's separate religious status. This would not have been a politic thing to say to the Latin Church, especially after Bessarion's change of heart. Hence the Latin is an urban affirmation of the official position on tradition and authority in the Church, with the hint that the disagreement was one over details:

Oportere maiores nostri dixerunt, qui ea tempestate fuere, qua oriri haec dissensio cepit, in rebus fidei, his acquiescere quae nobis a sacris litteris tradita sunt; in quibus omnis fidei veritas aut plane explicit(a) est, aut latens erui haud difficulter potest.

δεῖ γὰρ ἔν γε τοῖς περὶ πίστεως, μηδεμιᾶς μὲν οὔσης ἀνάγκης, μηδέ τινος κινδυνεύοντος, καὶ ἠρεμουσῶν τῶν αἱρέσεων, μένειν ἐπ᾽ αὐτῶν τῶν παραδοθέντων, ἃ μὲν ἀποκεκαλυμμένως, ἃ δὲ καὶ συνεπτυγμένως περιεχόντων τῶν θείων δογμάτων καὶ οὐδὲν ὅ τι ὀρθοδοξίας οὐ περιεχόντων ἐν ἑαυτοῖς.[26]

Each text contains the essential element of respect for tradition, but the implied rebuke to the Greeks for 'acquiescing in division' becomes in the Latin a mere reference to the times before the Great Schism. If the split was to be healed, and his own position presented in a reasonable light, two different cases had to be argued with the same text: the affair of the *Monumentum ancyranum* all over again.

Thus, in the passionate atmosphere of the Reformation, we can readily expect signal. The Reformers channelled the humanist dissatisfaction with the scholarship of the Vulgate and the growing regard for the current vernaculars. The initial stages were relatively innocuous: following Erasmus, critical Greek texts were produced and translated into both Latin and the vernaculars with all the care of the scholar. But as the Bible became the cornerstone of the Protestant effort to dislodge Rome, attempts at persuasion of the laity resulted in much oblique translation. In answer to accusations of bias from Gregory Martin, who was head of the team that produced the Douai–Rheims Bible, William Fulke, Master of Pembroke College, Cambridge, writes that it is absolutely necessary for a translator 'that hath regard to interpret for the ignorant peoples instruction' to use dynamic equivalence, a sentiment worthy of the Lollards.

But the signal aim flourished even in the literal versions of Geneva and Rheims, for, within the bounds of literality, the outlet for dynamic techniques necessary to make the text readable provides ample opportunity for interpretation.

One of the central issues of the Reformation was the nature of the Ministry and the translation of the Greek word, πρεσβύτερος. For the Catholics, the Ministry was primarily sacrificial, while for the Protestants it was a teaching ministry. Hence, the Catholic Bibles use the word 'priest', and Luther glosses his *der Eltesten* 'id est Der Priester oder Priesterschaft'. To a man, the English Protestants use *Elder*, occasioning Gregory Martin to accuse them of deceit and wilful concealment of traditional doctrine: The reply from the Protestants was crisp (Fulke 1583, 219):

> This word, *priest*, commonly taken for a sacrificer and the same that *sacerdos*, and by you translated, there was good occasion to use the world, *elder*. . . .

Obviously translators bear a large part of the responsibility for the deepening divisions of Christendom consequent on the Reformation. The Bible was not the only weapon at the disposal of religious persuasion. The effect of the signal aim on technique can be seen in the French version of Calvin's *Institutes of the Christian Religion*:

> Combien que i'ay desia enseigné en partie comment la foy possède Christ, et comment par icelle nous jouissons de ses biens, toutefois cela seroit encore obscur, si nous n'adioustions l'explication des fruites et effets que les fidèles en sentent en eux.

Unlike the Thomas Norton version (for this, see page 75, above), Calvin's is a version for the marketplace. Hence there is more attempt at flow: *effectuum* is rhythmically glossed to *fruits et effets*, and there is the modification of the vague pronoun *nos* to *les fidèles*, a deliberate sheeting home of the reference to Calvin's followers. We find similar 'marketplace' translations of important documents like Luther's Augsburg Confession, whose translator, John Taverner, had collaborated on the Bishop's Bible, and finally went to the stake.

As in the Middle Ages there was considerable attention paid to translation of hymns. Hymns spread from Lutheran sources, sufficient cause for both Catholic and Anglican Churches to avoid them. Indeed, the only traditional hymn surviving in the *Book of Common Prayer* is the *Veni creator spiritus* in the Ordination service. As far as English was concerned, the stronghold of congregational singing was in Scotland, where the Wedderburn brothers published an eminently successful collection drawn from Reformation and pre-Reformation sources. On the continent evangelical success with hymns prompted some attempts in the establishment Churches. In France, some of the most appealing Latin hymns of the de Santeuil brothers were translated from the Paris Breviary for lay use. Here is the first verse of one from the Common of Apostles, translated by Saurin in 1699:

> Est-ce ainsi que tu prens des Ministres habiles,
> Arbitre souverain des ames et des corps?
> Dans des vases vils et fragiles
> Commets-tu tes riches trésors?

It would seem that the French was set to music after it was translated, there being no traditional tune inseparably associated with the de Santeuil text. Contemporary though the Latin is, it is treated in a way that heightens the involvement of the singer. First, the statements of the Latin are made into rhetorical questions, a very strong type of affirmation in this religious context. The other expansions have the same type of strong involvement: *arbitre des ames et des corps* is a logical and telling expansion of *arbiter*, as is *riches trésors* of *opes* and *vils et fragiles* of *vilibus*. Technically, there is nothing here very different from the symptom translation in vogue in literature.

Anglicans and English Catholics kept aloof from this, and the development of English hymnody fell into the hands of Charles Wesley and his collaborators, who fuelled the Methodist movement with hymns from Lutheran and Moravian sources.

Anglicans were brought to hymnody by the crisis of the Oxford Movement in the 1830s. The point at issue was the essential Catholicism of the Anglican Church, an issue difficult to defend in the face of the Catholic insistence that the Apostolic succession had been broken in the time of Edward VI, and in view of the flourishing anti-Romanism awakened by the Catholic Emancipation Act of 1829. In his Anglican days, John Henry Newman had brought the attention of the Movement to the Roman Breviary, in which traditional hymns had their place beside psalms and patristic readings. The Apostolic status of the Anglican Church was to be affirmed by a return to the pre-Reformation practice of hymn-singing and a reintroduction of the old Latin hymns from the York and Sarum rituals. It followed that pre-Reformation hymns could not be divorced from their ancient melodies, and, where there had been a difference between Roman and English practice, it was the English that was followed.

Therefore the melody assumed by John Mason Neale (1818–66) in his translation of the twelfth-century *Rosy Sequence* is taken from the Sarum *Graduale,* not the Roman (see over).[27] Our example shows a technique little different from that of Saurin, but it would seem that in certain respects Neale's task was easier. For the unashamed Romanticism of the English shows an unexpected kinship to the emotional mysticism of the original Latin. There is a definite appeal to Victorian sentimentality and veneration for the great past. The kinship with Shelley's Goethe or even Morris's Vergil is close. By the sour-grape principle the odd Catholic attempts to mine ancient hymnody, spearheaded by Cardinal Newman, were swamped in the floods of religious balladry of Father Faber; and did not come to light until after the liturgical reform of 1969.

In its own way, Catholic work was of much the same quality and followed, in some respects, the same norms. Among the papers of Gerard

Je- su! the ve- ry thought is sweet

In that dear name all heart-joys meet

But oh! than ho- ney swee-ter far

The glimp- ses of his pre-sence are,

Manley Hopkins, Robert Bridges discovered this version of *Jesu dulcis memoria*, translated probably with the Roman melody in mind:

> Jesus to cast one thought upon
> Makes gladness after he is gone
> But more than honey and honeycomb
> Is to come near and take Him home.

It is a very personal vision of the hymn, especially in the highly imaged reference to taking Communion in the last line. But this work and that of others such as Ronald Knox did not take hold; it is significant, perhaps, that it was former Anglicans who tried to introduce this sort of hymnody.

In the Roman Catholic Church agitation for vernacular liturgy began during the 1930s. The feeling during the 1950s was summed up by a Dominican priest, Chéry, who presented the case for and against in a remarkably balanced account. In coming down on the side of the vernacular he shows a mixture of symbolic and signal reasoning. On one hand, the rarity of good Latinity among Catholics precludes understanding, and the necessary use of a vernacular Missal blocks effective participation of the sort enjoyed by the early Christians, for whom liturgy was active, not passive. Against this, there is the danger of disturbing ingrained habits, the inevitable artistic loss, and the effect on Church uniformity. Chéry's thought was to be reflected in the Vatican II Constitution on the Sacred Liturgy, promulgated in 1966, which accords permission for change without issuing a directive. When it came to implementing the Constitution, the directives to the translation teams included the following principle:

The prayer of the Church is always the prayer of some actual community assembled here and now. It is not sufficient that a formula handed down from some other time or region should be translated verbatim, even if accurately for liturgical use. The formulas translated must become the genuine prayer of the congregation and in it each of its members should be able to find and express himself.

Roman Catholic practice was largely influenced by similar work going on in other religious communions: the main problem was creating a liturgical vernacular where none had existed before, for hitherto, official liturgy had always been in Latin.

When put into practice, there were two phases of the work: the first was exegesis, the second actual translation. Influenced in spite of themselves by discussions of religious language such as Hulst (1963) and Wils (1963), the Roman Catholic translators presented the highly formalized Latin texts to the twentieth-century worshipper. Here is the Palm Sunday collect in French and English:

> Dieu éternal et tout-puissant,
> pour monter au genre humain
> quel abaissement il doit imiter,
> tu as voulu que notre Sauveur,
> dans un corps semblable au nôtre,
> subisse la mort de la croix:
> Accorde-nous cette grâce
> de retenir les enseignements de sa passion
> et d'avoir part à sa résurrection.

> Almighty, ever-living God,
> you have given the human race Jesus Christ our Saviour
> as a model of humility.
> He fulfilled your will
> by becoming man and giving his life on the cross.
> Help us to bear witness to you
> by following his example of suffering
> and make us worthy to share in his resurrection.

In following the requirement of the Consilium on the Liturgy (1969, 15) that such texts should be intelligible 'even to the less educated', these collects use a restricted code. The intricate subordination and balance of the Latin is replaced by a paratactic organization, more so in the case of the English than in that of the French. This rejection of formality is in direct contrast to older prayer texts, like the same text from the Book of Common Prayer (see page 176, below) and the English version of St. John Chrysostom (see page 187). For the older assumption was that divine worship required a formal, elaborated code. To the Romans, with a long tradition of sacral language formed by pagan temple ritual, law-court oratory and the ceremonial of the Imperial court, this had been the fitting approach to the divine. To a modern it is somewhat out of place, especially as one of the aims of the liturgical reform was to lessen the distance between God and Man. Hence, to reduce the level of formality, both texts remove the ornamental epithet, *propitius*, and concretise the imagery. French, being a more ceremonial language, attempts a unified flow through the text, but joins with the English in suppressing subordination. Technically we are not far from the practice of Ezra Pound.

A translator is no more accurate in determining the actual function of his text than the ordinary person speaking. Attempts at objectivity are particularly difficult, as few original texts are completely objective. At this stage, however, we have not enough evidence to discuss the effect of translations on people's attitudes to original and author, though it is obvious that translators have attempted, and at times succeeded, to direct the development of science or religion. This is particularly obvious in the case of Christianity, which has depended largely on translated texts for both doctrine, liturgy and discipline. For the moment we are concerned with the questions asked by Forster (1958, 5):

> . . . what is the purpose of the text in the original language? What means does the author employ to realise this purpose? . . . can I as a translator use the same means within the framework of my own language? If not, which can I use?

In general, translation as symbol demands a literal technique; an attempt at objective reporting of what was said. Signal translation usually demands oblique translation, and the risk of misunderstanding by the public is high, not to speak of the risk of inaccuracy. Symptom is in an ambiguous position, owing to the differences in relationship the translator sets up with his author. In the case of Catullus (see page 192, below) and Goethe (see page 93) the translator manages such close identification with the author that the essential of self-expression in symptom is satisfied by a carefully nuanced literality; in other translators we find varying degrees of freedom at the service of symptom. Therefore before attempting to relate the perceived function of translation and the actual effect, translation techniques should be examined.

Four

Approaching the Text

The translator's 'aggression', his interpretative movement into text to find what it has to offer and under what conditions, begins with his choice of source and target languages: the source language of the text is not necessarily that of the author; the target language not always the translator's native language. His second group of decisions, a continuous preoccupation, is judging the integrity of the text and understanding it. The third, likewise constant, is the use that can be made of dictionaries and other aids in isolating and interpreting the lexical and grammatical units in the text.

4.1 SOURCE AND TARGET LANGUAGE

At the beginning of our period, the native language of the translator was not an issue: the Jewish translators of the ancient world had either Greek or Hebrew as their native language; in classical Rome, the great translators were obviously Latin-speaking, but the translators of the *Monumentum ancyranum* and the first Christian Latin translators could have been Greeks. After a relatively short period when Latin speakers like St. Hilary and St. Jerome dominated our field, we enter a period when nobody translating into Latin spoke it natively.

Likewise, the language of the source text was taken for granted. It became an issue only when Jerome lost patience with the Septuagint and, much to the alarm of Augustine, went to the original Hebrew. While Jerome's concern was with the *hebraica veritas*, Augustine's was with the reaction of the Christian community to unfamiliar features in Jerome's Latin text: his attitude is that of a pastor who had to deal with a somewhat slow-witted flock; whatever experience lay behind his translation discussions in his Sermons on the Psalms must have been sobering. In letter 71 to Jerome in 403, he expresses fears of confusion that could arise when Jerome's version began to replace those taken from the Greek. To avoid these, and give some guide to preachers and exegetes, he asks in Letter 28 that Jerome adopt the scholar's compromise, since followed by other Bible translators, of citing Hebrew and Septuagint readings in footnotes.

But the tradition of second-hand translation set up by the early Christian translators was not ended by Jerome. Owing to the high rate of loss of official documents for various causes, misplaced Greek or Latin originals were often replaced by translations of the translation; so that, in using these documents, one can never be sure which is the original and which is the translation. The other important use of translated versions as originals was in the translation of Greek philosophy from Arab versions. It was in this way that Aristotle reached prominence. But at his first appearance in medieval schools he was suppressed; and his partisans blamed the fact that he had passed through the hands of two groups of translators. While Roger Bacon, for one, wanted to get rid of translation and translators altogether, the more usual attitude was that of Albertus Magnus, the preceptor of Thomas Aquinas, that it was safer to translate Aristotle from a Greek original than from an Arabic (*De anima* 1.i.5). But, as far as translation into vernacular languages was concerned, one translated from the most accessible version: Oresme, for instance, and his colleagues worked from Latin versions of Aristotle.

Second-hand translation continued among the early Greek Humanists. In essence the situation was the same as it had been in southern Italy during the twelfth century: only Greeks were bilingual in Latin and Greek, and so we have translation away from the mother tongue as a matter of course. Some translators, for instance Bessarion, redrafted so radically that there is very little interlingual interference. Others, for instance Argyropylus (1415?–1487?), show the normal mixture of interference and over-sensitivity to borrowings and calque that are characteristic of second-language writing. In the passage on page 143, below, there is the calque, *fere plurima*, and the use of *affectus*, a hyper-urbanism for the usual philosophical term, *passio*. Nor was the sixteenth century averse to this, one of the most famous versions of this kind being Thomas North's English version of Amyot's French Plutarch. Such translation arose from ignorance of the original source language; with the surge in interest in Greek at the beginning of the fifteenth century, it became more and more suspect. The touchiness of the Humanists about the competence of their predecessors gave rise to repeated statements from Bruni Aretino on, that a translator should have mastery of both source and target languages. It seems to have been Luther who for the first time assumed that one translated satisfactorily only towards one's own language (cf. Schwarz 1963, 18).

As usual, the most murderous arguments settled round the Bible. There were few who found it objectionable that both Reformers and counter-Reformers translated it into Latin; and Diodati's French version of his Italian Bible seems also to have passed without comment. But the Roman Catholic insistence on treating the Vulgate as the standard original attracted Protestant scorn, despite Martin's statement (1582, 17) that the

Greek had been kept in view 'to resolve the ambiguity that is some time in the Latine'.

Though men of letters assumed from this time on that one translated towards one's own language except as an exercise, there were exceptions. We have seen that Latin remained an international language of science until the end of the eighteenth century, the first important natural- or social-science text not translated into Latin probably being Adam Smith's *Wealth of Nations*. In religion, the eighteenth-century interest in patristics occasioned a large number of Latin translations of the Eastern Fathers, the most important being the Benedictine editions of the 1740s, which were reprinted during the nineteenth century by l'abbé Migne. Just as significant, at least in England, was translation from vernacular poetry into classical verse, for instance the version of *Paradise Lost* by Thomas Power (1660–1700):

> Illicitos vetita decerptos arbore foetus,
> Et patris antiqui noxam, qua concidit omnis
> Progenies, devota alieno crimine morti;
> Et sedem amissam; donec dator ille salutis
> Morte sua redimens animas, foelicibus hortis
> Addicat puras, & avita sede reponat; . . .[1]

One important motivation was to teach the target language and its composition techniques. Our present example is a fairly competent epic hexameter in which Milton's stock evocation of the Homeric or Vergilian Muse sits well. Given Power's purpose of revealing Milton to the world outside England as a great poet, such care in adopting parallel conventions in an international language was to be expected.

But, among the Romantics, congenial though a Roman Epic dress may have been to Milton himself, it was not through such translations one sought truth. The contrast between Power's classical pastiche and Chateaubriand's anglicized French is very clear. Besides, translation into a language other than one's own had little relevance to casting light on the original. Already Herder had been assuming that translation away from one's own language was not worth discussing; and after his time it has been axiomatic that one will work towards one's own language. One can hardly say the same for the source language. The many who had the temerity to translate the early Romantics from French versions were brought to book in the preface to an anonymous early English version of Goethe's *Werther* (Long 1915, 178):

> That an original loses by translation is obvious to everyone who reads two languages; and that this should be the particular case with the present work,

is not wonderful, when we find the translator own himself ignorant of the original language it was written in. . . .

Practice and attitudes have fluctuated violently on this issue. From the end of the nineteenth century it has become common to translate poetry in rare languages from English cribs. There have been some disasters, as the Robert Graves version of Omar Khayyam. But the essential act here is not one of translation, but one of literary creation from an unpolished original. It is doubtful whether this is translation in the full sense: as it is more in the nature of a thorough-going revision, whether it belongs in this book is a moot point.

But the Tridentine canonization of the Vulgate left a fruitful ground of controversy as the Roman Catholic Church barricaded itself behind St. Jerome. But under the changed conditions of the twentieth century, Catholic translators began working directly from the Hebrew and the Greek, instead of merely using them to check the accuracy of Jerome's Latin. The stamp of Papal approval was put on this practice by the encyclical, *Divino afflante Spiritu*, in 1944; and the Knox English Bible (1947–49) remains the last important version from the Vulgate.

4.2 ENTRY INTO TEXT

No matter what the state of an original, intelligible or not, corrupt or sound, one assumes that it makes sense, that the sense is worth saying. More attitude than act of faith, this trust, Steiner's first movement, permeates the entry into text. Vivier (1975, 60) calls the poetical translator 'un lecteur', whose reading is 'un acte mental au cours duquel il tâchera de ne point trahir'. Clearly, the scientific translator is under similar constraints: Holmstrom (1957, 31) reminds his readers that a technical translator must be able to reason about the subject of his text and read his source language so well that he can gauge the author's intentions and fall in with them. There are three elements in this *lecture du texte*: the first is to ensure that the text before one is as the author wrote it; the second is extracting the significance of linguistic and expository form in relation to the message. Each one of these elements depends on what follows it. As far as textual criticism is concerned, a good critic works not only according to the authority of the various recensions he has access to, but also from his knowledge of the intent and customs of his author.

Hence we find a major difference between Augustine and Jerome: Augustine, the objective theologian, first ensures the integrity of text by the usual method of comparing recensions; and then assesses what the text means. This is based on the translator's expertise in his subject (cf. *De doctrina christiana* III.i.1), which, when put into action, comes down to judging whether words were used in simple or transferred senses. In Jerome, we have what looks like the same two stages; but 'what the text means' also includes 'how it means': where Augustine rejected the link that ancient rhetoric placed between matter and style, Jerome twisted it to his own ends behind a smokescreen of piety.

The key passage is in his letter to Pammachius, where he speaks about the *proprietas verborum* and the sheer difficulty of transferring it. With it we can compare the many other passages where he notes that the style and euphony of the original are to be compensated for, provided that sense is not disturbed. Hence, his translations from the Greek Fathers and others are in the Ciceronian vein of recreating the author's rhetorical panache. In ascribing his literality in the Vulgate to the traditional attitude to the Word of God, however, he is only partially honest. By classical precedent, he had to reproduce the stylistic quality of the Greek in his Latin. The unpolished quality of Hellenistic Greek had an exact counterpart in colloquial Low Latin, and, by literality, Jerome could do three things at once: satisfy the scruples of a flock who had the Jewish reverence for the Word of God, translate in an objective reporting fashion, and satisfy his own scruples by recreating a style concordant with the matter.

Jerome, then, looks forward to a whole string of translators, mostly literary, who take style as an inseparable aspect of the message; but it was the Augustinian assumption that ruled the Middle Ages. Important as skill in language was, concern with matter and doctrine was seen to be the centre of the translator's work; and style, or attempts to reproduce it, were presumed to get in the way.

Scientific competence was the problem fixed on by Roger Bacon as the essential issue in translation. In a sweeping condemnation in his *Opus maius*, he lays the contradictions in the thought of Aristotle, as the Middle Ages knew him, squarely at the door of translators who had insufficient knowledge of both language and matter. But the centre of the problem for some translators remained the question of accuracy of original text. By the fifteenth century it was well known that Biblical texts varied in their rescensions, and the Lollards tried to forestall condemnation by scholarship:

> First the simple creature had much travail with divers fellows and helpers to
> gather many old Bibles, and other doctors and common glosses, and to
> make one Latin Bible some deal true; and then to study it off the new text
> with the gloss and other doctors as he might get, and especially Lyra on the
> Old Testament. . . ; the third time to counsel with the grammarians and old
> divines of hard words and hard senses how they might best be understood
> and translated, the fourth time to translate as clearly as he could to the sense

and to have many good fellows and cunning at the correcting of the translation.

And much good it did them. For there is always a subjective element of judgement in good criticism, and their scholarship did not save them from condemnation.

The necessity for textual criticism was obvious to the Humanists, especially in the light of their attempts to react against the medievals. Erasmus and Latomus referred to Jerome's search for the *Hebraica veritas* and saw as a remedy to faulty translation, 'inspectio codicis linguae primariae' (Latomus 1518, 11).

It is obvious that the Renaissance textual critics were concerned with interpretation as a part of text establishment. This became of crucial importance in Bible translation through the question of authority: and in a backhanded reference to the Catholic arguments from Jerome and Augustine, Fulke reminds his readers that

> How the Fathers of the Church used words it is no rule for the translators
> of the scriptures to follow, who oftentimes used words as the people did
> take them, and not as they signified in the apostles' time.

While textual criticism as a scientific procedure developed its own norms, translators were beginning to apply standards of their own to the issues it treated. Dryden's prefaces to Vergil and other Roman poets note the importance of knowing the original intimately and intuitively and react very sharply to accusations of falsification.

Both Dryden and Pope show by their notes and prefaces that both *signifiant* and *signifié* were subject to assessment. Dryden (1685, 254) argues that poets differ from each other not only in content but also in style and that those who have forced Vergil and Horace into the same English style have falsified them. The root problem is one of interpretation: few have improved on Tytler (1790, 64):

> A good translator must be able to discover at once the true character of his
> author's style. He must ascertain with precision to what class it belongs;
> whether to that of the grave, the elevated, the easy, the lively, the
> florid. . . .

This done, one can then proceed to a choice of style in the target language. At the same time, protests against the purely philological type of criticism abound. The most slashing appears in the first long footnote to Pope's *Iliad*:

> This Disposition of finding out different significations in one thing, may be
> the effect of either too much, or too little Wit: For Men of right

Understanding generally see at once all that an Author can reasonably mean, but others are apt to fancy Two Meanings for want of knowing One. Not to add, that there is a vast deal of difference between the Learning of a Critick, and the Puzzling of a Grammarian.

Pope's own footnotes show that he did his best to combine the two. His version of *Odyssey* xviii. 136–7 is:

For man is changeful as his bliss or woe,
Too high when prosperous, when distrest too low.

His footnote on the passage is a curious mixture of good textual criticism and typically eighteenth-century intuition:

> 163. *For man is changeful as his bliss or woe.*] Most of the interpreters have greatly misrepresented these words,
> Τοῖος γὰρ νόος ἐστὶν ἐπιχθονίων ἀνθρώπων
> Οἶον ἐπ᾽ ἦμαρ ἄγῃσι.
> They thus translate it, *talis mens hominum, qualem deus suggerit*; or "Such is the mind of man, as Heav'n inspires:" but this is an error, for *οἶον* cannot refer to *νόος*, but to *ἦμαρ*, and the sentence is thus to be render'd, *Talis mens hominum, qualem diem deus inducit*; that is, "The mind of man changes with the complexion of the day, as heaven sends happiness or misery;" or as in the translation,
> For man is changeful as his bliss or woe,
> To high when prosp'rous, when distress'd too low. ⟨163–4⟩
> The Reader will be convinc'd that the construction requires this sense, by joyning the præposition with the verb, *ἐπὶ* with *ἄγῃσι*, and rendring it, *οἶον ἦμαρ ἐπάγῃσι*; nothing being more frequent than such a division of the præposition from the verb amongst the *Greeks*. It must be allow'd, that *Homer* gives a very unhappy, yet too just a picture, of human nature: Man is too apt to be proud and insolent in prosperity, and mean and abject in adversity; and those men who are most overbearing in an happy state, are always most base and mean in the day of affliction.

The rejected interpretation is that of Chapman and Spondanus, and the arguments adduced by Pope are quite definitely taken from the 'Puzzling of a Grammarian'. The rest is a deliberate assertion of the eighteenth-century right to cross the i's and dot the t's in a way reminiscent of Caecilius Statius and the medieval *Pater noster*.

By the end of the eighteenth century the passions aroused by the Reformation had, to some extent, cooled. Under the influence of classical scholars, the approach to Biblical and other religious texts had changed so that, while translators kept in mind the question of divine inspiration, they treated the task as little different from translations of classical texts: as

Bishop Newcome in his 1792 proposal for the revision of the Authorized Version put its:

> The critical sense of passages should be considered and not the opinions of any denomination of Christians whatsoever. The translators should be first philologists, and not controversialists.

This case is argued by George Campbell in his Tenth Dissertation (Campbell 1789, I. 495–500). There he analyses the faults of Arias Montanus, St. Jerome, Castalio and de Bèze. The first he dismisses as inaccurate because of literality. The others have all sinned in the approach to text: Jerome, because he worked from uncritical manuscripts; Castalio because, in forcing a Classical Latin style on the Bible, he failed to perceive the importance of style in carrying the message; and de Bèze because 'he is more solicitous of accommodating Scripture to his sentiments than his sentiments to Scripture'.

By the beginning of the nineteenth century, not only was there considerable activity in lexicology, but the science of textual criticism had become a group of fairly accurate techniques, most rather mechanistic. And when the Romantics speak about *philologische Arbeit*, this is not what they mean. Their focus is rather empathy with the author and sensing of his times and intent through the living shell of his language.

It was in the clash between these two types of *Philologische Arbeit* that lay the grounds of the famous quarrel between Matthew Arnold and F. H. Newman, of the University of London, over Homer. Matthew Arnold began it by attacking Newman's translation on the following grounds (1861, 149):

> The translator of Homer should be penetrated by a sense of the four qualities of his author: he is eminently plain and direct, both in the evolution of his thought and in the expression of it, that is both in his syntax and his words; that he is eminently plain and direct in the substance of his thought, that is in his matter and ideas; and finally that he is eminently noble.

Having stated common ground, Arnold then challenged the classical establishment by saying that, if these qualities are to be preserved 'the translator must without scruple sacrifice where it is necessary verbal fidelity to the original' (ibid. 223). He then characterizes as contrary to the aim of simplicity the use of archaic language, attempts to reproduce Homer's compound epithets, and artificial 'poetic' language. Newman (1861, 56) replied that, far from doing justice to Homer, Arnold's ideas and practice actually wronged him:

Homer never sees things in the same proportions as we see them. To omit his digressions, and what I may call his 'impertinencies', in order to give to his argument that which Mr Arnold is pleased to call the proper 'balance', is to value our own logical minds over his picturesque but illogical mind.

To which Arnold (1861, 259) replied with the artist's suspicion of the scholar:

Perplexed by his knowledge of the philological aspect of Homer's language, encumbered by his own learning, Mr Newman misses the poetical aspect, misses that which alone we are concerned.

The main points at issue were form and style, both protagonists being well aware that these two automatically involved affective content.

Arnold's own efforts were variable in quality. Newman (1861, 68) seized his opportunity:

When Mr Arnold denies that Homer is ever prosaic or homely, his own specimens of translation put me into despair of ever convincing him; for they seem to me a very anthology of prosaic flatness.

For Newman, a typical classicist of his time, the fact that Homer was ancient by even Greek standards, had to be shown in English: 'Mr Arnold appears to regard what is *antiquated* as *ignoble*. I think him, as usual, in fundamental error. In general the nobler words come from the ancient style' (ibid. 84). The problem is what was seen, and also how it was to be represented. Arnold aimed at simplicity of language, an approximation to Victorian English: in his own defence, he quotes *Iliad* viii. 560–4 in English hexameters:

So shone forth, in front of Troy, by the bed of Xanthus,
Between that and the ships, the Trojans' numerous fires,
In the plain there were kindled a thousand fires, by each one
There sate fifty men, in the ruddy light of the fire;
By their chariots stood the steeds, and champed the white barley,
While their masters sat by the fire and waited for morning.

Newman, following the principle that Homer was archaic, even by Greek standards, had sought to transmit that by careful use of archaisms, a slightly more complicated style and a long ballad metre. It is doubtful whether either man ever forgave the other for his treatment of Homer, or for the aspersions cast in the quarrel. But the issue is not one of skill or linguistic knowledge: neither man was a rank amateur. The important things here was contrasting ways of approach. Arnold used his knowledge of Greek, and saw in Homer a fellow-poet with many of the human insights Arnold himself had. Thus Arnold applies a Victorian reasonable-ness to the problem of the horses waiting for morning: it is their masters who do so, and Homer attributes this to the horses by metonymy. But for Newman, Homer was an ancient, approached as such. There are, in fact, few better illustrations of the indeterminacy of translation than this child-ish display of one-upmanship from the pair of them.

What perceptive criticism could entail is shown by Amadée Pichot (1796–1877), who made it his business 'à faire connaître la pensée littéral de Byron'. Here is the opening of *English Bards and Scottish Reviewers*:

> Resterai-je toujours auditeur bénévole? . . . Fitzgerald braillera d'une voix enrouée ses aigres distiques dans une taverne, et je n'oserai rimer de peur que les Revues d'Ecosse ne me traitent d'écrivassier et ne dénoncent ma Muse?

> Still must I hear?—shall Hoarse Fitzgerald bawl
> His creaking couplets in a tavern Hall,
> And I not sing, lest, haply, Scotch reviews
> Should dub me scribbler, and denounce my muse[2]

Pichot has had the discernment to see in the opening an echo of Juvenal's first Satire which denounced the poetasters infesting the salons of imperial Rome: 'Semper ego auditor tantum?' (Am I always to be only a listener?). And Juvenal's memories of *raucus Codrus* (hoarse Codrus) are sheeted home to Fitzgerald in Pichot's French.

Pope had seen intuition as a respectable tool in criticism; this had been reaffirmed by Arnold against Newman, and is taken as basic by Stephen MacKenna (1872–1934), who writes in his preface to Plotinus:

> Plotinus is often to be understood rather by swift rushes of the mind—a mind trained to his methods—than by laborious word-racking investigation.

Here is his beginning to the *Second Tractate*:

> Since Evil is here, 'haunting this world by necessary law', and it is the Soul's design to escape from Evil, we must escape hence.
>   But what is this escape?
>   'In attaining Likeness to God', we read. And this is explained as 'becoming just and holy, living by wisdom', the entire nature grounded in virtue.

> Ἐπειδὴ τὰ κακὰ ἐνταῦθα καὶ τόνδε τὸν τόπον περιπολεῖ ἐξ ἀνάγκης, βούλεται δὲ ἡ ψυχὴ φυγεῖν τὰ κακά, φευκτέον ἐντεῦθεν. Τίς οὖν ἡ φυγή; θεῷ, φησιν,

ὁμοιωθῆναι. Τοῦτο δέ, εἰ δίκαιοι καὶ ὅσιοι μετὰ φρονήσεως γενοίμεθα καὶ ὅλως ἐν ἀρετῇ.[3]

MacKenna's problem is to present Plotinus as an ethical teacher, while avoiding, as far as possible, anything other than Platonic overtones. He signals the quotations from Plato by inverted commas; an elementary piece of criticism. There are problems, however, with the concepts of Evil and God. Personifying evil to translate τὰ κακὰ is a dangerous game, as is translating θεῷ, which does not have a definite article, as 'God' instead of 'a god'. He draws back from a completely Authorized Version flavour to the passage, however, by avoiding the temptation to translate δίκαιος as *righteous*, a typically Biblical word, and by using *just*. The problem is one of sensing Plotinus in a way that shows his kinship to Christian teaching while avoiding making a Christian of him.

In his editions of Manilius and Juvenal, A. E. Housman uses the traditional methods of text and *scholia* comparison up to a point. His forewords to both editions stress, however, that, in the last analysis, it is not only the number or respectability of recensions that has the deciding voice; but the editor's own intuitions of what the author would have written. This was not a licence to return to the unbridled wilfulness of Richard Bentley's editions of Horace, but an effort to point out that editing was not merely a reckoning up of accounts, but the understanding and sympathetic presentation of an author.

Housman had little to do with translation as such, and it is difficult to know if his ideas had any direct influence. But his critical principles reappear in Ezra Pound. Not that Pound approved of Housman, or was aware of how close their thought was on the matter. Comparison between Pound's essay on Cavalcanti (1930–1) and the Housman prefaces show that both wished to make the original speak for itself by using one's intuition on variants instead of merely applying rules. But intuition has to be rooted in knowledge, and knowledge guided by intuition. The requirements outlined by Battles (1963, 94) are by no means extreme:

> He who would translate Calvin must be a biblical translator first. Then he must know his Greek and Latin poets, philosophers and historians. The Church Fathers must be his intimates. He must profess too some knowledge of Roman and Canon Law, of scholastic theology, of medieval history. He must steep himself in the Reformation era. . . .

As an example of the meshing of knowledge and intuition, let us examine Matthew xxvi. 30, the beginning of the agony of Christ in Gethsemane.

The Greek is: Καὶ ὑμνήσαντες ἐξῆλθον εἰς τὸ Ὄρος τῶν Ἐλαιῶν. The point at issue is the exact force of the aorist participle, ὑμνήσαντες (having sung). Knox, working from the Vulgate has, 'And so they sang a hymn', commenting that 'it is no part of the translator's business to alter, on however good grounds, his original' (1949, 2). Yet is this merely ducking the question? For what is referred to here is the Great Halel, the Passover hymn of praise based on Psalms 113–18 which ends the Passover ritual. Other modern versions are more specific. The New English Bible (1961) has: 'After singing the Passover Hymn'. Other versions do not commit themselves as gravely: the French Jerusalem Bible (1956) and the English (1966) have 'Après le chant des psaumes', and 'After psalms had been sung'; the Spanish of Nacár-Colunga (1944) reads 'Y dichos los hymnos', and the Catalan of the Benedictines of Montserrat (1928), 'I, després de l'himne'. The whole problem of rights and duties in the face of a readership that does not have the social knowledge of that of the original is posed here and translators have gone for different types of specificity: the Ecole de Jérusalem leaving the impression that the psalms concerned were at the choice of the singers, and the Spanish and Catalan versions, through the article used, showing that it was a rubric that was being followed.

In scientific translation, textual criticism was concerned with elimination of errors. Eighteenth-century translators had not scrupled to change authors' mistakes, and the translator's rights and duties in the face of faults in text remains a conundrum. One assumes that a technical translator knows his field; and, indeed, most technical translators before the twentieth century were practitioners in the field and translators by accident. As twentieth-century translators are not so well placed, certain commercial translators request that, in the case of a difficult text, the translator be sent pertinent drawings and figures, with some references to related material (see Gingold 1966, 143). As in literary and religious translation, the attitude in technical translation had gradually changed from seeking out errors to forestalling them by interpretation.

4.3　SEGMENTATION

The act of translation begins from assumptions about the unit of translation. Two interlocking criteria operate here: integrity of message, and cohesion of utterance. The question of unit resembles the Chinese Box puzzle, with units of larger relevance giving way to smaller. Few would disagree with the Catholic liturgists on this (Consilium 1969, 3):

> The translator must always keep in mind that the unit of translation is not the individual word, but the whole passage. He must therefore be careful that his translation is not so analytical that it exaggerates the importance of particular phrases while it obscures or weakens the meaning of the whole.

And, indeed, this warning is found in translators with other purposes, for example Meschonnic (1973, 322), who sees the centre of translation theory as having passed from *l'unité-mot* to *l'unité-texte*.

The term, segmentation, is that of Sydney Lamb (1961a); for Vinay and Darbelnet (1958) it is *découpage*. In a linguistic sense this is isolating the smallest unit of meaning: Vinay and Darbelnet take as equivalent *unité de pensée*, *unité lexicologique* and *unité de traduction*, and deliberately avoid equating 'unit of translation' with word. However, throughout the history of translation there has been a conflict between rhetorical and linguistic considerations. In general, where small units are considered within the context of large units, translation tends to be 'free'; where small units are considered for themselves, and their structure given minimal importance, translation is 'literal'. The need to take as large a compass of unit as possible was clear to Jerome, who, in his preface to Ezechiel claims to be translating 'per cola et commata'.[4] i.e. through the large unit. In general, Augustine clearly agreed with this, as in his comment on Psalm lxxvii. 69 that expressions like *in saeculum* can be treated as a unit. But, in certain particulars, he sees bound morphemes as units of translation, as in Greek verbs compounded with prepositions, for which he demands separate translations.

There is little to suggest that Augustine's thought on the practice of segmentation was original. Christian translation from the *Pastor Hermae* (see page 99, above) and Hilary of Poitiers (page 69) seems to provide the basis for Augustine's requirements. Indeed, strict as the segmentation of this period is, both the anonymous translator of the *Pastor Hermae* and Hilary show some flexibility in interpreting segments: the use of two words for one, already remarked in the *Pastor Hermae*, and the calquing of Hilary. The virtue developed by Augustine, Jerome and Rufinus was flexibility: following this early practice, they defined the unit at the meaning level rather than through its form, and then descended to words and morphemes only when the energies of meaning dictated. In medieval technical translation this did not always take place. Despite quoting precedent from St. Jerome, Joannes Scotus Erigena in general takes the word as his unit, even when Greek has reduced it to a bound morpheme. His results are not happy, as in the beginning of his version of Pseudo-Dionysius:

Omne datum optimum, et omne donum perfectum, desursum est, descendens a Patre luminum: Sed et omnis Patre moto manifestationis luminum procession, in nos optime ac large proveniens, iterum ut unifica virtus restituens nos replet et convertit ad congregantis Patris unitatem et deificam simplicitatem.

«Πᾶσα δόσις ἀγαθὴ καὶ πᾶν δώρημα τέλειον ἄνωθέν ἐστι καταβαῖνον ἀπὸ τοῦ πατρὸς τῶν φώτων.» Ἀλλὰ καὶ πᾶσα πατροκινήτου φωτοφανείας πρόοδος εἰς

ἡμᾶς ἀγαθοδότως φοιτῶσα πάλιν ὡς ἐνοποιὸς δύναμις ἀνατατικῶς ἡμᾶς
ἀναπλοῖ καὶ ἐπιστρέφει πρὸς τὴν τοῦ συναγωγοῦ πατρὸς ἑνότητα καὶ θεοποιὸν
ἁπλότητα.

Despite claiming Jerome as his authority and model, Joannes does not
translate like Jerome. His unit is either word or morpheme so that his Latin
becomes difficult. For example, the word Πατροκινήτου is decomposed
into its lexical elements constructed in what looks like an ablative absolute,
Patre moto, where the verb seems to have deponent force. Reliance on the
smallest grammatical unit possible has produced lack of sense. The opposite tendency can be seen in the medieval Ovid texts where each sentence is
taken as a unit and translated without regard to linguistic matching of
smaller units within it.

The Cicero–Jerome doctrine appears again in Leonardo Bruni Aretino.
Bruni Aretino and his colleagues obviously allowed for nesting units of
variable size at structure level, and were well aware of the role of structure
in bringing about understanding: in the *De recta interpretatione* he repeats
almost word for word Cicero's doctrine on *cola* and *commata*. But one can
detect also an awareness of the importance of units as small as the word
within these environments: otherwise it would be impossible to explain
the close literality of Bruni Aretino, who was typical of the time. But the
issue of segmentation was one fully operative. One aspect of segmentation
was linkage within clauses and phrases. Chapman begins his *Iliad*:

> Achilles' banefull wrath resound, O Goddesse, that imposed
> Infinite sorrowes on the Greekes, and many brave souls losd
> From Breasts Heroique—sent them farre, to that invisible cave,
> That no light comforts; and their lims to dogs and vultures gave.
> To all which Jove's will gave effect; from which first strife begunne
> Betwixt Atrides, king of men, and Thetis' godlike Sonne.

In his note on line 5, Chapman attacks the usual reading of the Greek πᾶσι
as an adjective qualifying οἰωνοῖσι, and makes of it part of the parenthetical
statement about the will of Zeus:

> Κύνεσσιν, οἰωνοῖσι τε πᾶσι (Διός, &c.) is the vulgar reading, which I reade:
> Κύνεσσιν οἰωνοῖσι τε (πᾶσι Διὸς δ᾽ἐτελείετο βουλὴ) because πᾶσι, referd to
> κύνεσσιν &c., is redundant and idle—to the miseries of the Greekes by Jove's
> counsell, grave and sententious.

There is little on segmentation theory that was not already part of larger
discussions of rhetoric. There is no firm theoretical basis until the seventeenth century.

The basis was the *pensée*, which underlay the linguistic sign. In the words of Rollin (1725, III. 3), *pensées* were the images of things, and words images of *pensées*. However, this did not mean that in translation, the *pensée* was identical to the word: it referred more to the sense group. Thus in the Vergil of de Marolles (see page 89, above) we seem to be in the free world of the medieval Ovids and the Roman dramatists. There is this difference, however, that his freedom is contained within strict segmentation: thus *verba* becomes *la douceur de son entretien*, and *vultus*, *les traits de son visage*. And within many other *pensées* there is one-to-one lexical matching. As well, especially in classical languages, translators were well aware of the possibility of discontinuous signs: the Pope comment on *Odyssey* xviii. 136–7, is basically a justification of a certain choice of segmentation. A glance at the *scholia* on this passage shows that both interpretations are very old; and, indeed, Cicero, as we have seen, exemplifies the opposing view.

Strictness in segmentation did not, therefore, preclude any type of equivalence as long as the basis of the target text was a translation unit. Many translators show an unconscious use of the Hjelmslev *figurae* in dealing with semantic units. Hopkins, for instance (page 106, above), decomposes the Latin *memoria* into *think* and *absent*, and thus these two *figurae* appear distributed between the first and second line in Hopkins's English: '. . . to cast one thought upon . . . after he is gone . . .'.

There was little advance in the theory of segmentation until the twentieth century with the followers of Bally: Marouzeau (1931, 70) followed the strict line that the internal structure of the segment has to be kept, as it indicates the expressive priorities of the original. As an example of bad translation he gives for *admiratio et studium* (admiration and zeal) *une admiration passionée*: the Latin is analytic and the French synthetic. What would he have said to Hopkins? But in all its rigour, this attitude remained rare; more typical was the opinion of people outside the Bally school, for instance, Hilaire Belloc:

> It is of high importance to render idiom; and idioms of their nature demand translation into another form from that of the original.

And it is this, strongly coloured, as all French scholarship is, by the rigorous attitudes of classicism, that we find in Vinay and Darbelnet (1958) 37:

> Nous considérons comme équivalents les termes: unité de pensée, unité lexicologique et unité de traduction.

Until this point it was assumed that a unit of translation was primarily a lexical element. Vinay and Darbelnet, working from Malblanc, develop their theory of segmentation (*découpage*) along functionalist lines. They distinguish four types of unit: *unités fonctionelles*, *unités sémantiques*, *unités dialectiques* and *unités prosodiques*. The only one which is strictly semantic is the *unité sémantique*; all are *unités prosodiques* and the other two have direct relevance to grammar. Much the same type of division from an aggressively anti-mentalist viewpoint is found in Catford (1965).

In an anthropological context, we find the same thing in American structural linguistics with Voegelin's 'translation span contours'. Like the *unités* of *stylistique comparée*, these are functional segmentations; but, unlike them, they are separated one from the other for the precise purpose of translation. In view of the radical differences between Amerindian languages and English in syntax and the needs of the anthropological linguist, this would seem logical. And it was taken up by workers in machine translation. In a way closely paralleling the work of *stylistique comparée* and the theories of Catford, machine translators rejected the sentence as the unit, aiming at the smallest efficient unit, which was often the morpheme. However, these small units were always considered in their environments; and through concepts such as 'nesting' and 'structure', the insights of *stylistique comparée*, which depend more on intuition than on a rigid analysis method, were validated by the more mechanical approach of machine translators. In both groups, the isolation of the sense-unit depended not only on 'meaning', but also on function in text. It is instructive to compare Malblanc, Jumpelt, and Vinay and Darbelnet with the work of machine translators like Sydney Lamb and Paul Garvin on this point.

Beside this linguistic approach there was a rhetorical one, where the most important element was the discourse unit. This is what Belloc (1931, 26) means when he speaks of a translator 'blocking out' his work; and Pound with his concept of 'blank words' put in to fill out the discourse unit. In a letter in W. H. D. Rouse written in 1935, he says:

> I don't see that one *translates* by leaving in unnecessary words; that is, words not necessary to the meaning of the *whole* passage, any whole passage. An author uses a certain number of *blank* words for the timing, the movement, etc., to make his work sound like natural speech.

True to the difference in priority between the linguistic and literary theorist, the important question for the literary man is the final overall effect, and hence, we find among a large number of them the firm conviction that the only unit worth considering is the largest one, either verse line or whole discourse unit. In this literary principle, as laid out by Shattuck especially, linguist and literary theorist are approaching the same reality from different angles.

Most discussions of segmentation depend on semantic and grammatical meaning; but because in speech, features of sound are the palpable signs of functional segmentation, questions about the phonetic concerns of an artistic translator slip in and out of the literature. The earliest remarks are either negative or defensive: Renaissance translators are full of slurs on the sound of other languages, while later writers become interested in the differences of sound between languages: Addison, for instance, remarks that the intonations of excitement in Italian resemble those of anger in English, and counsels caution. From an interest in the random effects of onomatopoeia, through the Romantic theory of language as λόγος, developed a view of the translation segment that was not completely semantic in nature. Both Wirl (1958, 23) and Jumpelt (1961, 53) take the sound of a word as part of its content (*Inhalt*). For Zukovsky (see page 56, above) the phonetic image is the meaning in a segment like *vetuli* (translated as *wet to lee*). His problem is that he does not take as much care over phonology as over phonetics, so that suprasegmental features (accent, etc.) are not represented. Film-dubbing uses the same approach, but here the articulatory movement becomes the material to be translated. Phonology is irrelevant, so that, as in Zukovsky, meaning is derived from the phonetics of the passage. Indeed the only relevant element to be segmented is the movement of the lips: the unit is then a sound associated with the lip shape (cf. Rowe 1960, 118):

> In *Portes de lilas* the doltish Juju realises at last that Barbier, the unscrupulous gangster whom he has befriended, has been courting Maria, the barman's daughter, only in order to obtain money to flee the country. Juju decides to put a stop to it: Nôn, nôn, çâ v̊â pâs—Nŏ, nŏ, ĝiv̊e ît báck. Diacritical marks refer to the shape or position, i.e. the visual aspects of the lips: o rounded; ∧ open; ø half-labial (f,v); full labial (m,p,b).

It is, however, rare for the translation segment to be defined phonetically: it is usually defined phonologically, its boundaries and, to some extent, grammatical function and meaning being set by factors of intonation and juncture; hence the Vinay–Darbelnet concept of a prosodic unit, which has very little to do with poetry. Even where a translator does not voice the text, his phonological sense will guide his segmentation; in verse translation where one attempts to reproduce the metre and rhythm, intonation can become critical. The most difficult problems are in translation to music. Where the original composer has let his lyric set his musical rhythm and colour, the translator has to sense the colour of each segment in relation to its place in the melodic and sometimes harmonic structure.

Though it had long been a commonplace of good criticism that one could not separate language from style, it was only since the *Neuidealismus* represented by Walter Benjamin that the distinction between *signifiant* and *signifié* was collapsed, as, for instance, in Meschonnic (1971, 349) on Nida:

> La 'langue'—la 'littérature', ou la langue—la culture, ou le sens—la forme: il n'y a pas deux choses dissociables, hétérogènes. Quand il y a un texte, il y a un tout traduisible comme tout.

The most revealing aspect of Meschonnic's criticism of Nida is his constant reference to the *signifiant–signifié* dichotomy as *pré-Saussuréen*. This seems to be based on Saussure's image of *signifiant* and *signifié* being as closely linked as two sides of paper, and ignores completely the arbitrary nature of the link. In so doing, he redefined completely the linguistic unit of translation. It had usually been semantically or grammatically defined; and formal factors, though often tools by which one made the segmentation, were subsidiary. In Benjamin and Meschonnic both form and content of a segment were given equal importance and both were to be reproduced if the segment of the target text was truly to reflect that of the source.

In seeing literature as the sole function of language, these theorists came into conflict with those for whom the passing of information was the predominant function, as Meschonnic points out at many key points in his attack on Nida. The point here is a difference in what has been considered relevant in the translation unit. In texts perceived as having a symbol aim, the translation unit will be primarily one of information; in those having a symptom function, the translation unit will very often be one in which the form has precedence over content. How it is handled depends primarily on how the translator perceives its function, rather than what it is in itself.

4.4   AIDS TO THE TRANSLATOR

One tends to think of translators working with their dictionaries before them; to some extent this has been true. But long before dictionaries appeared, translators called on experts in the subject of their texts; engaged in lexicological research or consulted previous translations with different grades of purity.

In translating the Hebrew Old Testament, Jerome employed a rabbi as informant. It would seem that all Jerome was after was linguistic help: 1,000 years later, Wycliffe's team seems to have included not only experts in Latin but also theologians. Two centuries afterwards, correspondence between Luther, Melancthon and Spalatin shows that, although Luther took final responsibility for the German Bible, an incredible amount of consultation on theology, language and customs went on. John Bois' notes show another variation in the pattern. All the members of his company were noted biblical scholars and theologians, but certain members, for example Andrew Downes, Professor of Greek at Cambridge, were obviously there for linguistic rather than theological skill. Another important variation was that the texts from the companies underwent further revision from a revising panel before publication, an example followed to this day. Modern biblical translation into 'exotic' languages shows a variant imported from linguistic fieldwork. Nida (1961, 1964) describes the traditional team of biblical scholars and theologians, but adds to the team a native informant whose task is to check proposals for stylistic worth as a guide to the translator who has had to work between two foreign languages. A variant on this in technical translation is consultation of the author: tributes to the presence of the author range from Coste's acknowledgement of Locke in his 1700 preface to Horguelin (1966, 18), who points out that in government departments, at least under Canadian conditions, the author of a difficult document is often accessible for consultation.

The second type of prop is what has become the ubiquitous dictionary. Translators of the mid twentieth century, especially those working in literature, discussed their expectations of dictionaries in some detail. Valèry Larbaud (1946, 92) expected a dictionary, even a bilingual one, to 'contenir tout l'usage, littéraire et parlé, de ses deux idomes: langues des auteurs des différentes siècles . . .'. While not going as far as this, others expected to find in a good bilingual dictionary a wide range of examples and explanatory matter (Iannucci 1951, 195).

There is little mention, if any, of dictionaries before the sixteenth century and they seem to have drifted into translation from the classroom. The best translators never used dictionaries on their own: Luther, for instance, had a collection of Hebrew and Greek lexicons, the Erasmus New Testament in Latin, and some handbooks on preaching and biblical interpretation. Almost a century later, the translator companies of King James I of England worked from an immense reference library which seems to have contained most of the contemporary Latin and Greek dictionaries, the most important translations of the Bible (including the Roman Catholic version), and a large range of secondary material. We have a fair index of their behaviour from the notes of John Bois on the Pauline Epistles. His authorities range from the Fathers to classical authors; for example his note on Romans iv. 17 runs:

κατέναντι οὗ ἐπίστευσε i.e. ὁμοιῶς (Chrysostom) Sic *Apocalypse* xiii. 12 τό ἐνώπιον exponitur ab Aretha per ἀκολούθως.[6]

And on *Romans* xii. 8, he quotes a tag from Plato's *Apologia*, furnished by Andrew Downes, to clarify the meaning of Paul's Greek. Like manuscripts, dictionaries were weighed, and they suggested renderings rather than imposing them. Let us look at *Romans* iii. 5: εἰ δὲ ἡ ἀδικία ἡμῶν θεοῦ δικαιοσύνην συνίστησι, τί ἐροῦμεν; On this verse Bois has:

> συνίστησι established, confirmed. Vide Constantini Lexicon s.v. συνίστημι.

But in the final text we find:

> But if our unrighteousness *commend* the righteousness of God, what shall we say?

One cannot expect the same standards from other great translators of the time. This is evident in George Chapman (1559?–1634) who claims to have 'translated according to the Greeke, in iudgement of his best commentaries'. Among the dictionaries he used were the *Dictionarium* of Calepinus (1502) and Joannes Scapula's popular abridgement of Henri Estienne's *Thesaurus linguae graecae*. His use of Scapula was a little too assiduous, readings in his translation often being taken from the relevant entry. For example, on *Iliad* xiv. 516–17, he has:

> Atrides' javelin chac't
> Duke Hyperenor, wounding him in that part that is plac't
> Betwixt the short ribs and the bones that to the triple gut
> Have pertinence.

> Ἀτρείδης δ' ἄρ' ἔπειθ' Ὑπερήνορα, ποιμένα λαῶν,
> οὖτα κατὰ λαπάρην, διὰ δ' ἔντερα χαλκὸς ἄφυσσε
> δηώσας·[7]

This is a direct translation of Scapula's gloss on λαπάρη:

> Dicitur ea pars corporis quae posita est inter costas nothas, & ossa quae ad ilia pertinent.[8]

Out of this sort of behaviour grew two attitudes towards dictionaries: compilers found it in their interest to act as their own advocates, and preface after preface is full of self-praise and recommendations for use. We find a sourer note in Jean Leclerc (1688, 327):

> Les idées, qui sont attachées aux mots et aux phrases, changent si fort selon les occasions où on les emploie, et les manières de parler ausquelles on les joint, qu'il n'y a point de Dictionnaire qui puisse marquer toutes les significations et tous les changemens qui y arrivent.

And this caution remains through the next century: Tytler (1790, 11) reminds his readers that assiduous reading is a more comprehensive guide to a language than dictionaries, and Alonso Ortiz prefaces his translation of Adam Smith with the statement that, where necessary, he has preferred his own linguistic sense to 'la scrupulosidad del Diccionario'.

One can nevertheless guess at the influence wielded by dictionaries in translation by inspecting translations into Latin verse. One of the most important was the *Gradus ad Parnassum* (1670), which was still being published in the early nineteenth century. Its baleful influence is quite obvious from several passages in the Cowper translation of Prior and Power's Milton. In most cases, where there is an ornamental epithet with no warrant in the English, it comes from the list given in the *Gradus*. In the Prior (see page 90, above), *vigiles* is a stock epithet for *oculi*. The problem was not with the *Gradus*, whose authorities and scholarship are respectable, but with its users, who took citing of classical epithets as an instruction to use them at all times. In Power's Milton (see page 111, above) *Foetus*, usually the young of an animal, is glossed by the Thomas Elyot Dictionary of 1538 as: 'The product of generation, somtyme the fruit of trees', and this is repeated in the *Gradus*; *noxa* (harm), which means *crime* in its transferred sense, comes from dictionaries like Estienne, the *Gradus* and Elyot, who take *crime* to be the primary meaning.[9]

Translators had to struggle with the attitude that the dictionary was the final arbiter of usage. Especially in the case of technical dictionaries, this principle is doubtful. Marouzeau (1931, 29ff) begins from the principle that 'l'élève doit savoir lire son dictionnaire . . .', referring mainly to the necessity of approaching a dictionary entry with all the tools at the disposal of a literary critic assessing the authority of an edition. It was generally agreed that, despite the excellence of much bilingual lexicography, one should always cross-check in unilingual dictionaries; and the old attitude to the dictionary we see among the Authorized Version translators reappeared.

To supplement the dictionary and to suggest interpretations, many translators worked, especially in literature, with other translations at their elbow. The translators of the Authorized Version used their 'cribs' with considerable care; but some of their contemporaries were not so scholarly. Let us look at Chapman's Homer again. One of his props was the Latin–Greek edition of Homer by Jean de Sponde (Spondanus), whose influence was not always good. Thus in *Iliad* xvii. 599, he translated ὀστέον by *mouth*, a misreading of the Latin *os*, meaning both *bone* and *mouth*. And in *Iliad* xi. 624, Hecamede *prepares a potion*, a direct quote from Spondanus, who has *praeparabat potionem* for Homer's τεῦχε κυκειῶ.

Though the level of scholarship among seventeenth-century translators was higher, cribs are much in evidence, and even confessed to. Joseph

Webbe's Cicero letter (see page 88, above), he says himself, was translated with French and Italian versions in view. Does his phrase, 'but I
above the rest', reflect Manutius, 'ma io piu de gli altri' (see page 168,
below)? Dryden, for similar reasons, translated his *Aeneid* from the Ruaeus
edition. For Ruaeus's prose paraphrase in Latin, Dryden was obviously
grateful. Opposite *Aeneid* IV. 3–5 Ruaeus has:

> Multae virtutes Aeneae, et multae gloriae eius redit [sic] in mentem: vultus
> eius et sermo inhaerent impressi animo, et haec cura non permittit
> tranquillam quietam corpori.[10]

Comparison with the Dryden version on page 89, above, shows only one
lexical borrowing from Ruaeus: *imprinted* for *infixi*, which neatly destroys
Vergil's metaphor, but Dryden's smoothing out of the picture owes much
to the rather soulless prose of Ruaeus.

Ironically, the modern scientific explosion and the difficulty of keeping
terminology records abreast of what is going on, have occasioned technical translators to return to the ancient and medieval techniques of compil-
ing their own lexicons from their reading. There are many medieval
scientific treatises on science and medicine with a bilingual or trilingual
glossary attached. In a sincere attempt to come near the truth, Melancthon
assembled a coin collection to help him to establish the nature and value of
biblical money, but few have gone as far as that, before or since. The more
usual drill is to read technical material. This has two purposes: the first is to
keep oneself up to date on the terminology itself; the second is to see the
terminology concerned in its proper context (cf. Schorp 1963, 334). And,
indeed, in the minds of some translators, this method of proceeding
replaced the dictionary in many circumstances: Maillot (1970, 123), for
instance, takes for granted that recourse to a dictionary will take place only
in exceptional circumstances, but that it is, for all that, a necessary tool.

Operationally, 'trust' and 'aggression' cannot be separated from
Steiner's later stages of 'incorporation' and 'restitution'. There are elements of both in the way one goes about the concerns outlined here: the
skills brought to bear on text establishment are determined by understanding of the author and by one's expectations of what can be done within the
frame of the target language.

Five

Linguistics and Lexicon

The Saussurean link between *signifiant* and *signifié* is so much a part of the folklore of modern linguistics, that one forgets that, from at least St. Augustine on, this dualistic model of the sign presupposes the active presence of speaker or hearer. As it is traditionally described, formal equivalence so emphasizes the link between *signifiant* and *signifié*, that one tends to forget its conventionality through institutionalizing the link. Dynamic equivalence plays up the conventional and arbitrary nature of the sign by concentrating on response, on the presence of the person. Though the usual assumption is that the linguistic sign is an instrument,[1] Heidegger's sacramental view of words and their structures as *signum efficiens* exists in germ as early as Augustine, and is made clear by the preface of the Geneva Bible (1560) where Whittingham distinguishes between meaning and properties of words. In the next three chapters, therefore, equivalence is assumed to include not only reactions of *signifiant* and speaker towards the *signifié*, but also the effects that each element in the triangle of *signifiant*, *signifié* and speaker has on the rest of the triangle.

5.1 LEXICAL TECHNIQUES

After isolating and interpreting his units of translation, their values and their role, the translator proceeds to incorporation and restitution with his eye on Jerome's *proprietas linguae*. His choice of equivalence rests on the expressive aims of the source language, compared with the resources of the target. Technically, formal equivalence depends on one-to-one matching of small segments, on the assumption that the centre of gravity of text and translation lies in the *signifiant* for terminological or artistic reasons. The archetypal statement of the first is Boethius's declaration in his preface to Prophyry that he translated for matter rather than to preserve graces of style. And when Bruni Aretino attacked the medieval Aristotles in the *De recta interpretatione* of 1420, the Boethius doctrine was quoted to him by Alonso, Archbishop of Cartagena, who told him that the measure of a good translation was not its elegance, but the degree to which it kept 'the simplicity of the matter and the strict properties of the words'.

Yet, how 'scientific' was this attitude? How much did it owe to the ancient Jewish and Platonic doctrines of the all-powerful Word which reappears in Meschonnic (1973, 365):

> La traduction comme texte est un travail dans les chaînes du signifiant. Elle produit un texte si ce qu'elle produit ne se construit et ne se maintient que dans l'ambivalence de ses conflits: conflit d'une logique de l'ambivalence du signifiant avec une logique de l'identité du signe, conflit entre texte-départ et texte-arrivée.

Again the idea of struggle one finds in the Old Testament prophets, and, among translators, in Jerome, Day Lewis and Bonnefoy. But in keeping to strict consistency in the use of terms, the translator's language had formative power. This is quite clear in Philo Iudaeus and Roger Bacon, who saw exactness in terminology as a mainspring of transmission of science and the word of God. It is preached with violent enthusiasm by Daniel Huet (1661), followed with ferocious virtue by Vladimir Nabokov, and put forward as the only way to salvation by Benjamin and Meschonnic.

In practical terms the only difference in segment handling between these two persuasions among literal translators lies in their attitude of borrowing, an issue relevant only if *signifiant* and *signifié* are not the same thing. Few translators have allowed a borrowing to stand naked: they are usually assimilated morphologically and become part of the standard vocabulary if a need is felt. A subsidiary type of borrowing is *calque*: the adoption of source-language patterns in the target language (cf. Vinay and Darbelnet 1958, 47), as Hilary's *unigenitus* for μονογενῆς.

Dynamic equivalence seeks for the word of the source text a unit equivalent in communicative function. Such equivalences are not necessarily free: it suffices, as Marouzeau (1931, 43) remarks, that one 'not lose sight of' the target text and its modes of expression. Discussions of dynamic equivalence among American structuralist translators take for granted that verbal equivalences function within two contrasting sociolinguistic structures, in which the concepts denoted by the words in question have culturally peculiar value.[2] The Lévi-Strauss concept of things as symbols shows through Nida's discussion of Romans xvi. 16 where the Greek φίλημα (kiss) becomes a 'hearty handshake'. Clearly, the liturgical symbol of the non-sexual kiss has been missed, because the non-conformists have not preserved the liturgical structure in which it had meaning; and another structure, based on twentieth-century social behaviour, has been substituted for St. Paul's Christian assembly. Vinay and Darbelnet's discussion of the French and English attitudes to wine (1958, 192) rests on a similar structural approach to cultural facts.

Both the Geneva tradition and the American structuralist tradition agree that the essential element behind dynamic equivalence is perception: *modulation* and *adaptation* are both 'adjustments of language to experience', in the terms of Nida (1964, 239). Vinay and Darbelnet (1958, 51) define the first as 'une variation dans le message, obtenue en changeant de point de vue, d'éclairage'. There are excellent examples in the changes of imagery in Yonge's version of Guarini (see page 195, below): *mirando* becomes *marking*, *che adora* is *that to his heart was nearest*, both of them a stylization through an understated image. *Adaptation*, on the other hand, 's'applique à des cas où la situation à laquelle le message se réfère n'existe pas dans la langue d'arrivée, et doit être créée par rapport à une autre situation, qu'on juge équivalente'. It depends on socially functional matching of culturally peculiar objects, as in the handling of Plato's δικαστήριον (law-court) by Henricus Aristippus (see page 141, below) and Marsilio Ficino (see page 172). Reflecting the life of the South Italian royal courts, Aristippus uses *consistorium* (the room in which Pope or Emperor presided over official business.). Ficino reflects rather the Papal court of the early Renaissance, in which the term *curia* was used as a court of justice, or an administrative entity. Indeed, his use should be compared with that of Bartholomew Clerke on Castiglione.

In using modulation, one assumes that the *signifié* remains the same in both languages, but that its expression is culturally peculiar. The Vinay–Darbelnet classification of modulation is based on variations of metaphor, metonymy and synecdoche:

(a) abstract ⇄ concrete;
(b) cause   ⇄ effect;
(c) means   ⇄ result;
(d) part   ⇄ whole;
(e) part   ⇄ another part;
(f) reversal of point of view;
(g) rethinking of intervals and limits;
(h) sensorial modulations;
(i) manipulation of form, aspect and use;
(j) change of geographical reference;
(k) change of comparison or symbol.

This would seem to exclude from modulation, choices among possibilities offered by polysemy: e.g. the handling of the different senses of πυλῶνα in our versions of Luke xvi. 19; and the exploitation of a subsidiary sense of *pestilentia* (plague or storm) in the Old English Psalm 1 on page 142, below. Though *adaptation* consists in substituting an equivalent *signifié*, in practice the distinction between it and *modulation* is far from sharp: in the Homer couplet from Cicero on page 81, for instance, one would be hard-pressed to define the use of *lustrare* as one or the other, while *Iuppiter* for Zeus is clearly a cultural adaptation.

5.2   APPLICATION OF LEXICAL EQUIVALENCE

There are three ways of seeking lexical equivalence: one can attempt to translate completely literally; one can attempt completely consistent dynamic equivalence; or one can mix the two at need.

Few translators are so literal that they eschew dynamic techniques altogether. Most texts with almost completely formal lexical equivalence are concentrated in the early Christian period and the Middle Ages. Jerome's Biblical manner is typical: here is his text of Luke xvi. 19–21:

> Homo quidam erat dives, qui induebatur purpura et bysso: et epulabatur quottidie splendide. Et erat quidam mendicus, nomine Lazarus, qui iacebat ad ianuam eius, ulceribus plenus. Cupiens saturari de micis, quae cadebant de mensa divitis, et nemo illi dabat: sed et canes veniebant, et linguebant ulcera eius.

Literal though this translation is, it illustrates that formal equivalence still demands choice. There is a borrowing, *bysso*, and, like the *Vetus latina* (see page 69, above), Jerome translates πυλῶνα (gate, porch or door) as *ianuam* (door). He also adopts the synecdoche *epulabatur* (feasted) for εὐφραινόμενος (indulged himself), a dynamic equivalence the *Vetus latina* allowed itself. But, it is the differences that are interesting, for they do not step outside formal equivalences: there is no reason except instinct for translating πτωχός as *mendicus* (beggar) rather than the VL *pauper* (poor) or πρὸς as *ad* (at) instead of *ante* (in front of).

But in this matter, the archetypal statement is that of Boethius on page 71, above: here is how he handles the opening of Aristotle's *Categories*:

> Aequivoca dicuntur quorum nomen solum commune est, secundum nomen vero substantiae ratio diversa, ut animal homo et quod pinguitur. Horum enim solum nomen commune est, secundum nomen vero substantiae ratio diversa; si enim quis assignet quid est utrique eorum quo sint animalia, propriam assignabit utriusque rationem.

> Ὁμώνυμα λέγεται ὧν ὄνομα μόνον κοινόν, ὁ δὲ κατὰ τοὔνομα λόγος τῆς οὐσίας ἕτερος, οἶον ζῷον ὅ τε ἄνθρωπος καὶ τὸ γεγραμμένον· τούτων γὰρ ὄνομα μόνον κοινόν, ὁ δὲ κατὰ τοὔνομα λόγος τῆς οὐσίας ἕτερος· ἐὰν γὰρ ἀποδιδῷ τις τί ἐστιν αὐτῶν ἑκατέρῳ τὸ ζῴῳ εἶναι, ἴδιον ἑκατέρον λόγον ἀποδώσει.[3]

Like Hilary of Poitiers (see page 69, above), Boethius is seeking precise transmission of information through exact terminology. His technique, modelled partially on that of Cicero, was to take a Latin word which covered part of the semantic field of the Greek, and rigorously keep to it, as in *aequivoca* for ὁμώνυμα. Boethius was classicist enough to avoid borrowing.

Administrative registers of classical languages did not suffer from this ban to the same extent: the Greek text of the *Monumentum ancyranum* (A.D. 14) shows considerable borrowing of Roman social and legal terminology, e.g. πατρίκιος for *patricius* (nobleman); though there are some attempts to use a native Greek vocabulary, as ὕπατος (senior) for *consul*. Christian Latin followed the popular language in borrowing heavily for the new concepts brought in: words like *apostolus, diaconus, presbyter* and even *ecclesia* rapidly becoming part of first the juridical vocabulary and then the common Christian vocabulary. This did not go unnoticed by St. Augustine, whose justification of Hebraisms such as *alleluia, amen, racha* and *hosanna* rested on Christian treatment of words whose sacral flavour was intensely difficult to translate. One should note the intense avoidance of words with pagan overtones: there is no attestation of *flamen*, and at first, little of *sacerdos*, words both strongly associated with pagan worship.

With the strong philosophical and technical bias of the Latin Middle Ages, Boethius came to dominate translation into Latin. However, both borrowing and calque became a feature of medieval translation. From Arabic scientific works eleventh- and twelfth-century translators imported into Latin common terms like *algebra, alchemia* and *alkali*, while allowing the Latin *acidus* (sour) to acquire a technical meaning. The extent to which borrowing dominated terminology did not escape the sharp comment of Roger Bacon (1271?, 467), who noted that now scientists had to know Greek and Hebrew as well as Latin. This is exemplified in the *Ethica nova*, a late twelfth-century translation of the *Nichomachean Ethics*:

> Omnis ars et omnis doctrina, similiter autem et operatio et proheresis, boni alicuius optatrix est.[4]

Though one copyist glosses the word as *eligencia*, the Greek προαίρεσις is clearly borrowed. On the same passage in the Grosseteste translation, there is the revealing comment on *doctrina*, that several translators read *methodus*, again a direct borrowing from the Greek. Not that borrowing was a constant feature: in Grosseteste's literal opening of *De caelo*, it is absent:

> Scientia de natura fere plurima videtur circa corpora et magnitudines, et horum passiones atque motus, adhuc autem circa principia.

But there is a high degree of calque, both semantic and grammatical: for instance *passio* for πάθη, and *fere plurima* for σχεδὸν ἡ πλείστη. Not that this necessarily excluded dynamic equivalences: in our extract from the *Ethica nova, doctrina* is a mild modulation, while *optatrix esse* (to be an element wishing) is a modulated transposition of ἐφίεσθαι (to actively seek).

Vernacular translators acted the same way. The Oresme version of Grosseteste's Latin reads:

> La science naturele, presque toute, est des corps et des magnitudes, qui sont, et de leurs mouvements et de leurs passions ou qualitez, et encore de quelconques principes ou causes de tele substance.

Oresme might have been uneasy about his borrowing of *passions*, for he glosses it with *qualitez*. But, if the vernaculars were to have a technical vocabulary, this was the obvious method. It came to be of particular importance in medicine. For instance, in the anonymous French version of Henri de Mondeville's treatise on surgery (1314?), we read:

> . . . la premiere ruille est que nous devon plus tost entendre a restraindre les fleux de sang, et avant que entendre a la cure de la plaie.

> . . . prima regula est, quod prius et plus debemus vacare ad retentionem sanguinis quam ad curam vulneris.[5]

Here, though the only obvious borrowing is *cure* (curam), *fleux* seems to be an adaptation of *fluxus* (flow); and, throughout the work, *membre* is used in the technical sense of the Latin *membrum* (limb).

During the Renaissance, this choice remained open to technical translation. For example, in the Euclid translations of the sixteenth and seventeenth centuries, the terms ἀμβλυγώνιος (obtuse-angled) and ὀξυγώνιος (acute-angled) were dealt with in two ways, apart from Luca Paciolus (1509) who avoided the issue (as had Boethius 1,000 years before) by writing *qui obtusum habet angulum*. Zamberti (1505), Christopher Clavius (1574) and David Gregory, Savilian Professor of Astronomy at Oxford (1703), all borrowed the terms as *amblygonius* and *oxygonius*: while Joannes Scheubel (1550) and Federico Commandino (1572) calqued, writing *obtusiangulus and acutiangulus*. The same division remained in vernaculars: David Henrion (1615) and Claude-François de Challes (1720) write *amblygone/oxygone* and *obtusanglé/acutanglé* respectively. In English the modern *obtuse-angled* does not appear until 1733 in Samuel Cunn's translation of Commandino's Latin version.

In some literary and religious translation borrowings appear as part of the normal growth of the language: Chaucer, for instance, experimented with the French words, *gré* and *pris* in this passage from the *Romaunt de la Rose*:

> The mater fair is of to make;
> God graunte in gree that she it take
> For whom that it begonnen is!
> And that is she that hath, y-wis,
> So mochel prys; and ther-to she
> So worthy is biloved be,
> That she wel oughte of prys and right,
> Be cleped Rose of every wight.

> La matire en est bone et noeve:
> Or doint Diez qu'en gré le reçoeve
> Cele por qui ge l'ai empris.
> C'est cele qui tant a de pris,
> Et tant est digne d'estre amée,
> Qu'el doit estre Rose clamée.[6]

But within two centuries translators were suffering from extremely pain-ful qualms of conscience on this matter, and the issue of 'inkhorn terms' rose to plague a Europe which was gaining confidence in its own lan-guages. The struggle was between those who wished to borrow to make their languages worthy rivals of Latin, and those who were sure that they could do without recourse to such borrowing. In England, the crusade against borrowing was taken up by Sir John Cheke, who first laid down the rule promulgated some centuries later by the Fowler brothers: 'Use the Anglo-saxon word in preference to the Romance'. Cheke had powerful allies. The Thomas Wyatt translation of Petrarch's sonnet on Caesar and Hannibal shows extreme reluctance to use long words, and none of the borrowing that was so guyed by Rabelais's *écolier limousin*:

> CÆSAR, when that the traitor of Egypt
>   With th' honourable head did him present,
>   Covering his gladness, did represent
>   Plaint with his tears outward, as it is writ.
> And Hannibal eke, when fortune him shytt
>   Clean from his reign, and from all his intent,
>   Laugh'd to his folk, whom sorrow did torment;
>   His cruel despite for to disgorge, and quit.

> So chanceth it oft, that every passion
>   The mind hideth by colour contrary,
>   With feigned visage, now sad, now merry;
> Whereby if I laugh at any time or season,
>   It is for because I have no other way
>   To cloke my care, but under sport and play.

And yet, this translation is as literal as any of the Romantic interlinear versions of 300 years later, and keeps the sonnet form without strain.

The nub of the discussion was readability. Chaloner, in his preface to Erasmus's *In Praise of Folly*, 'eased the sowre sense of the Latin with some manerlier English words', and his English (see page 143, below) shows no evidence of borrowing. But the issue was not black and white: while Etienne Dolet's fourth rule demands avoidance of borrowing, two years later he admits in his preface to Cicero's letters that if one is to keep 'la vénérable antiquité', terms relating to social and public institutions are to be kept: so in his translation of Cicero's letter to Tiro (*Ad fam.* xvi. 3), he writes *les Ides de Novembre* where Joseph Webbe and Manutius use 'the fifth of November'.

The religious implications of the issue were particularly grave. Catholic attempts to fight Protestant error had led them to reiterate their dependence on tradition as a basis for doctrine, and, as in the early Church, both borrowing and calque offered an exact, unambiguous link with doctrinal tradition. Objections by William Fulke and the translators of the Authorized Version settled round accusations that Catholics were deliberately obscure to protect traditional misreadings of God's Word. Doctrine inevitably coloured translation disputes: one concerning borrowing centred round the issues of veneration of the saints and statues in churches. Gregory Martin (1582, 32), stung by Protestant objections to Church art, flatly denied that pictures and statuary were idolatrous, while attempting to turn the attack into a consideration of translation economy:

> Are not *idol, idolater, idolatrie* plaine English words? What needs that circumstance of three wordes for one, *worshipper of images*, and *worshipping of images*?

Religious questions aside, by Dryden's time, the issue of inkhorn terms was to be channelled into the question of need, and what borrowing was doing to the language.[7] Technical translators borrowed with a clear conscience. Marcel de Boulenc (see page 86, above) shows borrowings such as *sel de tartre, huile de vitriole*, because there were no native terms. The result was a scientific terminology spread by translators, especially in medicine; not that all the words so transmitted survived: in Keill's 1698 translation of Nicholas Lemery's *Cours de chymie* (Paris, 1696), we find:

> Pour forth your dissolution into a glass-cucurbite. . . .
>
> Versez votre dissolution dans une petite cucurbite de verre.

Both *dissolution* and *cucurbite* have been replaced, the first by *solution*, the second by *retort*. But where there was a standard technical vocabulary, as in ship-handling, obviously there was no need to borrow. Hence Stone's Pitot (see page 173, below) uses normal English navigation terms. The nuanced later seventeenth-century position is clear from the behaviour of Thiele and Coste towards the Latinized vocabulary of Locke (see page 167). In cases where Latin, French and English share the same word (e.g. *sensation*), it is used, but with a difficult concept like *mind*, the target language vocabulary follows the native traditions (i.e. *anima* in Latin, and *esprit* in French).

Under the impetus of nineteenth-century developments, alternately favouring and forbidding formal equivalence, the issue of borrowing fades before the more general question of total formal equivalence in lexicon, persisting in legal translation, especially in texts with binding force; see this extract from a League of Nations Treaty between France and Poland (1926, 141):

Judicial documents . . . shall be transmitted by the Polish diplomatic or consular agents to the 'Procureur de la République' within whose area the recipient of the act resides or the *commission rogatoire* is to be executed.

Les actes judiciaires . . . seront transmis par les agents diplomatique ou consulaires au procureur de la république dans le ressort duquel se trouve le destinataire ou dans le ressort duquel la commission rogatoire doit être exécuté.

All the hallmarks of formal equivalence are there: refusal to change the direction of the linguistic sign, closeness of grammatical form wherever possible, and borrowing of culturally peculiar terms.

Objections to formal equivalence come largely, at first, from literary translators. In his prologue to the *Aeneid*, John Stanyhurst has:

. . . thee first applying of a word may ease me in thee first place, so perhaps, when I am occasioned to use thee selfe sayme word elsewhere, I may as much bee hindered, as at thee beginning I was furthered.

As still, in the twentieth century, Knox (1949, 12) found it necessary to describe keeping to one translation for one word a 'capital heresy'. Traditional attacks on unrelieved formal equivalence rise from the need to be fully understood, and from the realization that words and their semantic fields vary according to language. But the issue is far from black and white: it depends on the aim of the translator. On anthropological translation Dell Hymes writes:

. . . smoothness of translation may deceive, representing too conventional an equivalence, or command of selection in only the target language, while roughness of translation may reveal, since it may reflect interference from the true patterns of selection in the source language.

And with this, Buber, Benjamin and Meschonnic may well agree. In essence, however, the translation behaviour of a ferocious opponent of literal translation like Cicero, is ample indication that the boundary between dynamic and formal equivalence is far from strict.

There are few discussions of dynamic technique in Cicero; the most germane here being that at the beginning of *De finibus bonorum et malorum* II. The crux is the Latin translation of the Greek ἡδονή in the context of Epicurean philosophy. In adopting the obvious translation, *voluptas*, he makes the point that, like ἡδονή, it means 'joy in the heart, and the pleasant turmoil of pleasure in the body'; but can differ from Epicurean usage by being regarded as *res vitiosa*. He rejects *laetitia*, which does not have as wide a sense. The lesson?—*vim verborum tenere*, and this *vis verborum* is not merely referential but affective, not merely denotation, but also connotation. The result is a delicate balance between matter and language based on two questions: What did the original say? How do I transmit it to my readers?

Though dynamic equivalence on the lexical level is not at first a feature of Latin prose translation, the Cicero Homer (see page 81, above) shows the extent to which it was used in classical verse translation. His translation of ἦμαρ by *lumen* is a reflection of the polysemy of the Latin *dies* (day or light), which makes possible the modulation in *lustravit* with its sacral overtones. While Cicero's sensitivity to the resonance of the Greek words in Homeric contexts leads him to modulate with his eyes on Roman evocations of the sacral, his sense of resonance in philosophical prose led him just as infallibly to control dynamic techniques to conform with the *vis verborum*. But, at the end of the Silver Latin period, modulation is common in prose, for example in the Latin translation of pseudo-Aristotle *De mundo*, attributed to Apuleius (A.D. 123–?). Here is the opening of chapter 2:

> Mundus omnis societate caeli et terrae constat et eorum natura quae utriusque sunt; vel sic, mundus est ornata ordinatio dei munere, deorum recta custodia. Cuius cardinem—sic enim dixerim κέντρον—robustum et immobilem genetrix atque altrix animantium omnium habet tellus.[8]

Apuleius's problem is a terminological one. As he was writing for a public that was linguistically sophisticated and largely bilingual, at least one sense of most of his Latin vocabulary is derived from parallel implications in the Greek: σύστημα and *societas* can mean a coherent assembly of either objects or people; ἑστία and μήτηρ (tutelary deity and mother, respectively) are well translated by *altrix* and *genetrix*, though the focus is skewed: *altrix* means one who takes care of, and *genetrix*, one who begets, both concepts being narrower than those represented by the Greek words. In one case, there is a double translation: φυλαττομένη undergoes a double modulation: from the idea of *things guarded* to task or responsibility (*munere*) and to guard duty (*custodia*). Finally there is modulation by metaphor: κέντρον (focal point) becomes *cardinem* (hinge).

His virtuosity would probably not have pleased Cicero, whose discip-lined sense of the *vis verborum* had given equal play to formal and dynamic equivalence. Jerome's regard for Cicero and imitation of his philosophy of translation was unashamed. In translating the Fathers, Jerome shows a much higher degree of dynamic technique than in the Vulgate; an example followed, in spite of all his protestations of purity of intent, by Rufinus. Their reason was *aemulatio*. Rivals to God were as unwelcome to Jerome as to any orthodox theologian; but both he and Rufinus could set out to rival the Fathers. In Jerome's Origen (see page 45, above), there are a large number of modulations: πρόχειρος (ready) becomes *promptus*, which adds the idea of *quick*, μελλητής (a person slow to do something) becomes *dissimulator*, which has the idea of slowness through neglect or deliberate oversight. There is also a vestige of the classical idea of concealment which is picked up later in the passage in the word *tacens* (silent). The principle invoked in Jerome's Epistle 106 is one of partnership expressed through parallelism in language function. Despite his disapproval of Jerome, we find the same thing in Rufinus's Basil (see page 100, above): ἐν κοινῷ τῶν ψυχῶν ἰατρείῳ (in the common cure of souls) becomes *ex communi quodam sanctitatis fonte* (from a certain common fount of holiness), an attempt to drive home Basil's point by varying his imagery. On a more down-to-earth level, ἴαμα is translated in two different ways: *sanitas* and *remedia*, the first version modulating cause to result, the second being formal in equivalence.

The bitter quarrels of this period left behind them a lingering sense that dynamic equivalence added meanings; which was often given as a cause for literal translation; but even a tender conscience was no protection. In his foreword to Plato's *Phaedo* (1156), Henricus Aristippus writes that he followed word for word in order to avoid 'intrudere novos sensus'. And yet his own perceptions of text and language drew him away from literality on several occasions, as in para. 59:

> Ego tibi a cardine experiar narrare. Semper enim ante his diebus
> consuevimus venire et ego et alii ad Socratem, collecti a primo oriente in
> consistorium in quo causa acta est—proximum erat carceri. . . .

Although the translation uses formal equivalence to the point that a separate crib is not necessary for the Latin, the translation of ἀρχῆς by *cardine* (hinge) shows a modulation by metaphor, which is comparable with Apuleius's reading of *cardo* for κέντρον. Just how unwelcome this type of dynamic equivalence was to medieval copyists we can gauge by the variant reading, *principio*, an exactly formal equivalent.

In vernacular translation of the time, however, both modulation and adaptation are common. As in the Jehan de la Vignay *Evangélaire*, they can appear in the body of a translation that depends largely on formal equivalence: the only clear case of adaptation in the extract on page 82, above, is *bougeran* for *byssus*, and *roigne* is a modulation by synecdoche for *ulcera*. In circumstances such as these, the English Bibles were as cautious. In the opening of the twelfth-century Old English version of Psalm 1 in Cotton MS Vesp. D. vii taken from Jerome's Gallican Psalter, we find:

> Seli bern, that noght is gan
> In the rede of wicked men;
> And in strete of sinfull noght he stode,
> Ne sat in setel of storm un-gode.

> Beatus vir qui non abiit in consilio impiorum, et in via peccatorum non stetit et in cathedra pestilentiae non sedit.[9]

Strete for *via* (road) shows the importance of the medieval street as a village meeting-place. *Cathedra*, a chair for dignitaries, is transformed into the lowly settle or backless stool. For the same passage, this time taken from the Hebrew Psalter of Jerome, the contemporary French *Psautier d'Eadwin* has:

> Beoneuret le heom ki ne alat el conseil de feluns; e en la veie des pecheurs ne stout e en la chaere des escharnisseurs ne sist.

The different handling of *impius* in the two texts illustrates the principle that the link between *signifiant* and *signifié* takes some resonance from the person who uses it. The English translation is a weak modulation that removes the specifically religious sense *impius* has in medieval Latin. But *felun*, in a translation produced for the Norman-French nobility, amplifies this religious sense by direct evocation of the feudal oath. *Fel* covered every sort of derelection of duty conceivable to the medieval aristocrat. But as duty to overlord, family and state were all included in duty to God, the change of image involved in *fel* is peculiarly appropriate to feudal society.

Like Cicero, the medieval Bible translators could use dynamic lexical technique to create a whole new picture. In a twelfth-century French version of I Kings xvii. 36, David arrives on the battlefield in time for Goliath's challenge to the Israelites. In true knightly fashion he asks:

Ki est cest ord paltunier ki feit tels repruces a la gent Deu?

Qui est iste Philistaeus incircumcisus qui ausus est maledicere exercitui Dei viventis?[10]

In the *C iansons de geste, paltunier*, originally meaning a footsoldier, came to mean a person lacking all the virtues of chivalry. It therefore comes to mean 'pagan' and so is appropriate to describe the Philistine. For what the pagan Saracen was to the medieval Christian, the Philistine was to the Jew. Similarly, *gent*, the vassals of a ruler bound to him by the feudal oath, is a social equivalent for *exercitui*, the Jewish people of God bound to serve him by a special dispensation.

Humanist translators approached dynamic lexical equivalence with varying enthusiasm. Humanist prose uses it rarely: the Joannes Argyropylus version of Aristotle's *De caelo* differs little from the Moerbeke–Grosseteste:

Scientia naturalis fere plurima circa corpora et magnitudines atque horum affectus motusve, et insuper circa principia quae sunt substantiae talis, versari videtur.[11]

Affectus for the medieval *passiones* is a purist's quirk. Budé (see page 72, above) and Bruni Aretino (see page 162) are as reluctant. But Humanist verse experimented willingly. Braccese (see page 83) has several striking modulations by synecdoche, e.g. *Niliacus* for *d'Egitto* and *docet ut pagina prisca* for *sì come è scritto*. This pattern of differing latitude for prose and verse recalls Cicero's practice, but the rule was not hard and fast.

For sixteenth-century translation, like the medieval, filtered the original through the perceptions of the translator. The chastened literality of More and Lily (see page 194, below) contrasts with the sudden high colour of Wyatt's 'fortune him shytt Clean from his reign' (see page 137), and the spicing of even literal technical translation by evocative language: in the Geneva Bible passage quoted on page 74, λαμπρῶς (sumptuously) is imaged to *wel and delicately*. Though many translators tended to be unfettered by the scruples of a scholar, unlike their medieval forebears, they consistently used dynamic equivalence together with strict segmentation. Chaloner's opening of the *Praise of Folly* runs:

Howe so ever men commonly talke of me (as pardie I am not ignoraunt what lewde reports go on FOLIE, yea even amongst those that are the veriest fools of all) yet that I am she, I onely (I saie) who through myne influence do gladde both the Goddes and men, . . .

Utcumque de me vulgo mortales loquuntur, neque enim sum nescia, quam male audiat STULTITIA etiam apud stultissimos, tamen hanc esse, hanc inquam, esse unam, quae meo numine Deos atque homines exhilaro, . . .[12]

Chaloner's picture is reversed from Erasmus's. By his *male audiat*, Erasmus represents Folly as having to listen to scolding; in his *lewde reports go* Chaloner changes focus to the dissemination of calumny, which Folly may or may not hear at first hand. Similarly, the *enim* in the second clause, merely a rhythmic link, becomes the amused expletive *pardie*, adding considerable pace to the passage.

The importance of perception as a base of modulation, and the risks entailed to the whole atmosphere of the work are clear in Marlowe's outrageous Ovid. Here is part of *Amores* I. v:

What arms and shoulders did I touch and see,
How apt her breasts were to be pressed by me!
How smooth a belly under her waist saw I!
How large a leg, and what a lusty thigh!

Quos humeros, quales vidi tetigique lacertos!
    Forma papillarum quam fuit apta premi!
Quam castigato planus sub pectore venter!
    Quantum et quale latus! quam iuvenile femur![13]

A most unsubtle change from the medieval view of Ovid as an arbiter of love to a picture of him as an amusing rake, which so incensed the Archbishop of Canterbury that Marlowe's book was publicly burnt. Ovid's appreciation is partially aesthetic, an element that Marlowe's modulations remove: *forma papillarum* (which can be taken in the double sense of *shape* or *beauty of her breasts*) becomes merely *breasts*, and *iuvenile* (youthful), again partially aesthetic, becomes the frankly sensual *lusty*, while *castigato* meaning slender and aesthetically pleasing, is left out altogether.

Not that all translators were as unbridled as this, however. De Baif's translation of Terence's *Eunuchus* reflects a courtly urbanity:

O bon Dieu qu'un homme devance
Un autre homme! La differance
Qu'il y a d'un homme entendu
A un fat! . . .

Di immortales, homini homo quid praestat! Stulto intelligens,
Quid praestat! . . .[14]

Homme entendu and *fat* for *intelligens* and *stulto* modulate mere intelligence to *savoir-faire*, a courtly virtue. Similarly, the sixteenth-century versions of Horace Odes I. v on page 145, above, produce their changed views of the scene by modulations: *comam* (a lock of hair) is diluted to *cabellos* by Luis de León, and sensorially modulated to *tresse* by de la Porte. Both French and Spanish modulations of *urget* depend on metonymy: Luis de León's *ciñe* gives an idyllic tone to the affair, while de la Porte's *presse* is somewhat sleazy. It was necessary that translators of this period make of their originals sixteenth-century documents: like the medievals, they did not see accuracy apart from the cultural ambience of the readership. We find, therefore, his responsibilities interpreted in relation to the public: De Baïf and Luis de León are writing for well-bred aristocrats; de la Porte and Chaloner for the sort of person who filled the Globe of an afternoon; and Marlowe for his tavern cronies.

In a similar way much technical translation was in the marketplace. The linguistic sophistication of aristocratic audiences is evident in the Machiavelli translations of the sixteenth and seventeenth centuries. In an anonymous translation ascribed to Bedingfield, we find:

> I will not discourse of popular estates, of these I have spoken more att large in an other place, I will nowe intreate only that sort of governmente which Princes have, and so knytting upp the devisions I will follow my purpose of settyng downe howe that kynde of state may best be governed and maynteyned.

This should be compared with the Latin of Silvestro Tegli (1560):

> Ommittam de Rebuspublicis disserere: de his alias fusius diximus. Nunc dumtaxat orationem ad principatum convertam, & quae superius iam orsus eram retexens (qua oratione scilicet principatus hi gubernari ac retineri possint) narratione institutam disputationem persequar.[15]

> Io lascerò indrieto el ragionare delle republiche, perché altra volta ne ragionai a lungo. Volterommi solo al principato, e andrò tessendo gli orditi soprascritti, e disputerò come questi principati si possono governare e mantenere.

Amelot de la Houssaye's version of this passage (1683, 3) is:

> Je me passerai de parler des républiques, dont j'ai traité ailleurs amplement, et je m'arrêterai seulement à la Principauté. Je dis donc, qu'il est bien plus facile de conserver des Etats Héréditaires, que des Etats nouvellement conquis.

The translators' first problems are metalinguistic: the concept of republic was for Machiavelli based on the city-states of Italy: hence Bedingfield's *popular estates* and the French *république*, though the Latin *respublica* is not quite the same thing. Likewise, given the nature of the Roman principate, Tegli's *principatus* is only approximate. The French *état héréditaire* is a definite reading in of detail: princely states are not necessarily hereditary, though to the seventeenth-century Frenchman this fine distinction would not have made much difference. The interesting modulation of the passage is the English *knyttyng upp*: was it influenced by the etymological sense of Tegli's *retexens*? In any case it adds a pictorial dimension that *tessendo* does not have, giving it just the right racy touch for a Tudor audience used to verbal conceits.

Some modulations and adaptations acted as rhythmic glosses, in that they both explained the meaning of a term, and added weight and drive to the sentence. It was a common mannerism: for λαμπρῶς Geneva (see page 74, above) has *wel and delicately* and Luther (page 176), *herrlich und in freuden*; Calvin (page 104) for his own *effectuum* has *fruits et effets* and Lambin (page 183) writes *via atque institutio* for Aristotle's simple μέθοδος. Others were used as explanations in text. Amyot was particularly fond of this intercalation of definition: cf. 'tribun militaire, c'est à dire, Capitaine de mille hommes de pied', from his life of Cato the Censor. The third explanatory function of modulation was heightening the effect of the message by evocation of famous authors. In Bartholemew Clerke's Latin translation of Castiglione (see page 183, below) the Horatian *aurea mediocritas* is used for Castiglione's *una certa mediocrità difficile*, a not inapt touch considering how the two men valued lack of ostentation. In the same spirit, Theodore Bathurst (d. 1651) went to work on the last section of Spenser's *Shepheardes Calendar* with the final ode of Horace's Third Book before him:

> En opus exegi, cunctos quod duret in annos,
> Temporis intactum morsu, diuturnius aere;[16]

> Lo I have made a Calendar for every year,
> That steele in strengthe and time in durance shal outwear. . . .

Exegi means *completed*, not *made*; and steel is not the Horatian bronze; to a public more familiar with Horace than Spenser, such dynamic equivalences would have been more artistically telling than a strictly 'accurate' translation.

During the next 200 years, the equilibrium reached between reader and author was further tipped in favour of the reader. The general attitude, as we find it in Cowley's introduction to Pindar and in D'Ablancourt on Tacitus, was that social and cultural differences, especially between two societies separated in time, demanded dynamic techniques absolutely.

But, though the attitude of cultural peculiarity was one shared with the Middle Ages and the ancient dramatists, as during the sixteenth century, one took considerable care in segmentation. Translation units often have double relevance: on top of their semantic content, there are formal repercussions. In his preface to Vergil (1648), Perrin describes how, to give a fitting translation of *Aeneid* II. 360:

Nox atra cava circumvolat umbra,

he took the frequency of /a/ as an auditory image of darkness, substituting French back vowels and /r/:

La sombre nuict autour roule son ombre creuse.

When dealing with the semantics of Perrin's work, as with Dryden and de Marolles (see page 89, above), it is difficult to distinguish dynamic equivalence from variations on a theme: it is clear that *ulcère* (*vulnus*) and Dryden's *Flame* (*ignis*) are modulations, but Dryden's last line recalls the freedom of the Roman dramatists and the medieval Ovids. Like Ezra Pound, these translators catered to the 'mental baggage' of the readership. This is very clear in Cowley's *Pindarique Odes* (1656):

> Queen of all harmonious things,
> Dancing words and speaking Strings,
> What God, what Hero wilt thou sing?
> What happy man to equal glories bring?

> Ἀναξιφόρμιγγες ὕμνοι,
> τίνα θεόν, τίν᾽ ἥρωα, τίνα δ᾽ ἄνδρα κελαδήσομεν.[17]

Cowley's notes to this passage from the Second Olympian show all the virtues and faults of the seventeenth century. There is little concrete here that is unexplainable; but Pindar's peculiarities have to be balanced against the seventeenth-century passion for reason in all things.

> 1. Whereas Pindar addresses himself to his *Song*, I change it to his *Muse* which, methinks, is better called Ἀναξιφόρμιγξ, then the Ode which she makes. Some interpret ἀναξιφόρμιγγες passively as subjects of the *Harp*, but the other sense is more *Grammatical*.

Hence, his modulations depend on attitude to language rather than on cultural fact: the idea of mastery in the first word becomes *Queen*, φόρμιγξ (*lyre*) in the same word is modulated by metonymy to *strings*, ὕμνοι to *words*. The issue is expanding an extremely compressed image for a century that, while understanding compression, was repelled by it.

Translators were not always as serious as this, nor did they take liberties as broad. In the Urquhart–Motteux translation of Rabelais (1653, 72) Maistre Janotus arrives to claim his bells:

> Master Janotus, with his hair cut round like a dish à la Caesarine, in his most antic accoutrement liripipionated with a graduate's hood, and having sufficiently antidoted his stomach with oven marmalades, that is bread and .holy water of the cellar, transported himself to the lodging of Gargantua, driving before him three red muzzled beadles, and dragging after him five or six artless masters, all thoroughly bedraggled with the mire of the streets.

The manner here uses little modulation, *graduate's hood* and *driving* being mild examples of the genre. But the handling of *maistres inertes* is worthy of Rabelais himself. In its union of meaning and form the French is a pun turning on the common sixteenth-century pronunciation of *inerte* with a low vowel. Urquhart changes the focus of the resulting reference to *maistre ès arts* by decomposing the word *inertes* into its morphemes, translating *in-* by the privative, *-less*, and bodily transferring the broadly pronounced syllable, *-ertes*, thus modulating the semantic content of *inert* to *unsophisticated*. In a similar vein, Tobias Smollett (or his Grub Street writer) makes of Gil Blas's mother 'qui n'étoit pas dans sa première jeunesse', the butt of a tavern joke: 'she was no chicken'.

What these two shared with pillars of respectability like George Campbell was a lively sense of the human dimension of language. Campbell starts from this principle (1789, I. 450):

> The translator's only possible method of rendering words justly is by attending to the scope of the author, as discovered by the context, and choosing such a term in the language which he writes as suits best the original term in the particular situation in which he finds it.

Though the issues of 'inkhorn terms' was still relatively hot, he dismisses it as irrelevant, asking only that the vocabulary chosen should have 'the same plainness, simplicity and perspicuity' as that of the original (ibid. 566). This means refusing to be bound by any hard and fast theories of 'original and true' senses, except that of observed usage (ibid. 576). According to this principle,

> The exact import of many of the words and combinations of words made use of in the language will never be perfectly comprehended by one who is totally unacquainted with the history of their religion, law, polity, arts, manners, and customs. (Ibid. 32.)

Campbell distinguishes four ways of dealing with institutions peculiar to Biblical societies:

(1) adopting the word from the original language;
(2) using a neutral equivalent;
(3) using a translation based on equivalent function determined by context;
(4) exact conversion into a dictionary equivalent.

The technique to be used is governed by three considerations:

(1) there are situations where the properties of the original thing designated are essential to the functional sense;
(2) there are situations where it is of no importance;
(3) there are situations where the relationship of the thing to other objects of the same class is important (Campbell 1789, I. 341).

In general, he is reluctant to borrow a Greek term, or to convert it into contemporary functional equivalents: this second procedure is a comment, and besides, in using it, one often ends up with nonsense. Thus in Matthew xxii. 19, where Christ asks the Pharisees to show him the 'coin of tribute', a Roman *denarius*, Campbell (ibid. 346) assesses it at sevenpence-halfpenny, and notes that this translation is impossible, as no English coin ever had this value. Less radically, an accurate translation, without being absurd, often misses the point. In Matthew v. 15, the size of the bushel under which the candle is placed is of no consequence, what is important is that it obscures the light (ibid. 345). His own translation, therefore, is: 'A lamp is lighted to be put, not under a corn-measure, but on a stand.' And in the parable of the servants and the talents (Luke xix. 13), he shows how exact mathematical conversion of ten talents into thirty-one pounds five shillings merely overloads the story with needless detail (Campbell 1789, I. 347–8).

At times his refusal to allow modulation or adaptation is based on a shrewd assessment of ways in which people will react to a difficult situation. In John vi. 7 where Christ feeds the multitude on five loaves and two fishes the disciples remark: '*Διακοσίων δηναρίων ἄρτοι οὐκ ἀρκοῦσιν αὐτοῖς, ἵνα ἕκαστος βραχύ τι λάβῃ.*' Campbell's comment (1789 I. 344) is:

Nothing can be more natural than the expression, 'Two hundred denarii would not purchase bread enough to afford every one of them a little.' This is spoken like one who makes a shrewd guess of what he sees. Whereas, nothing can be more unnatural than, in such a case, to descend to fractional parts and say, 'Six pounds, five shillings would not purchase . . .' This is what nobody would have said, that had not previously made the computation.

By a peculiar conjunction of terms, the Romantic goal of *Erklärung* coincides with the Vinay–Darbelnet definition of modulation as a change in *éclairage*. Modulation, indeed, is not uncommon in the 'interlinear version': in the Goethe translation on page 93, *häßlich* and *nachdenklich* both give Goethe's colour to *laid* and *rêvant*: the first is an emotional reaction to bad weather and the second specializes *rêvant* to *musing*. Poetic translators modulated freely, as in Shelley's version of the Archangel's Hymn from Faust (1822):

> The sun makes music as of old
>   Amid the rival spheres of Heaven
> On its predestined circle rolled
>   With Thunder speed; the Angels even
> Draw strength from gazing on its glance,
>   Though none its meaning fathom may:–
> The world's unwithered countenance
>   Is bright as at Creation's day.

The sobriety of Shelley's modulation can be seen by comparison with the de Nerval version on page 49, above: *tönt* (resounds) becomes *makes music* and *chante, Reise* (journey) becomes *circle* and *course*. But despite Goethe's admiration for his version, de Nerval's *'interprétation'* recalls the *belles infidèles* of the previous century, while Shelley's version embeds his modulations in a formal equivalence matrix.

Near the end of the century, traces of the Romantic approach were still to be seen under a freer appeal to dynamic equivalence. Classicists tended to carry over into English modulation by rhetorical equivalence. Charles Stuart Calverley (1831–84), a Cambridge don with a fair reputation among his peers, shows in his English version of de Santeuil the influence of classical rhetoric:

> O Lord, through instruments how weak
> Thou workest out thy sovereign will.
> Frail earthen vessels thou dost seek
> And with thy choicest treasures fill.

The manner is not unlike that of *Hymns Ancient and Modern*, but there are some close influences of the Romantic goal of *Erklärung*: *choicest treasures* for *opes* (goods) and *earthen vessels* for *vasis* are both types of metonymy not very far from Shelley's *Creation day* for *ersten Tag*. Yet for Calverley the technique was obviously learnt in the Latin composition class; for Shelley from the Romantic tradition.

In other nineteenth-century poetic translation, modulation was used to efface cultural differences. In Neale's *Jesu dulcis memoria*, for instance, hints of the Roman doctrine of the Real Presence in the word *praesentia* are hidden behind the mystical theology relating to the continual presence of God to those who seek him: both are equally respectable, even to a Catholic. Horace's Pyrrha (see pages 84 and 94, above) and her lover undergo cultural metamorphoses by modulations. Some modulations, however, had unforeseen results. Take, for instance, Michele Leoni's Italian version of Julius Caesar III. ii:

> Romani, amici, m'ascoltate: io vengo
> A pergere gli uffizi a Giulio estremi;
> A laudarlo non già: dopo la morte
> Degli uomini gli error vivono, e spesso
> Le bell'opre con lor sotterra vanno.

> Friends, Romans, Countrymen, lend me your ears:
> I come to bury Caesar, not to praise him:
> The evil that men do, lives after them,
> The good is oft interred with their bones.[18]

Shakespeare's imagery, as so often with continental translators, is toned downed considerably. The strong element of adaptation in Leoni's imagery accounts for his *pergere gli uffizi estremi* for *bury*. In so doing he is closer to the historical reality than Shakespeare: Caesar was not buried, but given a riotous cremation, an act the Italian is vague enough to cover. Was this deliberate?

Modulation was the plaything of classicists, especially in England. Here, from Robert Tyrrell of Dublin, is the beginning of Falstaff's account of the Gadshill fiasco from *Henry IV*:

> Tum tres simii tunicis herbeis viri,
> dis meis invitis, homines intestabiles,
> a tergo adorti, valide me infestis petunt
> machaeris; nam adeo tenebricosa nox erat
> non hercle nosses digitos tuos. . . .[19]

> But, as the devil would have it, three misbegotten knaves in Kendal-green came at my back, and let drive at me; for it was so dark, Hal, that thou could'st not see thy hand.

The modulations have two purposes. One is to situate the translation within the genre: *simii* (apes) is a recognized Plautine word of abuse, and deals happily with *knaves. Intestabiles* (abominable, untrustworthy) is a possible equivalent to *misbegotten*. But, remembering that devils did not exist in Roman theology, he writes *dis meis invitis* (against the will of my tutelary deities), and makes the figure turn on another view of the population of the spirit world.

It is in this game of virtuosos that the difference between the nineteenth and eighteenth century is thrown into the highest relief. The Ingram translation of Prior (see page 96, above) modulates with a broad wink at both the wigs and powder of the eighteenth century and Latin love poetry. In some modulations he agrees with Cowper (see page 90): in others, he differs, but his intentions are made clear by the use of *depereo* in his last line. In Classical Latin this word is found mainly in Plautus and in two Catullus Odes (35 and 100), where the word has either an amused or a sleazy tone depending on who the real flame is: most of those with whom Classical poets constructed the word transitively, tend to be undesirables or teenagers in the throes of calf-love. So while Cowper took the situation seriously, Ingram uses this satiric word to cock a snook at both Prior and Chloe.

In general, twentieth-century translation shows a high degree of modulation, but some caution as well; which does tend to dampen the atmosphere. Gennaro Perfetto's account of the arrival of Janotus (1914, 85) is a mixture of deft modulations and bewildered begging of the question:

> Maestro Giannotto, tonduto alla cesarine, vestito del suo liripipion teologale, e con lo stomaco ben antidotato di cotognata di forno ed acqua benedetta di cantina, si recò all'abitazione di Gargantua, menandosi innanzi tre *vitelli* col muso rosso, e trascenandosi dietro cinque ou sei maestri *inerti*, molto infangati a benefizio della economia.

As Urquhart before him had to face an unholy series of puns, so had Perfetto: his handling of *vedeaux* and *inertes* shows powerless desperation; but *cotognata*, a country wine, is happy, as is *trascenandosi*, meaning *to drag with some asperity*. *Economia* for *mesnaige* is a perceptive synecdoche, and his adaptation of *teologale* for *à l'antique* fits both linguistic and metalinguistic context. As the century went on, the use of lexical modulation came very close to the Renaissance ideal of remaking the original in socially correct terms. In a letter to Debenham written in 1919, Mackenna echoes Campbell's sentiments on literal translation as forcing on English resources foreign to it. And in discussing Pound, Mason (1963, 297), in surmising that sense can only be made out of an original by 'creative decisions', has a comment on the incapacity of the literal translator whose offhandedness can only be paralleled in Cicero's *De finibus*. The modern expression of this attitude is Ezra Pound's principle of transmitting 'wot the author means' rather than 'what he sez'. Pound himself modulates freely: in his Du Bellay sonnet (see page 53, above) modulation has two purposes: the obvious one is to produce changes in viewpoint or image: as *findest* for *aperçois*, and *transient and seaward bent* for *vers la mer s'enfuit*. But this second example with its rush of short vowels, shows Pound's concern with reproducing effects of sound. There are, it would seem, no actual reproductions of sound in this sonnet. Most translators used modulation lexically only: MacKenna's Plotinus, for instance: while τὰ κακὰ is personified to *Evil*, ἐξ ἀνάγκῆς is modulated through the metonymy, *by necessary law*, which plays down the element of blind inevitability in the Greek.

Technical and religious translation rediscovered this freedom later in the century; and linguistic discussions like those of Catford, Nida, Vinay–Darbelnet, Jumpelt and Maillot follow after the fact: for technical translation was modulating freely, as in this extract from the Canada Council Research Grant Application form for 1969:

> Les subventions offertes par le Conseil au titre de l'aide à la recherche visent d'abord à aiderⱼles spécialistes attachés à des universités canadiennes. Cependant, les chercheurs non employés par une université peuvent y être admissibles s'ils possèdent le même degré de compétence et si leur travaux offrent le même intérêt.

> The Research Grants Programme is offered by the Council primarily to meet the needs of career scholars in Canadian universities. Researchers not employed by a university may qualify, however, if their applications meet the same standards of judgement as to the scholarly merit of the project and the competence of the individual.

The modulations of this passage are directed towards creating a piece of clear administrative prose: the cliché, *career scholars*, is replaced by the less-imaged synecdoche, *spécialistes*; the active, *qualify*, becomes the passive, *être admissibles*. The French removes even the slight colouring of the English by striking back to the basic elements of the ideas.

Linguistically the conflict is one of different ways of visualization: English, with its *plan du réel*—better called *plan du visuel*—seeks out detail in a way the analytical French *plan de l'entendement* refuses. Yves Bonnefoy, writing in his Postface to *Hamlet* (Paris, 1962, 237), puts forward a theory of poetic diction which is exactly parallel:

> La poésie anglaise, celle de Shakespeare en tout cas, ne se refuse au réalisme des archétypes que pour mieux suivre tous les mouvements de notre inlassable liberté. . . . Toute autre est la poésie française. Dans la plupart des oeuvres de cette poésie plus prudente, plus secrète, il est sûr que le mot ne semble poser ce qu'il désigne que pour exclure aussitôt de l'espace du poème tout ce qui n'est pas désigné.

Bonnefoy believed himself worsted by the rich colouring of the Shakespearean word: here is Ophelia's reply to Laertes in *Hamlet* I. iii:

> L'impression que m'ont faite vos bons conseils
> Veillera sur mon coeur. Mais, mon chere frère,

N'allez pas imiter ces coupables apôtres
Qui nous montrent le dur chemin épineux du ciel
Tandis qu'eux-mêmes, impudents assouvis,
Suivent parmi les fleurs le sentier des plaisirs
Sans se soucier de leurs propres sermons.

I shall the effect of this good lesson keep
As watchman to my heart. But, good my brother,
Do not, as some ungracious pastors do,
Show me the steep and thorny way to heaven;
Whilst like a puff'd and reckless libertine,
Himself the primrose path of dalliance treads,
And recks not his own read.

Bonnefoy's modulations, like those of Valéry's Vergil (see page 165, below) and the Canada Council passage just quoted, exemplify Taine's image of French as a language with the quiet tones of a pencil drawing. Bonnefoy's *conseils* for *lesson*, *dur* for *steep* and *impudents* for *puff'd* are copybook *plan de l'entendement*. The same thing can be said for Valéry's *art* for Vergil's immediate *carminibus* (poems). By this reduction to non-pictorial elements, Bonnefoy achieves his *poésie plus prudente*. But even more important, in some images where the French keeps a pictorial aspect, the vectorial element in the image is reversed: Shakespeare's *watchman* is in Ophelia's heart looking out; Bonnefoy has the image of surveillance from outside looking in. Shakespeare's *primrose path* is one made of flowers, Bonnefoy's has flowers beside it. The persistence of classical attitudes in French translation can be gauged by comparing Bonnefoy's dilution of Shakespeare's imagery with that of Voltaire (see page 199, below). There also, the pictorial aspect of English is modulated to a 'more prudent' set of images: 'like a thing infirm' becomes '*avec effroi*'; 'riv'd' becomes *renverser*. Voltaire, like Bonnefoy, does not flee from metaphor: he merely tames it.

In other languages, modulation was guided by different imperatives. Schadewalt (see page 189) uses the peculiarly Roman patronymic, *Alciden*, for Heracles, and the personification of Venus for love. As both his source and target languages were Classical, he has few problems of level of intensity of imagery. On the other hand, Day Lewis has to deal with a source language with Classical restraints on intensity of imagery. Hence his incidence of modulation is high, and he sharpens the image in each case: *venis* becomes 'life's blood' by metonymy; and the image in *carpitur* (to be picked at) is changed to 'biting'. The problem is one of translating one's own image of the original into terms acceptable to the audience for which one writes, not forgetting, of course, that one become the archetype of one's own audience.

At times, translators use modulation to teach. This can be of particular importance in religious translation, especially in liturgical work. There is a particularly inspired example in the *Draft Book of Common Prayer* (1977) for the Episcopal Church in North America. The contemporary version of the Palm Sunday Collect reads:

> Almighty and everliving God, in your tender love for the human race you sent your Son our Savior Jesus Christ to take upon him our nature, and to suffer death upon the cross, giving us the example of his great humility: Mercifully grant that we may walk in the way of his suffering, and also share in his resurrection.

The Latin, *habere documenta*, ultimately derived from the verb *doceo* (I teach) is translated by *retenir les enseignements*, and *following his example* (see page 107), both entirely adequate. But the above version modulates with an eye on the Psalms when it writes 'walk in the way of' (cf. Psalm 1 on page 142, above). The Latin term itself is a cliché, common from late Classical times to Aquinas. But the Hebraism, *walk in the way of*, places the spirituality of Holy Week against the whole of its Old Testament and Pauline background; and, moreover, to an English-speaking audience, it savours of John Bunyan and the familiar Twenty-third Psalm.

For Benjamin and Meschonnic, this type of thing was beside the point, as such acclimatization denied the essential inseparability of *signifiant* and *signifié*. But Meschonnic's own practice, despite his concern for *l'unité-texte*, worked by interpretation of the segment. In his version of Genesis i. 2, he translates the Hebrew *tohu vavohu* as *boue et trouble*. Imitation of the sound values is only one of the elements of dynamic equivalence; the semantic component comes from the Targum commentaries, which describe the primeval chaos as 'une confusion informe de la masse liquide primitive'. As this modulation is based on the source language rather than the target, it goes some considerable distance towards Meschonnic's aim of achieving a continuity between source and target through treating each linguistic sign as a single, double-faceted unit.

Clearly, the lexical techniques of translation were not discovered by modern linguistics, merely described. No matter the period or genre, the basic lexical technique is formal equivalence. Texts whose lexical equivalences are completely formal are, however, rare: they are most likely to be found among scientific and technical translators of the Middle Ages and seventeenth centuries. Likewise, texts with completely dynamic equivalence are equally uncommon, those of the pre-Classical dramatists and the medieval poetic translators being clearly examples of Dryden's imitation, which he excludes from the genre of translation. The balance between formal and dynamic equivalence in the lexicon of a given text depends more on the balance it is seen to achieve between the language functions

156 Linguistics and Lexicon

discussed in Chapter 3 than on differences between source and target languages: in general, the more objective the information the translator seeks to impart to his reader, the less he uses dynamic equivalence techniques. But comprehensive judgements on relevance and dosage of lexical equivalence types are of little interest if taken without reference to structural equivalence and its modalities.

Six

Linguistics and Translation Structure

Formal structural equivalence reproduces the grammatical features of the source text: in the Scotus Erigena passage on page 121, for example, the Latin follows the Greek, even to calquing: the Hellenism, *Patre moto*, is not analysable by normal grammatical rules. On the other hand, dynamic structural equivalence, concerned solely with communicative function, normally abstracts from formal structural identity. The first type of equivalence is the structural aspect of literal translation, and the second, the result of transposition.

Early versions of transposition are based on three principles enunciated by Albert Sechehaye:

(1) Toute idée, quelle que soit sa catégorie naturelle au point de vue de la logique, peut être ramenée à la catégorie de l'entité;
(2) Toute idée de relation et toute idée de procès peut être exprimée adjectivement;
(3) Toute idée de qualité peut être transposée dans la catégorie de procès.

These three principles from *La structure logique de la phrase* (1926) have pragmatic forerunners in the Lollard concerns with understandable English syntax and in the discussions of *métamorphose* in Charles Batteux.

During the twentieth century direct application of these principles to translation theory comes in Panneton (1947): a version of transposition for use in language teaching had been discussed by Darbelnet (1949–50). Hence in Vinay and Darbelnet (1958, 16) transposition is defined as *procédé par lequel un signifié change de catégorie grammaticale*. Following criticism from Richard Bausch that this definition was too narrow, Félix Kahn (1971–2, 29) redefined transposition as: 'Procédé qui consiste à faire correspondre à un signifié de la langue de départ un signifié de la langue d'arrivée que relève d'une classe de substitution linguistique différente'; as his typology makes provision for morphological changes, we follow it here:

(1) Changement de classe de mots:
e.g. Goethe's *nackdenklich* (an adjective) for Diderot's *rêvant* (participle) (see page 93, above).
(2) Changement de catégorie grammaticale:
e.g. Dryden's *fed* (a past) for Vergil's *alit* (present) (page 89).
(3) Changement de fonction syntaxique:
e.g. Shelley's *The Angels draw strength* for Goethe's *Gibt der Engeln Starke* (indirect object becomes subject) (page 150).
(4) Changement de rapport syntaxique:
e.g. Marcel de Boulenc's *Voyla comme se faict* for Crollius's *ita habetur*, in which a principal verb becomes a subordinate verb (page 86).
(5) Changement de plan de langue:
e.g. Rufinus's *divinitus inspirata* for θεοπνευστης (word for bound morpheme) (page 100).

The Firthian parallels to these, as found in Catford (1965), are *class-shifts, intra-system shifts, structure shifts, unit shifts* and *level shifts*. Apart from the philosophical difference in sign theory, there is an important boundary difference, in that Catford (1965, 73) does not allow intonation a role in transposition, while Vinay and Darbelnet assign it a most important part in grammatical segmentation and function.[1]

Although Vinay and Darbelnet distinguish between *agencement* and *message* (roughly syntax and discourse), there is little reason to do so in discussing translation operations. The key concept here is *démarche*, the expressive priorities of phrase or sentence as signalled by word order, grammatical linkage, rhythm and semantic trust. Grammatical orders do not impose shapes on *démarche*; indeed the vectorial sense of a *démarche* usually determines grammatical selection. There are, then, two levels of *démarche*: that within sentence, clause or phrase we term 'internal *démarche*', that within the paragraph 'external *démarche*'. On both levels linkage is grammatical, and thus amenable to both formal and dynamic equivalence.

There is, however, a second distinction to be made: that between *démarche* in fixed-word-order languages and free-word-order languages. In the first, for example, French, English and German, *démarche* units fall into binary divisions termed *thème*, and *propos* by Bally, *theme* and *rheme* by Prague linguists, or *topic* and *comment*. But in the second, Latin and Greek for instance, freedom of word placement makes this binary division impossible and emphasis is sought by final or initial placement.

Our third distinction, more applicable to external than to internal *démarche*, is according to manner of articulation and grammatical subordination favoured by individual languages. Following Albert Dauzat, we distinguish between *langues liées* and *non-liées*. The first, through preference for *le plan de l'entendement*, usually adopt an analytical order of exposition with explicit linkage. The others, preferring the *plan du réel*, move in an impressionistic order, and have little need of explicit linkage.

The function of articulation being to carry the reader through the text, the translator usually remakes discourse or *démarche* patterns in a way his readers will find not only acceptable, but also congenial. Knox (1949, 37) saw this as his most serious problem:

> Easy enough to notice, as most of the modern translators do, when there is some positive Hebraism to be avoided; . . . It is a harder part of the translator's job to notice the negative effect produced by the absence of English mannerisms.

The discourse links (*charnières*) at his disposal are classed in two ways by Vinay and Darbelnet (1958, 222–6): according to function and form:

Function:
charnière de rappel (link with what precedes);
charnière de traitement (link with what follows);
charnière de liaison (non-vectorial link);
charnière de terminaison (signal of end of a series).

Form:
charnière explicite;
charnière implicite;
charnière de simple liaison;
charnière zéro.

Charnières are not necessarily conjunctions: they are any unit that creates a link between other units on the level of the *signifié*. Their utility rests on two concepts shared between stylistics and grammar: the first is movement between statements, what seventeenth-century French critics called *l'ordre des pensées*; the second, the need felt by speakers to sign-post the direction of this movement by the form and function of *charnières*.

6.1 Modulated Transposition

A unit of translation is often modulated and transposed at the same time. In the Cicero snippet from Plato (see page 163, below), there is a complex series in the second sentence, of which the most straightforward is the ablative absolute, *causa remota* (with the cause absent/removed), in which the Greek preposition, χωρὶς (without), is lexicalized by the Latin past participle, *remota* (removed). It would seem that such variants of transposition, not uncommon in Classical translation, became rare in medieval philosophical texts: one of the few examples occurs in the *Phaedo* of Henricus Aristippus (see page 141, above): ἡ δίκη ἐγένετο becomes *causa acta est*, in which the aorist middle, ἐγένετο (took place), is transposed to a passive, *acta est* (was tried). It was, of course, irrelevant to medieval free translation which ignored strict linguistic segmentation. But between these extremes, it had its uses. In the Poitiers version of the Rosy Sequence (see page 193, below), line 4 takes the noun group, *eius dulcis praesentia*, and transposes it to the verb group, *te contempler glorieux*. But, assuming that Christ is only truly present to him who is already in Paradise, the translator has modulated the idea of presence to contemplation, theologically very questionable.

Probably under the influence of Erasmus's *De copia verborum*, modulated transpostion became very common, and further explored possibilities that medieval translators had overlooked. Golding's *without avenging it* for *sine poena* (see page 199, below), Stanyhurst's *carcks* for *cura* (page 195), de Baïf's *La difference qu'il y a* for *Quid praestat* (page 194) demonstrates how by this technique the original colour could be read up or down. Let us demonstrate from two versions of More's *Utopia*, the English by Robynson (1573) and the French by Sorbière (1643):

> Husbandrye is a scyence common to them all in generall, both men and women, wherein they be all experte and cunnynge. In thys they be all instructe even from their youth; partly in scholes with traditions and preceptes, and partly in the contrey nighe the cytye, broughte up as it wer in playing, not onlye beholdynge the use of it, but by occasyon of exercisynge their bodies practising it also.

> Il n'y a qu'un seul mestier commun aux hommes et aux femmes: c'est l'agriculture, laquelle personne n'ignore. Car tous l'apprennent dès l'enfance; partie dans l'escole avec méthode; partie aux champs d'alentour de la ville, mettans eux-mesmes la main à la charruë par forme d'exercice, et regardans aussi travailler les vieux laboureurs.

Robynson has two striking modulated transpositions. The first, *they be all experte and cunnynge* for *nemo est expers*, modulates a negative statement to a positive, with the consequence that the singular of the Latin must be transposed to a plural. Its most interesting feature, however, lies in its concern for sound: it provides a rhythmical cadence to the topic sentence of the paragraph, and, despite the fact that *expers* and *experte* are contradictory, *experte* does suggest the sound of the original. The second modulated transposition is *with traditions and precepts* for *traditis praeceptis*. Such a transposition, an adjectivized past participle to a coordinate noun, is a grace of composition recommended by most textbooks of Latin composition.[2] The main interest of this example, however, lies in replacing the simple teaching (*traditis*) of the original by a concept of education one finds in both ancient Rome and the British public school: that of handing on the *mos maiorum* and national ethos through the school system. Again, the pivot is the concordance of sound between *traditis* and *traditions*.

In comparing Sorbière's treatment of the same two sentences, one finds little of interest in the first. In the second, however, *avec méthode* for *traditis praeceptis*, a modulated transposition also, imparts a strong Cartesian flavour, *méthode* being perhaps the central educational and philosophical concept of the French seventeenth century.

Especially among poets who sought to rethink imagery, modulated transposition becomes a valued tool. During the eighteenth century it degenerates into embroidery, not regaining subtlety until the late nineteenth century. Tyrell's *dis meis invitis* for *as the devil would have it*, already quoted as a modulation (page 151), transposes an adverbial clause to an ablative absolute. Our two late nineteenth-century versions of *Jesu dulcis memoria* are comparable: in Neale's second line *Dans* becomes *in that dear name* and *cordis gaudia* the almost pre-Raphaelite *heart-joys*. But Hopkins, with the strongly literal and personal Eucharistic theology of the Roman Catholic, gives to the noun, *praesentia,* a mystical intimacy: Christ is especially present when one "takes him home" after receiving the Sacrament.

As did sixteenth-century uses of this resource, twentieth-century uses often exploit qualities of sound. The Pound modulation, *transient and seaward bent* for *vers la mer s'enfuit*, transposes the verb to two adjectives and *vers la mer* to the adverb, *seaward.* The short sounds of *s'enfuit* give an impetus to the French which achieved in English by Pound's succession of short vowels and plosive consonants. We find the order of technique, with a totally different result in von der Vring's image of Dianeme's eardrop "sunk from your soft ear". By writing *der Rubin, ob unbedankt/Er untern zarten Ohr schwankt*, von der Vring transposes the past participle to a finite verb, and modulates *sunk,* a verb whose sound suggests stillness, to *schwankt* which implies movement; for the percussive sounds of the German give an auditory impression opposed to the nasal consonants at the end of the English word. Thus, while Herrick's still ruby suggests a poised and elegant Dianeme, von der Vring's swinging one implies vivacity.

The implication by all who have used this technique is that content is inseparable from form, that the word is therefore a *signum efficiens.* But our examples in this section make it clear that the relationships between target *signifiant* and *signifié* depend on the insight and vision of the translator rather than on any unaided properties of language.

6.2 SYNTAX AND INTERNAL 'DÉMARCHE'

Traditional discussions of structural equivalence have usually confined themselves to grammar. Yet it would seem more useful to discuss structure in terms of three approaches to relationships between syntax and *démarche*: the first is reproducing word order and syntax by formal structural equivalence; the second, abandoning both syntax and *démarche* through transposition; and the third, producing an approximation to the original *démarche* by controlled transposition.

The first alternative is a constant, but, in its strict form utilizing calque, relatively rare. It was a mannerism of early Jewish and Christian translation and survived through the early Middle Ages, gradually to be stigmatized as the refuge of the unskilled. Its second form, represented by Boethius (see page 134, above) is relieved by mild transposition: for instance, γεγραμμένον, a participle, is transposed to a clause, *quod pinguitur*. This is the variant usually termed 'literal translation'. A third form dispenses with both calque and transposition. It is found in the more perceptive of the medieval philosophical translators, Robert Grosseteste for instance. It had a champion with a difference in Bruni Aretino, who nuanced medieval literality by commenting perceptively on the role of the ear in determining what was good, strongly implying that content and form were operationally inseparable. Like most Humanist productions, his *Nichomachean Ethics* is formal in equivalence, the only structural differences being the postponed *-que* for the καὶ of the first line in Greek and the *et . . . et* in the second line:

> Omnis ars, omnisque doctrina
> similiter autem et actus et electio: bonum quoddam appetere videtur.[3]

For all his noisy disapproval of the medievals, this first sentence is identical to that of the Grosseteste translation (1270?). But what Aretino sought and achieved was a structurally rhythmic sentence that was both formally and functionally equivalent to the original Greek. Both the Greek and its Latin translation fall into three structural groups shown by the format adopted here. The first two, joined by a weighty *charnière* (ὁμοίως δὲ/similiter autem) make up a complex subject, whose predicate is the third group. The word order of the Latin corresponds almost exactly with the Greek, as does the syllable count. The solution of Aretino and Grosseteste had its supporters during the sixteenth century, and, indeed, well into the seventeenth: both Juan Luis Vives in the *De ratione dicendi* and Huet (1661) make the case that style quality can only be preserved by literality, an argument that goes well beyond the concern of men like Norton for content. It appears later in a different form with different priorities in Benjamin and Meschonnic.

The second alternative, that of abandoning both *démarche* and syntax, accords overriding importance to semantic content and a subsidiary role to the *signifiant*. Cicero (*De optimo genere oratorum* v. 14) speaks of his duties as weighing out words for the reader, not counting them out, so that their force is kept. Thus, in examining transposition as an instrument, one must keep in mind Cicero's *verba appendere*: transposition and reorganization of *démarche* depend only partially on language differences: they follow from an act of interpretation.

Cicero's own prose is as elegant as his poetry and more restrained. In the following passage from Plato's *Timaeus*, for instance, he assumes that the stress-point of Plato's first sentence is fate or necessity (ἐξ ἀνάγκης), and of the second, origin (γένεσιν). Hence, he places both these ideas in the most emphatic part of his Latin sentence, the end, and transposes to do so:

> Omne autem quod gignitur ex aliqua causa gigni necesse est; Nullius autem rei cause remota reperiri origo potest.

> πᾶν δ' αὖ γιγνόμενον ὑπ' αἰτίου τινος ἐξ ἀνάγκης γίγνεσθαι. Παντὶ γὰρ ἀδύνατον χωρὶς αἰτίου γένεσιν σχεῖν.[4]

Sir Thomas Wyatt's treatment of Petrarch (see page 137, above) is not at all different. Within the sonnet form, which to a certain extent determines his rhetorical units and the direction of their thrust, he attempts to mould his *démarche* to allow for rhyme and rhythm. Thus his second line is inverted, but is the emphatic placing of 'present' a compensation for the solemnity of *face il don*? Is the same remark to be made about his eighth line which uses the same technique? The answer lies in Wyatt's ear, rather than in the text on paper. Likewise, in translating from vernacular poetry into Latin, the early Humanist poets did much the same thing. Braccese (see page 83, above) shows a wide range of technique, from the modulated transposition of *proditor Niliacus* (*traditor d'Egitto*), an adjective referring to the Nile, for a prepositional phrase referring to Egypt, to the simple change of number in *gaudia* for *allegrezza*: *gaudium*, a cretic, would have been impossible in elegiacs. For metrical purposes the free word order of Latin is abused by Braccese, there being many dislocations that are ungrammatical: the handling of the conjunctions in lines 2, 4 and 5 are all schoolboy methods out of difficult situations.

In the examples quoted, only a certain number of sentences have been reorganized in both grammar and *démarche*: but among sixteenth-century

drama translators (cf. de Baïf on page 144, above) this was already changing. Especially in France, writers, over-conscious of vernacular peculiarities, deliberately avoided the original form where at all possible. The
best of them sought to parallel the power of the original *démarche* by
compensating for the pressure points of the sentence. Dryden's picture of
Dido (see page 89), for example, completely reverses the Latin *démarche*
by changes in grammatical function: the instrumental ablative of *gravi . . .
cura* becomes the English subject (*Anxious cares*) and the nominative *regina*
becomes the direct object. In the Latin, *cura*, at the end of line and sense-
group, is in an emphatic position made more so by its disjunction from the
adjective, *gravi*. As these effects are impossible in English, Dryden com-
pensates by making it the grammatical subject of a strong metaphorical
statement.

This type of approach was not restricted to poetry, being exploited and
recommended for prose from the beginning of the seventeenth century.
Despite attention to the universals of grammar, there was considerable
awareness of differences between language. Discussions within Port-
Royal did not distinguish between style and grammar. On the principle
that the beauty of French consisted in *l'étendue des mots* and that of Latin in
concision (Coustel 1687, 194), Lemaistre de Sacy required that both the
word order and sentence structure of the original should be abandoned
when necessary. His norms were universally respected. The Antonio
Medinella y Porres version of *Utopia* (1637) consistently reverses *démarche*.
As in Robynson's English, the *thème* of the first sentence becomes *La
agricultura*, while in the second it is the idea of teaching that comes
first:

> La agricultura es ocupación común á hembras y varones, la qual saben y
> excitan sin distinction. Enséñansela desde su menor edad por preceptos de la
> escuela, y por exercicio en el campo que está mas vecino á la ciudad como
> por entretenimiento, no solo mirando, pero manejándolo, y empleando las
> fuerzas del cuerpo.

Ironically enough, while the Romantics were exploring the interlinear
version for literature at the end of the eighteenth century, some scientists
were looking into this type of translation for textbooks. Hence, beside
Hermbstädt's literal version of Lavoisier (see page 171, below), we can
place the 1793 English version by Robert Kerr (1755–1813), a Fellow of the
Royal College of Surgeons:

> That every body, whether solid or fluid, is augmented in all its dimensions
> by any increase of its sensible heat, was long ago fully established as a
> physical axiom, or universal proposition, by the celebrated Boerhaave.

While the French sentence rises to the statement of Boerhaave's axiom, the English sentence falls from it by reversing the order of the French *thème* and *propos*.

Although this type of approach was developed no further and its life in science was short, it was to remain a standard manner among literary translators until the 1950s. Pound (1920, 273) writes:

> It seems to me that English translators . . . have been deaved with syntax, have wasted time, involved their English, trying first to evolve a definite logical structure for the Greek, and secondly to preserve it, and all its grammatical relations in English.

In his preface to Vergil's Eclogues, Paul Valéry (1871–1945) sees syntactic problems as inevitable:

> Le poète français fait ce qu'il peut dans les liens très étroits de notre syntaxe; le poète Latin dans la sienne si large, à peu près ce qu'il veut.

In this opening of Vergil's Nineth Eclogue, the original rising period becomes a falling period. The final placement of *omnia . . . servasse Menalcan*, an impressively emphatic place in Latin, is reflected by initial displacement, equally emphatic in French:

> On m'avait dit pourtant, qu'en faveur de son art,
> Ménalque conservait toute la pente douce
> Qui mène mollement des hauteurs jusqu'à l'onde
> Et l'antique hétraie aux cimes foudroyées.

> Certe equidem audieram, qua se subducere colles
> Incipiunt mollique iugum demittere clivo,
> Usque ad aquam et veteres, iam fracta cacumina, fagos,
> Omnia carminibus vestrum servasse Menalcan.[5]

Despite what he says, syntax is not the only reason for his sentence reorganization: the length of his Alexandrine and placement of *caesura*, are just as important in determining the shape of Valéry's sentence and its sense-divisions.

The third approach, and by far the most common, is preserving *démarche* by altering syntax. It seems to have been an offshoot of the application of *l'ordre naturel* to language teaching. In translation, it is first discussed at length by Charles Rollin (1725). Through Charles Batteux (1747–8), the principle spread to England and probably to Spain, for it appears in Capmany (1776). The first analyses of this technique were misunderstood, as those hostile to the principle of imitating word order assumed that it entailed imitating syntax, which was not the point at all. Batteux (1747–8, v. 215), in condemning 'le latinisme dans une composition française, et le gallicisme dans une composition latine', accounts for them in a working definition that still has some cogency. He takes it for granted that word order is prior to syntax: for, as he remarks, authors have their reasons for preferring one order of matter to another. More important than that, however, is his nod towards his own version of universal grammar (ibid., 219):

> Qu'on ne doit point toucher à l'ordre des choses, soit faits, soit raisonnements, puisque cet ordre est le même dans toutes les langues, et qu'il tient à la nature de l'homme plutôt qu'au génie particulier des nations.

In Port-Royal terms, this 'ordre des choses' was part of the *syntaxe du régime*, while adapting to it was the duty of the *syntaxe de convenance*. The grammatical changes required, Batteux termed *métamorphoses*, giving as an example the Latin cliché, *fieri solet*, which he translates *il arrive ordinairement*, in which *fieri*, an infinitive, becomes a main verb and *solet*, the main verb, becomes an adverb. This is, of course, the modern transposition. Batteux's only control is that the *pensée* must keep the same life.

Unlike a large number of translators, Batteux was well aware of how to put his principles into practice. Here is a passage from Aristotle's *Poetics*, which starts with an extreme transposition, ἔτι (*as well*) becomes the verb, *il reste*, and the final participle becomes the finite verb, *ils imitent*:

> Il reste une troisième différence, qui est la manière dont on imite. Car en imitant les mêmes objets, et avec les mêmes moyens, le poète peut imiter tantôt en racontant simplement, et tantôt en se revêtant de quelque personnage, comme fait Homère, ou en restant toujours le même, sans changer de personnages, ou enfin de manière que tous les personnages soient agissans et représentent l'action de ceux qu'ils imitent.
>
> Ἔτι δὲ τούτων τρίῃ διαφορὰ τὸ ὡς ἕκαστα τούτων μιμήσαιτο ἄν τις. καὶ γὰρ ἐν τοῖς αὐτοῖς καὶ τὰ αὐτὰ μιμεῖσθαι ἔστιν ὁτὲ μὲν ἀπαγγέλλοντα, ἢ ἕτερόν τι γιγνόμενον ὥσπερ Ὅμηρος ποιεῖ ἢς ὡς τὸν αὐτὸν καὶ μὴ μεταβάλλοντα, ἢ πάντας ὡς πράττοντας καὶ ἐνεργοῦντας † τοὺς μιμονμένους †.[6]

Perceptive as Batteux was, his practice and that of his contemporaries outruns his theory. For Batteux's concern was merely word order, while contemporary practice was equally concerned with the directional sense of *démarche*. It seems to have made little difference what the languages in question were. In the Locke sentence below, the *thème* ends at *Knowledge*, and each of the two halves in turn fall into *thème* and *propos*. This division is emphasized in the Latin version of Gottfried Thiele by gathering up all that precedes in *ea est*, a *charnière de rappel*. Coste's French, on the other hand, while doing the same thing with *c'est*, punctuates to give the impression that the main division is after *Retention*:

> L'autre faculté de l'esprit, par laquelle il avance plus vers la connoissance des choses que par la simple Perception, c'est ce que je nomme *Retention*: Faculté par laquelle l'Esprit conserve les idées simples qu'il a reçues par la Sensation ou par la Reflexion.

> Proxima facultas animae, per quam in cognitione adipiscenda ulterius proficit, ea est, quam *Retentionem* voco, sive *Idearum* simplicium conservationem, quas a sensatione aut reflexione recipit.[7]

> The Next Faculty of the Mind, whereby it makes a further Progres towards Knowledge, is that which I call *Retention*, or the keeping of those simple *Ideas*, which from Sensation or Reflection it hath received.

Of the two versions the Latin is closer to Batteux's aims than the French. But the need felt by the two *langues liées* to show explicitly linkages in thought, results in constructions like *in cognitione adipiscenda* (in obtaining knowledge) a lexicalization of *towards Knowledge* and Coste's use of *Faculté* in opposition to *Retention*.

Though discussed for the first time, it seems, by Batteux, the principle of using dynamic structural equivalence to preserve *démarche* is found in early translations such as Jerome's Patristic work (see page 45, above). A thousand years later, when translators were in the process of reconciling the lessons taught by the Humanists with the different grammatical resources of modern languages, those who wished to avoid literality were already as skilled as Batteux: witness Estienne Delaigne's French version (1531) of Caesar's *De bello civili*:

> Cesar dictateur tenant congregation pour eslire officiers fust esleu consul auec ensemble P. Servilius. Or estoit ce l'année en la quelle Cesar pouvoit par les lois estre consul.

> Dictatore habente comitia Caesare, consules creantur Julius Caesar et P. Servilius; is enim erat annus, quo per leges ei consulem fieri liceret.[8]

Caesar's Latin, in spite of itself, suggests a rigged election, probably because he is so careful to put in an explanation for his conduct in a following sentence. Delaigne's French follows the Latin almost word for word. But, to allow this, the ablative absolute at the beginning becomes the subject of the French sentence, a transposition involving a change in flexion, grammatical function and grammatical relation, and the rest of the translation follows with a combination of interlinearity and dynamic syntactic technique. From the point of view of *démarche*, the French sentences are not remarkable in themselves: they can be broken down into a series of internested assemblies of *thème* and *propos*. But these proceed from a text where the vectorial lines of force are the contrary: *César . . . officiers* is definitely a complex *propos*, the *déterminé* in Bally's terms: in Latin, however, it was the *determinant*, an ablative absolute modifying the following clause.

In the face of texts like this, translators and their critics were more conscious of grammatical differences than of concordance in the order of ideas. In spite of his attention to this aspect of translation, quite obvious from his Erasmus, Chaloner sees fit to defend himself against criticism for the grammatical adjustments which made his preservation of *démarche* possible:

> Wherein I chose rather to be counted a skante true interpretour, than otherwyse to touch thynges, which were better unsayed, as long as it hurted not the grace of the boke though they were ommitted. Likewise in my translation I have not peined myself to render worde for worde, nor proverbe for proverbe, whereof many be Greke, such as have no grace in our tong but rather markyng the sence, I applied it to the phrase of our Englishe.

English was not the only language where sixteenth-century translators used this technique: it is found in French and Italian as well. Both the Aldus Manutius and Etienne Dolet versions of Cicero *Ad fam.* XVI. 5 use transposition and modulated transposition (e.g. *se verrai gagliardo* and *si je te voy sain* for *si valebis*) to ensure the integrity of Cicero's word order and level of prose:

> Tutti ci struggiamo, ma io piu de gli altri, per uoglia di vederti quanto prima, ma in buoni termini, il mio Tirone. per il che non ti dar fretta veruna. reputerò di haverti ogni hora veduto, se verrai gagliardo. io posso far senze dell'opera tua: & però non credere, che tanto l'utile proprio mi spinga a desiderare la tua sanità, quanto l'amore, ch'io ti porto. Sta sano, Cicerone.

> Nous desirons touts, & moy principallement, de te veoir en bref en bonne santé, amy Tiro. Mais ne te haste point, ie te voirray assez tost, si je te voy sain. Ie me puis passer de ton service, mais ie desire, que tu soys en santé tant pour toy, que pour moy, amy Tiro. A Dieu.

Reference to the Webbe translation, which is, admittedly, somewhat later, does not show much difference in principle, though Webbe does show more expansiveness: 'but in no case without your health' is a gloriously seventeenth-century circumlocution for *sed valentem*.

The technique of these three is not very different from that of Batteux 200 years later. Indeed among some of his contemporaries working between modern languages, the typically seventeenth-century padding one finds in Batteux was stripped: Sir Thomas Nugent's Montesquieu of 1750 (the same year as the original was published in Geneva) is a good example:

> Substitutions are a restraint to commerce; the power of redemption produces an infinite number of processes; every estate in the land that is sold throughout the Kingdom, is, in some measure, without an owner for the space of a year.

> Les substitutions gênent le commerce; le retrait lignager fait une infinité de procès nécessaires; et tous les fonds du royaume vendus sont au moins, en quelque façon sans maître pendant un an.

The element of transposition in *are a restraint to* and *produces* is obvious; and each sentence in both languages can be cut the same way into *thème* and *propos* with the same directional relationship between them. Not that, even at this stage, this was restricted to technical work: Smollett's Gil Blas (see page 174, below), Houbigant's Bible (page 77), and Herder's Shakespeare (page 47) use the same approach.

From these writers to Goethe's Diderot (page 93) is an easy jump. As transpositions Goethe has *meine Gewohnheit bleibt*, a modulated transposition for *c'est mon habitude*; *abends*, an adverb, for the prepositional phrase, *du soir*; and the inversion, *Mich sieht man* for the foregrounding construction, *c'est moi qu'on voit*. Clearly, though Goethe's interlinear version aimed at identical word order and a similar sense of direction in the sentence, formal syntactic equivalence was sacrificed where he deemed fit and, indeed, Goethe's typology distinguishes the interlinear version and literal translation.

From this point, as we have seen, theoretical approaches to sentence construction take two paths. The first, that of Henri Weil (1844), deriving from the Batteux tradition, seems to have had little effect outside classics, the last discussion of him being by Tolman (1901). The other tradition, not completely unconnected with Romantic speculation, was the mid-nineteenth-century *Völkerpsychologie*. Both extended Batteux's theoretical concern with mere word order by visualizing the sentence as movement and thrust: Weil sees the sentence as proceeding from *notion initiale* to *but*; and von der Gabelentz in terms of psychological progression. Not surprisingly it is in philosophical translation that the interlinear version continues; take, for instance, the 1862 Paris translation of Kant's *Logic* (Leipzig, 1838) by Joseph Tissot (1801–76), dean of the Faculté des lettres at Dijon:

Tout dans la nature animée ou inanimée se comporte suivant des règles, mais ces règles ne nous sont pas toujours connues.

Alles in der Natur, sowohl in der leblosen als auch in der belebten Welt, geschieht nach Regeln, ob wir gleich diese Regeln immer kennen.

The original German sentence is organized to highlight *Regeln* at the end of the first clause, and progresses to the idea of knowing at the end of the second. To bring about the same progression, the German active verb is translated by a passive, and its subject made into an indirect object. The result is that *diese Regeln*, which is the object of *immer kennen*, becomes *ces règles*, at once grammatical subject and *thème* to the second member of Tissot's sentence. Despite the many theoretical approaches developed by twentieth-century linguists (see chapter 2), translators since have added few practical refinements.

6.3 ARTICULATION

There are three approaches to external *démarche* and articulation: formal structural equivalence, dynamic equivalence resting on structural units on the same level as those of the source text, and dynamic equivalence resting on units of different structural levels.

In its pure state, the first solution, formally equivalent structural linkage, is often characteristic of symbol translation. Certainly, early Christian translation, with its perpetual *autem* and *enim* for any Greek particle, ignores their vectorial function. This unenterprising approach continues in scientific and administrative texts throughout the Middle Ages to reach a peak actually among Latin scientific translators of the seventeenth and eighteenth centuries. One such was van Schooten, whose treatment of Descartes's Geometry ranges from the readable to the extract cited on page 76, above. Here the formally equivalent linkage and structure produces an involved schoolboy Latin lacking the directional clarity of Descartes's French.

But such failures as van Schooten were not inevitable: Humanist translators, while fastidiously literal in their linkage, were fully conscious of its functions. Guillaume Budé, for instance (see page 72, above), translates δὲ καὶ in Aristotle's second sentence by *etiam*, an almost literal *charnière de traitement* with the same strong directional sense as the Greek. For certain purposes, Humanist practice remained among Renaissance translators: Erasmus, in his New Testament for instance, adopted a chastened literality, guided by the classical sense that any type of language use required its own style. This feeling was one of the ideological elements that prevented the Romantics from being completely happy with literality: and in the work of German scientific translators, it brings about an obvious continuation of the articulation techniques of Bruni Aretino, Nugent and Houbigant. Indeed, Sigismung Hermbstädt's (1760–1833) translation (Berlin, 1803) of Lavoisier's *Traité élémentaire de chimie* (Paris, 1789) is, by contrast with Kerr (see page 164, above), more interlinear than Goethe's Diderot:

Es ist ein beständiges Phänomen in der Natur, dessen Allgemeinheit bereits durch Boerhaave sehr gut festgeseßt werden ist: daß wenn mann irgend einen festen oder flussigen Körper erwärmt, er in seiner Ausdehnung nach allen Seiten zunimmt.

The lineal descendant of this is technically the Meschonnic version of Genesis: but what Bruni Aretino and Hermbstädt do by literal handling of subordination and *charnières*, Meschonnic attempts through representing phonological and syntactic features by typographical space. Here is Genesis i. 2:

Et la terre   était boue   et trouble
et l'ombre   à la surface du remous
                       Et le souffle de Dieu   recouvre
la surface de l'eau.

On this passage Meschonnic (1973, 451) comments: 'La disposition typographique est ici capitale pour écrire la diction des accents disjonctifs (*ta'amim*) de l'ébreu. . . . Le langage biblique est pris d'abord pour et par sa matérialité. Cette matérialité est prise comme une diction, prosodie et rythme dominant, inséparables de la signification. . . .' Hence visual impression is taken to compensate for the loss of the auditory effect of the Hebrew.

Our second technical approach to external *démarche* is transposing to produce discourse units on the same grammatical level. When both source and target languages have the same or similar *démarche* preference and roughly similar grammatical resources, dynamic equivalence on the same discourse level is relatively simple. We have already quoted Jerome on segmentation *per cola et commata*; this he ascribes to Cicero, who seems to have practised it without discussing its repercussions on translation.

For Cicero's translations show strong feeling for the directional sense of articulation. Homer's couplet on page 81, above, grammatically falls into two weighted halves, linked by the correlatives τοῖος and οἷον. Cicero's translation does the same: *quali* is a *charnière de traitement* picking up the dependency left open by *Tales*.

One of the signs of the maturation of Christian Latin was such respect for articulation. Ambrose's Latin version of St. Basil (see page 81), literal though it is, makes some attempt to interpret rather than reproduce the Greek articulation pattern. *Etenim*, here a *charnière de traitement*, through its strong vectorial sense, signals the importance of the rest of its sentence. The minor *charnière*, δè, in the last member, which, though grammatically unnecessary, adds a certain weight to its phrase, is translated by the adversative, *sed*. In the syntax of the clause, the degree of dynamic equivalence is striking. The final result is a paragraph segment which climaxes as the idea of God's creating the world.

From such work is descended the medieval style of subordination. In both Latin and vernaculars it tends to have much less flair, and to drift back towards literality.

To the Humanists, then, the rambling medieval period was anathema. The ideal is discussed at considerable length by Bruni Aretino, whose stylistic discussion revolves around the problems of finding a Latin sentence shape which will both recall that of the original Greek and have rhetorical cogency in Latin. On these grounds, his *Nichomachean Ethics* set an impossibly high standard. The usual fault was to forget that the thrust of Latin and Greek is subtly different, and that grammatical equivalence is only a beginning. In its technique, then, Ficino's *Phaedo* is not very different from that of Aristippus:

> Conabor equidem a principio omnia enarrare. Solebamus quotidie diebus superioribus ad Socratem proficisci, ego atque alii, convenientes mane in illa curia, in qua et iudicium factum fuerat; carceri enim erat proxima.

Apart from unclassical constructions like the dependent present participle, *convenientes*, there is a consistent lack of thrust and unity in the sentence. The Latin is still being suited to an ear tuned to medieval stylistic sense, though there is an overlay of humanist sensitivities to post-Classical vocabulary.

The Classical element is obvious in the choice of *charnières*: *enim* for γὰρ is hardly remarkable, but the opening with *equidem* does show some sense of the classical need for continuity between sections of a document. But Bruni Aretino's requirements that the translated text was to be the mirror image (*effigies*) of the original leads to adopting a falling construction in the Latin, always a difficult sentence-type to keep moving in that language. And indeed, at every comma of the Ficino passage there is a natural stopping place with yet another clause tacked on.

This was, however, a transitional stage, and Renaissance Latin translation attained an almost Ciceronian subtlety. Articulation in both Classical and vernacular languages rested on a good deal less on formal equivalence. And even when it was used, the effects could be variable. Thus, in Thomas North's opening of Plutarch's *Romulus* there arises an ambiguity in the

English that the French avoids through its possession of gender in relative pronouns:

> The Historiographers doe not agree in their writings, by whom, nor for what cause, the great name of cittie of Rome (the glorie whereof is blowen abroad throughout the worlde) was first geven unto it. For some thincke. . . .

> Les historiens ne s'accordent pas a escrire, par qui ne pour quelle cause le grand nom de la ville de Rome, la gloire duquel s'est estendue par tout le monde luy ait esté premièrement imposé: pource que les uns tiennent. . . .

North assumes that the subordination patterns in Amyot's French will work in English and follows them closely, but *whereof* for *duquel* naturally has as its antecedent *Rome* not *name*.

During the seventeenth century the problem of sentence and clause linkage received considerable critical attention, most of it revolving round the question of adapting the long Latin period to French and English. As did Jerome before him, Udall, echoed many times by translators outside England, claimed to use stylistic adjustments to allow for the foibles of his readers (Amos 1920, 94):

> I have in some places been driven to use mine own judgement in rendering the true sense of the book, to speak nothing of a great number of sentences, which by reason of so many members, or parentheses, or digressions as have come in places, are so long that, unless they had been somewhat divided, they would have been too hard for an unlearned brain to conceive.

Modern language translation did not have to submit to the same theorizing as Classical, and so the treatment of subordination was less predictable, witness the English translation (London, 1743) of Pitot's handbook on navigation (Paris, 1731) by Edmund Stone (d. 1768):

> When a Ship at Rest is set in Motion by the action of the Wind upon the Sails, her Velocity or Way will increase by little and little, until the Action of the Water upon her Prow and Body, becomes equal to that of the Wind upon the Sails, and since Action is directly contrary and equal to Reaction, the Direction in which she is drove back by the Water which she meets, must always be the same as the Line of the moving Force, and this is the whole point of the whole Theory of the Working of a Ship, that is, the mean Resistance, of the Water against the Ship must be equal and directly opposite to the mean Force of the Wind upon the Sails, whereby the Axes of Equilibrium of the Resistance of the Water, and the Force of the Wind directly corresponds in a right Line.

Lorsqu'un Vaisseau en repos est mis en mouvement par l'action du vent sur les voiles, sa vitesse ou son sillage doit augmenter et s'accélérer peu à peu jusques à ce que l'action de l'eau sur la prouë et le corps du Vaisseau soit égale à celle du vent sur les voiles; or l'action étant toujours égale et directement opposée à la réaction, la direction selon laquelle le Vaisseau est repoussé par l'eau qu'il rencontre, doit être toujours la même que la ligne de la force mouvante. C'est ici le point principal de toute la théorie de la manoeuvre; c'est à dire, que la résistance moyenne de l'eau contre le Vaisseau doit être égale et directement opposée à la force moyenne du vent sur les voiles, pour que les axes d'équilibre, de la résistance de l'eau, et de la force du vent se réspondent directement en ligne droite.

Even in a technical handbook, French tends to rhetoric; so that *or*, a *charnière de traitement*, and the participial phrase following, are translated as a clause of reason: *since Action*. . . . The introduction of the last sentence, *c'est ici*, is transposed to *and this is* (the phrasal accent must fall on *this* to make sense of the sentence); a strong *charnière de terminaison*, signalling the point of what went before.

  Such dynamic changes were often used to give pace to a translation. In the following passage from Smollett's *Gil Blas* (London, 1750; original, Paris, 1715), the grammatical subordination of the second sentence to the first shows recognition that the second sentence acts as *propos* to the *thème* of the first in the scheme of discourse:

My father, Blas of Santillane, after having carried arms many years for the service of the Spanish monarchy, retired to the town in which he was born, where he chose a wife among the second-rate citizens, who, though she was no chicken, brought me into the world ten months after her marriage.

Blas de Santillane, mon père, après avoir longtemps porté les armes pour le service de la monarchie espagnole, se retira dans la ville où il avoit pris naissance. Il y épousa une femme de chambre qui n'étoit pas dans sa première jeunesse, et je vins au monde dix mois après leur mariage.

The French *charnière de rappel* is *y* (*il y épousa*). Smollett's behaviour is in line with Batteux (1747–8, v. 220) who justifies keeping subordination and clause linkage because 'cette liaison est la vie des pensées et l'objet principal de celui qui parle'. It is also a sign of the movement away from considering mere word order towards the *démarche* it signals. We see it in Jean-Antoine Roucher's translation (Paris, 1790, 7) of Adam Smith's *Wealth of Nations* (London, 1776), which was meant to provide a fiscal policy for the new French Republic:

Le développement des forces productrices du travail, c'est à dire l'addresse, l'activité et l'intelligence qui par-tout aujourd'hui l'appliquent et le dirigent, semble être l'effet de la division du travail, ou du soin qu'on a pris de distribuer en plusieurs mains les différentes branches d'un seul et même ouvrage.

The greatest improvement in the productive powers of labour, and the greatest part of the skill, dexterity and judgement with which it is anywhere directed or applied, seem to have been the effect of the division of labour.

Roucher was aware of what he was doing. His preface has a curious resemblance to Thomas Salusbury's stated intent to write for Gentlemen:

Mais aujourd'hui que le sphère de nos connaissances s'est aggrandie, et avec elle le circle de nos idées, j'ai cru qu'une traduction où l'on aurait tâché de réunir la fidélité à l'élegance, et cette précision modérée, qui, bien loin de nuire à la clarté, la rend, pour ainsi dire, plus visible encore. . . .

Roucher's translation of the first *and* in the passage by *c'est à dire* is grammatically questionable, though in rare instances, *and* can be an introduction formula for a definition: the long and otiose definition tacked on the end of this passage would suggest that Roucher did take this coordination as an explanatory one. By the end of the eighteenth century, then, this type of dynamic equivalence had developed to the point that it could handle both word order and *démarche* either accurately or inaccurately depending on the acuteness of the translator.

Our third manner of articulation, changes in the structural level of sentence segments and *charnières*, is not obvious until one began to translate into vernacular languages. For translation between Classical languages, with their arch-type *démarche*, and the linear *démarche* of vernaculars, with their nested *thèmes* and *propos*, offer rich possibilities. Our first examples are found in vernacular medieval hymns. In the Digby version of *Jesu dulcis memoria* (see page 193, below), the second line converts the Latin dislocation of the noun group by transposing *dans vera gaudia* (giving true joy) to *tant resiouys* (adverb–verb), and the objective genitive, *cordis*, is made the direct object and *propos*. The third and fourth lines of the Poitiers version realign *démarche* by changing the comparative linkage: in Latin it pivots on the preposition, *super*, which looks forward to *dulcis*; in French, on the conjunction, *que*, which looks back to *plus doulcereux*.

For the Renaissance translator for the popular market, the possibilities offered were exploited to the limit. Chaloner's Erasmus plays devastatingly with the Latin linkage and progression of ideas. In our snippet on page 143, *neque enim*, despite being grammatically a coordinating conjunction, from the point of view of *démarche*, introduces a logically subordinate idea, which Chaloner then translates as a digression, marks off by punctuation, and introduces by the modulated transposition, *pardie!* For Chaloner, visualizing Folly as a soapbox orator or a hell-fire preacher, both of whom the sixteenth century knew well, obviously thought his translation out in auditory terms: the strongest English charnière is *yea even* for an inoffensive *etiam*. Indeed, *even* alone would not have the weight to introduce the *among veriest fools of all* (for *apud stultissimos*).

Likewise, in more sober prose, rhythm and intonation are notable features of English articulation. At its simplest, as in the Bedingfield translation of Machiavelli (see page 145, above), *perché*, a *charnière de rappel*, though omitted on paper, is compensated for by the natural intonation of the passage it introduces. Such radical changes of level to be found especially in liturgical work. In the Book of Common Prayer, Cranmer, or whoever translated the Collects of the Roman Missal, produced this version for Palm Sunday:

> Almighty and everlasting God, which of thy tender love toward man, hast sent our Saviour Jesus Christ to take upon him our flesh, and to suffer death upon the cross, that all mankind should follow the example of his great humility: mercifully grant, that we both follow the example of his patience, and be made partakers of his resurrection: through the same Jesus Christ our Lord.

The most striking dynamic realignment of subordination is the transposing of the gerundival purpose phrase, *ad imitandum humilitatis exemplum*, to a full clause, and moving it from the beginning of its clause, an emphatic position in Latin, to the end of its clause in English, an equally emphatic position. At the same time, the arch construction of the Latin clause is transformed into a linear arrangement of *thème* and *propos*, with a marked recitation rhythm. In a simpler vein, Luther and the Authorized Version used dynamic articulation techniques, when necessary, to produce a series of sentence patterns arranged in two balanced halves. Here again is Luke xvi. 19–21:

> Es war aber ein reicher Man, der kleidet sich mit Purpur und koestlicher Linwad, und lebet alle tage herrlich und in freuden. Es war aber ein armer, mit namen Lazarus, der lag fur seiner Thuer voller Schweren, und begeret sich zu festigen von den brosamen, die von des Reichen tische fielen. Doch kamen die Hunde, und lecketen im siene schweren.

> There was a certain rich man, which was clothed in purple and fine linen, and fared sumptuously every day. And there was a certain beggar named Lazarus, which was laid at his gate full of sores, And desiring to be fed with the crumbs which fell from the rich man's table: moreover the dogs came and licked his sores.

The first adjective clause of the English and German ('which was clothed

. . ./der kleidet sich . . .') is a transposition of a coordinate Greek principal clause, the second half of which, a coordinate statement in both target languages, is a Greek participial phrase.

In poetical translation, balance such as this, metre and form, all become pretexts for realigning and filling out complex sentences, not only to retain *démarche*, but also to use up the chosen metrical form. Both Cowper and Power (see pages 90 and 111) find that their verse forms dictate structure: Cowper, for instance, has no choice in his first line but to put the object of his final clause before *ut* if he is to use those words. Working in the opposite direction, Dryden, Perrin and Pope ironically do the same thing to avoid having statements spill over the bounds of the heroic couplet and Alexandrine.

Prose was not forgotten in this awareness that languages had different ways of operating. In a manner prefiguring the doctrines of the School of Prague and *stylistique comparée*, Burnouf (1828, 22) writes that the idea in a foreign language always comes in a way contrary to the habits of the target language. One could, however, pay so much attention to language differences that one distorted the message. For all his carefulness over language standards, Burnouf's elegant subordinations at the beginning of Tacitus *Annales* i. 3 do no justice to the savage innuendo of Tacitus' prose. By very tight articulation, Tacitus makes two acts of nepotism into one monstrous crime: Burnouf splits the sentence into two urbane balanced periods. Moreover, Tacitus sees Agrippa's status as boon companion to Augustus as a crime added to his low birth: Burnouf makes it a compensation. Later discussion of articulation, e.g. that in Weil (1844) and Tolman (1901), followed Batteux on the matter. By the 1920s Marouzeau (1924, 189) was branding attempts to keep the order of the original *un fâcheux préjugé*, yet in 1931 (45) he writes, 'Supprimer la subordination, c'est supprimer les rapports entre les idées, donc une partie de la pensée de l'auteur.' Most of this theorizing followed widespread use of fully dynamic articulation, even in technical translation. A fair sample of the turn-of-the-century manner is Edward Suddard's English translation (London, 1906, 18) of Charles Widor's textbook on orchestration (Paris, 1904):

> Flutes are made in several keys. At the Paris Exhibition (1900) was to be seen a Bass Flute, tuned an octave below the standard instrument, but, unfortunately, it was almost impossible for the lips to bring out the lower notes.

> Il existe des Flûtes dans plusieurs tons. A l'exhibition de Paris (1900), figurait une Flûte basse accordée à l'octave inférieure, mais ne permettant guère, malheureusement, aux lèvres de faire sortir les sons graves.

The two salient points of this are, first, the preference for the passive in

English; and, second, the realignment of the grammatical coordination of the second sentence resulting from the transposition of *permettant* to a verb–adjective group. The rest of the twentieth century shows little improvement on this.

In any translation unit, the type of equivalence used on structural levels is not necessarily determined by the predominant lexical equivalence type: we have seen how some medieval and Humanist translators set dynamically equivalent lexicon within formally equivalent structure; and, conversely, how Cicero and Jerome used dynamic structure with formal lexicon. Further, dynamic equivalence in small structural units can be used either to keep the *démarche* of the discourse unit through recreating order and vectorial sense, or to transform it completely. Obviously, though twentieth-century linguistic analysis has produced comprehensive descriptions of translation mechanisms, 'modern' structural techniques, like lexical, are as old as translation itself.

In what, then, does evolution of translation technique consist?

Except for the shortest, the extracts so far examined show a variety of mechanisms—comparison of the versions of Luke xvi. 19–21 and of the opening of *Aeneid* IV, for instance, makes it clear that, even if individual operations come from the same repertoire, the ways in which they are combined vary according to period and purpose. For differences between languages provide merely for a range of solutions: it is up to the translator's professional conscience as to type of equivalence chosen for semantic and grammatical aspects of each unit, and the resulting mixture of techniques. Nor do the linguist and his analysis direct the conscience of a translator. For, in treating his source and target texts as complex signs, he is guided in his choice of linguistic techniques by the interplay he sees between the complex *signifié* and *signifiant* of the original and by the relationship between form and message he wishes to create in the target text.

Seven

Message, Style and Form

Notwithstanding Boethius and his spiritual descendants, style is never irrelevant; indeed, on style depends perception of the communicative priorities of one's text. This has been a preoccupation shared by all types of translators. To take merely the modern period, where Pound, in a letter to W. H. D. Rouse in 1935, sees the 'narrative flow' of a poem as essential, Knox (1949, 29) demands that a translator reproduce 'the argument running through your piece', and Jumpelt (1961, 171) bases the final judgement of a translation on the three requirements of simplicity, clarity and adequacy.

There are three broad criteria on which relevance of style is judged: that style conforms to matter, that style is selected to suit readership, that style reflects author. The first, an essential element in ancient rhetoric, reappears in the Humanists, and, during the twentieth century, forms part of both the Prague School theory of functional style and Halliday's concept of register.[1] The second, another element in the functional theories of both the Prague linguists and Halliday, first appears in St. Augustine, who directed his writings in the elevated style towards the educated, and those in the low to the ordinary Christian. The third, that style is the man, is a critical commonplace going back at least to Longinus' Περὶ ὕψους (first century A.D.). Clearly, choice between translation operations can hardly be said to depend on contrastive linguistics, governed as they are, by these three criteria.

7.1 PROSE

Translators adopt two approaches to the style of the original: they either imitate it through extended formal equivalence, or they use a target-language style deemed functionally equivalent.

Strict formal equivalence outside technical translation often rests on the assumption that style is the man. This is argued especially vehemently by Nabokov (1955), and is brought forward by Morgan (1956, 37) on Goethe:

Any writer has the right to write as his pen points and it is not our business, not even our advantage, to reshape him according to our notions of what really good writing is.

The intimate union between message and form thus implied, arising from the wisdom of language as sacrament and λόγος, expects a formal equivalence version to evoke both matter and form of the original. Thus Meschonnic's Genesis (see page 171, above) seeks not merely to transmit, but also to recreate the biblical formless void by building French auditory and semantic patterning after the original Hebrew. Though elements of this go back to Philo Iudaeus, one of the first absolute prescriptions of literality for stylistic reasons is the ferocious critique by Huet (1661) of his literary contemporaries and their free habits. It suffices here to recall Houbigant (see page 77) as an outstanding practitioner of Huet's principles, and to note the distance between desire and performance in 'literal' translators such as Chateaubriand (see page 93), whose work reflects Milton's biblically tinged English because it is spiced with dynamic equivalence, not in spite of it.

While one can assume that the author, had he written in the target language, would have used a style grammatically akin to his original, the other approach to this 'projective fabrication', as Steiner calls it, takes equivalence to derive from function, and further, not to flow from specific sister structures. Therefore, though in his version of Plato (see page 163, above) Cicero's lexicon is formally equivalent, he uses dynamically equivalent structure. Equally important to its thrust, the Latin is organized in rhythmic units whose syllable count is the same as the Greek, and which end, like the Greek, in *clausulae*:[2] The first is a spondee–cretic (*autem quod gignitur*), the second a trochee–spondee (*gigni necesse est*) and the third, a choriamb leading to a trochee–cretic (*remota reperiri origo potest*). True to the functional perspective, none of these are formally the same as the Greek *clausulae*.

The later style, represented by Apuleius (page 140) shows a studied use of *clausulae* to ornament and slow the pace. *Utriusque sunt* (trochee–cretic), *recta custodia* (spondee–cretic), and *omnium habet tellus* (paean–trochee) are all characteristic of the highly ornamented Silver style that reacted against Ciceronian restraint. But the evolution of the language was cutting the ground from under these vestiges of classicism; and the quantitative *clausulae* was being replaced by the accentual. Indeed our Apuleius examples can be read either way.

Thus it is the Ciceronian precedent, not the Silver-Latin development of it, that the Christians followed. Jerome's Origen, for instance, uses *clausulae* to mark both direction of argument and grammatical divisions in a text noted for dynamic equivalence.[3] Not that this was peculiar to Jerome: in the Ambrose and Eustathius versions of St. Basil (page 81), there are *clausulae*, a number of them matching the Greek, e.g. *nàrratúro* and *nàrratúrus* for διηγεῖσθαι. But under his surface polish Jerome had attitudes formed, not only by reading the *De optimo genere* which he quotes against Rufinus, but also by absorbing Cicero's other rhetorical works. Especially in *De finibus*, Cicero underlines the duty of following the manner of the original through dynamic equivalence: and this, in Patristic texts, Jerome does. But, in his Biblical work, Jerome realized that with formal equivalence he could reflect the movement of Biblical Greek: thus, through a rhetorician's paradox he reconciled Cicero's congruence of style and matter with Augustine's norm of fitting style to audience. For, like Augustine, Jerome exploited a sociolinguistic restricted code to allow for wide variations of linguistic sophistication in the laity. To appease his Christian conscience, however, he explains his Vulgate manner through the traditional principle that in Scripture even the word order was a divine mystery. Little wonder then that the less subtle Rufinus accused him of bad faith and casuistry.

In medieval translation, there are few attempts at functional stylistic equivalence in Latin, the only notable attempt quoted being the Anastasius Bibliothecarius account of the condemnation of Photius. In the vernaculars, however, there are the remarkably embroidered verse translations of prayers and the redrafting of standard works like Ovid and Vergil, according them the more leisurely oral tradition of medieval story-telling. It is only late in the Middle Ages that we find attempts at combining both formal and functional equivalence in style: Chaucer's *Romaunt de la Rose* is a case in point.

The Humanists, then, who sought to reconcile functional parity with formal resemblance, were on tested ground, even if the theoretical postulates were different. Bruni Aretino, for instance, argues the typical Humanist position that, as specific topics demand special styles in both Greek and Latin, so the movement of the Greek should show through his Latin. Hence, in his Aristotle (see page 162, above), dynamic lexicon is set in formally equivalent structure, resulting in a version whose three segments have the same thrust, syllable count and intonation as the Greek. And, like our Cicero Plato, each segment is marked off by a *clausula* though Aretino's are the accentual variety (*cursus*): the first (*omnisque doctrina*) is a *planus*, the second (*actus et electio*) a *tardus*, and the last, a *velox*.

Functional stylistic imitation of this almost literal type continued into the sixteenth century (cf. Erasmus, page 74, and More, page 194, below). It was, however, more to contemporary taste to create rhythmic flow by dynamic equivalence. Not that formality was necessarily the aim: the Becke translation of Erasmus (see page 46, above) aims at the informal, chatty rhythm of speech through dynamic approaches to both lexicon and grammar. Similarly, the Italian, French and English translations of

Cicero's correspondence attempts to give some flavour of Cicero and his friends in sixteenth-century terms. Both Manutius and Dolet attempt to catch the tone of conversation in letters between friends through subtly coloured dynamic equivalence: the almost slangy *ma in buoni termini* for *sed valentem* in Manutius, or the *A dieu* in Dolet's French for *Vale*, are attempts to write a prose whose tone and rhythm was as relaxed as that of Cicero. That this continued into the early seventeenth century is abundantly clear from Webbe's version of the same passage (see page 88, with its rhythmic gloss of *so you come lustie and strong* for *si valebis*.

In French, it seems to be a particular feature of religious controversy, as in Calvin (see page 104, above), who rounds off his sentence cadences with synonyms. In English, translators experimented with *cursus*.[4] In most work, examples occur haphazardly. It may be coincidence that the modulated transpositions discussed in Robynson's More (see page 160) are both *cursus plani* and fall at important cadence points; but in texts meant for public recitation, such rhythmic features were deliberately exploited. For example, the English Collect on page 176 falls into two major divisions, marked by colons in both Latin and English. In the Latin, the ritual adjectival clause stating the Palm Sunday theme ends with *subíre fecísti*, a *cursus planus*, to which corresponds *exámple of his great humílity*, a *tardus*; and both Latin and English end on a *tardus*: *consórtia mereámur/partákers of his resurréction*.

While this type of functional parity depended on imitating expository features of the source text, there surfaced attempts at justifying literal translation on the same grounds. This is found in the Geneva Bible, and also in Gregory Martin's preface to the Rheims Bible:

> There is a certain majesty in these speeches and therefore both the Latin and the Greek keep them, although it is no more the Latin or Greek phrase than the English.

To many this was not a welcome doctrine: Luther's *Sendbrief* consistently mocks the calque and literal translations of his predecessors, demanding that the prose style used be equivalent in function. For among literary translators, it had remained the norm: Becke's Erasmus, for instance (see page 46, above) is an excellent example of this marketplace translation, following as it does the norm to be trumpeted forth by Denham in his *Aeneid*:

> Therefore if Virgil must needs speak English, it were fit he should speak not only as a man of this nation, but as a man of this age.

For the learned market, some translators could not see past Cicero. *De optimo genere* v. 14, in which he takes translation as conforming to the norms of oratory, was plagiarized countless times. But desire often outran performance. For instance, Bartholomew Clerke (1537–90), translating Castiglione into Latin, does not argue for his Ciceronian style beyond descanting on his love for Cicero as an author; but how Ciceronian was he? Let us look at the beginning of his passage on women:

> Intermissis itaque animi virtutibus (quas illi cum nostro Curiali communes esse oportet), prudentia, magnanimitate, continentia, reliquisque nonnullis, quae omnibus ex aequo foeminis conveniunt, ut sunt illa, synceram modestamque esse, mariti facultates, familiam, liberos sollicite curare: illud praeterea in Aulica requiritur, ut iucunda quadam affabilitate in omni sermone, cum omni hominum genere utatur, tanta loci, temporis, personae, reliquarumque rerum consideratione, nihil ut exactius, tanta morum, actionisque modestia, nihil ut suavius, tanto acumine ac facilitate, nihil ut concinnius, appareat cumque se in omni tum dicto, tum facto pudicam, prudentem, dulcem, iucundam, argutam ostenderit, tum difficilem & scopulosam, sed tamen vere auream mediocritatem conservet, quam utrisque contrariis septam & quasi obsessam, sine scelere praeterire non potest.[5]

Clerke illustrates how reverence for Cicero was centred on vocabulary—though *aulica* is the only un-Ciceronian word here, by Ciceronian standards the structure of the passage is loose. Castiglione had organized his long Italian sentence into two parts divided by colon after *famiglia*. His first part, a prepositional phrase, is taken over almost literally into Latin, so that through its linear progression Clerke's phrase jerks towards the colon after *curare* without ever attaining a point of climax. The Latin main clause likewise lacks Ciceronian impetus and unity through its large number of natural stopping places. Beside this, the Tegli version of Machiavelli (see page 145, above), so criticized by Amelot de la Houssaye, nevertheless shows the essential element of Ciceronian style, i.e. attainment of clarity through making the sentence rise to a central point of unity: the phrase *disputationem persequar*. Another solution to the style problem is demonstrated by Gottfried Theile who uses another Ciceronian style element, the balancing of the sentence round a central fulcrum, in this case the phrase *ea est*.

But Latin style of the time was affected by some composition customs of vernacular languages, and a Renaissance equivalent to the Asiatic style affected by Apuleius grew up in the late sixteenth century. There are traces of it in the Aristotle translations of Denis Lambin (1516–72):

> Omnis ars, omnisque docendi via atque institutio, itemque actio et consilium, bonum aliquod appetere videtur.[6]

Comparison with the Grosseteste-Aretino version of this passage (see page 162) shows the same care for balance, but a certain squeamishness in the face of simplicity. The Aristotelian balance of the subject is transformed into a triple subject where *via atque institutio* for μεθόδος is balanced by *actio et consilium* and *omnisque* balances *itemque*.

Unwelcome as it was to rabid Ciceronians, Cicero was not the only writer of good Classical prose. The more broadminded of sixteenth-century Latinists were well aware that different subjects, even in Cicero, had different styles, and there were many who demanded that the mania for Cicero should be tempered by the classical filter of suitability of style to subject. Hence, in his preface to Hippocrates (1543), Johann Hagenbut (Cornarius), Dean of the Faculty of Medicine at Jena, notes that Ciceronian norms were neither worth the trouble, nor suitable to medical prose, and sneers politely at the 'new sect of men' who imitated Cicero in all things. His opening to *De diaeta* reads:

> Si quis mihi ex prioribus, qui de diaeta humana ad sanitatem conferente scripserunt, recte cognovisse, ac omnia per totum, quantum humanae menti possibile est, conscripsisse videretur; satis esset mihi aliorum laboribus, quos nossem recte habere, uti, prout singula utilia esse viderentur.
>
> εἰ μὲν μοί τις ἐδόκει τῶν πρότερον συγγραψάντων περὶ διαίτης ἀνθρωπίνης τῆς πρὸς ὑγιείην ὀρθῶς ἐγνωκὼς συγγεγραφέναι πάντα διὰ παντὸς ὅσα δυνατὸν ἀνθρωπίνη γνώμη περιληφθῆναι, ἱκανῶς εἶχεν ἄν μοι, ἄλλων ἐκπονησάντων, γνόντα τὰ ὀρθῶς ἔχοντα, τούτοισι χρῆσθαι καθότι ἕκαστον αὐτῶν ἐδόκει χρήσιμον εἶναι.[7]

The Greek falls into two balanced halves at the word περιληφθῆναι. Cornarius adopts the ground-plan of the Greek sentence, signalling the balance by the use of *satis* as a *charnière de traitement*, and the separation by the typical rhythmic use of a semi-colon after *videretur*. Within the subordinate clause, the dependent indirect statements are placed before the main verb in a manner typical of Classical Latin. In the principal clause, the important fact, that of using older authorities insofar as they were useful, is placed last, as it is, for Hippocrates, both justification and *modus operandi*. But, as in the Clerke passage there are stylistic infelicities which militate against functional adequacy: for example, the dangling clause at the end, beginning *prout*, gives the impression of being tacked on rather than being, as it is in Greek, an integral part of the sentence.

To a lesser extent, the Renaissance continued the medieval practice of verse translations of prose works. If one excepts the Latin Bible in Hexameters (1604) by the Bishop of Oxford, John Bridges, most of it is vernacular work and skilled. Its most urgent application was in the reformed churches of Geneva for whom hymns, as human documents, were not fit for divine worship. As the problem was pastorally an acute one—congregational participation was much easier through music—a number of illustrious translators, including Sir Philip Sydney and Clément Marot, produced verse psalms.

Precedents come from the constant reference to singing in the Psalter itself and in St. Paul: hence the preface of the Bay Psalm Book (1640):

> . . . if in our English tongue wee are able to sing them, than as all our English songs are in metre, soe ought David's psalms be translated into metre.

The metre chosen was the Ballad metre:

> The Lord to mee a shepheard is,
>   want therefore shall not I.
> Hee in the folds of tender-grasse,
>   doth cause me down to lie

In prose, the metrical element in stylistic equivalence did not survive to the sixteenth century. Practice, then, centred on adopting the same *démarche* with a high degree of formal equivalence, Smollett, Nugent and Campbell, for instance, attempt the style of their originals by embedding dynamically equivalent vocabulary in mainly formal structure. From this point of view, there is little new in the behaviour of Romantic translators, although, admittedly, their theory is of another order entirely. By the middle of the nineteenth century, then, many had learnt from the Romantics how to attain an illusion of literality by making the sense of direction, register and pace of the original felt. To compare with Goethe, Tissot and Hermbstädt, all of them searching for the interlinear version, here is the beginning of Victor Cousin's fourth lecture on Kant (Paris, 1844), translated in the grand lecture-room style by one A. G. Henderson (London, 1854):

> You now know the reform that Kant intended to introduce into metaphysical science; you also know what, according to him, is the true end of that science, and the only legitimate method by which it can be prosecuted. Both the end and the method he has taken care to establish, with the most perfect precision, in the Introduction, an analysis of which I have already presented you with, and which has already made you familiar with some of the essential principles, as well as with the phraseology of the Kantian philosophy. You can now therefore more rapidly follow me in the exposition of the 'Critique of Pure Reason'.

> Vous savez quelle réforme Kant entreprend dans la métaphysique; vous savez quel est, pour lui, le véritable but de cette science: ce but, Kant a pris

soin de l'établir lui-même, avec une parfaite précision, dans l'introduction que vous connaissez. En même temps, cette Introduction vous a initiés à plusieurs des principes essentiels et à une partie du langage de la philosophie kantienne. Maintenant donc, vous pouvez me suivre plus rapidement dans l'examen de la *Critique de la raison pure.*

Henderson's method depends, like that of the sixteenth-century translators referred to in this section, on visualizing the circumstances of delivery. If one sets aside Henderson's additions, which are rhythmic rather than explanatory in aim, the progression of this paragraph, from the first link-sentence with the last lecture, to the mention of the *Critique of Pure Reason*, follows that of Cousin and achieves its close-knit character through careful reproduction of Cousin's *charnières* and, as far as possible, a reproduction of Cousin's sentence rhythms.

The care in preserving the flow of ideas owes much to the example of Goethe's *Interlinearversion*, as in the Diderot passage on page 93, above. And we find exactly the same nuanced literality in Tissot (page 169), working some twenty years later. Clearly, the boundary between translation genres, insofar as style was concerned, meant little at this period.

While the Romantics were identifying stylistic imitation with sentence order, there was again growing a manner that adopted functionally equivalent style. Peculiarly enough, it is first exemplified in certain scientific translations of the end of the eighteenth century: Kerr's Lavoisier (see page 164, above), with its exact terminology set in reversed *démarche*, is a case in point. In literature, it is particularly exemplified by classicists: a century later, on the assumption that, had Plautus written the Falstaff speech in *Henry IV*, Tyrrell translated Shakespeare's prose into Plautine *senarii* with all the comic stylistic conventions of the genre.

This sensitivity to function set in train disenchantment with Wardour Street English. Within the discipline of classics, ventures beyond its formal approach result in searches for functionally equivalent style: as that of Phillimore (1873–1926), who asks that the translator find the 'pitch' of his author and choose his English style in consequence (Phillimore 1919, 14). And not before time: Wardour Street English was under informed and persistent attack as a baneful influence on the language sense of the young person exposed to it; and, as John Middleton Murry (1925) proclaimed in *Pencillings*, '. . . it is almost as difficult for a classical scholar to write a piece of hard clean English, as it is for a camel to pass through the eye of a needle'.

Usually, approaches to style varied between formal and functional equivalence. Mackenna (1917, xxiii) sees direct imitation of style as a goal to be sought only if the text and its matter are amenable. For Plotinus, it was not seen as useful, or even relevant. But in religious texts written in ancient languages, the vernacular crib had the difficult task of being both literal and functionally equivalent. Here is the opening of John Chrysostom's Anaphora in an early twentieth-century English version:

> It is meet and right to praise Thee, to glorify Thee, to bless Thee, to give thanks to Thee, to worship Thee, in all places of Thy dominion, for Thou art God ineffable, incomprehensible, invisible, inconceivable, existing always as Thou dost exist, Thou and Thine only-begotten Son and Thy Holy Spirit.

Literal this is, but not to a fault, for, as with the Bible some 300 years before, the slight archaism in vocabulary and imported grammatical features, like the post-position of the last string of adjectives gives a ceremonial pace to the English.

By the 1940s, Knox (1949, 36) remarked that the Bible should 'speak to Englishmen not only in English words but in English idiom'. He gives us a Christ who is an upper-class raconteur, a rabbi who speaks English with the quiet grace of the gentleman. With this approach to style we can compare the Canada Council passage on page 153, in which the administrative French register matches in function that of the original English. Both Knox and the French translator use formal equivalence as a base, but where clarity, elegance and parity of function require, spice it with dynamic.

While translators remained sensitive to both the ideas of the original and its stylistic flow, this type of behaviour did not jar. But for all that, failure rates were high. We have already seen the result of Burnouf's redrafting of Tacitus in *une langue perfectionnée*. His error—misinterpreting the ramifications of sociolinguistic codes—was repeated by liturgical translators in the Roman Catholic Church after Vatican II. In most Christian liturgies, formal worship translated the sense of occasion by elaborated code characteristics. Thus, in the Palm Sunday Collect, the complicated subordination, an elaborated code characteristic, leads the worshipper through the ritual relative clause, whose function is to set the background of the liturgical celebration, to the main meat of the prayer, which, in this case, is the final clause. This progression is respected by the Book of Common Prayer through both grammatical and rhythmic balance. The post-conciliar English versions of our Collect break the formal progression by using coordination, a restricted code characteristic when used to this extent. But in changing the sociolinguistic code, translators were also changing the religious priorities of the prayer: Cloud (1964, 146) remarks of the draft versions circulating at the time that this sort of technique moves the emphasis of the prayer from the central petition to God to the subsidiary section detailing attributes, a telling demonstration of

Marouzeau (1931, 45), who points out that if a translator suppresses subordination, he is suppressing part of the thought of the original.

But the twentieth century, like the eighteenth, was aware of its own uniqueness. Roman Catholic translators had taken to heart the principle that literary and mystical work provoked different reactions in different audiences (cf. Bandini 1948, 64). The problem was conflict between views of style function; the authorities agreed with Nida that readership controlled style, and opted for a restricted code approach: their critics, however, seeing style in the ancient terms of congruence between linguistic level and subject, sought an elaborated code.

In prose, then–apart from the extreme solution of verse for prose–our two solutions, the imitative and the functional, alternate. Imitative stylistic equivalence, into which, despite what he says, the Boethian attempt to ignore style enters, is a feature of translation where the aim was perceived to be unrelieved symbol–we find it almost continuously from the early Jewish Bible translators: the only attempts to depart from it occur in certain aspects of Royal Society prose in the mid seventeenth century and in the stylish translation of the late-eighteenth-century scientist. Functional correspondence is found in texts with multiple aims. Methods of attaining it vary from heavy use of dynamic equivalence, as in Cicero's completely recast Plato, to the nuanced literality of Knox, Campbell and Goethe.

7.2   POETRY

Most of what has been said about prose style is true also about verse, but with the added complication that verse style is associated with form. Here we follow Holmes (1970) in distinguishing four types of form: extraneous, organic, analogical and mimetic.

Extraneous form is usually associated with radical stylistic alteration: the polymetric *canticum* from Caecilius Statius' Menander (see page 79, above) is of a piece with the medieval Ovids. Their use of native verse forms with no regard to original line-length or stanza-type brings a different pace: in Caecilius a change from a sophisticated progression of ideas to a more earthy Roman view of helpless rage; in the medieval *Ars amoris* (see page 101) a rounding-out of detail. Among later translators, there are occasional examples of extraneous form: as in Calverley's use of Latin hexameters, not a lyric metre, to translate Tennyson's 'Tears, Idle Tears', and in the following version of an Anacreon ode by Wolfgang Schadewalt (1900–1974), Professor of Classics at Tübingen, who used an elegiac couplet to discipline the irregular stanza form of Anacreon (1970, I. 520):

Atrides studeo magnos et dicere Cadmum.
  Chorda tamen solam mota sonat Venerem.
Mutavi plectrum nervos chelyn. Usque ego canto
  Alciden: resonant usque fides Venerem.
Grandia iam valeant magnorum nomina regum.
  Nam quodcumque sonat chorda, sonat Venerem.

Θέλω λέγειν Ἀτρείδας,
θέλω δὲ Κάδμον ἄδειν,
ὁ βάρβιτος δὲ χορδαῖς
Ἔρωτα μοῦνον ἠχεῖ.
ἤμειφα νεῦρα πρώην
καὶ τὴν λύρην ἅπασαν·
κἀγὼ μὲν ᾖδον ἄθλους
Ἡρακλέους, λύρη δὲ
ἔρωτας ἀντεφώνει.
χαίροιτε λοιπὸν ἡμῖν,
ἥρωες· ἡ λύρη γὰρ
μόνους Ἔρωτας ᾄδει.[8]

Fine performance thought this is, it is achieved at the price of imposing through the elegiac couplet a cohesion on Anacreon he definitely does not want and by altering the proportions and pace of the poem.

Yet imposition of alien poetic forms is rare: it is much more usual to employ an organic form which arises out of the way in which the translation falls. As organic form follows from an act of interpretation, Holmes takes it to comprise evolution of original verse forms. While this is true, considering that the choice of prose can be critical commentary on the original, we are including prose versions here.

Dissatisfaction with the fidelity of verse translations of poetry runs through the Middle Ages as an undercurrent, surfacing occasionally as in John Trevisa's comment (1387?, 207) that prose chronicles were more accurate and easier to read than verse. Again as an undercurrent, it continues into the sixteenth century, becoming especially visible in French translations of Terence for the stage; Jean Bourlier introduces his *Adelphi* with sentiments Goethe would have approved of:

Pour lequel mieus entendre l'avons traduit en prose, afin de plus clerement monstrer le stile et manière de procéder, et le bon esprit, qu'avoit le Comique en la façon d'icelles, Car, à dire vray, la prose rend le principal sens, la phrase et l'esprit d'une matière, sans contrainte du langage plus facile, que le Rithme.

Correspondence is functional rather than imitative, Terence's graceful laconicness being replaced by a wordy courtliness more akin to the first verse translations of the next century. After more than a century of this, French artistic consciences uneasily sought atonement through prose, with varying results: the de Marolles account of *infelix Dido* is merely flat; *La boucle de cheveux enlevée* (1728) by Pierre François Guyot Desfontaines (1685–1745) ridiculous:

> Je chante une cruelle offense causée par l'Amour, et une querelle sérieuse née d'une hardiesse badine. Muse, c'est à Caryl que ces vers sont dûs; et je me flatte que Bélinde daignera les lire. Malgré la frivolité du sujet, je mériterai de grandes éloges, si l'une m'inspire et si l'autre m'applaudit.

> What dire offence from am'rous causes springs,
> What mighty contests rise from trivial things,
> I sing—This verse to Caryl, Muse! is due:
> This ev'n Belinda may vouchsafe to view:
> Slight is the subject, but not so the praise,
> If she inspire, and He approve my lays.[9]

Pope's first two lines are an epic cliché, the third and fourth a reminiscence of Vergil's *Eclogue* x. Through insensitivity or perhaps dislike of this incongruous mixture of epic and pastoral convention, Desfontaines has replaced epigrammatic acidity by flaccid earnestness. Obviously, the change to prose was merely treating the symptoms so well-described by Eléazar de Mauvillon:

> Les François ont fait revivre le goût naturel; ils ont chassé de leurs écrits les Jeux de Mots, les Pointes, les Hyperboles, et les Figures outrées.

One who was aware of this was a Jesuit latinist, Jacques Tarteron (1644–1720), who writes in his foreword to Horace that, because the conventions of French verse were so rigid, *le vers françois . . . approcheroit moins que la prose des beautés qui nous enlèvent dans Horace.* He was not alone: much the same thing was being said about German versions of Milton, cf. the *Critische Briefe* of Bodmer and Breitinger (1746). Tarteron's reason was that, owing to the freedom of the prose, one could, by a type of compensation (the word is his own), remake the piquancy of Horace. And, by a fortunate meeting of minds, his version of *Satires* I. ix (1685) is urbane, witty and biting:

> J'allois l'autre jour mon chemin par la ruë sacrée, rêvant, selon ma coûtume, à je ne sçai quelles bagatelles, dont j'étois tout occupé; lorsque certain Aventurier, que je connoissois que de nom, m'aborde, et me serrant la main: Hé bien, dit-il, le plus aimable des hommes, comment va la santé?

Ibam forte via sacra, sicut meus est mos,
Nescio quid meditans nugarum, totus in illis:
Occurrit quidam notus mihi nomine tantum,
Arreptaque manu: Quid agis, dulcissime rerum?[10]

In France, at any rate, there remained a large body of opinion in favour of
prose for verse: Pichot (1877, I. 220) for instance, on his Byron recalls
Tarteron:

Quelques personnes prétendent que la poésie ne doit être traduite qu'en
vers. Mais avec les entraves du rythme, qui pourrait être toujours fidèle?
D'ailleurs un grand poête consentira-t-il à ne jouer que le rôle ingrat de
traducteur, et l'humble prose ne vaut-il pas mieux que les vers médiocres?

The use of prose for poetry remains an option acceptable to Romantics, its
best-known example being Chateaubriand's *Paradise Lost*. But unlike
Pichot's Byron, Chateaubriand's Milton attempts the biblical weight of
the English. Like Goethe's Diderot, the passage quoted on page 93 is
literal only in appearance: the *démarche* of the original is kept but there are
grammatical reorganizations. For example, Milton's introductory *of* disappears, Chateaubriand's *chante* being transitive on the model of the Latin
epic cliché, and the collective, *woe*, becomes a less telling plural, *malheurs*.
But the long series of subordinations, the epic vocabulary (e.g. *séjour
bienheureux* for *blissful seat*) and the slow rhythm of the English, all appear
in the French. The success of this type of translation undoubtedly justified
Pichot's less ideological use of prose, and underlies the continuing support
of prose for verse among some modern French critics: cf. Marouzeau
(1931, 72):

Quand un vrai poète attaque à un poète, il le traduit volontiers en prose,
comme a fait Leconte de Lisle pour Horace.

In England, prose for verse is rarely defended before the nineteenth
century; indeed the normal attitude was that of Tytler (1790, 111):

To attempt therefore a translation of a lyric poem into prose, is the most
absurd of undertakings: for all those very characters of the original which
are essential to it, and which constitute its highest beauties, if transferred to
a prose translation, become unpardonable blemishes.

Despite continual skirmishing by English critics (e.g. Horne 1844) who
were inspired by the Romantics, it was not until the twentieth century that
a case for artistic verse translation was made out in English. There are two
main thrusts to the argument. Robert Bridges in *Ibant obscuri* argues for

prose Vergils from the imperfections of earlier verse translations, an echo of the French seventeenth-century attitude. The more usual reason for requiring prose was the Romantic one that new verse forms prevented adequate 'representation', as John Middleton Murry (1925) wrote in *Pencillings*, or that they were what Rieu called 'an alien design' in his preface to his 1949 version of Vergil for Penguin Classics. Akin to this was Northrop Fry's attack on verse translation in the 1964 *Arion* questionnaire:

> Poetical translations of classical poetry are all right as a literary exercise or a technical tour de force. As a guide to the poetry itself they are an abomination.

Organic form in verse is rare until the free-verse forms of the twentieth century: previous arguments in favour of verse forms assumed either analogical or mimetic forms. As with adoption of prose, the assumption is that style brings form. In discussing his *Aeneid* translation, Day Lewis remarks that, in modern English, we do not have a grand epic manner of the type open to Dryden and Pope. Thus, as his priority was the speaking voice of the story-teller, to keep the momentum of the poem he evolved a flexible line of six stresses rhymed in couplets: prose would not have allowed him to combine the onward pace of the poem with accuracy to both matter and manner. The result, as in the extract on page 97, is a translation which reproduces much of Vergil's free movement within a discipline imposed by the line form.

Our third approach to form is the mimetic, which attempts to retain the form of the source text. True, forms are not 'retained' in passing from one language to another, merely imitated by 'looking squarely at the original poem . . . to the exclusion of other considerations' (Holmes 1970, 95). Usually mimetic form, if it attempts the style of the original, will employ a high degree of dynamic equivalence, the reason being that the rhythm and flow of the original is an essential part of the message to be transmitted.

Mimetic form was used by the Romans without discussion. For instance, Catullus in his *Ode* 51 attempts Sappho's blend between sentence-pattern and verse-shape, even to having his first sentence spill over into the second stanza. In addition, certain key words, like *audit* and ὑπακούει (listens) occupy similar positions of stress:

> Ille mi par esse deo videtur,
> Ille, si fas est, superare divos,
> Qui sedens adversus identidem te
>   Spectat et audit
> Dulce ridentem, . . .

φαίνεταί μοι κῆνος ἴσος θέοισιν
ἔμμεν' ὤνηρ, ὄττις ἐνάντιός τοι
ἰσδάνει καὶ πλάσιον ἆδυ φωνεί-
σας ὑπακούει
καὶ γελαίσας ἰμέροεν, . . .[11]

There are, however, licences Catullus does not allow himself, like the divided word at the end of the third line.

Cicero's Homer (see page 81, above) is subtly different in that, though there are epic elements, like the adjective *auctiferas*, a nice Ennian touch, Cicero does not follow Homer's distribution of matter exactly from line to line, but organizes his correlative sentence round the strong caesura in his first line.

Similarly, among medievals translating hymns from the Divine Office, mimetic form demanded dynamic equivalence, and style questions tended to be ignored. Many of these versions sit relatively easily on the traditional plainsong melodies: for example the versions of the Rosy Sequence in Digby MS 149 and Poitiers MS 95:

Dulce memorie de Ihesu Crist
qui cel et tere et tut ben fist;
n'est altre ren en tut le monde
que veire ioie a home dunt.

Doulce memoire de Ihesus,
Tant resiouys le cuer piteux,
mais il n'est riens plus doulcereux
que te contempler glorieux.[12]

Fit the melodies these versions do, but there are peculiarities in the French stress patterns. The Latin is an accentual catalectic trochee; both French versions alternate iambic and trochaic lines. The second and third lines of the Digby version and the third line of Poitiers are definitely iambic, even if one allows for the fact that a Middle French iambic was much less obvious to the ear than the Latin; and the basis of French intonation was moving from stress-timing to syllable-timing.

In verse translation from vernacular works, mimetic form was the rule, it seems, but, as in our Chaucer extract (see page 137), the level of formal equivalence was much higher. A century later, Humanist translators also combined mimetic form with formal equivalence, but not without risk. Sir Thomas More (1478–1534) and William Lily (1468?–1522) both translated the same elegiac epigram from the *Greek Anthology*:

> Nudus in terra veni, sic nudus abibo:
>   Quid frustra sudo, funera nuda videns?   [More]

> Ingredior nudus terram, egredior quoque nudus,
>   Quid frustra studeo, funera nuda videns?   [Lily]

> γῆς ἐπέβην γυμνὸς, γυμνός θ᾽ ὑπὸ γαῖαν ἄπειμι,
>   καὶ τὶ μάτην μοχθῶ, γυμνὸν ὁμῶν τὸ τέλος.[13]

Of the two Lily's is the better. More's version is heavy owing to the large proportion of spondees and, as well, More opens with a trochee, *Nudus*, instead of the allowable dactyl or spondee. Lily has gone further, in that he has attempted to follow the Greek placing of dactyls and spondees exactly.

The classicist's example had followers; for the practice of Elizabethan madrigal translators was of a piece. In the Yonge translation of Guarini's text as set by Luca Marenzio, the play of equivalence is so set that, as is clear from the Bassus (see opposite), the tonic accents are placed mostly on long notes approached by changes in pitch, reflecting melodic patterns of English speech. It thus happens that Yonge's patterns of English intonation match the Italian, for Marenzio had obviously arranged his melody around the stress patterns of Guarini's text; and through the medodic pattern comes mimetic form.

> Tirsi morir volea
> Gli occhi mirando, di Colei che adora;
> Quand'ella che di lui non meno ardea,
> Gli disse: Ohimè, Ben mio,
> Deh non morire ancora
> Ché teco bramo di morire anch'io.[14]

This should not, of course be considered in isolation from other metrical borrowings from modern languages, nor, indeed, from the question of classical metres in English. The Roman adaptation of Greek metres to Latin was taken as a worthy precedent by Richard Stanyhurst in his *Aeneid* (1582). His own attempt at Dido tries to combine metrical imitation with reproduction of *démarche*, and, like the medieval hymn-writers before him, Stanyhurst's equivalences are free in the extreme:

Of 5 The firſt part.   XVI. BASSVS.   Luca Maranzio.

Hirſis Thirſis to die deſired,   marking hir eyes ẙ

to his hart was nea-   reſt, and ſhe that with his flame

no leſſe was fyred, ſayd to him,   oh harts loue deareſt, alas forbeare to dye now,

ij.   by thee I liue, with the I wiſh to dye too, to dye too,

by thee I liue, with thee I wiſh to dye too, to dye too.

But the queene, in mean while, with carcks quādare deep anguisht,
Her wound fed by Venus, with firebayt smoldred is hooked.
The wight's doughtie manhood leag'd with gentilitie nobil,
His woords fitly plac'd with his heu'nly phisnomie pleasing;
March through her hart mustring, al in her brest deepely she printeth,
These carcking cratchets her sleeping natural hinder.

On the surface, his verse seems to show proper classical caesura and play between accent and quantity. But the preponderance of trochaic rhythms gives the verse a heavy movement, and some casuistry is needed to scan it.

The nineteenth-century controversy over classical metrics, is connected with Romantic theories on interlinear versions. As a beginning, Herder's Shakespeare songs (see page 47, above) framed the more intangible aspects of *démarche* within English verse forms, setting a precedent followed by Shelley, Taylor and de Nerval in their versions of the Faust Archangels' hymn. This touched even translation into Latin verse: against the normal nineteenth-century practice, E. F. Haupt (1773–1843) used accentual verse with close imitation of metre and *démarche* through mild dynamic equivalence:

Ah, quis reddet dies faustos?
Quis primitias amoris,

Fructum vel unius horae?
Quis me reddet reducis?
Vulnus nutrio dolore,
Atque luctus inexhaustos
Affert fuga temporis?
'Ach,' quis reddet dies faustos
Meis desideriis.[15]

Ach wer bringt die schönen Tage,
Jene Tage der ersten Liebe,
Ach,. wer bringt nur eine Stunde
Jener holden Zeit zurück!
Einsam nähr'ich meine Wunde
Und mit stets erneuten Klage
Traur'ich um's verlorene Glück.
Ach, wer bringt die schönen Tage,
Jene holde Zeit zurück.

In spite of Goethe's expressed preferences for prose, other Romantics, chiefly Humboldt and Schleiermacher, saw formal imitation as necessary for faithful reproduction of the original. Imitation of the minutiae of rhythm, sound and form was an essential element of the translator's criticism of his original, a penetration to the inner core of language that transfer of meaning alone could not bring about.

At the end of the eighteenth century, following the pioneer work of Klopstock, German versions of classical stanza forms were widely used: the Binder version of Horace *Odes* I. v (see page 94, above) is a late-nineteenth-century example showing the difficulty of keeping accent and quantity separate, since in German as in English, long syllables attract accent. Peaceful as the advent of classical metres was in German, in England there was considerable controversy, the most noisy phase of which was the quarrel between Matthew Arnold and F. W. Newman. Arnold demanded the hexameter for Homer, while Newman chose an analogical ballad metre. The unspoken assumption, that probably added fuel to the quarrel, was that Arnold subordinated his classicism to a Romantic view of language creativity, while Newman took for granted an Aristotelian view of language as instrument separate from content. Arnold (1861, 285) claims that the hexameter was selected because he 'required certain Homeric characteristics in a translation of Homer', an argument with strong antecedents not only among the Romantics but running right back to the Romans. But the kindest thing that can be said about Arnold's version on page 117, above, is that the scansion is not obvious, and even, in the case of fire at the end of the line, depends on personal idiosyncrasies of pronunciation.

Perhaps the most thoroughgoing attempt to introduce classical metrics into English was that of William Johnston Stone (1899), who worked from phonetic analysis. Proceeding from the fact that English does have syllables of variable length, he distinguished quantity from accent, arguing that English-speakers were not used to taking quantity as pertinent. Then, noting that classical rules for determining quantity do not apply in English, he evolved a few of his own, based, like those in Latin and Greek, on the place of the accent in the word – accent preserved the quantity of a syllable: for instance, open syllables before an accent were long, and final open syllables except those in -*y* were long. After the savaging meted out to him by Housman, to which we shall refer later, the issue went underground in English to surface in Leishman's Horace (1956). In his introduction Leishman repeats all the traditional justifications for metrical imitation found in Matthew Arnold and Humboldt: what is new and important is his rephrasing of Stone's arguments in terms of sentence patterns through distinguishing between words in the dictionary and the words in action (Leishman 1956, 44). This, based on sound observation and analysis of English sentence intonation makes explicit much that is implicit from Stanyhurst to Stone.

In contrast to English, classical metres flourished in German, accompanied by constant imitation of vernacular forms. Little had changed from the Herder precedent of 200 years before, judging from the discussion between Süskind and von der Vring on the Herrick translation on page 61. The operative principles isolated there are the following: that the translator must adopt the tone and style of the original, that this inevitably means that he must find the same rhythmic flow, and that flow will dictate form.

Much of the post-Romantic discussion of formal imitation reappears, by accident or design, in discussions of musical translation. The insistence by the compilers of *Hymns Ancient and Modern* on keeping the original melodies is probably an unadmitted influence of Romantic authenticity on the religious importance accorded to the traditional nature of the Latin hymns. The best of these translators, and those working in other areas of musical translation, sought more than the rhythmic accuracy of the sixteenth century: they were guided by the characteristics of the melody and of its history. To judge the tenor of nineteenth- and early-twentieth-century discussions, let us look at J. Smith's Latin version of *Comin' thro' the Rye*.[16] The characteristic bounce of the melody and flippancy of the lyrics dictate careful placing of tonic accents around the Scotch snaps. Further, the syntax is elliptical, a mixture of Tacitus and Plautus, with comic touches, like the satiric *pupa* (doll) for *lassie*.

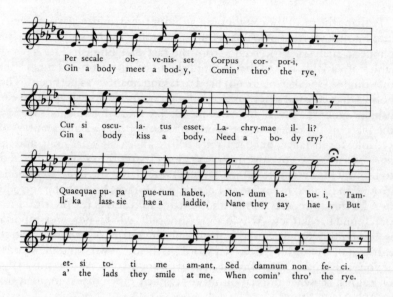

Per secale ob- ve-nis- set Corpus cor- por-i,
Gin a body meet a bod- y, Comin' thro' the rye,

Cur si oscu- la- tus esset, La- chry-mae il- li?
Gin a body kiss a body, Need a bo- dy cry?

Quaequae pu- pa pue-rum habet, Non- dum ha- bu- i, Tam-
Il- ka lass-sie hae a laddie, Nane they say hae I, But

et- si to- ti me am-ant, Sed damnum non fe- ci.
a' the lads they smile at me, When comin' thro' the rye.

Trifle though this is, there is little change in practice among Opera and
Lieder translators of the next sixty years. It is an excellent illustration of
Fox-Strangways (1921, 213):

> Words can sometimes do no more than not strike a jarring note; but that is
> a great deal. And to know what jars, or does not jar, we must consult the
> music, which has absorbed and epitomised the mood, and which, with the
> great songwriters, can not lie.

In contrast to mimetic forms, analogical form seeks to frame the translation in a form whose function is the same as that of the original. For the
rhythmic build of the target language does not always allow form to be
imitated, nor do forms always fulfil the same role.[17]

Latin poetic translation begins analogically, with the Livius Andronicus
Homer in Saturnians, the native Italic verse. But it was the fifteenth
century that established the analogical principle. In translating from vernaculars to Latin, it was assumed (cf. Braccese, page 83, above), that the
elegiac couplet was the translation equivalent of any lyric form, and the
hexameter of any epic or narrative form. In work into modern languages
most translators preferred native metres: one favourite was the fourteener,
the 'long metre' of the English Hymnal. Two notable translations in this
metre were Chapman's Homer (see page 122, above) and Golding's Ovid
(1567). Book VI of the *Metamorphoses* begins:

Tritonia unto all these wordes attentive hearing bendes,
And both the Muses learned Song and rightfull wrath commendes.
And thereupon within hirselfe this fancie did arise:
It is no matter for to prayse: but let ourself devise
Something to be commended for: and let us not permit
Our Majesty to be despisde without avenging it.

Praebuerat dictis Tritonia talibus aurem;
Carminaque Aonidum, iustamque probaverat iram.
Tum secum: 'Laudare parum est; laudemur et ipsae;
Numina nec sperni sine poena nostra sinamus.'

For both Golding and Chapman, the problem is one of filling up the space allowed in the metre, especially if one attempts to work line for line: both slow the style to fit form. Marlowe's Ovid (see page 144, above), on the other hand, with the iambic pentameter couplet, though working line for line, reproduces Ovid's compression even if, in the process, Ovid's comparative sobriety is lost. In French, after experiments with eight-syllable lines (Luc de la Porte, see page 84, above) and *dizains*, the Alexandrine became standard.

We have seen that French translators of the late seventeenth century opted for prose: what were they reacting against? The norm among those using verse was the strict Alexandrine, rhymed in couplets with a medial caesura. Of itself, it is not excessively spacious for Latin hexameters, but when, as Perrin's *Aeneid* does (see page 89, above) one translates one Latin verse in two French, narrative pace slows. There were some few who did translate line for line: faced with Shakespeare, Voltaire not without grumbling, used Alexandrine blank verse. Our example is from *Jules César* I. vii (1736):

N'êtes vous pas troublé, quand vous voyez la terre
Trembler avec effroi jusqu'en ses fondemens?
J'ai vu cent fois les vents et les fières tempêtes,
Renverser les vieux troncs des chênes orgueilleux;
Le fougueux Océan, tout écumant de rage,
Elever jusqu'au ciel ses flots ambitieux.

Are you not mov'd, when all the sway of Earth
Shakes, like a thing unfirm? O Cicero,
I have seen tempests, when the scolding Winds
Have riv'd thy knotty Oaks, and I have seen
Th'ambitious Ocean swell, and rage, and foam,
To be exalted with the threatning Clouds.[18]

With new form, came a new style, and Voltaire's Shakespeare is discip-lined by end-stopped lines and a diluted vocabulary. In English, the situation was not much different. Where French poets had come under the spell of the Alexandrine, English used the heroic couplet. Dryden's *Aeneid* and Pope's *Iliad* have an epigrammatic quality due to the end-stopped, rhymed couplets, quite different from the stylized simplicity of both originals. In Latin and Greek, likewise, the position of both hexameter and elegiac was consolidated, leading ironically to the same problems. The strongly classical manner of Milton survived, in some measure, his passage into Latin at the hands of Thomas Power (see page 111, above) and into Greek hexameters in John Plumptre's *Lycidas* (1797). Prior was not so fortunate: in Cowper's version of Prior (see page 90) the immense extra space left by the elegiac couplet demands filling, and, as we have seen, baroque ornament is piled on ornament.

Our problem was that, at this time, translation from Classical languages was used to teach grace in the mother tongue. But this training in style was to bring its own nemesis. Dryden had already been uneasy about the invariable Augustan manner, and he was to be followed by several who repeated the sixteenth-century reserves about rhyme, as, for instance, a certain P. Francis quoted by Draper (1921, 248):

> . . . the misfortune of our translators is that they have only one style, and
> that consequently all their authors, Homer, Virgil, Horace, Ovid, are
> compelled to speak in the same numbers and the same unvaried expression.

As a result, near the end of the century, formal authenticity became the watchword.

Apart from attempts to imitate form and use of prose, such searches for authenticity led down strange paths. Among English Classicists, Wardour Street English rose to caricature Romantic interlinearity by assuming that story-telling customs from ancient Rome, were equally valid in Victorian England. On his *Aeneid* (1866), which combines an enviable sense of Vergilian atmosphere with the grossest of Wardour Street English, John Conington writes:

> I have not indeed denied myself an occasional archaism, any more than
> Virgil himself has done, as I can not see that *mote* for *might* and *eyen* for *eyes*
> are any more objectionable than *faxo* for *fecero* and *aulai* for *aulae*.

While Conington and his colleagues tried to Romanize an archaic English, William Morris, in his Beowulf-tinged *Aeneid* (see page 95, above), had tried to match venerable Roman antiquity with venerable British. The French equivalent was the Homer experiment by Emile Littré, the lexicologist. He chose a reconstructed Old French for the following reasons:

C'est surtout à rendre avec rapidité et légérité des détails de récit et de conversation qu'excelle le français ancien, détails insupportables en vers s'ils avancent avec des articles, des particules et des conjonctions: lourdes béquilles dont le langage moderne ne sait pas se passer.

And, together with his Old French, he chooses the familiar epic conventions of the *Chansons de Geste* which are surprisingly Homeric:

Chante l'ire, ô déesse, d'Achille fil Pélée,
Greveuse et qui aux Grecs fit maux tant merveilleux
Livrant à Pluton l'ame maint guerrier généreux
Et le corps aux vautours et aux chiens en curée;
Ainsi de Jupiter s'accomplit la pensée,
Du jour où la querelle primerain fut levée
D'Atride roi des hommes, d'Achille fil des dieux.[19]

Though Littré's argumentation for this is almost purely linguistic, there are solid artistic reasons as well. The epic convention of the noble hero with his interminable genealogy, the aura of constant divine intervention, the warrior tradition, all are as proper to Old French as to Homer. Hence linguistic imitation is enshrined in analogical form.

It was from this sense that analogical form was adequate that attacks on classical metres arose in part. There was also the firm conviction of writers like Newman (1861, 9) that the predominantly consonantal nature of English made it too difficult. Tennyson (1863), for instance, argues from both points of view, seeking to justify by his own example the virtues of blank verse:

So many a fire between the ships and stream
Of Xanthus blazed before the towers of Troy,
A thousand on the plain; and close by each
Sat fifty in the blaze of burning fire;
And champing golden grain their horses stood,
Hard by the chariots, waiting for the dawn.

In a transparent reference to Arnold's version of this passage, he notes that the best of English poets 'have gone far to prove the impossibility of the task'; but the aura of *Mort d'Arthur* is hard to escape.

After a brief and successful fling with classical metres, C. S. Calverley examined the whole issue from a functional viewpoint. Taking as the essential element of classical metrics the rhythmic counterpoint between syllable length and stress accent, he comes to the conclusion that the different nature of both syllable length and accent in English precludes successful imitation of classical verse forms in English. In his damning review of Stone (1899) in the *Classical Review* Housman (1899) argues from the same premises that Stone's analysis of English intonation is not only unproven, but also improbable; and, with a hilarious comparison to playing cricket while standing on one's hands, closes the matter.

True, the nineteenth century did develop analogical forms that allowed the same space and almost the same disposition of material as the original: such are the analogical *Ad Pyrrham* versions on page 94, above. In Latin and Greek, classicists such as Sir Richard Jebb were widening the lyric repertoire of forms: fidelity to the original poet is to be achieved by choosing a classical model with characteristics similar to his. Such choice avoided eighteenth-century padding. Thus, when Ingram used the Second Asclepian for Matthew Prior's *Euphelia and Chloe*, the small compass allowed demands almost Horatian restraint and compression (see page 96, above). Problems rise when the original does not have classical qualities; because the intense economy of classical poetry takes uneasily to luxuriant romanticism, in his Latin version of Thomas Moore's *The Last Rose of Summer* (1969), Hermann Steinberger (1885–   ), prunes Moore's parallelism and makes his imagery more sober: the problem is lack of classical precedent for both subject and expression:

> Ultima aestatis rosa sola flores;
> A– – –iacent iamiam comites venustae;
> Non soror dulcis prope te rubescit,
>   Non gemit ulla– – –
>
> Non ego afflictam volo te dolere,
> Cum tenentur iam sociae sopore:
> Mortuas spargo foliis tuis, ut
>   Ipsa quiescas!
>
> Mox sequar vos: cum iam abiere amici et
> Indiget splendore corona amoris,
> Quis carens caris manet hoc libenter
>   Lurido in orbe?[20]

> 'Tis the last rose of summer,
>   Left blooming alone;
> All her lovely companions
>   Are faded and gone;
> No flowers of her kindred
>   Nor rosebud is nigh,
> To reflect back her blushes
>   Or give sigh for sigh.
>
> I'll not leave thee, thou lone one,

To pine on the stem;
Since the lovely are sleeping,
  Go sleep thou with them;
Thus kindly I scatter
  They leaves o'er the bed,
Where thy mates of the garden
  Lie scentless and dead.

So soon may I follow,
  When friendships decay
And from Love's shining circle
  The gems drop away.
When true hearts lie withered
  And fond ones are flown,
Oh! who would inhabit
  The bleak world alone.

Interestingly, Steinberger's technique is akin to the liturgical translators who trimmed the luxurious synonymy of the Roman Canon in the 1969 translations.

In the matter of poetic form then, there are two issues; the translator's approach to form and the relationship between form and style. After the pre-Classical period from Livius Andronicus to the dramatists whose approach to form was analogical, there is nearly 1,500 years in which translators worked almost entirely with mimetic form: Jerome's Hebrew Psalter in organic prose is the outstanding exception. Then, ostensibly because of phonological and structural differences, analogical form enters translation from vernacular poetry to Latin and while remaining in wide use until the present, attains the peak of its importance in England during the Augustan and post-Augustan period. Its two competitors are the organic prose of the French eighteenth century, which had repercussions elsewhere in Europe, and the mimetic form, particularly in translation from Classical languages, of German poetic translators. Extraneous form remains rare. Curiously enough, imitation of form did not automatically bring with it imitation of style: while the majority of mimetic translators take care to harmonize formal and stylistic imitation, medieval hymns and some nineteenth-century productions, like Matthew Arnold's Homer, are stylistically very different from their originals.

From the operational point of view, translation style, too, is subject to mimetic and analogical principles. Among translators, the choice between the two will depend very largely on assessment of purpose and value, on, in other words, balance between text, matter and readership. Solutions to the problem depend on resolving the Saussurean contradiction between the necessity and arbitrariness of the *signifiant–signifié* linkage in the linguistic sign. In the terms of our first chapter, this means determining whether the sign is sacramental or non-sacramental, i.e. whether features of the *signifiant* are part of the meaning of the *signifié* and thus, so inseparable from it that there are only identical and not functional equivalents.

Such cases are, however, rare. But there are contradictions. Boethius and other scientific translators, though proclaiming their disdain for style, have, as Jumpelt and other moderns remark, actually adopted a functionally equivalent style set by target-language conventions for scientific prose. Secondly, most style that is functionally equivalent adopts at least the word order of the original; exceptions are few: Cicero and some chemical translators of the end of the eighteenth century being the only ones that come readily to mind. Finally, in poetry, adoption of form does not mean adoption of style, and vice-versa. We have seen the loose style of the medieval hymn translations whose form is close to the Latin, and the tight Miltonic style of Thomas Power, in an analogical, not mimetic, form.

In the face of such variety of usage among translators, how has the balance between text and function, between language difference and bridging technique been characterized?

Eight

Rights and Duties: 'Fidus Interpres'?

Unless seen to be such, a sign is not a sign: for meaningful union between *signifiant* and *signifié* takes place in the sight of human observers. Though a few, for instance Housiaux (1967) and Levý (1969), accept this three-cornered sign relationship of St. Augustine as a basis for translation models, the more usual theoretical models are those of the de Marolles, Nida and Catford type, which sacrifice form to reader response, and those proposed by Huet, Benjamin and Meschonnic, for whom the original relationship between matter and form is to be kept at all costs. Axiomatic though it is, fidelity in translation is thus a bone of contention.

8.1 Fidelity, Spirit and Truth

As a technical concept, fidelity begins under a cloud, equated with literal translation: *fidus interpres* is the slighting term Horace applies to the literal translator in *Ars poetica* 133. Our second term, spirit, comes from Jerome and Augustine. Jerome, in his preface to the Pentateuch, asks his readers to assist him with their prayers, so that he can translate the Bible *eodem spiritu* (with the same spirit) as that with which it was written; and in *De civitate dei* xviii. 42, Augustine, referring to the legend that the seventy translators of the Septuagint all produced identical versions, emphasizes that 'in truth, there was the one spirit in all of them.' Our third term, truth, is also found in Jerome, whose espousal of the *Hebraica veritas* (the authentic Hebrew text) so distressed Augustine.

In the history of European translation, these three terms have been inextricably tangled. Until the end of the seventeenth century, fidelity most often means formal equivalence. Horace remained to haunt translators: when Joannes Scotus Erigena, to defend himself against the *culpam infidi interpretis*, loudly proclaimed his literality, a copyist with a wry sense of humour and knowledge of Horace wrote *fidi interpretis*. Lemaistre de Saci, recommending in 1647 that one should *suivre la fidélité sans blesser l'élégance et l'élégance sans blesser la fidélité*, signals the end of unquestioning acceptance of literality as fidelity. Already, in 1708, Samuel Clarke, translating Rohault's Physics into Latin, writes that through showing less concern for the words, he sought to render the author's meaning *fideliter et dilucide*. The fate of spirit is almost parallel. While the Latin word can mean creative energy proper to literature, Augustine clearly means the Holy Spirit. In the face of both meanings, Jerome, being Jerome, probably deliberately equivocated.

It is truth that is the most interesting of these terms. As spirit and truth are intimately connected in Augustine's theology (cf. *De doctrina christiana* III.xxvii.38), he seems to differ from Jerome, who probably meant by *Hebraica veritas* the authentic Hebrew text. Augustine, judging from his teaching on linguistic signs, means content. Boethius then, in distinguishing violently between *incorrupta veritas* and beauty of style obviously takes truth to be literality. Almost immediately after Boethius, Dionysius Exiguus, a member of the *Vivarium*, followed the *fidem sententiarum*, 'because he knew of nothing more valuable than the truth'. And, as Dionysius is as literal as Boethius, his *fides* and *veritas* clearly both mean literality. Yet, by the ninth century, in the rescript of Abbot Hilduinus, on one side, truth is identified with the words of the text: on the other, there is a promise to 'transmit the delightful flavour of the author's truth and understanding'. An ambiguous reference to content?

Further, 300 years later, in one of his several diatribes against translators, Roger Bacon writes that if a translation is to be true (*vera*), the translator must know both languages, and the science he is to translate. He then implies with a sneering reference to *Ecclesiasticus* xxxi. 9 that few do: 'Quis est hic et laudabimus eum? Fecit enim mirabilia in vita sua.' After him, *veritas* equates to content: by writing in his prologue to Vegetius that he was going to give *la pure vérité de la lettre*, Jehan de Vignay was not promising literality: his graphic behaviour in the Luke passage on page 82, above, shows his 'truth' is insight into realities signified by linguistic signs. This is how matters stood until the seventeenth century.

By 'fidelity', 'spirit' and 'truth', one denotes the translator's commitment. Such commitment, as indeed any responsibility, is shaped by the authority structure, 'personal' or 'positional', under which the translator places himself. Within personal authority structures, one takes responsible autonomy and retains power of decision, while positional structures impose formal patterns of obligation.[1] Commitment, then, based on a personal authority structure, gives rise to translation behaviours akin to an elaborated sociolinguistic code: the translator's approach to text is multi-dimensional, author or reader-centred and subjective. Where, however, the translator sees the relation between him and the text as positional, the approach is that of restricted sociolinguistic code: unidimensional, text- and object-centred and objective. Thus, depending on the type of authority his text exercises over the translator, fidelity will mean either collaboration or servitude.

It is Horace who best sums up the duty of a translator: in *Ars poetica* 131–5, he forbids the poet to venture where 'modesty forbids or the laws governing the work' (*operis lex*). As the central point of discussion, *operis lex* means two things: the first, always taken for granted, is communicative purpose, that is, the author's balance between symbol, symptom and signal. Only in the light of this can the second element in the *operis lex*, relationship between matter and form, have any significance. Thus the first hermeneutic movement, trust, is best interpreted within Ebeling's concept of responsibility and right to speak. True, one does approach the text with trust, but trust for what? Depending on whether the author offers the translator room for objective intellectual commitment or a chance to participate in some creative act, the movement of trust is a decision to be either slave, collaborator or master.

Thus, considering that the *operis lex* of the Bible was determined by its divine authorship, the commitment of Jewish and early Christian translators was that of servitude—what other authority structure but the positional did God exercise? Likewise, from Boethius on, technical and philosophical translators adopted positional relationships, laying claim to an objective and unidimensional trust. But, despite claims to objectivity, performance varies. Joannes Scotus Erigena is certainly subservient to his text, as is Boethius. Jerome's Biblical manner allows for minor discretion: the reading of *ianua* for πυλῶνα is an example. But there is a constant taking of initiative in so-called literal texts. We have seen Henricus Aristippus produce perceptive metaphor, and Jean de Vignay paint a grisly picture of the health of Lazarus. But even in legal texts, literality is varied at will. In the Old French Justinian on page 35, above, there are the odd calque and borrowing, (e.g. *volentés* for *voluntas*; and *esciences* for *scientia*), but beside them there are modulations, like the change of image in *perdurable* (long-lasting) for *perpetua*, and *ferme* for *constans*.

But such discretion was controlled by the fear of betraying the author's intention; for there were medieval translators who acted as masters of their authors. As did the pre-Classical dramatists, such translators did not allow authors abroad unchaperoned: where Caecilius Statius had dressed Menander in a more homely Roman image, so medieval translators, for example Jacques d'Amiens and Jehan de Malkaraume, bowdlerized and medievalized Ovid.

In explaining why freedom does not necessarily lead to abuse of the author, Roscommon's figure of friendship is most important. The essence of friendship, as Ebeling, Buber and C. S. Lewis point out, is shared insight, not domination. This was the Roman translator's *operis lex*: Catullus' Ode 51 is a painful sharing and redirection of Sappho's jealousy for the husband of one of her lovers: the Cicero extracts are Roman penetrations to the Homeric sense of the sacral and the Platonic view of creation. The operative importance of the personal authority structure of friendship is nowhere clearer than in Jerome. Though his attitude to the Bible was a positional one, his Ciceronian handling of content and form in Origen shows how far he had adopted a personal attitude to the Fathers.

So far, personal authority structures had resulted in free translations, and positional structures in literal translation. This dichotomy began to change during the late Middle Ages. The variable was interpreted experience: where the translator could visualize in his own terms, or add understanding on several dimensions, he stretched fidelity beyond the literal: hence the gusto of the battle scenes in the medieval Old Testaments (see page 143, above) and the heavily elaborated mystical theology of prayer and hymn texts. The fifteenth-century Humanist added another dimension, an approach to style through formal equivalence. Bruni Aretino treated Aristotle's philosophical texts as both symbol and symptom through a peculiar blend of collaboration and servitude: he followed the movement of the original, yet took the responsibility to select both formal and dynamic equivalence as necessary. Indeed such personal interpretation of the *operis lex* seemed to many the final argument against literal translation. Amos (1920, 146) quotes a certain W. L. Gent as saying:

> Some readers I make no doubt they will meet with in these dainty mouthed times, that will tax me with not coming resolved word for word and line for line with the author. . . . I used the freedom of a translator not tying myself to the tyranny of a grammatical construction but breaking the shell into many pieces, was only careful to preserve the kernel safe and whole from the violence of a wrong or wrested interpretation.

For the Renaissance translator of this type saw responsibility to text in terms of an exigent readership: fidelity was becoming a multidimensional concept for which a personal authority structure, by which one balanced regard for author, reader and language, was the only one possible.

To be sure, a large number of translators, especially before religious texts, adopted a positional relationship. Thomas Norton explained his treatment of Calvin this way:

> And they that watte what it is to translate well and faithfully, specially in matters of religion, do know that not the onely grammaticall construction of the words sufficeth, but the very building and order to observe all the advantages of vehemence and grace, by placing or acount of wordes, maketh much to the true setting forthe of a writer's minde. In the end, I rested upon this determination, to follow the wordes so neere as the phrase of the English tongue would suffer me.

And his text, as we have seen, is as literal as possible without offending against the language. But in the passion of the sixteenth-century religious situation, the boundaries between collaboration and servitude broke down under the pressure of the signal aim. Thus it is that all Biblical translators of the time, with, perhaps, the exception of Erasmus, mistake their own degree of objectivity and accuse opponents of a subjectivity they were not consciously guilty of. Even the revered Authorized Version came in for abuse from other Protestants. In his preface to Galen, Nicholas Culpepper attacks the companies for blasphemy and presumption:

> They have added certain thousands of words both in the Old Testament and the New, thereby corrupting in many places the sense of the Holy Ghost, in all places conveying it like a nose of wax to their own present judgement, and if you ask them why they did so, they will tell you it was to make sense of it; Blasphemous wretches, did the Spirit of God when it penned the Scriptures pen nonsense?

This is very much a positional approach to the authority of the text, which is taught at considerable length by Huet. Indeed, the whole of Huet can be summed up in one precept which has haunted translators ever since: if a translator is to be faithful, he must leave nothing to his own judgement (Huet 1661, 27).

But the sixteenth century had brought into the marketplace the conviction that fidelity went beyond words. Early seventeenth-century critics then redefined 'spirit', removing the theological sense it had had in Jerome. Thus, as the creative energy of the work which was to be sought on the terms of the target language, it came to denote a personal attitude to the original rather than a positional attitude: Antonio de Medinella, for instance, separates spirit from words, and Dryden in the preface to the *Sylvae* distinguishes 'drawing the outlines true' and 'making it graceful . . . by the spirit which animates the whole'.

The basic problem is one of culture clash. Alexander Tytler's discussion makes it clear that fidelity is not to be positionally judged by formally matching words and expressions, but by the functional approach of whether the translation is acceptable to the public to which it is directed (Tytler 1790, 147):

'Πάντως, θαρσαλέη, κύον ἀδεές, οὔ τί με λήθεις
ἔρδουσα μέγα ἔργον, ὅ σῇ κεφαλῇ ἀναμάξεις. . . .' (*Odyssey* xix. 91–2)
These opprobrious epithets, in a literal translation, would sound extremely offensive from the lips of the περίφρων Πηνελόπεια whom the poet has painted as a model of female dignity and propriety. . . . Of this sort of refinement Mr Hobbes has no idea; and therefore he gives the epithets in their genuine purity and simplicity:

> Bold Bitch, said she, I know what deeds you've done,
> Which thou shalt one day pay for with thy head.

We can not fail, however, to perceive that Mr Pope has, in fact been more faithful to the sense of his original, by accommodating the expression of the speaker to that character which a modern reader must perceive to belong to her:

> Loquacious insolent, she cries, forebear!
> Thy head shall pay the forfeit of thy tongue.

As during the Middle Ages, fidelity was now a multidimensional concept: indeed, it is somewhat more complex. For, though the eighteenth-century translator, no matter his field, sought to link reader and subject or genre, he was careful to allow the original text some control over his version, as in Campbell (1789, 445–6):

> The first thing, without doubt, . . . is to give a just
> representation of the sense of the original. . . . The second thing is, to
> convey into his version, as much as possible, in a consistency with the
> genius of the language which he writes, the author's spirit and manner, and
> . . . the very character of his style. The third and last thing is, to take care,
> that the version have, at least, so far the quality of an original performance,
> as to appear natural and easy. . . .[2]

In Campbell, then, positional attitudes are coupled with behaviour more appropriate to a personal authority structure, a characteristic of a large number of late-eighteenth-century translators. As, therefore, such translators took responsibility for judging what is valuable in the author, from this flows a long controversy over the translator's right to correct his original, with, on one side, Maillet-Lacoste (1843, 23), who refused to 'languish with his author', to Menéndez y Pelayo (1900?, I. 48):

> . . . uno versión, como fiel espejo que ha de ser del original, debe reproducir
> todas suas desigualidades, incongruencias y asperas, su pena de degenerar en
> imitación o parafrásis.

After the beginning of the nineteenth century, scientific translation partly drew back from the personal attitude a man like Kerr had to Lavoisier, without, however, going consistently towards literality. In literary translation, fidelity follows intangibles, rather than units of the text. Indeed the letter of the text is expendable, provided that the function of the version vis-à-vis the reader is the same as that of the original: in this particular, MacKenna meets Cicero, and Pound is at one with Batteux.

Though there was still intense fear of paraphrase, translators, having taken it for granted that the differences between source and target languages brought responsibility for interpreting the author's intentions, accepted the attendant risks. Indeed Belloc (1924, 153) sums up almost the whole history of discussion on this point with his distinction between spirit and letter:

> Good translation must . . . consciously attempt the spirit of the original at the expense of the letter. Now this is much the same as saying that the translator must be of original talent; he must himself create; he must have power of his own.

Fidelity, then, was the obligation of deciding what was important, and the choice of how this was to be reproduced or represented in the target text. Much depends on the insight the translator brings to his text, on the balance perceived between meaning, sound and form. Since Cicero there has been a persistent implication that, as *signifiant* and *signifié* are function-ally indissociable, there are universal rhetorical and poetic devices based on natural links between sound and meaning. In *De oratore* III.lvii.216, Cicero tells his reader that every impulse of the mind has its own facial expression, sound and gesture. And, on Cavalcanti, Pound writes:

> As for the verse itself, I believe in an ultimate and absolute rhythm as I believe in an absolute symbol or metaphor. The perception of the intellect is given in the word, that of the emotions in the cadence. It is only in the perfect rhythm joined to the perfect word that the two-fold vision can be recorded.

Operatively, the problem here is that considerable linguistic freedom has been claimed in the interests of preserving the expressive priorities of the source text. The reasoning is one based on personal responsibility. Levik (1970, 168), for instance, speaks of liberty as necessary to avoid being sidetracked by details. And in this he echoes Gide's letter to André Thérive (1928), in which Gide speaks of the absolute necessity of *incessants détours* if the translator is to write a text equivalent to that of the author.

This is at its most obvious in song translation. Instrumentally, trans-lators are bound to a certain play of rhythm and tone colour: the question has been discussed at considerable length. But under the instrumental problem is the more significant question of how to reproduce the implica-tions of tone and harmonic colour. From medieval hymns to opera, translators have had to balance sense against sound; and film dubbers have had to work within the confines set by lip-movements. In neither case has there been a mechanical or easy way towards equivalence, or any way the author can avoid taking responsibility. The following passage from Spaeth (1915, 295) speaks for itself:

> In his famous setting of the 'Erlkönig', Schubert makes use of a number of dramatic devices which the careful translator must imitate if possible. The terror-stricken cry of the child, for instance, is intensified in the phrase 'Siehst, Vater, du den Erlkönig nicht?' by the position and sound of the word *nicht*. But this phrase has been translated, 'Seest, father, thou the Erlking, alas!' A pitful subterfuge, even supposing that an actual child could have used such an exclamation as 'alas!'

In competition with this personal approach, especially in Germany, is the hermeneutic theory that turns on the ancient meaning of *Geist* (spirit) as the mystical bringer of truth. As we have seen Herder's own practice (cf. his Shakespeare on page 47, above) was to seek *Treue* by allowing the word order of the original to influence the structure of the translation. For only in this way could one preserve the life-giving *Geist* of the original. The most significant Romantic discussions are in Schleiermacher (1813) and von Humboldt (1816), in which *Treue* is defined as the 'veritable character of the original' that continues its life through the version. And, in an image used a century later by Walter Benjamin, the original 'shines through' the version.

It is to be expected that the attitude of the Romantics and their heirs is a positional one: Goethe's image of the translator as a prophet among his own people demands truth through subjection to the original writer, not merely to his ideas but to his *ipsissima verba*. The first is characterized by Schleiermacher as *dolmetschen* and only the second, as *übersetzen*, a distinction that runs through German translation criticism since. The crux of the matter is what Schadewalt (1927, 253) and Rüdinger (1938, 181) call *Individualität*, which can only be attained if, as well as being *sinngetreu*, the translation is *wortgetreu*. Thus Buber (1954, 351) criticizes the great Biblical translations, the Vulgate, Luther's Bible, and the Authorized Version, for being so concerned with meaning that they do not give a true sensory impression of the original Hebrew and Greek. Indeed, if one goes further along this road one comes to Benjamin and Meschonnic for whom the *matérialité* of language, the physical aspect, the manner of signification, is exalted over signification itself.

This essentially positional approach entails the restricted-code reaction to social control: for it assumes one dimension, denying the duality of the linguistic sign and obeying abjectly without presuming an intention beyond the form of words. To this, one contrasts the behaviour of MacKenna and Pound, whose insistence on the essential creativity of translation assumes the personal responsibility of finding intention behind the symbol. And, indeed, arguments in favour of this approach during the 1960s invoke the image of translator as slave only to reject it.

The root of the argument over fidelity is, then, the almost theological point of whether translators owe subjection or collaboration. Probably the most complete attempt to give some philosophical sense to the question is that of Steiner (1975, 300ff), where the test of fidelity is taken to be 'significant exchange' and 'conservation of the energies of meaning':

> The translator, the exegetist, the reader is *faithful to* his text, makes his
> response possible, only when he endeavours to restore the balance of forces,
> of integral presence, which his appropriative comprehension has disrupted.

As a member of the target-language community, the translator shares its resources and as a member, perhaps temporary, of the source-language community, he attempts to supplement them. The translator's role as a bridge between cultures is discussed at least as early as Terence. His mission, however, is not the passive one this image would suggest, but one of actively changing the target-language culture: again, Cicero knew this. The problem has always been the means: on one side, one preaches liberty (Levik 1970, 168):

> . . . seule la traduction basée sur le principe de la liberté au nom de la
> fidélité peut remplir les hautes missions de l'art de traduire, à savoir:
> (1) être un intermédiaire entre les peuples, les conduire vers l'amitié
>   s'appuyant sur la compréhension mutuelle;
> (2) enrichir le trésor de la poésie nationale;
> (3) assurer la survie des poètes.

On the other, the positional approach (Ayala 1965, 16):

> Aquélla que se propone conducir a los lectores hacia el original traducido,
> trasladando con la maxima fidelidad su estructura externa. . . .

The problem is two views of 'the energies of meaning': that which ignores the reader or takes him for granted, and that which includes him.

More serious than this is the constant refusal of translation theorists, both literary, linguistic and religious, to question the aims they assign to translation. The reader is not at all contingent; and as Buber and Ebeling well saw, the first evidence of any energy in meaning is its effect on him, and, according to Newton's first Law of Motion, his effect on it. The second energy of meaning is the play in the *signifiant* between its *significations et valeurs*, and, by the same principle, the effect of *signifié* on *signifiant*. These can only take place within communicative intention: thus, an attempt at objectivity, a positional approach in our terms, will produce a different character from a subjective, personal approach.

Therefore, one agrees with Steiner that the usual instrumental arguments between literal and free translation are contingent. While agreeing also that translation depends basically on a hermeneutic motion, one usefully supplements the Heideggerian paradigm by developing Buber and Ebeling. Every hermeneutic movement into text is an assessment of communicative aim, of balance between I and Thou. Steiner's conservation of the energies of meaning is then Horace's *operis lex*: the translator seeks to find in the translation the same equilibrium between *signifié*, *signifiant* and human user as in the original text and not to represent the original as something it is not.

8.2   IS TRANSLATION POSSIBLE?

In the light of this last statement, controversy is inevitable. The original reason given for the impossibility of translation is that languages are different: as Sirach tells the readers of *Ecclesiasticus*:

> I ask its readers to come well-disposed to their task, and to follow me closely, making allowances for me whenever I seem to have failed in the right marshalling of words, as I pass wisdom on at second hand. Hebrew words lose their force when they are translated into another language.

We find no such qualms among classical translators: indeed Cicero seems to have believed in a universality of rhetorical devices based on natural links between sound and meaning: in the *De oratore* III.lvii.216 he writes that every idea and emotion has its own natural form of expression. But Jerome obviously felt the weight of disapproval, and Augustine confessed that, because of lack of matching resources, unfamiliar Hebrew words like *amen*, *alleluia* and *hosanna* should be borrowed.

The disasters attending Aristotle's introduction into European universities in the thirteenth century were taken by Roger Bacon (1271?, 475–80) as irrefutable proof that translation of Greek philosophy into Latin was doomed by the differences between Arabic, Greek and Latin. So far, arguments had concerned objective texts: forty years later, as the foundations were laid for the Humanist movement, Dante and his circle argued from the loss of energy in the Latin versions of the psalms, that literary translation was impossible too (1308?, 15):

> Sappia ciascuno, che nulla cosa perlegame musaico armonizzata si può della una loquela in altra trasmutare, senza rompere tutta sua dolcezza e armonia.

E questa à la ragione perche Omero non si muto di Greco in Latino, come l'altre scritture che avemo de loro; e questa à la ragione per che i versi del Psaltero sono senza dolcezza di musica e d'armonia; che essi furone trasmutati d'Ebreo in Greco, e di Greco in Latino, e nella prima trasmutazione tutta quella dolcezza venne mano.

An instrumental view of the problem, granted, but one with a vision wide enough to require refutation. Thus Bruni Aretino a century later attacks the medieval statement that language differences were insurmountable as a smokescreen for incompetence.

While Bruni Aretino proclaimed, as Roman Jakobson was to do much later, that there was no resource lacking in any language for adequate translation, the translators of the Renaissance were not as categorical: Latomus (1518, 12) recognized that certain properties of Latin and Greek were peculiar to them, and Roger Bacon's metaphor of racking wine with its attendant risk of souring reappears, leading to a Morton's Fork mentality: Du Bellay (1549, 64–5), while complaining that a close translation refuses the same grace, notes that an attempt at *le Naïf* will inevitably be stilted.

Thus, by the end of the sixteenth century, discussions on the possibility or impossibility of translation revolved around a primitive contrastive linguistics and around the idea of 'spirit', either preserving it, as Power had hoped in his Milton (1691), or putting it back in the manner of Denham's Vergil (1632). Under this was the strong difference between those like Huet, who castigated every translator who did not adopt positional attitudes, and the normal run of translators, whose acceptance of personal authority structures left them free to aim at functional rather than formal equivalence. This was not achieved merely through selective linguistic equivalence, but also through acclimatizing the foreign work to a whole new build of metaphysics and rhetoric.[3]

Under the impetus of the Romantics, however, the rules were subtly changing. The theory of the interlinear version following so quickly on universalist language theories made the linguistic aspect of the question contingent. But seeing that language was λόγος, as a piece of literature continued the life of the author, so it set up resistance to translation. All the ideas expressed in Humboldt on language and literature as history of a people come out in Hugo (1864, 1442) writing on his son's French version of Shakespeare:

Shakespeare résiste par le style: Shakespeare résiste par la langue. Est-ce là tout? Non. Il résiste par le sens historique; il résiste par le sens légendaire.

The Romantics, as we have seen, aimed at remaking the work itself in the target language and, on those grounds, despite their fascination with translation, despaired. Hence, at the end of the century one could claim with Marc Monnier that the translation should not reproduce the original, while yet being able to discharge its functions. Thus, for William Morris, translation was to aid in purging the ugliness of late Victorian England: therefore, as Vergil had embodied the ancient virtues of Rome, albeit at the behest of Augustus, Morris and his group gave England a Vergil in Victorian English with touches of Anglo-Saxon. After all, Vergil had read and imitated Ennius.

But did this resolve anything?

Not for Benedetto Croce. Working from the aesthetic role of language he found falsification to be inevitable in translation. He blames translators for 'pretending to effect the remoulding of one expression into another, like a liquid poured from a vase of one shape into a vase of another'. Further, in his view, the translator puts the original 'back in the crucible and mingles it with the personal characteristics of the so-called translator' (Croce 1902, 68). As far as his somewhat incoherent statements can be interpreted, he puts the translator in a most untenable position by rejecting both the freedom of his contemporaries in literature, the closeness of the technical translator, and the hermeneutic approach. Adopting a personal view of the translator's responsibility will inevitably lead to abuse of freedom: adopting a positional is asking the impossible. Readers of Dante linked with Croce the passage quoted from the *Convivio*, and Crocean fears haunted the century.

Similar reserves had long been expressed by ethnolinguists. In a series of articles on Bible translation, A. F. Chamberlain (1901, 166) had argued that the 'inborn genius' of a people cannot be transferred perfectly, a Humboldtian theme that had been discussed by Vossler, among others. Channelled in other ways by the climate left by Sapir and Bloomfield, this attitude culminates in statements like that of Punya Sloka Ray (1962, 182): 'Translation is impossible in theory, if not in practice'; and in the cruel epigram from Ida Rhodes, a prominent researcher in machine translation: '. . . the words *translation* and *mistranslation* which connote the same concept'.

The body of contrary opinion remained strong. The reasoning is essentially based on personal authority structures which allow the translator to substitute. Carne-Ross (1964, 27) gives expression to this by recommending 'transposition' as a critical concept because 'translation is at present being saddled with an improper obligation: it is supposed to "give you the original".' The predominant line of reasoning in support of this position is the production of a profit-and-loss balance: Malblanc (1967, 287), for instance, distinguishes between a 'correct' and an 'exact' translation, seeing the first as always possible, the second as not always acceptable.

Whether translation is possible or not, turns on the concept one has of fidelity, which we have linked to the Bernstein concepts of positional and personal authority. If one is to define translation as conservation of the energies of meaning, what is the energy and what the meaning? For, in a real sense, the translator has many cards stacked against him. Here, Quine's indeterminacy of translation is crucial, resting as it does, not only on the multiplicity of relationships possible between word and object, but also on the unpredictability of human reactions to signs, linguistic and otherwise. But is translation the meeting of strangers that Quine envisages? It is here that Roscommon's figure of friendship is so important, for no matter how distant, friendship rests on shared insight and experiences. It is insight that ensures that through their freedom Cicero, Chaloner and MacKenna are as true to their originals as Chaucer, Bruni Aretino and Hermbstädt who are literal. And through lack of insight, Zukofsky converts Catullus into Gertrude Stein, and Michel de Marolles etiolates Vergil's Dido. Hence the contingency of instrumental arguments. If the translator's expectation of the author matches that the author had of himself, through this basic insight the translator will take him on his own terms, and Jakobson's values and message, Steiner's energies of meaning, will be preserved.

The responsibility of translation, then, begins with understanding the *operis lex*. Its first aspect is communicative function, the balance, in Buhler's terms, between symbol, symptom and signal. The second is then assessing, in the light of this balance, values in the message. As in daily encounters with other people, this assessment asks what the other is willing to give and why. And parallel with this assessment is that of self: am I capable of translating this author on his terms and, indeed, am I interested? Trust, then, establishes relationships, assesses values, asks whether the author's meaning has a sufficiently interesting stock of energy before one's own measure of oneself. From this flows the translator's intention, his terms of reference which drive him towards the unidimensional, objective, positional relationship, or the multivalued, subjective, personal relationship. It is here that fidelity or infidelity starts.

For, balancing himself against his own conception of the *operis lex*, the translator determines the limits of his own discretion. The point made by translators as distant as Cicero and Ezra Pound is that refusal to exercise discretion in certain texts is as radical an infidelity as faulty understanding of lexicon: in other words, using a positional or symbol approach where a personal or symptom approach is appropriate, and vice-versa, effectively precludes good translation. It would seem that texts that are obviously technical have been translated in a consistent manner since at least Boethius: a positional, literal approach has been used. The controversies and vilifications of previous ages have come about in other types of translation through changes in boundaries between genres and communicative purpose, and consequently in assessment of responsibility. Each age in cases of doubt sees the balance of personal versus positional differently.

And cases of doubt are legion. Because utterances seldom have only one of the three aims of Buhler, and sensitivities to language vary from society to society, documents like the Bible, Aristotle's philosophical works or Vergil have been translated in ways reflecting, not only the competence of the translator, but the ideology and the needs of the age. In this, the Classical age, the sixteenth century and the modern period have, in general, balanced their own creative sense against text itself. It is only in the pre-Classical period, the Middle Ages and the poetry of the seventeenth and eighteenth centuries that the translator has blatantly overriden the judgement of the author with his own. The opposite behaviour, treating literary texts as if they were objective, is found only at the end of the Middle Ages and after the Romantics. If there is a moral responsibility in translation, it flows from initiative appropriately or abusively taken, from correct or incorrect assessment of the original.

There are no total multidimensional translations: in all communion, private areas lie hidden, and, even where a work does not resist translation in certain periods, each age seeks new values in what has gone before. For this reason, great books have been translated countless times, the versions reflecting different insights. Hence there abound translations that have conserved the energies of meaning enough to transform language or intellectual activity: Jerome's Vulgate, Moerbeke's Aristotle, Luther's Bible, the Authorized Version . . . the list is long. But equally, such translations float on a sludge of failures where the flow of energy between theme, language and reader has been distorted by alien values and made to yield a false message.

Nine

Theory of Translation?

Had translation depended for its survival on theory, it would have died out long before Cicero. Yet its practice has always assumed principle, the professional conscience of 2,000 years being summed up in Roman Jakobson's 'translator of what messages? betrayer of what values?'

It is only by tracing translators' perceptions of message and values that theory is anything but a pipedream. For in all utterances, 'message' and 'values' are generated within Augustine's and Saussure's relationship between *signifiant*, *signifié* and speaker–hearer. In normal speech behaviour, interpretation being as active as speech, the hearer experiences the intent and content of another's utterance through the signs received. In translated utterances, however, the hearer of the target text experiences the original only indirectly. According to Jiri Levý's model quoted on page 64 above, the target-language reader actively interprets the translated text by an experience deemed parallel to the translator's recreation of the original; and this is itself parallel to the original drafting by the author. In short, the translator teaches his public to 'read' the original (cf. Govaert 1971, 436, quoted on page 34), leading him through Buber's 'language experience', a concept at the centre of Levý's model.

Of the three branches of theory, that detailing purpose is by far the richest. In contrast, theoretical models of translation technique, though the subject of scattered comment since Roman times, are not systematized coherently until the twentieth century. But the translator's repertoire of operations was complete well before Cicero. The third aspect of theory, coordination of aims and technique, has been discussed since Cicero, but it is doubtful whether anyone will ever better Batteux and Campbell in their discussions of expressive priorities and ways of attaining them.

If translation is as basic to language as has been claimed by Vossler and other hermeneutic theorists including Steiner, it follows that its many genres are as interesting to a comprehensive theory as the traditional literary orientation. Citroen (1966) is wrong to deny the existence of two 'professions' among translators: indeed, if there were not at least two, translation could not reflect as well as it does the multiplicity of language experience. Multiplicity of genre does not preclude unified theory; unity in theory does not deny variety in genre.

Distinctions between technical and literary translation are deceptively easily exemplified, but simplistic: indeed, one would be hard put to it to see what is essentially technical about late-eighteenth-century science texts like Kerr's Lavoisier (see page 164, above). Likewise administrative and religious texts show all shades of objectivity: the objectivity of the *Vetus latina* highlights the flagrant bias of the great sixteenth-century Bibles, the blatant propaganda of Augustus's Greek *Res gestae* sits ill with the accuracy of the League of Nations treaties.

The basic variable is not one of subject matter, but one of intent. The translator assesses the function in Buhler's terms of his source text; he judges his responsibility in relation to his reader, even if, as in the case of Benjamin, that means ignoring him. And from this balance he takes up a positional or a personal attitude to the text. Some translators of peculiar flexibility have adopted either to suit their text: witness Jerome's contrasting attitudes to the Bible and the Greek Fathers. The controversy surrounding Jerome is typical of the way in which the surface issue of literal versus free has been taken to be a theoretical issue rather than an indication of a basic attitude towards language itself and the source text.

If language is taken as 'object-centred' or purely informational, the translator will suppress any awareness of aims other than symbol, and will therefore be able to find some reason for literal handling. This technical approach is not restricted to technical translation, nor does its justification rest on language theory alone: assumptions of the essential objectivity of language signs have been bolstered by the theological argumentation of Jews and Christians, by the artistic theories of the Romantics, by the needs of scientists. In a sense, this is a null-form solution to theory, as its proof is an appeal to authority, an acceptance of duties but no rights in the most extreme cases. On the other hand, the constant thread running through artistic translation theory is a view of language as 'person-centred' or multidimensional: Quintillian's *aemulatio*, Roscommon's image of friendship, Boswell's contrast between Homer's bassoon and Pope's flageolet, Steiner's hermeneutics, all assume that the essential function of language is sympton or signal, all place the translator face to face with his author. Such an attitude also transcends genre. As this person-centred attitude implies near-equality at least between translator and author, it accords the responsibility to interpret the multidimensional language use of the original.

Given the traditional focus of translation theory on intent, theory-building has been the province of the man of letters. Acceptance of multiplicity of intent brings questioning; from questions come judgements; from judgements, theory; from theory, experimentation. Hence the wide range of technique in creative translation, and the constant examination of aims and methods. As those who submit themselves to a unidimensional view of language abdicate the right to assess the sign at more than face value, they need not question, and theory becomes irrelevant except as a pragmatic description of operations. It is indeed unfortunate for the development of theory that the person-centred view of language behaviour has been seen as contradictory to the object-centred, and that partisans of these extremes consider they have the whole truth.

In adopting an aggressively personal attitude towards their originals, the pre-Classical Roman dramatists took a summary view of content with a somewhat cynical view of Roman receptivity to Greek sophistication. Like Shakespeare, they had a public to please, and theoretical discussions, beyond counterattacks on critics, were not of interest. A century or so later, in the anti-commercial atmosphere of aristocratic Rome, Cicero discusses his translation practice according to a view of language and literature strikingly parallel to that of Cecil Day Lewis. Where Lewis had sensed emotional parallels between his attitude to England and Vergil's to Rome, Cicero writes that any translator of Demosthenes must become Demosthenes: his own public career furnished ideal conditions for such a venture, giving full opportunity for the development of the statesman's insight in troubled times. As we see in *De finibus*, Cicero took for granted that language structures differed radically, so that translation from Greek meant bending Latin to express to the full his insight into matter and manner of the original. This productive rivalry between intimates is Quintilian's *aemulatio*. It is a typically classical concept; for while the pre-Classical dramatists deliberately interposed themselves between author and public, Cicero and the Latin translators of the next 200 years sought to express parallel matter through parallel language resources.

As with the pre-Classical dramatists, there is doubt whether the Jews and early Christians had any interest in theory. Their attitude was positional: God being the author of the Bible, man was necessarily inferior; God being the author of truth, the Bible account was objective. Therefore there was no leeway for discussion on the relationship between things and language signs. By their attempts to harmonize Jewish and Roman thrusts of translation practice, Jerome and Augustus mark a watershed. For both men, translation was essentially a teaching activity: but they differed on the modalities of teaching.

Augustine makes a clear distinction between meaning and language. Meaning is assumed to be a constant, and language is a series of signs which acts as a channel between concept and hearer. In translation, as concepts are shared between languages, the sign structure of the translation must reflect that of the source text if error is to be avoided. But the demands of clear teaching forbid unnuanced adoption of positional relationships. The existence of synonymy in the translator's language resources is discussed and exemplified several times in the *Enarrationes in Psalmos*. For Augustine good translating demanded judgement. Augustine, then, marks the beginning of theory: he left an elementary model of transfer which had considerable influence in the theological disputes of the fourteenth century. More importantly, his adaptation of Aristotle's theory of signs was to recur until our own day.

Jerome, the Ciceronian, had, one suspects, little time for theory. Yet his wider view of meaning and purpose of text prompted him to draw up a typology of translation based on distinctions in attitude and purpose. In texts in which *aemulatio* could be fitting, such as the Greek Fathers, he adopted, instinctively it seems, a personal attitude, and followed Ciceronian precedent. In Biblical texts, however, he behaves traditionally, using the normal positional argument that one does not tamper with God's word, and consoling his Ciceronian self by the reflection that his Vulgate style reflects that of the Septuagint.

By his severely positional stand, Boethius marks a decisive crisis in Western translation, which then enters on 500 years of rigid pragmatism and objectivity. For Boethius, translation was object-centred, and therefore one abdicated one's right to judge. The Boethian attitude to textual matching is found exemplified in Henricus Aristippus, whose reason for close formal equivalence is the typically positional fear of betraying the author's meaning. Naturally, the promising theoretical developments in Augustine, occurring between the lines in Jerome's many discussions of his practice, were cut off; and the early medieval rule of thumb dispensed with theory and its disturbing questions.

The first attempts at theoretical discussion after Boethius occur in specific crises. Acting on the assumption that translators should act as a bridge between the warring sections of the Christian church, Humbertus de Romanis suggested in 1260 that a model of translation could be built on scholastic theories of language; but beyond some acute comments in Aquinas nothing came of it. Similarly, a century later, the Lollards sought to defend themselves by an amateurish examination of the issues of translation and failed. These attempts are notable as concentrating on translation method, rather than translation aim. The aim was still objective information, but medieval language theory provided a basis for questioning modes of transmission.

From about the tenth century there is considerable vernacular translation of poetry. The manner is not unlike that of Terence and his contemporaries, and attention to theory is as rudimentary. Not that there lack statements on the translator's responsibility to author and public; but in an age that sought a reason for practically everything, translation somehow escaped the attention of the theorist.

In one particular, however, the medieval period left its mark on all discussions after it. The question of whether translation is possible or not is normally traced to Dante's *Convivio*, and most discussions since have quoted Dante's condemnation of translators who neglect form and rhythm. But, half a century before, Roger Bacon had based his case for impossibility on objective grounds of lack of matching between the intellectual content of words. The disasters befalling Aristotle and Aristotelians in the medieval universities are laid squarely at the door of translators, on the grounds that translation is impossible. Where moderns refer deliberately to Dante, Roger Bacon's case reappears in an unlikely Firthian garb in Catford. Not that belief in the impossiblity of translation has ever stood in the way of a determined translator.

But for all the practical activity of that thousand years, Boethius's statement that style and content are inimical is a poor basis for practice or theory. The atheoretical period he ushered in ceases abruptly after the fall of Constantinople in 1453. As the political situation of the Eastern Empire became more tenuous, refugee Greeks fled to the West, many of them setting up schools of rhetoric and study circles. The *De interpretatione recta* (1420?) of Bruni Aretino is a manifesto of these early Humanists. In essence, it is a return to Cicero's *aemulatio*, and an assumption of personal attitudes. The strength of the Humanists and of their sixteenth-century successors was insight into the purpose of the original, coupled with enjoyment. Even the casual reader of prefaces from *De interpretatione recta* to the equally belligerent dedication of the Authorized Version to James I, senses that the translator is aware of the various functions of language, has made a judgement of how they are exemplified by his text, and is out to share his enjoyment of his author with the public. As yet, theory remains incomplete, treating only the purpose for which one translated, and ignoring the practical exploration of techniques, that was pursued with such unbridled gusto.

For the 400 years from Bruni Aretino to the Romantics, the weight of translation theory lay in a contrastive rhetoric. From the beginning of the seventeenth century, especially after the work of Port-Royal on *grammaire générale*, the grammatical component was becoming more important. This is abundantly clear from the Port-Royal rules preserved by Nicholas Fontaine and from the voluminous notes appended by Pope, Dryden and Desfontaines to their translations. Translation theory begins to draw directly on grammatical theory in Charles Rollin; and by the appearance of Campbell (1789), there is considerable understanding of the theoretical bases of translation technique, and much perceptive comment on relations between technique and expressive purpose. As far as translation is concerned, the most important forerunners of Campbell are Batteux (1747–8) and Houbigant (1753).

Except for the fulminations of Huet (1661), who is almost medieval in his defence of literality, the period is marked by aggressive personal-authority attitudes. That Port-Royal and their German and English contemporaries abused their position is undeniable; but whether they could have survived if they had not is a difficult question. There are two remarkable features in the period: the first is the gradual equilibrium reached by the 1750s between literality and freedom in prose translation. Indeed Batteux and Campbell treat both extremes as equally offensive. The second, contradictory but convergent, is the abandonment of close literality in technical translation. This is particularly notable in the chemical translations from the University of Edinburgh, of whom Kerr and Keill are examples. The Romantic revolution, in translation as in literature, was brewing.

This, then, completes discussion of Steiner's first period. Though it is not a unit, empiricism is the characteristic found from the very beginning. It falls into five parts. The pre-Classical period, with the unbridled freedom of the Romans and the formal equivalence of the Jews, is echoed by the double manner of both medieval period and the seventeenth and eighteenth centuries. Resemblances are not merely technical, they are also attitudinal. Terence and Caecilius share with Jacques d'Amiens and the Augustans, regard for their originals, tempered by doubts of their ability to please the public unless thoroughly acclimatized. The early Bible translators prefigure both Boethius and Daniel Huet in their conviction that the translator is at the mercy of his text. But, whereas attempts to found theory fail during the Middle Ages, and the Classical and Renaissance periods neglect the details of operations, the eighteenth century finishes with a relatively coherent body of theory, whose analysis of purpose and operations was true to the sober practice of prose translators from about 1750 on. Not unexpectedly, its rationalistic character and empiricism was its downfall in the Romantic climate.

Steiner's second stage, 'one of theory and hermeneutic enquiry', begins with Schleiermacher's *Über die verschiedenen Methoden des Übersetzens* (1813). This critical document, however, owes its main themes to Herder's *Fragmente* (1777), thereby ignoring the pragmatic legacy of the eighteenth century. Definite ideologies of translation date from this time. Romantic goals and distinctions were still to have a powerful influence on moderns such as Ezra Pound and Georg von der Vring, and still to be felt by the more empirically minded like Ronald Knox. Coherent and exciting though these Romantic theories of national and artistic purpose are, they actually mark a regression when measured even against Rollin, fifty years before. For their assessment of translation technique is not only inadequate, but completely out of step with what they were actually doing. At the root of the practice of the *Interlinearversion* is the task of keeping the order of sememes, the actual grammatical structure being reinterpreted and sacrificed if necessary. Granted, facets of style were often imported from the target language, but none suffer from grammatical calque, none are really strange, except for the solemn lunacies of Wardour Street English. In order to keep word order, the incidence of dynamic equivalence is high, too high for this manner to be considered first cousin to literality. At the root of the Romantic analysis of technique, such as it was, is the error refuted half a century before by Batteux: that similarity of word order demanded similarity of syntax. In essence there is nothing new about the *Interlinearversion*: it is fully developed in Houbigant (1753) and Smollett (1750). Nor is it peculiar to creative translation: it is found from Salusbury (1661) to Hermbstädt (1803). And its purpose and method had already been discussed by Batteux and Campbell.

For all that, however, the Romantics mark a decisive summation of the late-eighteenth-century revolt against the excesses of such as Pope and Desfontaines, a revolt affecting both literature and linguistics. In literature, they drew attention away from the translators' rights as a virtuoso to his duties as a skilled intermediary between literatures. Virtuosity was to be tempered by taste. To the technical aspect of theory, nineteenth-century historical linguistics contributed nothing. Despite the importance of his theories on word order, Weil too contributed nothing; and nineteenth-century descriptive linguistics has no effect until the publication of Bally's *Précis de stylistique* in 1909. Through Bally, the *Völkerpsychologie* was to pass on to the translation theory of both Geneva and Prague the strong Humboldtian influence under which it developed. Not only was this current isolated from literature; it also had little effect on rival linguistic theories. Both the American Structuralists and the London School of J. R. Firth were prevented by their anti-mentalist postulates from taking advantage of this work. Those translation theories developed in response to specific situations: the Americans developed translation theory in the context of anthropological research and Christian missionary activity; the English to fit the needs of colonial administration.

Isolation of theorist from theorist continues into Steiner's third period which begins after the Second World War. For individual schools of linguistics, it is one of consolidation, each school, beginning with Vinay and Darbelnet (1958), producing an extended account of its theory of translation techniques. Translation, following the literary discussions of Croce, Pound and Gide, gradually becomes a philosophical and epistemological problem. There is, as yet, little understanding of one group of theorists or translators by another, although dialogue does commence in Brower's *On Translation* (1966a) and Arrowsmith and Shattuck's *The Craft and Context of Translation* (1964).

We are still at the beginning of Steiner's fourth stage, whose essential mark is consolidation of theory. Beginning with Mounin (1963), the descriptions of process so far typical of the Prague and Geneva approaches to translation are related to underlying functions of language; and, as an extension of American and English work, sociolinguistics begins to take an interest in translation. It was natural, after the work of Cassirer, Buber and Heidegger, that interest would quicken in the Romantic theories of translation, and that important symbolist documents, like Benjamin (1923), would come out of obscurity. On this count alone, one would expect that the wall between man of letters and linguist, between aims and method, would begin to weaken.

And, indeed, exploration of what other theorists have to offer one's own discipline is the essential characteristic of the last ten years. Holmes (1970; the report of the Bratislava Conference on Translation as an Art, 1968) reads uncannily like the late-eighteenth-century critics in its insistence on the reciprocal relationship between linguistics and other language disciplines in translation theory. And the importance of hermeneutics to the work of Jakobson and Wandruszka is equally clear.

It is not difficult to see in the Romantic period a series of parallels to the goals, and often the manner, of Classical Rome and Renaissance Europe, or in the somewhat self-opinionated twentieth century, a mirror of the seventeenth and eighteenth centuries. For, while technical translators keep strictly to positional attitudes to their task, the latitude allowed themselves by their personal-attitude confrères varies from a sincere but illusory semblance of subjection to the original in Goethe, to Steinberger's obvious assumption of authority over Moore. We have thus come full circle: the modern Latinist, like the ancient, remakes his original, while the Septuagint translator's care for the very breath of the Hebrew reappears in Buber's and Meschonnic's translations of the Hebrew Bible.

Clearly, the repertoire of translation techniques has not evolved: there is little to choose between Cicero and Pound in range of dynamic techniques; Nabokov's formal equivalences would not seem strange to the translators of the *Vetus latina*. There is no satisfactory attempt at analysis before Batteux (1747–8), and the sophisticated modern analyses have not affected the practice of translation at all deeply. In this area there does seem to be the alteration R. H. Robins discerns in the history of linguistics itself between data-orientation and theory-orientation:[1] the data-oriented eighteenth century is followed by the theory-oriented nineteenth. Bally's early-twentieth-century work is data-oriented, while theory-orientation becomes important once Vinay and Darbelnet (1958) and Catford (1965) have made their mark.

It is only by recognizing a typology of function that a theory of translation will do justice to both Bible and bilingual cereal packet. It is obvious that the Dionysiac language theories of Heidegger are as inadequate as the empirical communication models of Nida. These both ignore the multifarious purposes of language: language can frustrate communication, act purely as a medium of information, or create new worlds for its users. As language lives through multiplicity of function, so does translation.

There is no more than apparent contradiction between the main thrusts of language theory: sacrament and instrument are both sign functions. In the context of language, let alone translation, exclusive attention to either of these aspects of sign function prevents theory from reflecting the reality of its object. Moreover, the central contribution of grammatical or linguistic theory is analysis of the manner in which are attained the goals sought by philosopher, critic or sociologist. That translation is an art, its theory a contribution to epistemology, is hardly grounds for denying the relevance of applied linguistics.

It is not merely to modern practice that theory applies. If a comprehensive theory be possible, it must seek the essential harmony between the practice of all ages and genres, and give a satisfactory analysis of differences. Such an ideal theory would grow from the hermeneutics of Buber and Ebeling. Both recognize a typology of language act, from deep communion to the automatic rituals of courtesy, from manipulation to communication. This aspect of hermeneutic theory, sensing of intent, is an important bridge between language philosophy and the pragmatic sociolinguistic theories of Bernstein, Halliday and Labov. For translation is as social an act as language, and as individual. Ebeling is doubly important, for almost alone among modern hermeneutic theorists, he has a clear vision of the interaction between linguistic philosophy and linguistics in language theory.

Just as features of an utterance reveal purpose and expressive needs, so do those of a translated text. The essential variable is what the translator sees in the original, and what he wishes to pass on. Each age and culture translates anew; by their contemporaries translators are judged according to criteria peculiar to time, place and genre. If the translator must be a man of other cultures besides his own, is it too much to ask that his critic be likewise a man who crosses frontiers of space and time? Such largeness of vision is rare. Yet it is indispensable to those who would presume to sit in judgement on colleagues of the past. For unless our modern attitudes are tempered by understanding of past criteria, have we any right to expect fair judgement from the future?

Appendix

Originals Translated by Several Hands

ARISTOTLE (*both from Oxford Classical Text*)

De caelo I.1 (268a):

Ἡ περὶ φύσεως ἐπιστήμη σχεδὸν ἡ πλείστη φαίνεται περί τε σώματα καὶ μεγέθη καὶ τὰ τούτων οὖσα πάθη καὶ τάς κινήσεις, ἔτι δὲ περὶ τὰς ἀρχάς, ὅσαι τῆς τοιαύτης οὐσίας εἰσίν.

(The science concerning nature is almost entirely about bodies, magnitudes, their changes and movements; and, as well, the principles which belong to such substances.)

Translators:
J. Argyropylos (1460?; repr. Paris, 1886), p. 143; William of Moerbeke and Robert Grosseteste (1271; *Aristotelis opera*, Venice, 1562–74, v) p. 135; N. Oresme (1377; ed. A. D. Menut and A. J. Denomy, *Medieval Studies* III (1941), 185–280 and IV (1942), 159–297), p. 136 (from the Latin of Moerbeke and Grosseteste).

Nicomachean Ethics I.1 (1094a):

Πᾶσα τέχνη καὶ πᾶσα μέθοδος, ὁμοίως δὲ πρᾶξίς τε καὶ προαίρεσις, ἀγαθοῦ τινὸς ἐφίεσθαι δοκεῖ.

(Every art and every body of knowledge, and likewise action and choice, seems to be in view of some good.)

Translators:
Bruni Aretino (1420?; repr. Paris, 1510), p. 162; Grosseteste (1270?; ed. R. A. Gauthier, *Aristoteles latinus* XXVI, Leiden and Brussels, 1972), p. 162; *Ethica nova* (ibid.), p. 135; D. Lambinus (1560?; ed. S. Maurus, repr. Paris, 1886), p. 183.

Pseudo-Aristotle, *De mundo* (ed. Bussemaker, Paris, 1854, III.627–42):

κόσμος μὲν οὖν ἐστι σύστημα ἐξ οὐρανοῦ καὶ γῆς καὶ τῶν ἐν τούτοις
περιεχομένων. λέγεται δὲ καὶ ἑτέρως κόσμος ἡ τῶν ὅλων τάξις τε καὶ
διακόσμησις, ὑπὸ θεῶν τε καὶ διὰ θεῶν φυλαττομένη. ταύτης δὲ τὸ μὲν μέσον,
ἀκίνητον τ' ὄν καὶ ἑδραῖον, ἡ φερέσβιος εἴληγε γῆ, παντοδαπῶν ζῴων ἑστία καὶ
μήτηρ.

(Now the universe is an agglomerate of heaven and earth and those things
belonging to them. This is also put in another way: the universe is a placing
and an ordering, kept in being by the gods and through the gods. The
central point of it, immovable and stable, is the fertile earth, being the
home and begetter of all living things.)

Translators:
Apuleius (A.D. 150?; ed. J. Beaujeu, *Apulée, Opuscules philosophiques*, Paris,
1973), p. 140; G. Budé (1534; Basle, 1557), p. 72.

BIBLE

Luke xvi. 19–21 (ed. Erasmus, 1524; repr. London, 1962); bracketed
passages taken from edition of A. Merck (Rome, 1958):

ἄνθρωπος δέ τις ἦν πλούσιος, καὶ ἐνεδιδύσκετο πορφύραν καὶ βύσσον
εὐφραινόμενος καθ' ἡμέραν λαμπρῶς· πτωχὸς δέ τις ἦν ὀνόματι Λάζαρος, ὅς
ἐβέβλητο πρὸς τόν πυλῶνα αὐτοῦ ἡλκωμένος καὶ ἐπιθυμῶν χορτασθῆναι ἀπὸ
[τῶν ψιχίων] τῶν πιπτόντων ἀπὸ τῆς τραπέζης τοῦ πλουσίου· [καὶ οὐδεὶς
ἐδίδου αὐτῷ·] ἀλλὰ καὶ οἱ κύνες ἐρχόμενοι ἐπέλειχον τὰ ἕλκη αὐτοῦ.

(Now there was a rich man, and he dressed in purple and fine linen,
feasting luxuriously every day. And there was a poor man, Lazarus by
name, who was stationed at the entrance to his house, covered with sores,
wishing to gorge on [the crumbs] that fell from the rich man's table. [And
nobody gave them to him.] But the dogs coming licked his sores.)
(Bracketed passages are omitted in most critical texts.)

Translators from Erasmus's Greek:
Authorized Version (London, 1611), p. 176; G. Campbell (London, 1789),
p. 77; Erasmus (1524), p. 74; Luther (1534; repr. Weimar, 1906–61), p. 176;
W. Whittingham *et al.* (London, 1576), p. 74.

Translators from longer Greek Text:
Jerome (383?; repr. Rome, 1592), p. 134; *Vetus latina* (quoted Augustine, Sermon 33a, *Corpus christianorum latinorum* XLI), p. 69.

Translators from Vulgate:
Jehan de Vignay (1340?; in Berger 1884, 226–7), p. 82; R. A. Knox (London, 1948), p. 52.

CALVIN

Institutes of the Christian Religion III.3 (3rd edn, 1560)

> Etsi iam ex aliqua parte docuimus quomodo fides Christum possideat, et per ipsum fruamur eius bonis: hoc tamen adhuc obscurum esset nisi effectuum, quos sentimus, accederet explicatio.

(Although we have already taught to some extent how faith possesses Christ, and how through him we enjoy its gifts, this however would still be unclear unless there followed an explanation of the effects which we feel.)

Translators:
Calvin (1561; W. Baum *et al.* (eds), *Corpus reformatorum* III, Halle, 1865), p. 104; T. Norton (1561; London, 1574), p. 75.

CASTIGLIONE

Il cortegiano (Venice, 1528):

> Lassando adunque che le virtú dell'animo che le hanno da esser communi col Cortegiano, come la prudenzia, la magnanimità, la continenzia, e molte altre; e medisimamente quell condizioni che si convegno a tutte le donne, come l'esser bona e discreta, il saper governar le facultà del marito e la casa sua e i figlioli quandi è maritata, e tutte quelle parti che si richieggono ad una bona madre di famiglia: dico, che a quella che vive in corte parmi convenirsi sopra ogni altra cosa una certa affabilità piacevole, perla qual sappia gentilmente intertenere ogni sorte d'omo con ragionamenti grati ed onesti, ed accomodati al tempo e loco, ed alla qualità di quella persona con cui parlerà, accompagnando coi costumi placidi e modesti, e con quella onestà che sempre ha da componer tutte le sue azioni, una pronta vivacità d'ingegno, donde si mostri aliena da ogni grosseria; ma con tal maniera di bontà, cha si faccia estimar non men pudica, prudente ed umana, che

piacevole, arguta e discreta: e però le bisogna tener una certà mediocrità difficile, e quasi composta di cose contrarie, e guigner a certi termini appunto, ma non passargli.

Translators:
B. Clerke (1571; London, 1612), p. 183; T. Hoby (London, 1561), p. 73.

CICERO

Ad fam. xvi. 5 (also numbered *Ad fam* xvi. 3) (ed. Stephanus, 1538–9):

Omnes cupimus, ego in primis, quam primum te videre, sed, mi Tiro, valentem. Qua re nihil properaris; satis cotidie te videro, si valebis. Utilitatibus tuis possum carere: te valere tua causa primum volo, tum mea, mi Tiro. Vale.

(We all wish, myself in particular, to see you as soon as possible, my Tiro, but well. In this matter, hurry nothing: I shall see you soon enough, if you are well. I can survive without your services. I want you to be well, first for your own sake, then mine, my Tiro. Farewell.)

Translators:
E. Dolet (Paris, 1542), p. 168; A. Manutius (Venice, 1563), p. 168; J. Webbe (London, 1620?), p. 88.

DE SANTEUIL

Hymn from Common of Apostles, Paris Breviary (1670?; repr. *Penguin Book of Latin Verse*, 332):

Supreme quales arbiter
Tibi ministros eligis,
Tuas opes qui vilibus
Vasis amas committere.

(Supreme ruler, what sort of servants do you choose for yourself, who love to entrust your treasures to worthless vessels?)

Translators:
C. S. Calverley (1870?; London, 1901), p. 150; J. Saurin (Paris, 1699), p. 104.

GOETHE

Faust, Archangels' Chorus (Weimar 1887, vol. 14–15):

Die Sonne tönt nach alter Weise
In Brüdersphären Wettgesang,
Und ihre vorgeschriebne Reise
Vollendet sie mit Donnergang.
Ihr Anblick gibt den Englen Stärke,
Wenn keiner sie ergründen mag;
Die unbegreiflich hohen Werke
Sind herrlich wie am ersten Tag.

Translators:
G. de Nerval (1828; ed. F. Baldensperger, Paris, 1932), p. 49; P. B. Shelley
(1822; *Complete Works*, ed. R. Ingpen and W. E. Peck, London and New
York, 1965, IV. 322), p. 150; B. Taylor (Cambridge, Mass., 1870), p. 94.

HOMER

(In cases of doubt the Oxford Classical Text has been taken as correct.
Otherwise originals are as noted below).

Iliad i.1–7:

Μῆνιν ἄειδε, θεά, Πηληϊάδεω Ἀχιλῆος
οὐλομένην, ἣ μυρί᾽ Ἀχαιοῖς ἄλγε᾽ ἔθηκε,
πολλὰς δ᾽ ἰφθίμους ψυχὰς Ἄϊδι προΐαψεν
ἡρώων, αὐτοὺς δὲ ἑλώρια τεῦχε κύνεσσιν
οἰωνοῖσί τε πᾶσι, Διὸς δ᾽ ἐτελείετο βουλή,
ἐξ οὗ δὴ τὰ πρῶτα διαστήτην ἐρίσαντε
Ἀτρεΐδης τε ἄναξ ἀνδρῶν καὶ δῖος Ἀχιλλεύς.

(Sing, Goddess, the accursed wrath of Peleus' son, Achilles, which
brought countless sorrows on the Greeks, and sent forth to Hades the
brave souls of heroes, and gave them [i.e. their bodies] as prey to all the
dogs and vultures. But the will of Zeus was fulfilled, from the time when
the first quarrel rose between the son of Atreus, king of men, and divine
Achilles.)

Translators:
Chapman (1598; ed. Allardyce Nicoll, Princeton, 1956; original, ed. Spondanus, 1583), p. 122; Littré (1847; original, ed. F. Wolf, Leipzig, 1817),

p. 201; Pope (1715–20; ed. M. Mack, London, 1967; original, ed. J. Barnes, Cambridge, 1711), p. 59.

Iliad viii.560–5:

> τόσσα μεσηγὺ νεῶν ἠδὲ Ξάνθοιο ῥοάων
> Τρώων καιόντων πυρὰ φαίνετο Ἰλιόθι πρό.
> χίλι᾽ ἄρ᾽ ἐν πεδίῳ πυρὰ καίετο, πὰρ δὲ ἑκάστῳ
> εἴατο πεντήκοντα σέλαι πυρὸς αἰθομένοιο.
> ἵπποι δὲ κρῖ λευκὸν ἐρεπτόμενοι καὶ ὀλύρας,
> ἑσταότες παρ᾽ ὄχεσφιν, ἐΰθρονον Ἠῶ μίμνον.

(So many fires, lit by the Trojans, appeared between the ships and the river Xanthus before Troy. A thousand fires shone in the plain. At each one sat fifty men, in the light of the bright fire, their horses eating white barley and oats stood by the chariots, awaiting the fair-throned morning.)

Translators:
Matthew Arnold (1816, 262), p. 117; Tennyson (1863, 708), p. 201.

Odyssey xviii.136–7:

> τοῖος γὰρ νόος ἐστὶν ἐπιχθονίων ἀνθρώπων
> οἷον ἐπ᾽ ἦμαρ ἄγῃσι πατὴρ ἀνδρῶν τε θεῶν τε.

a. (reading ἐπ᾽ as a preposition)
(For the mind of mortal men is such as day by day the father of gods and men directs.)

Translator:
Cicero (50 B.C.?; quoted in Augustine, *De civitate dei* v.8), p. 81.
b. (reading ἐπ᾽ as a particle separated from its verb)
(For the mind of mortal men is changeable as the day the Father of gods and men brings on.)

Translator:
Pope (1725), p. 115.

HORACE

Odes I.v. 1–5 (all editions used agree with the Oxford Classical Text):

Quis multa gracilis te puer in rosa
Perfusus liquidis urget odoribus
Grato, Pyrrha, sub antro?
Cui flavam religas comam,
Simplex munditiis? . . .

(What slender boy, scented with heady perfumes, courts you among the many roses in your pleasant bower, Pyrhha? For whom are you binding up your yellow hair, simple in its art?)

Translators:
(all versions are cited in R. Storrs, *Ad Pyrhham*, London, 1959): W. C. Binder (1855), p. 95; G. Chiarini (1916), p. 94; Luc de la Porte (1584), p. 84; Luis de León (1631), p. 84; Menéndez y Pelayo (1882), p. 95; L. Richault (1879), p. 95.

JESU DULCIS MEMORIA

Text and melody below from *Liber usualis* (Tournai, 1950). Melody on p. 106 from *Hymns, Ancient and Modern*.

(Jesus, sweet to the memory, giving true joy of heart; but above honey and everything is his sweet presence.)

Translators:
Anon. Old French (cited in Thomson 1942), p. 193; Hopkins (ed. R. Bridges, London, 1956), p. 106; Neale (1854; in *Hymns Ancient and Modern*) p. 106.

JOHN CHRYSOSTOM

Anaphora from Eucharistic Liturgy (original facing Leo Tuscus's Latin):

ἄξιον καὶ δίκαιον σὲ ὑμνεῖν, σὲ εὐλογεῖν, σὲ αἰνεῖν, σοὶ εὐχαριστεῖν, σὲ
προσκυνεῖν ἐν παντὶ τόπῳ τῆς δεσποτείας σου· σὺ γὰρ εἶ θεὸς ἀνέκφραστος,
ἀόρατος, ἀκατάληπτος, ἀεὶ ὤν, ὡσαύτως ὤ, σὺ καὶ ὁ μονογενής σου υἱὸς καὶ τὸ
πνεῦμά σου τὸ ἅγιον.

(English on p. 187 a sufficiently close crib.)

Translators:
Anon. (early 20th cent., London, n.d.), p. 187; Leo Tuscus (12th cent., ed.
Claudius de Sanctis, Antwerp, 1562), p. 72.

LAVOISIER

Traité élémentaire de chymie (Paris, 1789):

> C'est un phénomène constant dans la nature et dont la généralité a été bien
> établi par Boerhaave, que lorsqu'on échauffe un corps quelconque, solide ou
> fluide, il augment dans tous les sens.

Translators:
Hermbstädt, S. F. (Berlin, 1803), p. 171; Kerr, R. (Edinburgh, 1793), p.
164.

MILTON

Paradise Lost I.1–6 (1667; Oxford, 1958):

> Of Man's First Disobedience, and the Fruit
> Of that Forbidden Tree, whose mortal Taste
> Brought Death into the World, and all our Woe,
> With loss of Eden, till one greater Man
> Restore Us, and regain the blissful Seat,
> Sing, Heavenly Muse, . . .

Translators:
Chateaubriand (Paris, 1836), p. 93; T. Power (Cambridge, 1691), p. 111.

MORE

Utopia (London, 1516):

Ars una est omnibus viris mulieribusque promiscua: agricultura, cuius nemo est expers. Hac a pueritia erudiuntur omnes partim in schola traditis praeceptis, partim in agros viciniores urbi quasi per ludum educti, non intuentes modo, sed per exercitandi corporis occasionem tractantes etiam.

(One art is common to all men and women: agriculture, of which nobody is ignorant. This they are all taught from childhood, partly by rules taught in school, partly after having been taken into the fields right by the city as if in a game, not only watching, but also working as a chance to exercise their bodies.)

Translators:
G. Antonio Medinella y Porres (1637; Madrid, 1805), p. 164; R. Robynson (London, 1551), p. 160; S. Sorbière (Amsterdam, 1643), p. 160.

Ovid

Metamorphoses vi.1–4 (ed. Aldus Manutius, Venice, 1515–16):

Praebuerat dictis Tritonia talibus aures
Carminaque Aonidum iustamque probaverat iram.
Tum secum: 'Laudare parum est, laudemur et ipsae
Numina nec sperni sine poena nostra sinamus.

(Pallas had lent her ears to these words, and had approved of the songs of the Muses and of their just anger. Then, to herself: 'It is too little to praise. Let us be praised, and let our Godhead not be despised without punishment!')

Translators:
A. Golding (1567; ed. J. F. Nims, New York, 1965), p. 195; *Ovide moralisé* (14th cent.; ed. C. de Boer, Wiesbaden, 1966), p. 58.

Petrarch

Sonnet CII (facing Braccese translation):

Cesare, poi che'l traditor d'Egitto,
Gli face il don de l'onorata testa,
Celando l'allegrezza manifesta,
Pianse per gli occhi fuor, si come è scritto:

Ed Annibal, quando a l'imperio afflitto
Vide farsi fortuna sì molesta,
Rise fra gente lagrimosa e mesta,
Per isfogare il suo acerbo despitto;
E così avvem che l'anomi ciascuna
Sua passion sotto'l contrario manto
Ricopre co la vista or chiara or bruna.
Però, s'alcuna volta io rido o canto,
Facciol perch' i' non ho se quest' una
Via da celare il mio angoscioso pianto.

Translators:

A. Braccese (1490?; *Carmina*, ed. A. Perosa, Florence, 1943), p. 83;
T. Wyatt (1528; *The Poems of Thomas Wiat*, ed. A. K. Foxwell, New York, 1964, I. 13), p. 137.

PLATO

Phaedo 59d:

> *ΦΑΙΔ.* Ἐγώ σοι ἐξ ἀρχῆς πάντα πειράσομαι διηγήσασθαι. ἀεὶ γὰρ δὴ καὶ τὰς πρόσθεν ἡμέρας εἰώθεμεν φοιτᾶν καὶ ἐγὼ καὶ οἱ ἄλλοι παρὰ τὸν Σωκράτη, συλλεγόμενοι ἕωθεν εἰς τὸ δικαστήριον ἐν ᾧ καὶ ἡ δίκη ἐγένετο· πλησίον γὰρ ἦν τοῦ δεσμωτηρίου.

(I shall try to tell you everything from the beginning. For always, during the days before, we used to go to Socrates, I and the others, assembling before dawn in the room in which the trial had taken place—for it was near the prison.

Translators:

M. Ficino (1464; repr. Lyons, 1590), p. 172; Henricus Aristippus (1160; ed. L. Minio-Paluello, *Plato latinus* II, London, 1940), p. 141.

PRIOR

Euphelia and Chloe (original facing Ingram text):

The Merchant to secure his treasure,
Conveys it in a borrowed name:
Euphelia serves to grace my measure,
But Chloe is my real flame.

Translators:
Cowper (1779; *Cowper's Poetical Works*, ed. G. Gilfillan, Edinburgh, 1854, II. 231), p. 90; J. K. Ingram (ed. R. Y. Tyrrell, *Dublin Translations*, 348), p. 96.

RABELAIS

Gargantua ch. 18 (original, Lyons, 1608):

> Maistre Janotus, tondu à la césarine, vestu de son lyripipion à l'antique, et bien antidoté l'estomac de coudignac de four et eau béniste de cave, se transporta au logis de Gargantua, touchant devant soy trous védeaulx à rouge muzeau, et traisnant après cinq ou six maistres inertes, bien crottez à profit de ménage.

Translators:
G. Perfetto (Naples, 1914), p. 152; T. Urquhart (1653–94; ed. C. Whibley, *Tudor Translations* 24–6, New York, 1967), p. 148.

ROMAN LITURGY

Collect for Palm Sunday (Roman and Sarum Missals):

> Omnipotens sempiterne Deus, qui humano generi ad imitandum humilitatis exemplum Salvatorem nostrum carnem sumere et crucem subire fecisti, concede propitius, ut et patientiae ipsius habere documenta et resurrectionis consortia mereamur.

(Almighty, eternal God, who, for the human race, as an example of humility to be imitated, made our Saviour take flesh and undergo the cross, mercifully grant that we may be worthy to have the fruits of his suffering and a share in his resurrection.)

Translators:
Book of Common Prayer (London, 1552), p. 176; Draft Book of Common Prayer (Washington, 1977), p. 155; International Commission on English in the Liturgy (Washington, D.C. 1969), p. 107; Commission internationale liturgique pour les pays de langue française (Paris, 1969), p. 107.

VERGIL

Aeneid iv.1–5 (ed. Ruaeus, Paris, 1682; and F. A. Hirtzel, Oxford, 1900):

At regina gravi iamdudum saucia cura
Vulnus alit venis et caeco carpitur igni.
Multa viri virtus animo, multusque recursat
Gentis honos: haerent infixi pectore vultus
Verbaque, nec placidam membris dat cura quietem.

(But the queen, long since wounded by grave disquiet, feeds the wound with her veins, and is being worn away by the secret fire. The manifold worth of the man and the manifold honour of his family keep running through her mind: they cling, fixed fast in her breast, his face and words; and her disquiet allows no peaceful rest to her members.)

Translators:
C. Day Lewis (New York, 1952), p. 63; Dryden (1697; ed. J. Kingsley, London, 1958), p. 89; M. de Marolles (Paris, 1649), p. 89; W. Morris (London, 1876), p. 95; P. Perrin (Paris, 1648–58), p. 89; R. Stanyhurst (1582; ed. D. van der Haar, Paris and Amsterdam, 1933), p. 195.

Notes

CHAPTER I

1. See Gerhard Ebeling, *Introduction to a Theological Theory of Language*, trans. from German by K. A. Wilson (London, 1973), 154ff.
2. See Bloomfield, *Language* (1933; New York, 1961), 139. With this compare Firth, *Papers in Linguistics 1934–1951* (London, 1957), 181: '. . . we study language as part of the social process, and what we may call the systematics of phonetics and phonology, of grammatical categories or of semantics, are ordered schematic constructs, frames of reference, a sort of scaffolding for the handling of events.'
3. See G. Guillaume, *Leçons de linguistique 1948–49, Série A* (Québec and Paris, 1971), 105ff.
4. See W. Hirtle, *The Simple and Progressive Forms, an Analytical Approach* (Québec, 1967), 19.
5. Cf. P. Seuren, *Operators and Nucleus* (Cambridge, 1969), 103: '. . . a universal deep structure . . . would provide important insights into the process of translation. . . .' Contrast Steiner (1975, 105) who points out that as the distinction between formal and substantive universals is unclear, this goal has not been realized.
6. See N. Chomsky, *Aspects of the Theory of Syntax* (Cambridge, Mass., 1965), 30: 'The existence of deep-seated formal universals . . . implies that all languages are cut to the same pattern, but does not imply . . . that there must be a reasonable procedure for translating between languages.'
7. In this connection see Politzer (1956) on the three degrees of translatability: $M = M_1$ (identity); $M \neq M_1$ (lack of identity); M and M_1 share features or functions.
8. Cf. Buber (1923, 9): '. . . for in actuality, speech does not abide in man, but man takes his stand in speech and talks from there'. On Lévi-Strauss, see Umberto Eco, 'Social Life as a Sign System', in D. Robey (ed.), *Structuralism: an Introduction* (Oxford, 1973), 57–72.
9. See Vossler (1925, 181): 'Merely listening to and understanding the speech of my countryman and contemporary is a translation of his meaning into my own.' Compare Steiner (1975, ch. 1), and Edmund Leach, 'Structuralism in Social Anthropology', in Robey, op. cit. 37–56.
10. Cf. J. Wain, 'Poetry', in C. B. Cox and A. E. Dyson (eds.), (Oxford, 1972), 370: *The Twentieth-century Mind, 1: 1900-1918,* 'To the Symbolist, the ego is an encumbrance and action a mere toing and froing. His instrument is contemplation; he surrounds himself with stillness and non-event.' For a religious application see John of the Cross, *Ascent of Mount Carmel*, III.xiii.2.

11. Cf. Steiner (1975, 333): 'Ordinarily translation, even literary translation, moves on no such wilful lofty plane. It aims to import and naturalise the content of the source-text and to stimulate, so far as it is able, the original executive form of that content.'

CHAPTER 2

1. Cf. K. R. Bausch (1970, 14): 'Il nous paraît donc nécessaire de relier le problème de la qualité en traduction d'abord à la pratique de la linguistique différentielle, afin d'arriver ensuite à la discussion plus détaillée de son influence sur le but linguistique.' Contrast H. Meschonnic, quoted in Steiner (1975, x): 'La théorie de la traduction n'est donc pas une linguistique appliquée. Elle est un champ nouveau dans la théorie et la pratique de la littérature. Son importance épistémologique consiste dans sa contribution à une pratique théorique de l'homogénéité entre signifiant et signifié propre à cette pratique sociale qu'est l'écriture.'

2. Translation, ed. F. Olivier-Martin (Paris, 1935); original, ed. J. B. Moyle (Oxford, 1883). Both texts: 'Justice is a constant and perpetual will to give each person his rights; the practice of law and the knowledge of divine and human matters; the knowledge of the just and the unjust.'

3. And I do not mean by 'translation' merely a paraphrase, but struggle and rivalry over the same sense. Cf. also Marouzeau (1931, 71): '. . . en général, on s'inspirera de la langue courante, on repensera les idées de l'auteur latin en français d'aujourd'hui.'

4. *Patrologia graeca* XIII.255–514 (Latin and Greek in parallel columns).
   Latin text: 'God is quick to do good, but tardy to punish those worthy of punishment. In fact, when he can quietly without discussion of what is to come, punish those whom he has once judged worthy of death, he never does it. But, even if he has pronounced sentence, he says what it has always been proposed to him to say in order that those who had been condemned through sin, be freed through penance.'
   Greek text: 'God is prompt to do good, but in punishing those worthy of punishment, a delayer. For, though able to carry out in silence the punishment of those deserving punishment, he never does it. But, if he condemns, he says what is to his purpose, to liberate from his justice the guilty person.'

5. Translation, ed. H. de Vocht, *The Earliest Translations of Erasmus's Colloquia* (London, 1928), 3–51; original, Basle, 1519. Latin text: 'My warmest greetings, my dearest Xanthippe. And the same to you, my dearest Eulalia. You seem to be more lovely than ever.'

6. For a modern stand against Dryden's disapproval, see Steiner (1966, 54): 'Thus I take translation to include the writing of a poem in which a poem in another language (or in an earlier form in one's own language) is the vitalising, shaping presence; a poem which can be read and responded to independently, but which is not ontologically complete, a previous poem being its occasion, begetter and in the literal sense, *raison d'être*.'

7. Translation, ed. B. Suphan, *Sämmtliche Werke* (Berlin, 1877–1913), vol. 25; original, ed. Samuel Johnson (London, 1765).

8. Translation, Paris, 1827; original, ed. J. Naudet (Paris, 1819–20). Latin text:

'But Augustus, as support for his tyranny, named Claudius Marcellus, the son of his sister and still young, to the Pontificate and to a Curule Aedileship, and honoured Marcus Agrippa, a man of low birth and a boon companion in war and victory, with successive consulates.'

9. Translation, ed. H. Kenner, *The Translations of Ezra Pound* (London, 1953); original, ed. Société littéraire de France (Paris, 1919).

10. Translation, London, 1969; original, Oxford Classical Text. Latin text: 'Boy, server of the good old Falernian, pour out for me even dryer cups, as demands the law of Postumia, mistress of the feast, more tipsy than the tipsy grape. But you water, go from here to wherever you like, you destroyer of wine; and go away to puritans. This is pure Thyonian.'

11. Cf. Fréron (1755, 138) on Fielding's Tom Jones: 'Il est vrai que l'original est surchargé de tant d'excursions inutiles, et sans un peu d'indulgence, on auroit réduit cette masse énorme à un très petit volume.'

12. 'Pallas had given her ear to listen to this marvel that the Muse was recounting to her. She remembered the account of the nine Muses and the nine feet, and said that they were well avenged, and praised their argument, and that they were right and within their rights. Then she said to herself, so that nobody heard: "What good does it do me to praise you? Why do I let myself grow angry? I am very hurt and angry because Arachne insults me by her words and her skill, of which she is boasting. She is a beautiful worker and a fine weaver, and for this she does not deign to obey me. I shall go, certainly, to attack her, if she keeps up her defiance, if she does not show me reverence."'

13. Translation, Berger (1888, 26); original, Roman Missal. French text: 'Our Father who art in Heaven, your name be sanctified, may your eternal reign come; may you at all times reign more over us. Your will, may we all in common do it fully. Give us our bread of food, doctrine and penance, bread of sacrament of the altar, which guards from mortal sin. Give us pardon for our sins as we pardon others. Grant that we do not become slaves of sin, and deliver us from all evil. Give us these requests, who heaps us with all other favours.'

14. But cf. Francklin (1753, 4):

> Unless an author like a mistress warms,
> How shall we hide his faults or taste his charms,
> How all his modest latent beauties find,
> How trace each lovelier feature of the mind,
> Soften each blemish, and each grace improve,
> And treat him with the dignity of Love?

He footnotes: 'Roscommon says, "Chuse an author as you chuse a friend." Perhaps the image is better drawn from the livelier passion.'

15. Cf. Fränzel (1914, 190). For the same sentiment, cf. Cicero, *De optimo genere* ii.6: 'Therefore nobody who does not want to be like Demosthenes is an orator . . .'; de Golefer (1633, 14): 'Par ainsi un très scavant homme qui s'écoulera . . . dans les sentiments d'un sainct Thomas et d'un sainct Augustin deviendra semblable à eux en intelligence et peut-estre en probité.'

CHAPTER 3

1. Cf. Postgate (1922, 18): 'It is unfortunate that usage has not provided distinctive names for translation which primarily regards the author, and translation which primarily regards the reader. *Retrospective* and *prospective* would express the difference in their aim, *receptive* and *adaptive* the difference in their methods'; Belloc (1931, 10): '. . . two departments . . . *instruction*, the other *literary*'; and modern German critics, e.g. Schadewalt (1966, 683), who distinguish between *Übersetzer* (artistic translator) and *Dolmetscher* (technical or scientific translator).

2. Cited in H. B. Smith and P. Schiff, *Creeds of Greek and Latin Churches* (London, 1877; Greek and Latin on facing pages). Both texts: 'We believe in God, the Father, the ruler of all [Latin: the almighty], maker of all things visible and invisible. And in one Lord [Latin adds: of ours], Jesus Christ, the son of God, born the only Son of the Father, that is from the substance of the Father, God from God, Light from Light, True God from True God, born, not made, of one substance with the Father [Latin adds: which the Greeks call *homoousion*]. Through whom everything is made which is in Heaven and on Earth. Who for the sake of us men and for our salvation came down, took flesh, and suffered; and rose on the third day, and ascended into heaven; and will come to judge the living and the dead. And in the Holy Spirit. But those who say: "he existed when he did not exist", and "before he was born, he did not exist", and "that he was made from things not existing", or "from another substance" or "essence"; and those saying "changeable and mutable Son of God"; these the Catholic Church anathematises.'

3. For a crib of this Latin, see English version on page 187.

4. 'The universe is an assembly made up of heaven and earth, and of those things that are contained between them. The universe is also otherwise described as the order and system of all things which are kept in being by God and through God. Whose central point, immoved and stable, has come to be the earth, endowed with the fertility of life; for it is the seat and parent of every type of distinct living thing.'

5. There was a certain rich man, who dressed in purple and fine linen, and feasted splendidly every day. But there was a certain beggar, by the name of Lazarus, who lay near (at?) his door, all ulcerated, wishing to be sated with the scraps that fell from the rich man's table. But the dogs came and licked his ulcers.

6. Translation, Amsterdam, 1649; original, Paris, 1637. Given the literality of the Latin, a crib is unnecessary.

7. Annexed to his *Biblia hebraica* (Paris, 1753; Latin and Greek in parallel columns). Both texts: 'Love justice, you who judge the earth; think rightly of the Lord, and seek him in simplicity of heart. For he is found by those who do not test him; and he is present to those who do not lack trust in him.' (The Greek has participles where the Latin has adjectival clauses.)

8. Translation, 1877 (repr. *Complete Works*, London, 1915), 1095–121; original, ed. Dindorff (Leipzig, 1857).

9. Translation and original cited in Williams 1968, 363–4:
   Latin text: 'He is really miserable who cannot hide his misery in public; but my wife gives every indication of it by her appearance and her exploits, even if I keep silence. Apart from her dowry, she has everything one does not want.

He who is to be wise will learn from me, who, a captive in the hands of the enemy, while yet free am a slave, while my city and fortress are still safe. Am I to wish her health when she does her best to deprive me of everything I want? While I pant for her death, I myself live as a dead man among the living. She says I frequented the maid in secret. She accused me of it; and so by weeping, imploring, nagging and reviling she wore me down. I sold the maid. Now I believe that she is sowing the tale among her friends and relatives: "Which of you while still a slip of a girl could have got from her husband, what I have just now got as an old woman: that I have deprived my husband of his doxy?" That will be the subject of their meetings today. I will be torn apart by their gossip.'

Greek text: 'The lovely heiress can now sleep on either ear. A great and glorious deed has been done. From the house, she has expelled, as she wanted, the maid who troubles her, so that all should gaze only on the face of Krobule, so that, being my wife, she should be known as my ruler. And that face! "an ass among apes"—that's the proverb. I want to say nothing about that night that was the beginning of many evils. Would that I had not married Krobule who has a nose a cubit long, even if her dowry was ten talents. Then her temper: how can one stand it? By Zeus of Olympus and by Athene, never! So, quicker than you can say it, she got rid of that nice little serving-maid.'

10. Such are the minds of men, as the light with which Father Jupiter himself lights up the fruitful earth.' (For another interpretation, see Pope on p. 115.)

11. Ambrose (in *Basilii sancti patris nostri Opera omnia*, ed. J. Garnier, Paris, 1839): 'A suitable beginning for one about to relate the building of the world is to place before his account the principle by which visible things were set in order. For the creation of heaven and earth is to be related, and it did not come about by chance, as some have thought, but drew its origin from God.'

Eustathius (in *Patrologia latina* LIII.865–966): 'As a fitting beginning, he who was to relate the making of the world took the putting-together of the work done, making that the opening of his account. For the making of heaven and earth is to be related, not as being formed spontaneously, as some imagine, but as having obtained the causes of its own substance from God.'

Greek (listed in parallel columns to Ambrose translation): 'A fitting beginning to one about to relate the formation of the universe is to set before his account the cause of the ordering of visible things. For the making of heaven and earth is to be related not as being put together spontaneously, as some have imagined, but as taking its beginning from God.'

12. Ed. J. Hardouin, *Acta Conciliorum* (Paris, 1714), v. Both texts: 'Now, beloved brothers and fellow-priests, in the next act of this great and holy synod, it is declared how Photius, who, having come from the streets and marketplaces, invaded the Church of Constantinople by force, was admonished to submit, to confess his crimes by word and in writing, and to twice abjure his impious writings and acts against the holy Patriarch, Ignatius, . . .'

13. There was a man who was rich, and was dressed in purple and expensive material, and every day ate very fully. Now there was a beggar whose name was Lazarus and who lay at his door full of sores. And he wished to be sated with the scraps that fell from the rich man's table, and no man gave them to him; but the dogs came and licked his mange.'

14. Caesar, after the Egyptian traitor made the sad gift of the honoured head to him, hiding his obvious joy, as the ancient page teaches, pressed inert tears

from his eyes in public. Hannibal, after losing his high office by so many changes in fortune, was fated to see the sad deeds, while interiorly sad, pretending, laughed with tearful eyes, to better suppress grief in his groaning heart. Thus, under a changing cover, one hides all emotions and anxieties, now with a happy face, now with a sad. If ever I chuckle with unwelcome sorrow, and even if I sing songs, I do it since there is no way left to us, except this by which I hide tears and sadness.

15. Translation, 1661 (ed. G. de Santillana, Chicago, 1953); original, ed. F. Brunetti (Bari, 1963).

16. Translation, Paris, 1624, 6–7; original, Frankfurt, 1609. Latin text: 'Take, for example, four ounces of the whitest salt of tartar [potassium carbonate], dissolved several times according to the chemical art, filtered and coagulated with water of agrimony. Dissolve it in a vessel over the marble or by the use of a flame until it becomes an oil [i.e. a saturated solution]. Once you have this pure oil, take two ounces of oil of vitriol [i.e. concentrated sulphuric acid] rectified as well as possible, and introduce it onto the surface of the oil of tartar drop by drop in a large vessel. There there will be a white precipitate, moisture floating above it. The salt will be brought to dryness with a slow heat. In this way is produced white tartar, fixed in vitriol [potassium sulphate].' (Glosses mine. The process described is to add concentrated sulphuric acid to a saturated solution of potassium carbonate. Potassium sulphate precipitates out, and is then dried.)

17. Translation, London, 1652; original Basle, 1542. Greek text: 'Medicine is the knowledge of healthy things, harmful things, and things that are neither. It makes no difference if one says that it pertains to the sick.'

18. R. Shepherd, *Polyaenus's Strategems of War* (London, 1793), introduction: '. . . the extraordinary conduct of a neighbouring nation having provoked almost all Europe to arms; Great Britain of too much consequence in herself and her connections to remain an idle spectator of exertions calculated to involve the world in scenes of anarchy and confusion found it necessary to take the field. . . . At this period and in this state of things, the author hath been induced to hazard on the public the following pages.' Cf. also J. Roucher, *Recherches sur la nature et les causes de la Richesse des Nations* (Paris, 1790), I.vii: 'On demandoit depuis longtems une traduction françoise de l'ouvrage de M. Smith. On la demande surtout aujourd'hui, que l'assemblée Nationale s'occupe des moyens de régénérer la fortune publique, dilapidée par une longue suite de prodigalités et de malversations.' And this in spite of at least two other French translations in circulation at the time!

19. A merchant, so that he can deceive watchful eyes, sends his treasures across the sea under a false name. Softly and melodiously Euphelia sounds from my strings, but my prayers seek only you, Chloe.

20. Translation, 1805 (Weimar, 1964); original, ed. H. Dieckmann (Paris, 1957).

21. Under an assumed name, to allay his fears, the cautious merchant hides his treasures. My verses praise Emilia, but inwardly I die for Chloe.' Latin text in R. Y. Tyrrell (ed.), *Dublin Translations* (London and Dublin, 1890), 349.

22. *Patrologia graeca* II.819–1024 (Latin and Greek in parallel columns). Both texts: 'Hear now [Latin text adds 'foolish one'], how sadness tortures the [Latin adds 'holy'] spirit, and how it makes it well. When a doubter enters on some

business, and does not come to the end of it because of doubt, this sadness enters into the man, and makes the Holy Spirit sad, and troubles him.'

23. *Patrologia graeca* XXXI.1723–33 (Latin and Greek in parallel columns).

Latin text: 'Every divinely inspired writing is useful for teaching: for this very reason, Scripture was written by the Holy Spirit, because we are all to take for ourselves remedies for our own passions from this, as from some common fount of holiness. "For health", it says, "suppresses many sins."'

Greek text: 'All God-inspired writing is useful: for this reason things were composed by the Holy Spirit; so that, as in the common healing of souls, all of us men, each of us, should choose a remedy for his own suffering. "For," it says, "the remedy checks great sins."'

24. Translation, ed. G. Koerting (Leipzig, 1868); original, Oxford Classical Text.

French text: 'And have it so that she sees you weep tenderly and sigh deeply. Such things will very well soften her and move her to this, that she will have mercy on you.'

Latin text: 'And tears do good; with tears you will move adamant. Let her see, if you can, damp cheeks.'

25. This tract seems to have been popular among the English reformers, being reprinted in the middle of the sixteenth century. There is a modern edition by Curt F. Buhler, *Medium Aevum* VII (1938), 167–83.

26. *Oratio dogmatica de unione* (1450?; ed. E. Candal, Rome, 1958—Latin and Greek on facing pages).

Latin text: 'Our ancestors who lived at the time when this split began said that, in matters of faith, one must assent to those things that have been handed down to us by sacred writings, in which all the truth of faith is either fully explained, or, if hidden, can be sought in it without difficulty.'

Greek text: 'For it is necessary in those things concerning faith, there being neither necessity nor risk of acquiescing in division, to stand fast to those traditions, which, either clearly or in a hidden fashion, have complete truth about the doctrines of God in them.'

27. Gregorian hymns often had several melodies, depending on local custom. The melody appearing here is that taken from the Sarum ritual by *Hymns Ancient and Modern*; that in the Appendix is from the *Liber usualis* (the Manual of Gregorian Chant from the Roman Rite), which presumably is the melody Hopkins (see page 106, above) had in mind.

CHAPTER 4

1. The illicit offspring from the forbidden tree, and the crime of the ancient father by which the whole of his race fell handed over to death by another's sin, and the home lost until that giver of salvation, redeeming souls by his death, leads them purified into the happy garden and regains the ancestral home, . . .'

2. Translation, Paris, 1877, 347; original, London, 1809.

3. Translation, 1917–30 (London, 1962); original, ed. R. Volkmann (Leipzig, 1883). Greek text: 'Since evil things of necessity infest this world, and the spirit wishes to flee evil, it must go from here. What is this escape? To become, they say, like God: that is if we become just and holy through wisdom, and entirely in virtue.'

4. For definitions of these concepts, see Cicero, *Brutus* 162, and *Orator* 211.

Though Cicero does not apply these terms to translation as such, his discussions of their role in rhetoric is applicable to translation.

5. Translation, 860?, *Patrologia latina* cxxii.1029–194; original, *Patrologia graeca* iii.119–24. Both texts: 'Every good [Latin: best] gift and every perfect gift is from above, coming down from the Father of Light. But every Father-moved, light-showing influence, coming generously into us again, restoring us like a unifying strength, fills and changes us to the unity and god-making simplicity of the Father gathering us together.'
6. 'Before him whom he believed' that is, 'in like manner' (Chrysostom). Thus *Apocalypse* 'facing in the same direction' is explained by Arethas as 'in accordance with'.
7. But Atrides stabbed Hyperenor, the shepherd of the people, in the side, and the bronze let his bowels through. . . .
8. 1582 (repr. Amsterdam 1619). 'This is defined as that part of the body which lies between the short ribs and the bones that pertain to the lower abdomen.'
9. Cf. Elyot, s.v. *noxa*: 'peyne, offense or trespace; sometyme it signifieth hurt or harm.' Cf. also Estienne: 'Noxa est Peccatum, aut pro peccato poena.' (*Noxa* is sin, or punishment for sin.)
10. This passage is part of a prose paraphrase which is printed in the margins of the edition. 'The many virtues of Aeneas and his many stories return to her mind. His face and speech stick fast, imprinted on her mind, and this anxiety does not allow tranquil quiet to her body.'

CHAPTER 5

1. Cf. Vernay (1974, 211): 'Ainsi une linguistique de la traduction, si la linguistique proprement dit en constitue un élément essentiel, doit s'ouvrir a une sémiologie qui n'étudie pas seulement les signes porteurs de signification dans le cadre des structures linguistiques en question, mais leur rôle dans l'acte de communication et dans la vie sociale.' For a hostile enunciation, cf. Meschonnic (1971, 331); 'Nida oppose la "forme" à la "réponse". Il prend pour vérité–réalité–nature une distinction idéologique courante, selon laquelle la forme est opposée au sens et privée du sens.'
2. Cf. Nida (1964, ch. 8) and Edmund Leach, 'Structuralism in Social Anthropology', in D. Robey (ed.), *Structuralism* (Oxford, 1973, 37–54).
3. Translation, 510? (ed. L. Minio-Paluello, *Aristoteles latinus* i, Bruges and Paris, 1961); original, ed. I. Bekker (Oxford, 1837). Both texts: 'Equivocal is said of those things whose name only is common, and under that name the principle of substance is diverse, as in animal, man and what is drawn. For only their name is common, but under the name there is a different principle of substance. For if anybody assigns to them what they have which makes them animals, he also assigns their proper principle to each.'
4. 'Every art and every body of knowledge, and similarly both operation and choice, is a seeker of some good.'
5. Translation, 1314? (ed. A. Bos, Paris, 1897); original, ed. J. L. Pagel (Berlin, 1892). Both texts: '. . . the first rule is that we must first and more carefully look to the retention of the blood [French has 'restraining the flow of blood'] than to [French has 'before'] the treatment of the wound.'
6. Translation, 1372 (ed. W. W. Skeat, *The Complete Works of Geoffrey Chaucer*,

Oxford, 1899, I.93–259); original given ibid. French text: 'Its matter is good and new: now God grant that she, for whom I have taken it in hand, receive it in kindness. It is she who is of so high worth, and is so worthy of being loved, that she must be called Rose.'

7. See Dryden (cited in Proudfoot 1960, 231): "Tis true that when I find an English word significant and sounding, I neither borrow from the Latin or any other language; but when I want at home, I must seek abroad.' Cf. also Pope in the introduction to his *Iliad* (1715, 19): 'I speak of Homer's Compound-Epithets and his Repetitions. Many of the former cannot be done literally into English without destroying the Purity of our Language. I believe such should be retained as slide easily of themselves into an English-Compound, without Violence to the Ear or to the received Rules of Composition.' For a parallel concern in France, cf. Sorel (1667, 212): 'Si on doit avoir égard dans les traductions à ne se point servir de vieux mots, il faut avoir le mesme soin pour ne pas tomber dans l'autre extrémité, qui est de ne se vouloir servir que de mots nouveaux.'

8. 'The entire universe consists of an association of heaven and earth and of the nature of those things which belong to both; or thus: the universe is an ordering made by the responsibility of god, by the assiduous watchfulness of the gods. Its "hinge" (for thus I would translate κέντρον), robust and immovable, resides in the earth, the mother and nurse of all living things.'

9. English text, ed. J. Stevenson (*Anglo-Saxon and Early English Psalter*, Surtees Society, London, 1843, I;1) original on facing pages; original, Gallican Psalter (*Patrologia latina* xxix.123; French, cited in Berger (1884, 4); original, Hebrew Psalter (*Patrologia latina* xxix.1189). (The Gallican Psalter is that appearing in the Vulgate. The Hebrew Psalter, whose reading appears in brackets below, was a later version Jerome translated direct from the Hebrew.) 'Blessed is the man who does not go out in the counsel of the wicked, and does not stand in the way of sinners, and does not sit in the seat of pestilence [mockers].'

10. Translation, *Li quatre livre des Rois* (ed. E. R. Curtius, Halle, 1911); original, repr. Gutenberg, 1450–3. French text: 'Who is this filthy scoundrel who is making such reproaches against the people of God?' Latin text: 'Who is this uncircumcised Philistine who dares malign the army of the living God?'

11. 'Natural science almost entirely would seem to be concerned with bodies and magnitudes and with their changes or movements, and especially with the principles which belong to such substances.'

12. Translation, 1549 (ed. C. H. Miller, Early English Text Society, 257, London, 1965); original, 1501 (repr. Leyden, 1703). Latin text: 'No matter how mortals talk of me in public, and I am certainly not unaware of how badly Folly is talked of even among the most foolish, however, I am she, I say, I am the only one who by my divinity gladdens both gods and men, . . .

13. Translation, 1595? (*Marlowe's Plays and Poems*, New York and London, 1958); original, ed. Aldus Manutius (Venice, 1515–16). Latin text: 'What shoulders, what arms I touched and saw! The form of her breasts, how apt it was to be pressed! How flat a belly under a pleasing bosom! How large and what a side! How youthful a thigh!'

14. Translation, 1573 (quoted in Lawton, 1926, 522); original, Venice 1555. Latin text: 'Immortal Gods, how one man outshines another! How an intelligent man excels a fool! . . .'

15. Translations, N. Amelot de la Houssaye (Amsterdam, 1683); T. Beding-field(?), 1570? (ed. H. Craig, Chapel Hill, 1944); S. Tegli (Frankfurt, 1560); original, Vinegia, 1554. Latin text: 'I shall omit discussion of Republics: about these we have spoken further in another place. Now I shall turn the discussion to principates, and bringing together what I have already begun above (i.e. by what method principates are to be kept and governed), I shall pursue my intended discussion with this account.'

16. Translation, London, 1653, 146; original, London, 1586. Latin text: 'Behold, I have completed a work which will last for all ages, untouched by the bite of time, more lasting than bronze.' On Bathurst's *aere* for *steel*, cf. Horace, *Odes* III.xxx.1: 'Exegi monumentum aere perennius.' Cf. Pichot's use of transposition to recall Juvenal, p. 118, above.

17. Translation, London, 1656 (repr. Menston, 1971); original footnoted by Cowley. Greek text: 'Hymns ruling the lyre, what god, what hero, what man shall we celebrate?'

18. Translation, Milan, 1811; original, ed. C. Jenners, London, 1774.

19. Translation, ed. R. Y. Tyrrell, *Dublin Translations* (London and Dublin, 1890), 276; original facing. Latin text: 'Then three apes of men in green tunics, abominable fellows, against the will of my gods, appeared at my back, and vigorously came after me with hostile knives. For the night was so dark that, by Hercules, you would not have known your own fingers. . . .'

Chapter 6

1. Cf. *She did it*: translated by *C'est elle qui l'a fait*, where the intonational focussing of *She* must be compensated for by syntactic means in French. For a full discussion see Darbelnet (1971). The opposing point of view is based on M. A. K. Halliday, 'Categories in the Theory of Grammar', *Word* 17 (1961), 241–92.

2. The basis of Renaissance discussion is the Lorenzo Valla description of the passive force and nominal properties of the past participle in *Elegantiarum linguae latinae libri sex* (Gryphius, Lyons, 1544). lib. I.xxx; and the chapter in Erasmus, *De copia verborum* I.xxvi on syntactic methods of varying constructions.

3. 'Every art, and every body of knowledge, and likewise act and choice, seems to seek some good.'

4. Translation, B.C. 45?, ed. I. Verburg (Amsterdam, 1724); original, Oxford Classical Text. Latin text: 'But everything that is produced must needs be produced from some cause; for the origin of nothing can be found separate from its cause.' Greek text; 'Again, everything which comes into being, of necessity comes from some cause; for it is impossible for anything to have beginning without a cause.'

5. Translation, 1944 (Paris, 1956); original on facing pages. Latin text: 'Indeed, I had certainly heard that because of his songs, Menalcas had kept everything from where the hills begin to slope and leave the ridge with a gentle slope, as far as the water and the beeches with broken crowns.'

6. Translation, 1750 (repr. Brest, 1822); original, on facing pages. Greek text: 'There is still a third difference between them, that is, how they imitate each of

their objects. For truly, in representing the same objects, it is possible to imitate either by narrating, or by becoming another person, as Homer does, or by not changing and remaining in one's own persona, or by showing the characters as acting and carrying out what is imitated.'

7. Translations, P. Coste (Amsterdam, 1700); G. H. Theile (Leipzig, 1711). Latin text: 'The next faculty of the soul, through which it makes further progress in obtaining knowledge, is that which I call *Retention*, or the simple conservation of *Ideas*, which it has received from sensation or reflection.' Original, London, 1690.

8. Translation, Paris, 1531; original, ed. Beroaldus (Lyon, 1520). Latin text: 'The dictator, Caesar, holding elections, the consuls elected were Julius Caesar and P. Servilius. For this was the year in which by law he could become consul.'

9. Translation, from French, 1579 (repr. New York, 1967); original, Paris, 1559.

CHAPTER 7

1. For ancient discussions, see *Ad Herennium* IV.vii.11 and Quintilian X.i.4 and XII.x.58. The Cicero references are too scattered to be cited here. The most important Renaissance treatment is Erasmus's *Ciceronianus*. On Prague, see J. Dubský, 'The Prague Conception of Functional Style', in V. Fried (ed.), *The Prague School of Linguistics and Language Teaching* (London, 1972), 112–27.

2. *Clausulae* were rhythmic endings to major sentence divisions. They originally were composed of quantitative verse feet, being scanned as in verse. As the phonological features of Latin and Greek literature changed after the classical period, these were gradually replaced by *cursus*, i.e. metrical endings based on the accentual feet of popular and medieval verse. For a short discussion see the *Oxford Classical Dictionary* (2nd ed., London, 1970) s.v. Prose-rhythm.

3. The fourth-century *clausula* was a compromise between the classical quantitative form and the *cursus* we have seen in Bruni Aretino. In the Origen passage on page 45, *-éndum prómptus ést* is quantitatively a spondee–cretic and accentually a trochee–cretic; while *dìssimulátor*, taking into account the subsidiary accent on *dis*, is quantitatively and accentually a dactyl–trochee.

4. For a full discussion of *cursus* in English, see Croll (1919).

5. 'Leaving aside, therefore, for a short while, the virtues of soul (which should be common to her and our Courtier), to wit, prudence, magnanimity, continence, and the others, which equally grace all women, as are these: to be uncorrupted and modest, to diligently care for the property of her husband, for her household and her children: that in addition, in a lady of court it is requisite that she exercise a certain pleasant affability in every kind of conversation with every kind of person (she should act with so much consideration of place, time, person and other things, that nothing seems more punctilious; with so much modesty of conduct and action, that nothing seems more fetching; with so much ease and deftness, that nothing seems more elegant); and when she has shown herself in word and deed modest, prudent, sweet, pleasant and witty, let her keep the difficult and exacting, but truly golden mean, which, bounded and as it were blockaded, by both contrary qualities, can not be abandoned without grave fault.'

6. 'Every art, every way of teaching and instruction, and also action and intention, seems to seek some good.'

7. Translation, 1543 (repr. Venice, 1737); original, ed. Cornarius (Basel, 1538).

Latin text: 'If any among my predecessors who had written about man's diet and its relation to health, had seemed to know the truth and to have written everything accessible to human understanding; it would be enough for me to work from the labours of others I know to be right, insofar as each of them seemed to be useful.'

Greek text: 'If I believed that one of my predecessors had written everything about the diet to follow in order to remain in good health that it is possible for the human mind to grasp, and had known it well; it would be enough, having built on the work of others to use their work in the measure I judged each of them to be correct and useful.'

8. Both texts in Schadewalt (1970, 1.520–1).

Latin text: 'I long to hymn the great sons of Atreus and Cadmus. But my string when struck sounds only Venus. I changed plectrum, strings and shell. I continually sing of Hercules; continually my lute sounds Venus. The great names of kings are powerful. But whatever the string sounds, it is Venus.'

Greek text: 'I wish to sing of the heroes; I wish to hymn Cadmus. But the lyre has only Love in its strings. I lately changed strings and the whole lyre, and I sang of the deed of Hercules. But the lyre answered with Love. Praise heroes the rest of you; but my lyre sings only Love.'

9. Translation, 1728; both texts in *Oeuvres complètes de Pope* (Paris, 1779).

10. Translation, 1708 (repr. Paris, 1740); original, ed. E. A. de Martignac (Paris, 1678). Latin text: 'I happened to be going along the Via Sacra, as is my custom, thinking of some trifle or other, totally absorbed in it. Somebody known to me only by name came up and grabbed my hand: "How are you, my dear fellow?"'

11. Latin, 58 B.C.?, ed. M. Schuster (Teubner, Leipzig, 1954); original in Appendix. Latin text: 'He seems to me equal to a god, or even, if it is fitting, to surpass the Gods, who, sitting opposite you over and over again, looks at you and hears you sweetly laughing.' Greek text: 'To me he seems the equal of the gods, that man who sits face to face with you and hears you sweetly speaking near him and lovingly laughing.'

12. Digby 149: 'Sweet memory of Jesus Christ, who well made Heaven and Earth and all things. There is no other thing in all the world that gives true joy to Man.'

Poitiers 95: 'Sweet memory of Jesus, you so rejoice the sorrowful heart; but there is nothing sweeter than to contemplate you in glory.'

13. Greek and Latin texts in *Thomas Mori . . . opera omnia*, 1518 (repr. Frankfurt, 1963). More's Latin: 'I came naked on the earth, I shall go away naked. Why do I uselessly sweat, seeing a naked funeral.' Lily's Latin: 'Naked I enter the earth, and I leave naked. Why do I worry needlessly seeing a naked funeral.' Greek text: 'To the earth I came naked, naked I go from the earth; and what do I uselessly worry about, seeing the bareness of death.'

14. Translation in Yonge, *Musica transalpina* (London, 1588); original, Guarini, *Opere* (Verona, 1737–8). Reproduction by courtesy of the University Library, Cambridge.

15. *Gedichte Goethes ins Lateinische übertragen*, 1843 (Berlin, 1899); original on facing pages. Latin text: 'Ah, who will bring back the happy days? Who the first stirrings of love, or the fruit of one hour? Who will bring it back as it is

remembered? I feed the wound with my pain; and the flight of time takes away the pent-up grief. Ah, who will bring back the happy days to my desires?'

16. Translation, A. G. Abbie (ed.), *The Scottish Student's Songbook* (London and Glasgow, 1899). Latin text: 'Should a body meet a body through the rye, why, if there is a kiss, are there tears? Every doll has a boy. I do not yet have one, although they all love me. But I do not give a damn.'

17. Cf. Opitz (1624, 55): 'Eine guete art der uebung uber ist, das wir uns zueweilen auß den Griechischen und Lateinischen Poeten etwas zue ubersetzen vornemen: dadurch denn die eigenschafft und glanz der Wörter, die menge der figuren, und das vermögen auch dergleichen zue erfinden zue wegge gebracht wird.' Compare with the sixteenth-century discussions in Smith (1904), and modern discussions by Yves Bonnefoy in the Postface to his *Hamlet* and by Kochel 1970.

18. Translation, Paris, 1736; original, *Julius Caesar, a Tragedy as it is Now Acted at the Theatre Royal* (London, 1680).

19. 'Sing the anger, O Goddess, of Achilles, son of Peleus. It was calamitous, and it brought such astounding evil on the Greeks, handing over to Pluto the souls of so many noble warriors, and to vultures and wandering dogs their bodies. Thus was accomplished the intention of Jupiter, from the day when was raised the primordial quarrel between Atrides, king of men, and Achilles, son of the Gods.'

20. Both texts, *Vita latina* 37 (May 1969), 31: Latin text: 'The last rose of summer, you flower alone. Ah, already the lovely companions lie dead. No sweet sister blushes near you, none groans. I do not wish you to grieve afflicted, when your friends are held in sleep. I sprinkle the dead ones with your leaves, so that you yourself may rest. Soon I shall follow you: when friends have already gone, and the crown of friendship has lost its splendour, who, lacking those dear, remains willingly in this bleak world?'

CHAPTER 8

1. This discussion is based on Basil Bernstein, 'Social Class, Language and Socialisation', in P. P. Giglioli (ed.), *Language and Social Context* (Penguin Books, 1972), 157–78.

2. The same three requirements appear in Tytler (1790, 9) and Gourdin (1789, xliij). They also appear in the theory of the interlinear version as discussed by Goethe in *Dichtung und Wahrheit*.

3. Cf. the perceptive comment on Voltaire by Pons (1960, 118): 'Etre ou ne pas être devient sous la plume de Voltaire:
   Demeure, il faut choisir et passer à l'instant
   De la vie à la mort et de l'être au néant.
On ne saurait pas être plus naivement cornélien. C'est curieusement transposé sur le plan métaphysique, le style de la célèbre "apostrophe de Rodrigue au Comte".'

CHAPTER 9

1. R. H. Robins, 'Theory-orientation versus Data-orientation: a Recurrent Theme in Linguistics', *Historiographia linguistica* I (1975), 11–26.

Bibliography

1. DISCUSSIONS OF THEORY AND PRACTICE

Anonymous (15th cent.) *Lollard Tracts on the Bible* (Cambridge MS II. 6.26).
—— (1770) 'Remarks on the Translation of Antient Authors', *Gentleman's Magazine* 40, 510–11.
—— (1813) Critique of Tytler, *Essay on the Principles of Translation* (3rd edn), *Gentleman's Magazine* 83, 257–8.
—— (1820) 'Translation of the Bible', *Quarterly Review* 23, 287–325.
—— (1935) 'A Translator's Decalogue', *Journal of Education* (London) 67, 617.
—— (1958) *Abstracts of the Conference on Machine Translation, Moscow, 15–21 May, 1958* (JPRS/DC–241, Washington).
Adams, R. M. (1973) *Proteus, His Lies, His Truth: Discussions of Literary Translation* (New York).
Addison, John (1711) Letter 29, *The Spectator* (London, 1797), I. 161–6; Letter 229, ibid., III. 339–43.
Adkinson, B. W. (1967) 'The Role of Translation in the Dissemination of Scientific Information', in Citroen (1967, 91–103).
Aginsky, B. W. and E. G. (1948) 'The Importance of Language Universals', *Word* 4, 168–72.
Alegria, F. (1954) 'How Good is a Translation?' *Américas* 6.5 (May), 36–8.
Anastasius Bibliothecarius (9th cent.) *Sancta synodus septima generalis nicaena secunda, Patrologia Latina* 129: 195–8; *Collectaneae ad Ionnem Diaconem*, ibid., 557–62; *Epistola ad Aionem*, ibid., 729–30.
Anderton, B. (1920) 'Lure of Translation', in *Sketches from a Library Window* (Cambridge), 38–70.
Andreyev, N. D. (1964) 'Linguistic Aspects of Translation', *Proceedings of the 9th International Congress of Linguists* (The Hague), 625–38.
Antolkolskij, P. (1967) 'Quelques observations sur la traduction', in Citroen (1967, 83–8).
Arnaud, Paul (1967) 'La traducteur technique de l'avenir: Le documentaliste linguiste', in Citroen (1967, 109–17).
Arnold, Matthew (1861) 'On Translating Homer', in *On the Study of Celtic Literature and On Translating Homer* (New York, 1906), 141–300.
Arnott, P. (1964) 'Greek Drama and the Modern Stage', in Arrowsmith and Shattuck (1964, 113–28).
Arns, K. (1921) Über die Kunst der Übersetzung englischer Verse', *Zeitschrift für französischen und englischen Unterricht* 20, 12–27.
Arrowsmith, W. and Shattuck, R. (1964) *The Craft and Context of Translation* (New York).

Arrowsmith, W. (1964) 'The Lively Conventions of Translation', in Arrowsmith and Shattuck (1964, 187–213).

Ascham, Roger (1570) *The Scholemaster*, ed. E. Arber (1870; English Reprints VI, New York, 1966).

Astre, F. (1870) 'Aperçus critiques sur les traductions et les traducteurs', *Mémoires de l'Académie des Sciences de Toulouse* II. 135–50.

Saint Augustine (380–400?) *Enarrationes in psalmos*, Patrologia Latina 36/37: 68–1960.

—— (382?) *Epistola 28*, PL 33: 111–14.
           Epistola 71, PL 33: 241–3.

—— (427?) *De doctrina christiana*, PL 34: 15–122.

Aulus Gellius (A.D. 100?) *Noctes atticae*, ed. C. Hosius (Leipzig, 1903).

Ayala, F. (1965) *Problemas de la traducción* (Madrid).

Bacci, A. (1963) *Lexicon vocabulorum quae difficilius latine redduntur* (Rome).

Bachet de Méziriac, C.-G. (1635) *De la traduction*, *Ménagiana* (Paris, 1715), 411–60.

Bacon, B. W. (1925) 'Punctuation, Translation, Interpretation', *Journal of Religion* 4, 243–60.

Bacon, Roger (1268?) *Opus maius*, ed. J. H. Bridges (3 vols, London, Edinburgh and Oxford).

—— (1271?) *Compendium studii philosophiae*, *Fratris Rogeri Bacon opera quaedam hactenus inedita* (London, 1859), I. 393–519.

—— (1272?) *Grammatices graecae*, ed. E. Nolan and B. A. Hirsch (Cambridge, 1902).

Balcerzan, E. (1970) 'La traduction, art d'interpréter', in Holmes (1970, 3–22).

Bally, C. (1912) 'Stylistique et linguistique générale', *Archiv für des Studium der neueren Sprachen* 128, 87–126.

—— (1921) *Traité de stylistique française* (2nd edn, 2 vols, Paris and Heidelberg, 1937).

—— (1922) 'La pensée et la langue', *Bulletin de la Société de Linguistique de Paris* 23, 117–37.

—— (1932) *Linguistique générale et linguistique française* (4th edn, Berne, 1965).

Bandini, A. R. (1948) 'The Way of the Translator is Hard', *Catholic World* 167, 60–6.

Bar-Hillel, Y. (1962) 'Four Lectures on Algebraic Linguistics and Machine Translation', *Automatic Translation of Languages*, papers presented at the NATO Summer School, Venice, July 1962 (London, 1966).

Barrera-Vidal, A. (1971) 'La traduction en français moderne du prétérit simple et du prétérit composé espagnols. Essai d'analyse différentielle', in Bausch and Gauger (1971, 397–415).

Barzun, J. (1953) 'Food for the NRF or "My God! What Will You Have?"', *Partisan Review* 20:2, 660–74.

Bates, E. S. (1936) *Modern Translation* (London).

Batteux, C. (1747–8) *Principes de littérature* (6 vols, Lyon, 1802).

Battles, F. (1963) 'Englishing the Institutes of John Calvin', *Bable* 9, 94–8.

Batts, M. S. (1975) *Translation and Interpretation, a Symposium* (Vancouver).

Bausch, K. R. (1968) 'Die Transposition, Versuch einer neuen Klassification', *Linguistica Antverpiensia* 2, 29–50.

—— (1970) 'Qualité en traduction et linguistique dite différentielle', *Babel* 16, 13–21.

Bausch, K. R. and Gauger, H. M. (eds) (1971) *Interlinguistica: Sprachvergleich und Übersetzung*, Festschrift zum 60 Geburtstag von Mario Wandruszka (Tübingen).

Beekman, J. (1965) *Notes on Translation with Drills* (Summer Institute of Linguistics, Santa Ana, Cal.).

Beerbohm, Max (1903) 'Advice to Those about to Translate', *Saturday Review* 96, 75–6.

Bell, H. I and D. (1942) *Dafydd ap Gwilym – Fifty Poems* (London).

Belloc, Hilaire (1924) 'On Translation', *London Mercury* 10, 150–6.

—— (1931) *On Translation*, Taylorian Lecture (London).

Benjamin, W. (1923) 'Die Aufgabe des Übersetzens', in Störig (1963, 182–95).

Benson, A. C. (1924) 'Verse Translation', *Cornhill Magazine* 57, 586–98.

Bitaubé, P. J. (1770?) 'Réflexions sur la traduction des poètes', in *Oeuvres complètes de Bitaubé* (4th edn, Paris, 1804), I. 55–79; IV. 39–82.

Blixen, O. (1954) *La traducción literaria y sus problemas* (Montevideo).

Blount, T. P. (1694) *De re poetica or Remarks upon Poetry* (Hildesheim, 1969).

Bodmer, J. J. and Breitinger, J. J. (1746) *Critische Briefe* (Hildesheim, 1969).

Boethius (500?) *In isagogen Porphyrii*, ed. S. Brant, in *Corpus scriptorum ecclesiasticorum latinorum* 48 (Vienna and Leipzig, 1906).

Bogenschneider, H. J. (1959) 'Technischer Übersetzer und Technische Bibliothek', *Babel* 5, 200–206.

Bois, John (1605–8) 'Notes on the Authorised Version', ed. W. Allen, in *Translating for King James* (Nashville, Tenn., 1969).

—— (1655) *Veteris interpretis cum Beza aliisque recentioribus collatio* (London).

Bolinger, D. (1966) 'Transformation; Structural Translation', *Acta linguistica hafniensia* 9, 130–44.

Bonavia-Hunt, N. A. (1969) *Horace the Minstrel* (Kineton, England).

Bonnefoy, Y. (1962) *Hamlet*, Mercure de France, Paris.

Bonnerot, L. *et al.* (1963) *Chemins de la traduction, domaine anglais; du français à l'anglais, de l'anglais au français* (Paris).

Boudon, R. (1965) 'Lingua volgare e partizipazione attiva', *Traduzione dei libri liturgici* (Vatican City), 27–42.

Bovie, S. P. (1964) 'Translation as a Form of Criticism', in Arrowsmith and Shattuck (1964, 51–75).

Bridges, Robert (1916) *Ibant obscuri; an Experiment in the Classical Hexameter* (Oxford).

Brislin, R. W. (ed.) (1976) *Translation: Applications and Research* (New York).

Brower, R. A. (1966a) *On Translation* (New York).

—— (1966b) 'Seven Agamemnons', ibid., 173–95.

Brun, L. (1929) 'Contribution à l'étude de la traduction: d'une différence fondamentale entre le slave (le tchèque) et le français: l'imparfait', *Travaux du cercle linguistique de Prague* 1, 156–69.

Bruni Aretino, Leonardo (1420?) 'De interpretatione recta', *Humanistische philosophische Schriften*, ed. H. Baron (Berlin, 1928), 81–96.

Bryant W. (1972) 'A Comparison of Translation Styles', *META* (University of Montreal) 17, 160–4.

Buber, M. (1923) *I and Thou*, trans. R. G. Smith (New York).

—— (1954) 'Zu einer neuen Verdeutschung der Schrift', in Störig (1963, 322–68).

Burnouf, J.-L. (1826) *De la traduction* (Paris, 1861).

Caillé, P. F. (1960) 'Cinéma et traduction; le traducteur devant l'écran', *Babel* 6, 103–9.

Calverley, C. S. (1868) 'On Metrical Translation', *Works of C. S. Calverley* (London, 1901), 496–503.

Campbell, George (1776) *The Philosophy of Rhetoric* (2nd edn, New York, 1850).

—— (1789) *A Translation of the Four Gospels with Notes* (2 vols, London).

Capmany Suris y de Montpalau, A. (1776) *El arte de traducier el idioma francés al castellano* (Madrid).

Carlyle, Thomas (1828) 'Goethe's Collective Works', *Foreign Review* 1, 429–68.

Carmignani, G. A. F. (1808) *Dissertazione critica sulle traduzioni* (Florence).

Carne-Ross, D. S. (1962) 'Structural Translation: Notes on Logue's *Patrokleia*', *Arion* 1, 27–38.

—— (1964) 'Translation and Transposition', in Arrowsmith and Shattuck (1964, 3–28).

Cary, E. (1949) 'Défense et illustration de l'art de traduire', *La nouvelle critique* (June), 82–93.

—— (1956) *La traduction dans le monde moderne,* (Geneva).

—— (1960) 'La traduction totale', *Babel* 6, 110–15.

—— (1962–3) 'Pour une théorie de traduction', *Journal des traducteurs/Translators' Journal* 7, 118–27; 8, 3–11.

Cary, E. and Jumpelt, R. W. (eds) (1963) *Quality in Translation: Proceedings of the Third Congress of the International Federation of Translators* (New York)

Casagrande, J. B (1954) 'The Ends of Translation', *International Journal of Applied Linguistics* 20, 335–40.

Cassiodorus (560?) *Cassiodori senatoris institutiones*, ed. R. A. B. Mynors (Oxford, 1937).

Catford, J. C. (1965) *A Linguistic Theory of Translation* (London).

Cauer, P. (1893) *Die Kunst des Übersetzens* (Berlin, 1914).

Cermák, J. (1970) 'La traduction du point de vue de l'interprétation', in Holmes (1970) 23–42.

Chamberlain, A. F. (1901) 'Translation: a Study in the Transference of Folk Thought', *Journal of American Folklore* 14, 165–71.

—— (1910) 'Some Difficulties in Bible Translation', *Harpers Monthly Magazine* 121, 726–31.

Chéry, H.-C. (1951) *Le français – langue liturgique?* (Paris).

Cicero, Marcus Tullius (46 B.C.?) '*De optimo genere oratorum*', ed. A. S. Wilkins, in *Ciceronis Rhetorica*, II (Oxford, 1957).

—— (45 B.C.?) *De finibus bonorum et malorum libri IV*, ed. W. L. Hutchinson (London, 1909).

Citroen, I. J. (1959) 'The Translation of Texts Dealing with Applied Science', *Babel* 5, 30–3.

—— (1962) 'Specialisation in Technical and Scientific Translation', *Babel* 8, 66–71.

—— (1966) 'The Myth of Two Professions: Literary and Non-literary Translation', *Babel* 12, 181–8.

—— (ed.) (1967) *Ten Years of Translation* (Oxford).

Clas, A. (1971) 'L'opération traduisante', in Bausch and Gauger (1971, 607–9).

Cloud, D. (1964) 'The Problem of Liturgical Translation', *The Furrow* 15, 143–51.

Consilium for the Implementation of the Constitution on the Sacred Liturgy (1969) *Instruction on Translations of Liturgical Texts (Vatican City)*.

Cookson, G.M. (1923) 'On Translating Greek Tragedy', *Classical Review* 37, 146–8.

Corrigan, R. W. (1964) 'Translating for Actors', in Arrowsmith and Shattuck (1964, 129–46).

Coustel, P. (1687) *Règles d'éducation* (2 vols, Paris).

Craddock, J. T. (1971) 'The Translator's Tools', in Sykes (1971, 64–87).

Crim, K. R. (1972) 'Translating the Poetry of the Bible', *The Bible Translator* 23, 102–9.

—— (1973) 'Hebrew Direct Discourse as a Translation Problem', *The Bible Translator* 24, 311–16.

Croce, Benedetto (1902) *Aesthetic*, trans. D. Ainslie (London, 1962).

Cromer, E. B. (1913) 'Translation and Paraphrase'. *Edinburgh Review* 218, 102–14.

D. Z. (1771) 'An Essay on Translation', *Gentleman's Magazine* 41, 349–52.

Dante Alighieri (1308?) *Il convivio*, ed. M. Simonelli (Bologna, 1966).

Darbelnet, J. (1949–50) 'La transposition', *French Review* 23, 115–18.

—— (1952) 'Stylistique et traduction', in Vinay (1952, 105–15).

—— (1970a) 'Traduction littérale ou traduction libre?' *META* 15, 88–94.

—— (1970b) 'Dictionnaires bilingues et lexicologie différentielle', *Langages* 19, 92–102.

—— (1971) 'Accent de phrase et dialectique en anglais et français', in Bausch and Gauger (1971, 416–24).

Day Lewis, C. (1962) 'On Translating Poetry', *Essays by Divers' Hands*, ed. J. Richardson, Royal Society of Literature, London, 1963, 18-36.

de Golefer, G. (1633) *Du mérite et de l'utilité de la traduction françoise*, (Paris).

de Grandcombe (Boillot), F. (1949–51) 'Réflexions sur la traduction', *French Studies* 3, 345–50; 5, 253–63.

de Laudun D'Algaliers, P. (1597) *L'art poétique françois*, ed. J. Dedieu (Toulouse, 1909).

Delmont, T. (1890) *Cours de versions latines* (Lyons and Paris).

De Mauvillon, E. (1740) *Lettres françoises et germaniques* (London).

Dennet, H. (1965) *A Guide to Modern Versions of the New Testament* (Chicago, 1966).

Dent, E. J. (1921) 'Song Translations', *Nation* 29, 482–4.

de Stael-Holstein, Anne Louise Germanie (Necker) (1810) *De l'Allemagne* (Paris, 1853).

—— (1816) *De l'esprit des traductions*, in *Oeuvres de Madame de Stael* (Paris, 1821), vol. 17, 387–97.

Dickinson, G. L. (1929) 'On Translation', *Nation and Athenaeum* 46, 282–3.

Diderot, D. and D'Alembert, J. L. (1765) 'La traduction', in *Encyclopédie ou dictionnaire raisonné des sciences, des arts, et des métiers* (Paris and Neufchastel, 1751–65), vol. 16, 510–12.

Dionysius Exiguus (540?) 'Epistola ad Eugipium presbyterum', *Patrologia latina* 67: 345–6.

Dolet, E. (1540) 'Règles de traduire', ed. P. Rickard, in *La langue française au XVI siècle: Etude suivie de textes* (Cambridge, 1968).

Dostert, L. E. (1955) 'Problems of Translation', *Monographs on Linguistics and Language Teaching* 8.

Douglas, K. (1955) 'Problems in Literary Translation', *Georgetown Monographs* 8, 80–6.

Drinker, H. S. (1950) 'On Translating Vocal Texts', *Musical Quarterly* 36, 225–40.
Dryden, John (1661–79) *Essays of John Dryden*, ed. W. P. Ker (New York), 1961).
Du Bellay, Joachim (1549) *La deffence et illustration de la langue françoyse*, ed. E. Person (Paris, 1878).

Eliot, T. S. (1936) 'Baudelaire in Our Time', in *Essays Ancient and Modern* (London), 60–74.
Erasmus, Desiderius, *Opus epistolarum Desiderii Erasmi Roterdami*, ed. P. S. Allen (12 vols, London, 1906).
Ervin, S. and Bower, R. T. (1952–3) 'Translation Problems in International Surveys', *Public Opinion Quarterly* 16, 595–604.
Etkind, E. (1967) 'La stylistique comparée, base de l'art de traduire', *Babel* 13, 23–30.
Evans, O. E. (1976) *On Translating the Bible* (London).

Fang, Achilles (1966) 'Some Reflections on the Difficulty of Translation', in Brower (1966a, 111–13).
Ferry de Saint Constant, J. (1808–11) *Rudimens de la traduction* (2 vols, Paris).
Finlay, I. F. (1962) 'The Translation of Technical and Literary Material—Science versus Art?', *Babel* 8, 57–61.
Firbas, J. (1964) 'On Defining the Theme in Functional Sentence Analysis', *Travaux linguistiques de Prague* 1, 267–80.
Firth, J. R. (1956a) 'Linguistics and Translation', in *Selected Papers of J. R. Firth*, ed. F. R. Palmer (London, 1968), 84–95.
—— (1956b) 'Linguistic Analysis and Translation', ibid., 74–83.
Fitts, D. (1966) 'The Poetic Nuance', in Brower (1966a, 32–47).
Fitzgerald, R. (1964) 'Postscript to a Translation of the Odyssey', in Arrowsmith and Shattuck (1964, 303–51).
Fontaine, C. (1549) *Quintil Horatien ou La Critique de la Deffence de J. du Bellay*, in Person edn of Du Bellay (q.v.), 187–212.
Forster, L. (1958) 'Translation, an Introduction', in Smith, A. H. (1958, 1–28).
Fox-Strangways, A. H. (1921) 'Song Translation', *Music and Letters* 2, 211–24.
Francklin, T. (1753) *Translation, A Poem* (London).
Fréron, E. (1755) 'Nouvelles lettres angloises', *L'année littéraire* 8, 137–8.
—— (1762) 'Pensées angloises, Lettre III', ibid., 7, 45–62.
Freudenthal, H. W. L. (1942) 'The Problem of Translating', *Modern Language Journal* 26, 62–5.
Fromaigent, E. (1955) *Die Technik der praktischen Übersetzung: Deutsch–Französisch* (Zurich).
Fulke, W. (1583) *Defence of the Sincere and True Translation of the Holy Scriptures into the English Tongue*, ed. C. H. Hartshorne (Parker Society, Cambridge, 1843).
—— (1589) *Confutation of the Rhemish Testament* (New York; Boston, 1834).
Furley, D. J. (1958) 'Translation from Greek Philosophy', in Smith, A. H. (1958, 52–64).

Gachechiladze, G. R. (1967) 'Realism and Dialectics in the Art of Translation', *Babel* 13, 87–91.
Garnier, G. (1975) 'Time and Tense in French and English. Some Translation Problems', in A. Joly and T. Fraser (eds), *Studies in English Grammar* (Lille), 163–84.

Garvin, P. (1961) 'Syntactic Retrieval', in H. P. Edmundson (ed.), *Proceedings of the National Symposium on Machine Translation* (Englewood Cliffs, N.J.), 286–92.

Geoffroy, J.-L. (1783) 'Lettre VI', *L'année littéraire* 8, 73–102.

—— (1785) 'Lettre XII', ibid., 6, 216–32.

Gide, André (1928) 'Lettre à André Thérive', in *Divers* (Paris, 1931), 188–98.

Gingold, K. (1966) 'A Guide to Better Translations for Industry', *Babel* 12, 142–5.

Goddard, K. A. (1972) 'Translation and Bilingualism', *Babel* 18, 18–23.

Goethe, Johann Wolfgang von (1811–31) *Aus meinem Leben: Dichtung und Wahrheit*, ed. S. Scheibe, 2 vols, Berlin, 1970.

—— (1820) *Noten und Abhandlungen zum Divan*, excerpted *Babel* 11 (1965), 7.

—— (1827) Letter to Carlyle, *Goethebriefe*, Berlin, 1902–5, VIII. 178–82.

Goffin, R. (1968) 'La terminologie multilingue et la syntagmatique comparée au service de la traduction technique', *Babel* 14, 132–41.

Gorjan, Z. (1963) 'Men of Good Will', in Cary and Jumpelt (1963, 253–5).

—— (1966) 'Two Questions: "Is it Possible to Understand the Literature of a Foreign Language?" and "Is Translation an Adequate Mediator?"', *Babel* 12, 18–20.

Gottsched, J. C. (1730) *Versuch einer Critischen Dichtkunst*, in J. and B. Birke (eds), *J. C. Gottsched Ausgewältewerke* (Berlin and New York, 1973), vols VI.i, 113–493; VI.ii, whole vol.

Gourdin, F.-P. (1789) *De la traduction considérée comme moyen d'apprendre une langue et comme moyen de se former le goût* (Rouen).

Govaert, M. (1971) 'Critères de la traduction', in Bausch and Gauger (1971, 425–37).

Green, J. (1942) 'Translation and the "Fields of Scripture"', *American Scholar* 11, 110–21.

Gregory the Great (6th cent.) 'Epistola XXXIX ad Aristobolum', *PL* 77: 482; 'Epistola ad Narsum Religiosum', in P. Ewald and L Hartmann (eds), *Monumenta Germaniae Historiae*, Ep. I (Berlin, 1881), 474.

Grosier, J.-B. G-A. (1772) 'Critique of Cavailhon's *Orlando Furioso*', *L'année littéraire* 4, 289–324.

Gruppe, O. F. (1859) *Deutsche Übersetzungkunst* (Hannover, 1866).

Güttinger, F. (1963) *Zielsprache: Theorie und Technik des Übersetzens* (Zürich).

Haas, W. (1962) 'The Theory of Translation', *Philosophy* 37 (1962), 208–28.

Halliday, M. A. K. (1960) 'Linguistics and Machine Translation', in Halliday and A. M. MacIntosh (eds), *Patterns of Language: Papers in General and Applied Linguistics* (Bloomington, Ind., and London, 1966), 134–50.

Hardbottle, R. (1971) 'Practical Translating and Its Techniques', in Sykes (1971), 1–21.

Hébert, A. and Scott, F. (1970) *Dialogue sur la traduction* (Montréal).

Heffzallah, I. M. (1970) 'The Art of Translation', *Babel* 16, 180-7.

Heidegger, M. (1959) *On the Way to Language*, trans. P. D. Hertz (New York and London, 1971).

Heilmann, L. (1967) 'De officio arteque vertendi', in *To Honor Roman Jakobson, Essays on the Occasion of his Seventieth Birthday* (3 vols, The Hague), II. 901–9.

Herbert, J. (1964) *Manuel de l'interprète* (Geneva).

Herder, J. G. (1677) *Über die neuere deutsche Literatur* (Fragmente), in B. Suphan (ed.), *Sämtliche Werke* (Hildesheim, 1967), I. 131–532.

Higham, T. F. *et al.* (eds) (1938) *Oxford Book of Greek Verse in Translation* (London).
Hilduinus (835?) *Rescriptum Hilduini Abbatis ad serenissimum imperatorem, dominum Ludovicum,* in *Patrologia latina* 106: 13–22.
Hockett, C. F. (1954) 'Translation via Immediate Constituents', *International Journal of Applied Linguistics* 20, 313–15.
Hollander, J. (1966) 'Versions, Interpretations, and Performances', in Brower (1966a, 205–31).
Holmes, J. S. (1970) *The Nature of Translation* (The Hague and Paris).
—— 'Forms of Verse Translation and Translation of Verse Form', ibid., 91–105.
Holmstrom, J. E. (1955) 'How Translators Can Contribute to Improving Scientific Terminology', *Babel* 1, 73–9.
—— (ed.) (1957) *Scientific and Technical Translation and Other Aspects of the Language Problem* (Paris).
Hookham Frere, J. (1820) Review of T. Mitchell, *A Translation of the Comedies of Aristophanes, Quarterly Review* 23, 474–505.
Horace (Quintus Horatius Flaccus), *Opera Horati,* ed. E. C. Wickham (Oxford Classical Text, 1957).
Horguelin, P. A. (1966) 'La traduction technique', *META* 11, 15–25.
Horne, R. H. (1844) 'Remarks on Translation', *Classical Museum* 1, 398–403.
Houbigant, C.-F. (1753) *Biblica hebraica cum notis criticis et versione latina* (4 vols, Paris).
Housman, A. E. (1899) Review of *On the Use of Classical Metres in English* (W. J. Stone), *Classical Review* 13, 317–19.
Houziaux, M.-O. (1965) 'Pour une autonomie des recherches en traduction automatique', *Babel* 11, 118–21.
Howard, R. (1964) 'A Professional Translator's Trade Alphabet', in *The Craft and Context of Translation* (New York), 247–59.
Howerton, P. W. (1962) 'Technical Translations: Their Initiation, Production and Use', *Special Libraries* 53, 21–5.
Huebsch, B. W. (1942) 'Cross-fertilisation in Letters', *American Scholar* 11, 304–14.
Huet, P. D. (1661) *De interpretatione* (Stade, 1680).
Hugo, Victor (1864) 'Préface pour la nouvelle traduction de Shakespeare', in F. Bouvet (ed.), *Oeuvres complètes, Oeuvres critiques complètes* (Paris, 1963), 1441–4.
Hulst, A. R. (1963) 'Bible Translating into Dutch', *Babel* 9, 79–82.
Humbertus de Romanis (1274) 'Discourse at the Council of Lyons', in J. D. Mansi (ed.), *Sacrorum conciliorum nova collectio* (Venice, 1780), 24: 128–9.
Humphries, R. (1966) 'Latin and English Verse—some Practical Considerations', in Brower (1966a, 57–66).

Iannucci, J. E. (1959) 'Explanatory Matter in Bilingual Dictionaries', *Babel* 5, 195–9.
Ilek, B. (1970) 'On Translating Images', in Holmes (1970, 135–8).

Jakobson, R. (1966) 'On Linguistic Aspects of Translation', in Brower (1966a, 232–9).
Jankowsky, K. R. (1970) 'Lexicology and its Potential Contribution to the Theory of Translation', *Babel* 16, 135–42.

Jechová, H. (1970) 'La Perspective de la représentation littéraire et le problème de la traduction', in Holmes (1970, 43–6).

St. Jerome (Sophronius Eusebius Hieronymus), *Ad Pammachium* (Ep. 57), in I. Hilberg (ed.), *Sancti Eusebii Hieronymi Epistulae, Corpus Scriptorum Ecclesiasticorum Latinorum* (vols 54–6, Vienna and Leipzig, 1910–18), 54: 503–26.

—— *Ad Sunniam et Fretellam* (Ep. 106), ibid., 55: 247–89.

—— (380?) Preface to Eusebius, *Patrologia Latina* 27: 33–40.

—— (383?) Preface to Pentateuch, *PL*. 28: 147–52.

—— (384?) Preface to Isaiah, *PL*. 28: 771–4.

—— (386?) *Commentarium in epistolam ad Ephesios*, *PL* 28: 439–554.

John of Salisbury (1180?) *Metalogicon*, *PL* 199: 823–945.

Jumpelt, R. W. (1958) 'Fachsprachen—Fachwörter—als Problem der Dokumentation und Übersetzung', *Sprachforum* 3, 1–13.

—— (1961) *Die Übersetzung naturwissenschaftlicher und technischer literatur* (Berlin-Schöneberg).

—— (1963) 'Methodological Approaches to Science Translation', in Cary and Jumpelt (1963, 267–81).

Kahn, F. (1971–2) 'Traduction et linguistique', *Cahiers Ferdinand de Saussure* 27, 21–42.

Kallman, C. (1954) 'Opera in Translation: Some Notes on an Almost Impossible Craft', *Center* I. 1, 11–13.

Kallman, C. and Auden, W. H. (1962) 'Translating Opera Libretti', in W. H. Auden (ed.), *The Dyer's Hand* (New York), 483–99.

Kattan, N. (1975) 'Problèmes particuliers de la traduction de textes littéraires', in Batts (1975, 72–82).

Keen, D. (1957) 'Les mots intraduisables', *Vie et langage* 61, 178–82.

Kemp, F. (1965) *Kunst und Vergnügen des Übersetzens* (Pfullingen).

Kerman, J. (1964) 'Translation for Music', in Arrowsmith and Shattuck (1964, 147–64).

Kirk, R. (1969) 'Translation and Indeterminacy', *Mind* 78, 321–41.

Kloepfer, R. (1967) *Die Theorie der literarischen Übersetzung romanisch–deutsch Sprachbereich* (Munich).

Knight, D. (1966) 'Translation: The Augustan Mode', Brower (1966) 196–204.

Knox, R. A. (1949) *Trials of a Translator* (New York).

—— (1957) *On English Translation*, Clarendon Press, Oxford.

Kochel, V. (1970) 'The Problem of Verse Rhythm in Translation', in Holmes (1970, 106–11).

Koessler, M. and Derocquigny, J. (1928) *Les Faux Amis ou les trahisons du vocabulaire* (Paris).

Koschmieder, E. (1955) 'Das Problem der Übersetzung', *Corolla linguistica Festschrift F. Sommer* (Wiesbaden), 120–8.

Krzesowski, T. P. (1971) 'Equivalence, Congruence and Deep Structure', *Papers in Contrastive Linguistics*, ed. G. Nickel, Cambridge University Press.

Kuič, R. (1970) 'Translating English Romantic Poetry', in Holmes (1970, 182–91).

Kutzleb, H. (1941) 'Übersetzen', *Monatsschrift für das deutsche Geistesleben* (Nov.), 340–5.

Lamb, S. M. (1961a) 'Machine Translation Research at the University of California, Berkeley', in *Proceedings of the National Symposium on Machine Translation* (Englewood Cliffs, N.J.), 140–54.

—— (1961b) 'Segmentation', ibid., 335–42.

Larbaud, V. (1946) *Sous l'invocation de Saint Jerôme* (Paris).

Latomus, J. (1518) *De trium linguarum et studii theologi ratione dialogus* (Basle).

Lattimore, H. (1966) 'Practical Notes on Translating Greek Poetry', in Brower (1966a, 48–56).

Leclerc, J. (1688) 'Règles de critique pour l'intelligence des anciens auteurs', *Bibliothèque universelle* (Amsterdam, 1718), x. 309–20.

—— (1712) *Joannis Clerici ars critica* (3 vols, Amsterdam).

Lednicki, W. (1952) 'Some Notes on the Translation of Poetry', *American Slavic and East European Review* 11, 304–11.

Lefevre, A. (1970) 'The Translation of Literature: an Approach', *Babel* 16, 75–80.

Leishman, J. B. (1956) *Translating Horace* (Oxford).

Levik, V. V. (1970) 'La traduction et création littéraires', in Holmes (1970, 163–9).

Levý, J. (1967) 'Translation as a Decision Process', in *To Honor Roman Jakobson. Essays on the Occasion of his Seventieth Birthday* (The Hague) II.1171–82.

—— (1969) *Die literarische Übersetzung: Theorie einer Kunstgattung* (Frankfurt and Bonn).

L'Isle, W. (1623) *A Saxon Treatise Concerning the Old and New Testament* (London).

Littré, E. (1847) 'La poésie homérique et l'ancienne poésie française', *Revue des deux mondes* 19, 109–61.

Longacre, R. E. (1958) 'Items in Context, Their Bearing on Translation Theory', *Language* 34, 482–91.

Lupan, R. (1970) 'Sur l'esprit moderne dans l'art de traduire', in Holmes (1970, 150–6).

Luther, Martin (1530) *Ein Sendbrief vom Dolmetschen*, in *Werke* (Weimar, 1883–1970), xxx. 627–46.

—— (1531–3) *Summarien Über die Psalmen und Ursachen des Dolmetschens*, ibid., XXXVIII. 9–69.

Magnus, L. (1931) 'Hours in Undress: Translation', *Cornhill Magazine* 71, 244–54.

Maillet-Lacoste, P.-L. and Charma, A. (1843) *Polémique sur la traduction* (Caen).

Maillot, J. (1970) *La traduction scientifique et technique* (Paris).

Malblanc, A. (1944) *Vers une stylistique comparée du français et de l'allemand* (Paris).

—— (1968) *Stylistique comparée du français et de l'allemand* (Paris)

Manchester, P. T. (1951) 'Verse Translation as an Interpretative Art', *Hispania* 34, 68–73.

Mandefield, H. W. (1952) 'La science et le métier en traduction', in Vinay (1952, 65–83).

Marouzeau, J. (1924) 'La traduction et l'ordre des mots', *Revue des études latines* 2, 189–95.

—— (1931) *La traduction du latin* (4th edn, Paris, 1951).

—— (1935) *Traité de stylistique appliquée au latin* (Paris).

Martin, Gregory (1582) *Discoverie of the manifold Corruptions of the Holy Scriptures by the Heretikes of our Daies* (Rheims).

—— (1582b) *The New Testament* (Rheims).

Mason, H. A. (1963) 'The Women of Trachis and Creative Translation', in J. P. Sullivan (ed.), *Ezra Pound* (Penguin Books, 1970), 279–309.

May, J. L. (1927) 'Concerning Translation', *Edinburgh Review* 245, 108–10.

Melancthon (1522) Correspondence with Spalatin, in C. G. Brotschmeider (ed.), *Corpus reformatorum* (Halle, 1836), III. 563–84.

Menéndez y Pelayo, M. (1900?) *Juicios doctrinales. Antologia general de Menéndez y Pelayo* (Madrid, 1956), I. 37–288.

Meschonnic, H. (1973) *Pour la poétique* II (Paris).

Miko, F. (1970) 'La théorie de l'expression et de la traduction', in Holmes (1970, 61–77).

Milligan, E. E. (1957) 'Some Principles and Techniques of Translation', *Modern Language Journal* 41, 66–71.

Mommsen, T. (1858) *Die Kunst des deutschen Übersetzens* (Oldenburg).

More, Sir Thomas (1528) *A Dialogue concernynge Heresyes and matters of Religion made in the Yere of oure Lord MDXXVIII*, eds W. E. Campbell and A. W. Reed (London, 1927).

Morgan, B. Q. (1956) 'What is Translation For?' *Symposium* 10, 322–8.

Moritzen, J. (1921) 'Is the Translator Without a Literary Conscience?' *Bookman* 53, 133–5.

Mounin, G. (1955) *Les Belles Infidéles* (Paris).

—— (1963) *Les problèmes théoriques de la traduction* (Paris).

—— (1964) 'L'intraduisibilité comme notion statistique', *Babel* 10, 122–4.

—— (1976) *Linguistique et traduction* (Brussels).

Muir, E. and W. (1966) 'Translating from the German', in Brower (1966a, 91–6).

Mund, A. (1968) 'La traduction lyrique; Art, science et technique', *Babel* 14, 144–51.

Murray, Gilbert (1923) 'On Translating Greek', *Living Age* 318, 420–3.

Murry, John Middleton (1925) 'Classical Translations', *Pencillings* (Freeport, N.Y.), 128–37.

McFarlane, J. (1953) 'Modes of Translation', *Durham University Journal* 45, 77–93.

McKenna, Stephen (April 1919) Letter to E. R. Debenham, in E. R. Dodds (ed.), *Journal and Letters of Stephen McKenna* (New York), 153–6.

McQuown, N. A. (1960) 'Discussion on Symposium on Translation between Language and Culture', *Anthropological Linguistics* 2, 79–80.

Nabokov, V. (1941) 'The Art of Translation', *New Republic* 105, 160.

—— (1955) 'Problems in Translation: *Onegin* in English', *Partisan Review* 22, 496–512.

—— (1966) 'The Servile Path', in Brower (1966a, 97–109).

Nette, H. (1946) *Wort und Sinn* (Fulda).

Newcome, W. (1792) *An Historical View of the English Biblical Translations and the Expediency of Revising by Authority of our Present Translation* (Dublin).

—— (1796) *An Attempt towards Revising our English Translation of the Greek Scriptures* (2 vols, Dublin).

Newman, F. W. (1861) *Homeric Translation in Theory and Practice* (London and Edinburgh).

—— 'Essay on Poetical Translation', *Fraser's Magazine* N.S. 12, 88–96.

Newmark, P. (1957) 'Standards of Translation', *Journal of Education* 89, 248–50.

—— (1973) 'An Approach to Translation', *Babel* 19, 3–18.

Nida, E. A. (1945) 'Linguistics and Ethnology in Translation Problems', *Word* 2, 194–208.

—— (1961) *Comment traduire la bible*, trans. J.-C. Margot (Paris, 1967).
—— (1964) *Toward a Science of Translating with Special Reference to Principles and Procedures Involved in Bible Translation* (Leiden).
Nida, E. A. and Tabor, C. R. (1969) *The Theory and Practice of Translation* (Leiden).
Nietzsche, F. (n.d.) 'Zum Problem des Übersetzens', in Störig (1963, 136–8).
Nöel, J. (1966) 'Linguistics and Translation', *Revue des langues vivantes* 32, 525–31.

O'Brien, J. (1966) 'From French to English', in Brower (1966a, 78–92).
Oettinger, A. G. (1960) *Automatic Language Translation* (Cambridge, Mass.).
Opitz, M. (1624) *Buch von der deutschen Poetery* (repr. Halle, 1876).
Ortega y Gasset, J. (1945) 'Miseria y esplendor de la traducción', in *El libro de las misiones* (Buenos Aires, 133–72).
Outhier, J. J. (1802) *L'art de traduire le latin en français et le français en latin* (Paris).

Paepke, F. (1971) 'Sprach-, Text-, und Sachgemäßes Übersetzen: Ein Thesentwarf', in Bausch and Gauger (1971, 610–16).
Palsgrave, J. (1540) *The Comedy of Acolastus; Translated from the Latin of Fullonius*, ed. P. L. Carver, Early English Text Society, Old Series 202, Oxford, 1935.
Panneton, G. (1947) 'Graphique de l'art de transposer', in Vinay (1952, 29–46).
Paris, J. (1964) 'Translation and Creation', in Arrowsmith and Shattuck (1964, 77–91).
Pascher, G. (1965) 'Traduzioni e tradizione', *Le traduzioni dei libri liturgici, Atti del congresso tenuto a Roma il 9–13 novembre 1965* (Vatican City, 1966), 89–108.
Pasquier, E. (1576) *Choix de lettres sur la littérature, la langue et la traduction*, ed. D. Thicket (Geneva, 1956).
Pattison, E. W. (1860) 'Translation', *University Quarterly* 2, 124–35.
Paz, O. (1971) *Traducción: Literatura y literalidad* (Barcelona).
Péguy, C. (1908) 'Les Suppliants parallèles', in *Oeuvres complètes* II (Paris, 1920), 379–474.
Peletier du Mans, J. (1555) *L'art poétique*, ed. J. Boulanger (Paris, 1930).
Peyser, H. F. (1922) 'Some Observations on Song Text and Libretto Translation', *Musical Quarterly* 8, 353–71.
Phillimore, J. S. (1919) *Some Remarks on Translation and Translators* (English Association Pamphlet 42, London).
Philo Iudaeus (20 B.C.?) *De vita Mosis* (Loeb Classical Library, Cambridge, Mass. and London, 1935).
Plinius Secundus (A.D. 85?) Epistola VII. 9, *Pliny's Letters* (Loeb Classical Library, 1969), 501–7.
Pocar, E. (1964) 'Lektor und Übersetzer', *Babel* 10, 20–3.
Poggioli, R. (1966) 'The Added Artificer', in Brower (1966a, 137–47).
Politian, Angelo, (1486–7) 'Oratio in expositione Homeri', *Opera omnia* (Basle, 1553), 477–92.
Politzer, L. (1956) 'A Brief Classification of the Limits of Translatability', *Modern Language Journal* 40, 319–22.
Pope, Alexander (1714) 'To Edward Blount', in G. Sherburn (ed.), *The Correspondence of Alexander Pope* (London, 1956), I. 246.
Postgate, J. P. (1922) *Translation and Translators* (London).
Pound, Ezra, *The Letters of Ezra Pound (1907–1941)*, ed. D. D. Page (London, 1951).

—— *Literary Essays of Ezra Pound*, ed. T. S. Eliot (New York, 1954).

Pratt, A. W. and Pacak, M. G. (1969) 'Automated Processing of Medical English', in *Preprints of the International Conference on Computational Linguistics* (Stockholm).

Procházka, V. (1942) 'Notes on Translating Technique', in *Prague School Reader on Aesthetics, Literary Structure and Style* (Washington D.C., 1964), 93–112.

Purvey, John (attrib.) (1385?) 'On Translating the Bible', in A. W. Pollard (ed.), *Fifteenth-Century Prose and Verse* (New York and London, 1903), 193–9.

Quenneville, N. (1805) *Virgile à Jacques Delille, ou Dialogue des morts sur la traduction des six premiers livres de l'Enéide* (Paris).

Quine, W. V. (1960) *Word and Object* (Cambridge, Mass.).

—— (1966) 'Meaning and Translation', in Brower (1966a, 138–72).

Quintilian (A.D. 100?) *Institutionis oratoriae libri XII*, ed. L. Radermacher (2 vols, Leipzig, 1965).

Rabin, C. (1958) 'The Linguistics of Translation', in Smith, A. H. (1958, 123–45).

Raffel, B. (1971) *The Forked Tongue, A Study of the Translation Process* (The Hague).

Ray, Punya Sloka (1962) 'A Philosophy of Translation', *Babel* 8, 182–8.

Rescher, N. (1956) 'Translation as a Tool for Philosophical Analysis', *Journal of Philosophy* 53, 219–24.

Reyburn, W. D. (1969–70) 'Cultural Equivalence and Non-Equivalences in Translation', *The Bible Translator* 20, 158–67; 21, 26–35.

Rhodes, I. (1962) 'Syntactic Integration Carried out Mechanically', *Automatic Translation of Languages, papers presented at the* NATO *Summer School, Venice, July 1962* (London, 1966), 205–9.

Richards, I. A. (1932) 'Towards a Theory of Translating', in A. F. Wright (ed.) (1953) *Studies in Chinese Thought* (Chicago) 247–62.

Richens, R. H. and Booth, A. D. (1955) 'Some Methods of Mechanised Translation', in W. N. Locke and A. D. Booth (eds), *Machine Translation of Languages* (New York and London), 24–46.

Robinson, I. (1973) 'Religious English', in *The Survival of English: Essays in Criticism of Language* (Cambridge), 22–65.

Roguet, A.-M. (1965a) 'Problèmes des traductions liturgiques', *Etudes* 322, 369–79.

—— (1965b) 'I generi literari dei testi liturgici loro traduzione e uso liturgico', *Traduzioni dei libri liturgici* (Vatican City, 1965), 145–60.

Rollin, C. (1725) *De la manière d'enseigner et d'étudier les belles lettres* (4 vols, Paris, 1765).

Ronai, P. (1958) 'The Trials of a Technical Translator', *Babel* 4, 210–12.

Roscommon, Wentworth Dillon, Earl of (1684) *An Essay on Translated Verse* (London).

Rouse, W. H. D. (1908) 'Translation', *Classical Review* 22, 105–10.

Roux, R. (1954) 'De l'art de traduire les économistes', *Kyklos* 7, 354–94.

Rowe, T. L. (1960) 'The English Dubbing Text', *Babel* 6, 116–26.

Rudhart, J. (1964) 'Réflexions philosophiques à l'occasion d'un exercice de traduction', *Cahiers Ferdinand de Saussure* 21, 55–85.

Rüdinger, H. (1938) 'Problematik des Übersetzens', *Neue Jahrbücher für antike und deutsche Bildung* 1, 179–90.

Rufinus Aquiliensis (400?) *Apologia in Hieronymum*, ed. M. Simonetti (Alba, 1957).

Saint-Evremond (1674) *Réflexions sur nos traducteurs*, in *Oeuvres en prose*, ed. R. Ternois (Paris, 1966), III. 96–117.

Saint-Simon, M. H. de (1771) *Essai de traduction littérale et énergique* (2 vols, Haarlem).

Savory, T. (1957) *The Art of Translation* (Philadelphia).

Schadewalt, W. (1927) 'Das Problem des Übersetzens', in Störig (1963, 249–267).

—— (1957) 'Antike Tragödie auf des modernen Bühne', in *Hellas und Hesperien* (2nd edn, Zürich and Stuttgart, 1970), II. 622:71.

—— (1958) 'Aus der Wekstatt meines Übersetzens', ibid., 671–80.

—— (1966) 'Die Übersetzung im Zeitalter der Kommunikation', ibid., 680–8.

Scherer, E. (1876) 'De la traduction en vers', in *Etudes sur la littérature contemporaine* (Paris, 1886), v. 319–40.

Schleiermacher, F. (1813) 'Über die verschiedenen Methoden des Übersetzens', in Störig (1963, 38–70).

Scholz, K. W. H. (1918) *The Art of Translation* (Philadelphia).

Schopenhauer, A. (1861) 'Parerga et Paralipomena über Sprache und Worte', in Störig (1963, 101–7).

Schorp, A. (1963) 'Quelques critères de qualité dans les traductions techniques', in Cary and Jumpelt (1963, 333–47).

Schottel, J. G. (1663) 'Wie man recht verdeutschen soll', *Ausführliche Arbeit von der Deutschen Hauptsprache*, ed. W. Hecht (Tübingen, 1967), II. 1218–68.

Shattuck, R. (1964) 'Artificial Horizon; Translator as Navigator', in Arrowsmith and Shattuck (1964, 215–33).

Shillan, D. (1970) 'An Application of Contrastive Linguistics', *META* 15, 161–3.

Simpson, E. (1975) 'Methodology in Translation Criticism', *META* 20, 251–62.

Sliosberg, A. (1971) 'Quelques considerations sur la traduction médicale et pharmaceutique', *Babel* 17, 14–21.

Smeaton, B. H. (1958–9) 'Translation, Structure and Learning', *Journal des traducteurs/Translator's Journal* 3, 122–30; 4, 9–14.

Smith, A. H. (ed.) (1958) *Aspects of Translation* (London).

Smith, G. G. (ed.) (1904) *Elizabethan Critical Essays* (2 vols, London).

Smith, J. M. Powis (1926) 'Some Difficulties of a Translator', *Journal of Religion* 5, 163–71.

Smyth, T. Taggart (1949) 'The Art of Translating', in Vinay, (1952, 19–27).

Sorel, C. (1667) *Bibliothèque français* (Paris).

Souter, A. (1920) *Hints on Translation* (New York).

Spaeth, S. (1915) 'Translating to Music', *Musical Quarterly* 1, 291–8.

Spence, J. (1737) *An Essay on Mr Pope's Odyssey* (London).

Spolsky, B. (1962) 'Comparative Stylistics and the Principle of Economy', *Journal des traducteurs/Translators' Journal* 7, 79–83.

Steiner, G. (1966) 'To Traduce or Transfigure', *Encounter* 27:2, 48–54.

—— (1975) *After Babel* (London).

Stern, P. (1949–50) 'The Violet and the Crucible', *Cambridge Journal* 3, 389–405.

Stone, W. J. (1899) *On the Use of Classical Metres in English* (London).

Störig, H. J. (ed.) (1963) *Das Problem des Übersetzens* (Stuttgart).

Storr, F. (1909) 'The Art of Translation', *Educational Review* 38, 359–79.

Süskind, W. E. and von der Vring, G. (1963) 'Die Kunst der Übersetzung', in *Die Kunst der Übersetzung* (Munich), 9–40.

Sutor, Petrus (1525) *De translatione bibliae et novarum reprobatione interpretationum* (Paris).
Swadesh, M. (1960) 'On the Unit of Translation', *Anthropological Linguistics* 2:2, 39–42.
Sykes, J. B. (1971) *Technical Translator's Manual* (London).
Symonds, J. A. (1890) 'National Style', in *Essays Speculative and Suggestive* (2 vols, London), I. 268–331.

Taber, C. R. (1970) 'Explicit and implicit Information in Translation', *The Bible Translator* 21, 1–9.
Tallgren, O. J. (1924) 'Savoir, comprendre, traduire', *Neuphilologische Mitteilungen* 25, 162–86.
Tarnóczi, L. (1967) 'Congruence entre l'original et la traduction', *Babel* 13, 137–43.
Tennyson, Alfred (1863) 'Attempts at Classical Metres in Quantity', *Cornhill Magazine* 8, 707–9.
Terence (185–149 B.C.) *Comediae*, ed. J. Marouzeau (3 vols, Paris, 1947).
Terracini, B. (1951) 'El problema de la traducción', in *Conflictas de lenguas y de cultura* (Buenos Aires), 43–97.
Testard, M. (1975) 'La traduction du latin', in *Problèmes littéraires de la traduction* (Louvain and Leiden), 29–55.
Thalmann, M. (1925) 'Gestaltungsfragen lyrischer Übersetzung', *Die neueren Sprachen* 33, 321–32.
Thierfelder, F. (1955) 'Darf der Übersetzer den Text des Originals verandern?' *Babel* 1, 51–4.
Thomas Aquinas (1263?) 'Contra errores Graecorum', *Divi Thomae Aquinatis doctoris angelici opuscula omnia* (Antwerp, 1612), vol. I.
Thursfield, H. (1936) 'Translation', *Cornhill Magazine* 153, 482–6.
Toksvig, S. (1920) 'The Mutilation of a Masterpiece', *New Republic* 25, 113–15.
Tolman, H. C. (1901) *The Art of Translating* (Boston, Mass.).
Trevisa, John (1387?) 'Dialogue between a Lord and a Clerk upon Translation', in A. W. Pollard (ed.), *Fifteenth-century Prose and Verse* (New York, 1903), 203–10.
Tyrell, R. V. (1887–8) 'Translation as a Fine Art', *Hermathena* 6, 147–58.
Tytler, A. F. (1790) *Essay on the Principles of Translation* (New York and London, n.d.).

Ure, J. (1963) 'Types of Translation and Translatability', in Cary and Jumpelt (1963, 136–46).
Ure, J. Rodger, A. and Ellis, J. (1969) 'Soma=Sleep: an Exercise in the Use of Descriptive Linguistic Techniques in Literary Translation', *Babel* 15, 4–14.

Valeri, D. (1965) 'Qualche nota sul tradurre poesie *Lirici tedeschi*, 1959', *Babel* 11,7.
Valgimigli, M. (1916) 'Poesia e traduzione di poesia', in *Del tradurre e alteri scritti* (Milan, 1957), 22–59.
—— (1952) 'Del tradurre da poesia antica', ibid., 3–21.
van Doren, M. (1950) 'The Uses of Translation', *Nation* 170, 474.
van Hoof, H. (1962) *La Théorie et pratique de l'interprétation* (Munich).
—— (1971) 'Recherche d'un modèle d'analyse en traduction', *META* 16, 83–94.

(Second) Vatican Council (1963) *Constitution on the Sacred Liturgy*, *Documents of Vatican II*, ed. W. M. Abbot (New York, 1966), 137–82.

Vernay, H. (1974) *Essai sur l'organisation de l'espace par divers systèmes linguistiques: Contribution à une linguistique de la traduction* (Munich).

Vinay, J.-P. (1952) *A la recherche d'une traduction* Montreal, 47–63.

—— (1966) 'Stylistique et transformation', *META* 11, 3–14.

—— (1975) 'The Theory of Translation: Myth or Reality', in Batts (1975, 35–46).

Vinay, J.-P. and Darbelnet, J. (1958) *Stylistique comparée du français et de l'anglais* (Paris).

Virágh, Z. (1966) 'Linguistic Problems of a Jurist: Translation and Adaptation of Trademarks', *Babel* 12, 146–9.

Virtue, L. M. and Baklanoff, N. W. (1952) 'The Technique of Translation', *Modern Language Journal* 36, 396–401.

Vivès, J. L. (1531a) *De causis corruptarum artium*, in *Opera omnia* (Valencia, 1782; repr. London, 1964), vi.8–238.

—— (1531b) *De tradendis disciplinis*, ibid., 243–415.

—— (1532) *De ratione dicendi*, ibid., ii. 93–237.

Vivier, R. (1975) 'La traduction des poètes', in *Problèmes littéraires de la traduction* (Louvain and Leiden), 56–63.

Voegelin, C. F. (1953) 'From FL (Shawnee) to TL (English: Autobiography of a Woman', *International Journal of Applied Linguistics* 19, 1–25, 106–17.

—— (1954) 'Multiple Stage Translation', *IJAL* 20, 271–80.

Voltaire (1736) *Lettres philosophiques*, ed. G. Lanson (2 vols, Paris).

Voltaire, Jean-Marie Arouet de (1736) *Jules César, Oeuvres Complètes* (Paris, 1785) IX: 361–440.

von der Gabelentz, G. (1869) 'Ideen zu einer vergleichenden Syntax', *Zeitschrift für Völkerpsychologie und Sprachwissenschaft* 6, 376–84.

—— (1875) 'Weiteres zur vergleichenden Syntax', ibid., 8, 129–65, 300–38.

—— (1891) *Die Sprachwissenschaft*, ed. G. Narr and U. Petersen (Tübingen, 1969).

von Doderer, H. (1963) 'Réponse à l'enquête', in Cary and Jumpelt (1963, 193).

von Humboldt, W. (1816) 'Einleitung zur Agamemnon-Übersetzung', in Störig (1963, 71–96).

von Radecki, S. (1963) 'Vom übersetzen', in *Die Kunst der Übersetzung*, Munich), 40–76.

von Wilamowitz-Moellendorf, U. (1891) 'Was ist Übersetzen?' in Störig (1963, 139–69).

Vossler, K. (1925) 'Sprachgemeinschaft als Gesinnungsgemeinschaft', in Störig (1963, 196–219).

Walmsley, J. B. (1970) 'Transformation Theory and Translation', *International Review of Applied Linguistics* 8, 185–99.

Wandruszka, M. (1967) 'Implicitation et explicitation', *Revue des langues romanes* 31, 316–30.

—— (1968) 'L'aspect verbal, problème de traduction', *Travaux de linguistique et de littérature* 6:1, 113–29.

—— (1971) 'Nos langues; structures instrumentales—structures mentales', *META* 16, 7–16.

Warren, T. H. (1895) 'The Art of Translation', *Quarterly Review* 182, 324–353.

Weaver, W. (1949) 'Translation', in W. N. Locke and A. D. Booth (eds), *Machine Translation of Languages* (New York and London, 1955), 15–23.
Webbe, Joseph (1622) *An Appeale to Truth* (Menston, 1967).
Weightman, J. G. (1950) 'Translation as a Linguistic Exercise', *English Language Teaching* 5, 69–75.
Weil, H. (1844) *De l'ordre des mots dans les langues anciennes comparées aux langues modernes: Question de grammaire générale* (2nd edn, Paris).
Weisgerber, L. (1955) 'Das Dolmetschen und die sprachliche Verwandlung der Welt', *Babel* 1,7–9.
Wellard, J. H. (1928) 'The Art of Translating', *Quarterly Review* 250, 128–47.
Widmer, W. (1959) *Fug und Unfug des Übersetzens* (Cologne and Berlin).
Wilhelm, J. (1971) 'Zum Problem der literarischen Übersetzung', in Bausch and Gauger (1971, 617–27).
Will, F. (1973) *The Knife in the Stone* (The Hague and Paris).
Wils, J. (1963) 'Aspects of Sacral Language', *Babel* 9, 36–47.
Winston, R. (1950) 'The Craft of Translation', *American Scholar* 19, 179–86.
Winter, W. (1964) 'Impossibilities of Translation', in Arrowsmith and Shattuck (1964, 93–113).
Winthrop, H. (1966) 'A Proposed Model for Studying Message Distortion in Translation', *Linguistics* 22, 98–112.
Wirl, J. (1958) *Grundsätliches zur Problematik des Dolmetschens und des Übersetzens* (Vienna).
Wuthenow, R. R. (1969) *Das fremde Kunstwerk* (Göttingen).
Wycliffe, John (1377–8) *De veritate sacrae scripturae* ed. R. Buddenseig (3 vols, London, 1905–7).
Wyss, S. (1975) 'A Problem in Contrastive Linguistics: *chassé–croisé* Sentences or Deep Instrumentals as Surface Verbs', in A. Joly and T. Fraser (eds), *Studies in English* (Lille), 131–61.

Young, D. (1964) 'Summing up of a Round Table Discussion on Translation and Translators Held by the International PEN Club', *Babel* 10, 154–8.

Zeydel, E. H. (1941) 'Can We Rely on Translation?' *Modern Language Journal* 25, 401–4.
Zilahy, S. P. (1963) 'Quality in Translation', in Cary and Jumpelt (1963, 285–9).

2. SECONDARY SOURCES

Amos, F. R. (1920) *Early Theories of Translation* (New York).
Arnold, T. W. and Guillaume, A. (1931) *The Legacy of Islam* (London).
Atzert, K. (1908) *De Cicerone interprete graecorum* (Göttingen).

Baillet, A. (1685–6) 'Traduction', in *Jugemens des sçavans sur les principaux ouvrages des auteurs* (Paris), III.301–702.
Bardy, G. (1940) 'Traducteurs et adapteurs au quatrième siècle', *Recherches de science religieuse* 30, 257–306.
Beaulieu, C. (1904) 'Liste des dictionnaires, lexiques et vocabulaires français antérieures au *Thrésor* de Nicot (1606)', in *Mélanges Ferdinand Brunot* (Paris).

Bédoret, H. (1938) 'Les premières traductions tolédanes de philosophie—oeuvres d'Alfarabi', *Revue néoscolastique de philosophie* 41, 80–97.

Bellanger, J. (1892) *Histoire de la traduction en France* (Paris).

Benson, L. F. (1915) *The English Hymn, its Development and Use in Worship* (New York).

Berger, S. (1884) *La bible française au moyen âge* (Slatkine Reprints, Geneva 1967).

Bertelli, L. A. (1965) 'A Glimpse at the History of Translation in Italy', *Babel* 11, 76–8.

Berthelot, M. (1893) *La chimie au moyen âge* (Osnabrück, 1967).

Blatt, F. (1938) 'Remarques sur l'histoire des traductions latines', *Classica et medievalia* 1, 217–42.

Bluhm, H. (1965) *Martin Luther, Creative Translator* (St. Louis, Miss.).

Boas, M. (1962) *The Scientific Renaissance, 1450–1630* (New York).

Bonnard, J. (1888) *Les traductions de la bible en vers français au moyen âge* (Geneva, 1967).

Bottkol, J. M. (1942–3) 'Dryden's Latin Scholarship', *Modern Philology* 40, 241–54.

Bruce, F. F. (1970) *The English Bible, a History of Translations* (New York).

Butterworth, C. C. (1953) *The English Primers, 1529–1545* (Philadelphia).

The Cambridge History of the Bible (3 vols, Cambridge).

Carpenter, K. E. and Redlich, F. (1973) 'Research Possibilities in a History of Political Economy through a Bibliography of Translations', *History of Political Economy* 5, 268–83.

Cary, E. (1957) 'Théories soviétiques de la traduction', *Babel* 3, 179–90.

Casanova, C. (1938) *Luis de León como traductor de los clásicos* (London).

Clausen, A. (1827) *Augustinus sacrae scripturae interpres* (Copenhagen).

Cohen, J. M. (1962) *English Translators and Translations* (London).

Conington, J. (1861) 'The English Translators of Virgil', *Quarterly Review* 110, 73–114.

Conley, C. H. (1927) *The First English Translators of the Classics* (New Haven, Conn.).

Cook, A. S. (1925) 'The Odyssey, Seventh Book, as Known to Petrarch', *Philological Quarterly* 4, 25–38.

Coste, J. (1958) 'La première expérience de traduction biblique', *Maison-Dieu* 53, 56–88.

Courcelle, P. (1943) *Les lettres grecques en occident de Macrobe à Cassiodore* (Paris).

Croll, M. W. (1919) 'The Cadence of English Oratorical Prose', *Studies in Philosophy* 16, 1–54.

Crombie, A. C. (1967) *Medieval and Early Modern Science* (2 vols, Cambridge, Mass.).

Davril, R. (1956) 'Shakespeare in French Garb', *Shakespeare Jahrbuch* 92, 197–206.

Deanesley, M. (1920) *The Lollard Bible* (Cambridge, 1966).

de Bruyne, D. (1913) 'L'Itala de Saint Augustin', *Revue bénédictine* 30, 294–314.

de la Ville de Mirmont, H. (1903) *Etudes sur l'ancienne poésie latine* (Paris).

de Salas, P. (1965) 'La traducción de obras teatrales en Espanã', *Babel* 11, 19–20.

de Vaux, R. (1933) 'La première entrée d'Averroes chez les Latins', *Revue des sciences philosophiques et théologiques* 22, 193–245.

Draper, J. W. (1921) 'The Theory of Translation in the Eighteenth Century', *Neophilologus* 6, 241–54.
Dubeux, A. (1928) *Les Traductions françaises de Shakespeare* (Paris).
Duméril, E. (1933) *Le Lied allemand et ses traductions poétiques en France* (Paris).
Dunlop, D. M. (1960) 'The Work of Translation at Toledo', *Babel* 6, 55–9.

FitzMaurice-Kelly, J. (1911) 'Translation', *Encyclopedia Britannica* (11th edn, Cambridge), vol. 27, 183–8.
Fontaine, N. (1738) *Mémoires pour servir à l'histoire du Port Royal* (2 vols, Cologne).
Fränzel, W. (1914) *Geschichte des Übersetzens im 18 Jahrhundert* (Leipzig).
Fuchs, G. (1936) *Studien zur Übersetzungstheorie und -praxis des Gottschedkreises* (Freiburg).

Geyer, B. (1917) 'Die altenlateinischen Übersetzungen der aristotelischen Analytik, Topik, und Elenchik', *Philosophiches Jahrbuch* 30, 25–43.
Gneuss, H. (1968) *Hymnar und Hymnes im englischen Mittelalter* (Tübingen).
Grant, W. L. (1954) 'Ut universi orbi prodessent', *Phoenix* 8, 64–70.
Grasset, B. (1938) 'Traduction et traducteurs', *Revues des deux mondes*, 459–66.

Haskins, C. H. (1924) *Studies in the History of Medieval Science* (Cambridge).
—— (1927) *The Renaissance of the Twelfth Century* (Cambridge, Mass.).
Hatcher, O. L. (1912) 'Aims and Methods of Elizabethan Translators', *Englische Studien* 44, 174–92.
Heck, P. (1931) *Übersetzungsprobleme im Frühen Mittelalter* (Tübingen).
Hennebert, F. (1858) *Histoire des traducteurs français des auteurs grecs et latins pendant le XVIe siècle* (Gand).
Hermann, A. and von Soden, W. (1957) 'Dolmetscher', *Reallexicon für Antike und Christentum*, ed. F. J. Dölger *et al.* (Stuttgart), 4: 24–9.
Highet, G. (1949) *The Classical Tradition* (London).
Huguet, E. (1925) 'Les procédés d'adaptation chez Amyot', *Revue du XVIe siècle* 12, 44–78.
Hulubei, A. (1931) 'Virgile en France en XVIe siècle; éditions, traductions, imitations', *Revue du XVIe siècle* 18, 1–77.
Humbert, J. (1940) 'A propos de Cicéron traducteur du grec', in *Mélanges de philologie, de littérature et d'histoire ancienne offerts à Alfred Ernout* (Paris), 197–200.

Jacobsen, E. (1958) *Translation a Traditional Craft* (Copenhagen).
Johnson, F. R. (1937) *Astronomical Thought in Renaissance England* (Baltimore).
Jones, R. F. (1953) *The Triumph of the English Language* (London).
Jourdain, A. (1843) *Recherches critiques sur l'âge et l'origine des traductions latines d'Aristote*, rev. C. Jourdain (repr. New York, 1960).

Kehrein, J. (1853) *Kirchen- und religiöse Lieder aus dem zwölften bis fünfzehnten Jahrhundert* (Hildesheim, 1969).
Kelly, L. G. (1968) '*Contaminatio* in *Lycidas*; an Example of Vergilian Poetics', *Revue de l'université d'Ottawa*, 38, 587–98.
—— (1973) 'Linguistics and Translation in Saint Augustine', *The Bible Translator* 24, 134–9.

—— (1975) 'Saint Augustine and Saussurean Linguistics', *Augustinian Studies* 6, 45–64.

King, D. B. (1952) 'The Greek Translation of Augustus *Res Gestae*', *Transactions of the Wisconsin Academy* 41, 219–28.

Lacombe, G., *et al.* (1939–55) *Aristoteles latinus* (Rome).

Ladborough, R. W. (1938–9) 'Translation from the Ancients in Seventeenth-century France', *Journal of the Warburg Institute* 2, 85-104.

Lallemand, P. (1888) *De parnasso oratoriano* (Paris).

Larwill, P. H. (1934) *La théorie de la traduction au debut de la renaissance en France* (Munich).

Lathrop, H. B. (1967) *Translations from the Classics into English from Caxton to Chapman 1477–1620* (New York).

Lawton, H. W. (1926) *Térence en France au XVIe siècle* (Paris).

Lebègue, R. (1939) 'Les traducteurs en France pendant la renaissance', *Actes du troisième congrès de l'Association Guillaume Budé* (Strasbourg), 362–7.

Loane, G. N. (1939) 'Chapman and Scapula', *Notes and Queries* 176, 405–6.

Long, O. E. (1915) 'English Translations of Goethe's *Werther*', *Journal of English and German Philology* 14, 169–203.

Maier, I. (1966) *Ange Politien: la formation d'un poète humaniste (1469–1480)*, (Geneva).

Manitius, M. (1911–31) *Geschichte der lateinischer Litteratur des Mittelalters* (Munich).

Marrou, H. I. (1949) *Saint Augustin et la fin de la culture antique* (Paris).

Marti, H. (1974) *Übersetzer der Augustin-zeit: Interpretation von Selbstzeugnissen* (Munich).

Martimort, A. G. (1966) 'Essai historique sur les traductions liturgiques', *Maison-Dieu* 86, 75–105.

Matoré, G. (1968) *Histoire des dictionnaires français* (Paris).

Matthiessen, F. O. (1931) *Translation, an Elizabethan Art* (Cambridge, Mass.).

Mencken, F. O (1736) *Historia vitae et in litteras meritorum Angeli Politiani* (Leipzig).

Menéndez y Pelayo, M. (1878) *Humanistas españoles del siglo xvi*, in *Obras completas* VII (Madrid, 1941).

—— (1885) *Horacio en España* (2 vols, Madrid).

Meyer, P. (1896) 'Les anciens traducteurs français de Végèce et en particulier Jean de Vignai', *Romania* 25, 400–23.

Mezger, J. J. (1967) *Geschichte der deutschen Bibelübersetzungen in der schweizerisch-reformierten Kircher* (Nieuwhoop).

Monfrin, J. (1964) 'Humanisme et traductions au moyen âge', in A. Fourrier (ed.) *L'humanisme médiéval dans les littératures romanes du XIIe au XIVe siècle* (Paris), 217–47.

Mounin, G. (1964) *La machine à traduire: histoire des problèmes linguistiques* (The Hague).

Munteano, B. (1956) 'Port-Royal et la stylistique de la traduction', *Cahiers de l'association internationale des études françaises* 8, 151–72.

Murray, J. A. H. (1900) *The Evolution of English Lexicography* (London).

McGuire, M. R. P. (1967) 'Translation Literature, Latin into Greek', in *New Catholic Encyclopedia* (New York), XIV. 256–7.

Partridge, A. C. (1973) *English Bible Translation* (London).

Poncelet, R. (1957) *Cicéron traducteur de Platon: l'expression de la pensée complexe en latin classique* (Paris).

Pons, C. (1960) 'Les traductions d'Hamlet par des écrivains français', *Etudes anglaises* 13, 116–31.

Pound, Ezra (1917) 'Notes on Elizabethan Classicists', in T. S. Eliot (ed.), *Literary Essays of Ezra Pound* (London, 1954), 227–49.

—— (1920) 'Translators of Greek, Early Translators of Homer', ibid., 249–75.

Praz, M. (1956) 'Shakespeare Translations in Italy', *Shakespeare Jahrbuch* 92, 220–31.

Proudfoot, L (1960) *Dryden's Aeneid and its Seventeenth-Century Predecessors* (Manchester).

Purdie, E. (1949) 'Some Problems of Translation in the Eighteenth Century in Germany', *English Studies* 30, 191–205.

Quemada, B. (1967) *Les dictionnaires du français moderne 1539–1883: Etude sur leur histoire, leurs types et leurs méthodes* (Paris).

Radó, G. (1967) 'Approaching the History of Translation', *Babel* 13, 169–73.

Reu, M. (1934) *Luther's German Bible* (Columbus, Ohio).

Roddier, H. (1957) 'L'abbé Prévost et le problème de la traduction au XVIIIe siècle', *Cahiers de l'association internationale des études françaises* 7, 173–81.

Sabbadini, R. (1922) *Il metodo degli umanisti* (Florence).

Sandys, J. E. (1921) *A History of Classical Scholarship* (3rd edn, Cambridge).

Sarton, G. (1947) *Introduction to the History of Science*, III (Washington, D.C.).

Schoell, F. L. (1925) 'L'hellénisme français en Angleterre', *Revue de littérature comparée* 5, 193, 238.

Schwarz, E. (1933) 'Zweisprachigkeit in dem Konzilakten', *Philologus* 68, 245–53.

Schwarz, W. (1944a) 'The Meaning of *fidus interpres* in Medieval Translation', *Journal of Theological Studies* 45, 73–8.

—— (1944b) 'Translation into German in the Fifteenth Century', *Modern Language Review* 39, 368–73.

—— (1945) 'The Theory of Translation in Sixteenth-Century Germany', *Modern Language Review* 40, 289–99.

—— (1963) 'The History of the Principles of Bible Translation in the Western World', *Babel* 9, 5–22.

Scott, M. A. (1916) *Elizabethan Translators from the Italian* (Boston and New York).

Seigel, J. E. (1968) *Rhetoric and Philosophy in Renaissance Humanism* (Princeton, N.J.).

Selver, P. (1966) *The Art of Translating Poetry* (London).

Senger, A. (1971) *Deutsche Übersetzungstheorie im 18 Jahrhundert* (Bonn).

Setton, K. M. (1956) 'The Byzantine Background to the Italian Renaissance', *Proceedings of the American Philosophical Society* 100, 1–76.

Siegmund, P. A. (1949) *Die Überlieferung der griechischen christlichen Literatur in der lateinischen Kirche* (Munich).

Simon, I. (1964–5) 'Critical Terms in Restoration Translation from French', *Revue belge de philologie et d'histoire* 42, 853–79; 43, 902–26.

Starnes, D. T. (1937) 'Bilingual Dictionaries of Shakespeare's Day', *PMLA* 52, 1005–18.

—— (1954) *Renaissance Dictionaries, English–Latin and Latin–English* (Austin, Texas).
—— (1963) *Robert Estienne's Influence on Lexicography* (Austin, Texas).
Sühnel, R. (1958) *Homer und die englische Humanität* (Tübingen).

Taton, R. (1963) *Ancient and Medieval Science*, trans. A. J. Pomerans (London).
Thieme, K. (1955) 'Die geschichtlichen Haupt-typen des Dolmetschens', *Babel* 1, 55–60.
Thieme, K., Hermann, A. and Glässer, E. (1956) *Beiträge zur Geschichte des Dolmetschens* (Munich).
Thillet, P. *et al.* (1967) 'Translation Literature, Greek and Arabic', in *New Catholic Encyclopedia* (New York), XIV. 248–56.
Thompson, L. S. (1943) 'German Translators of the Classics between 1450 and 1550', *Journal of English and Germanic Philology* 42, 343–63.
Thomson, S. (1942) 'The *Dulcis Jesu memoria* in Anglo-Norman and Middle French', *Medium Aevum* 11, 68–76.

Underhill, G. J. (1899) *Spanish Literature in the England of the Tudors* (New York).

van der Vyver, A. (1931) 'Cassiodore et son oeuvre', *Speculum* 6, 244–92.
van Tieghem, P. (1917) L'année littéraire *comme intermediaire en France des littératures étrangères* (Paris).
Vigouroux, F. G. (1912) *Dictionnaire de la Bible* (5 vols, Paris).

Weiss, R. (1950) 'Translators from the Greek of the Angevin Court of Naples', *Rinascimento* 1, 194–226.
West, C. B. (1932) 'La théorie de la traduction au XVIIIe siècle par rapport surtout aux traductions françaises des ouvrages anglais', *Revue de littérature comparée* 12, 330–55.
Whibley, C. (1932) 'Translators', in *Cambridge History of English Literature* IV.1–25 (Cambridge).
Williams, G. (1968) *Tradition and Originality in Roman Poetry* (Oxford).
Witty, F. J. (1967) 'Translation Literature, Early', in *New Catholic Encyclopedia* (New York), XIV. 248–56.
Woledge, B. (1953) 'La légende de Troie et les débuts de la prose française', in *Mélanges de linguistique et de littérature romanes offerts à Mario Roques* (Paris), II. 313–24.
Wüstenfeld, F. (1877) *Die Übersetzungen arabischer Werke in das lateinische Seit dem XI Jahrhundert* (Göttingen), XXII #3.

Zuber, R. (1968) *Les 'belles infidèles' et la formation du goût classique. Perrot d'Ablancourt et Guez de Balzac* (Paris).

Index

The names of translators quoted and the page references to their translations are in italics.